WHAT STUDENTS ARE SAYING ABOUT *SPEAK UP!*

Easy to read, good fluidity, logical order, relatable examples and anecdotes.

—Sarah Le Clair, Student

I found it highly engaging. I wasn't bored or zoning out because the material kept my attention, unlike other textbooks I've used.

—Dana Schmitz, Student

The tone of the bo~'~ ~~el reassured about ~ted with taking Spe~

—Matthew Pac~

When I learned something new, it captivated me.

—Jon Hongpananon, Student

The images really helped me understand what the text was saying—like a visual summary.

—Olivia Baney, Student

Speak Up

AN ILLUSTRATED GUIDE TO PUBLIC SPEAKING

Douglas M. Fraleigh
California State University–Fresno

Joseph S. Tuman
San Francisco State University

With Illustrations by
Peter Arkle

Bedford / St. Martin's
Boston • New York

For Bedford/St. Martin's

Publisher for Communication: Erika Gutierrez
Executive Editor: Simon Glick
Developmental Editor: Ann Kirby-Paine
Associate Editor: Mae Klinger
Production Editor: Jessica Skrocki Gould
Senior Production Supervisor: Nancy Myers
Marketing Manager: Adrienne Petsick
Art Director: Lucy Krikorian
Text Design: Jerilyn Bockorick
Copy Editor: Jamie Nan Thaman
Indexer: Leoni Z. McVey
Cover Art: Peter Arkle
Composition: Nesbitt Graphics, Inc.
Printing and Binding: R.R. Donnelley & Sons Company

President: Joan E. Feinberg
Editorial Director: Denise B. Wydra
Director of Development: Erica T. Appel
Director of Marketing: Karen R. Soeltz
Director of Production: Susan W. Brown
Associate Director, Editorial Production: Elise S. Kaiser
Managing Editor: Shuli Traub

Library of Congress Control Number: 2010932996

For information, write: Bedford/St. Martin's, 75 Arlington Street, Boston, MA 02116   (617-399-4000)

ISBN: 978-0-312-62188-9

Acknowledgments

Acknowledgments and copyrights appear at the back of the book on page C-1, which constitutes an extension of the copyright page.

Joe

For my wife, Kirsten: With every new book, there are more reasons to appreciate your love and patience.

Doug

To my family, the source of inspiration for all of my writing.

BRIEF CONTENTS

ABOUT THE AUTHORS AND ILLUSTRATOR

DOUGLAS M. FRALEIGH is a professor and chair of the Department of Communication at California State University at Fresno. He is also on the faculty of Fresno State's Smittcamp Family Honors College and has taught public speaking courses for twenty plus years. Dr. Fraleigh has coached intercollegiate speech and debate at CSU Fresno, UC Berkeley, Cornell, and CSU Sacramento, and his research interests include freedom of speech, argumentation, and legal communication.

JOSEPH S. TUMAN is professor of speech and communication studies at San Francisco State University, where he has received the Jacobus tenBroek Society Award for Excellence in Teaching. Dr. Tuman has taught at the University of California at Berkeley, the New School, and University of PARIS II, and has published widely in the field of communication studies. He appears regularly on television news programs as a political commentator.

PETER ARKLE is a professional illustrator who grew up in Scotland and received a BA in illustration from St. Martin's School of Art and an MA from the Royal College of Art. Peter is a regular contributor to the New York Times, New York Magazine, Time Magazine, and Architect Magazine, and his work has appeared in many other publications. He lectures several times a year at high schools and universities across the United States. To see more of Peter's work, please visit www.peterarkle.com.

PREFACE

As longtime teachers of public speaking and as former coaches of forensics, we have spent more than forty combined years teaching students the value and power of speech in their own lives and in the shaping of our democracy and society. So when we started to think about creating a truly excellent new introduction to speech, we focused on making a textbook that would distill the best practices we have developed in our teaching while transmitting our passionate commitment to the craft and art of public speaking. Our goal was to create a book that would grab the attention of students in our own classrooms while meeting the teaching and learning needs of students, colleagues, and friends across the communication discipline.

We recognized that covering the vast field of public speaking—from classical rhetoric and contemporary communication theory to the specific steps of choosing and researching a topic, preparing an outline, and delivering a speech—can be a tremendous challenge given the time constraints of the course. Instructors need teaching materials that are comprehensive yet flexible enough to work with a variety of teaching styles. At the same time, students want a book that is engaging, fun, and affordable.

With these challenges in mind, our goal with *Speak Up* has been to provide excellent coverage of the topics that most books typically include while getting rid of the excess and offering unique coverage, suggestions, and illustrations that we strongly feel will be useful to students—and their teachers.

Now, we are especially proud to present this new and improved version of *Speak Up*. Over the last several years, we have been privileged to hear from many instructors and students who have reported that the first edition really worked for them as a teaching and learning tool—and we were honored to find that *Speak Up*'s approach and philosophy have resonated enough that the book has become one of the most successful new speech texts published in the last two decades. But even more important, the insightful feedback we have received from instructors and students has helped us to make the second edition even better. Based on this feedback, every change in the new edition, from fresh examples and illustrations to new end-of-chapter pedagogy and updated sample speeches, has been designed to help better meet the needs of speech instructors while capturing student attention and interest.

TRADITIONAL COVERAGE, COMPELLING WRITING, AND BRIEF, TOO!

We think of *Speak Up* as a traditional speech text—with a twist. The book's traditional organization and structure allow it to work seamlessly with most instructors' courses and syllabi—yet it offers unique coverage not found in other books along with truly useful suggestions for students on every step of the speechmaking process, from topic selection to delivery. And throughout, *Speak Up* pays special attention to helping students successfully adapt their messages to their audiences.

Yet great content doesn't matter if students don't read, understand, and retain it. We developed the writing style for our book with students in mind, using clear, accessible language that is at once friendly yet authoritative. We also took care to incorporate engaging examples, drawn from current events and our own experience. From beginning to end, concepts are illuminated with these vivid examples that touch on pop culture, politics, and watershed events that will resonate with students, such as the recent health-care debate and responses to the earthquake in Haiti. Familiar names and faces—from Ellen Page to Cesar Millan—firmly root in-text examples in the real world.

And with all this rich content, *Speak Up* is still about 25 percent briefer than most traditional competing texts, making it an accessible, easy-to-use learning tool for a wide range of students. With its accessible writing, lively examples, relatively brief chapters, and traditional organization, instructors can use *Speak Up* easily, no matter what books or materials they have used in the past.

ILLUSTRATIONS THAT REALLY WORK

Our goal has always been to create a book that offers not only superior coverage of public speaking concepts and skills, but one that today's demanding and time-crunched students actually *look forward* to reading. At the earliest stages of its development, we realized that illustrations could be a key to this challenge and could help make *Speak Up*'s art program more interesting—and more pedagogically useful—than image after image and page after page of students and professionals standing at podia.

This idea really gelled when we teamed up with the brilliant illustrator Peter Arkle, who brought to the project his wit, clever writing, and infallible line. Starting with rough ideas from us, Peter created illustrations that show the *workings* of each step in the speechmaking process, from action shots depicting motion or the passage of time to concepts difficult to represent with static photographs (such as how to use transitions or the importance of outlining). And in collaboration, we all made sure that the illustrations worked in tandem with the text itself—echoing it, elaborating on it, and offering true *visual explanations* for virtually every key concept in the book.

And you know what? Students and instructors tell us they *love* the illustrations. Students say the illustrations actually lead them to read more of the text *itself*, and that they serve as useful study tools when preparing for a speech assignment or studying for an exam. Instructors tell us they have an easier time teaching the material and that their students are getting more out of the class. These instructors affirm our hopes for the illustrations: they're fun and interesting, but they're also smart and pedagogically effective, and they are truly serious *learning tools* that lead to better outcomes for the vast majority of students.

A BOOK THAT STUDENTS CAN AFFORD

Speak Up's manageable, engagingly written chapters are paired with an affordable price, less than half the cost of most traditional introductory speech texts.

NEW TO THIS EDITION

- **More coverage of key topics typically given short shrift in competing texts.** From our experience teaching speech and coaching forensics, we've found that there are important topics that other introductory books seem to cover only in passing (or not at all). Many of these topics center on creating messages that are tailored to specific audiences, from aspects of choosing a topic that *really* connects with listeners to strategies for identifying prior exposure. We covered several of these key topics in the first edition, and based on positive instructor feedback, we've strengthened many of these areas even further:

  - **Audience analysis:** To bolster the book's consistent advice that speakers should build audience-centered messages, the new edition provides additional strategies for identifying prior exposure and seeking common ground plus a new section on socioeconomic status in the coverage of demographic analysis.

  - **Choosing a topic:** Additional material supports the message that speakers should choose topics that prove compelling to listeners, fit the speakers' own knowledge and interests, and factor in the speech context, while new ideas for speech topics include privacy in the electronic age, the nature of sleep disorders, the dangers of texting while driving, and many others.

  - **Persuasion:** More on the importance of strategic discourse, additional advice for framing arguments based on audience disposition, and new scholarship on the ethical use of *pathos*.

  - **Ethics:** An updated discussion of ethical codes from ethical absolutism to situational ethics, more on the distinction between legal and ethical speech, and a stronger emphasis on the rights and responsibilities that free speech entails.

  - **Impromptu speaking:** New coverage of impromptu speaking in the chapter on delivery gives students the tools they need to speak successfully on the fly—from advice on quickly organizing thoughts to dealing with in-the-moment communication apprehension.

- **Listening:** Updated coverage of listening from the speaker's perspective with more on encouraging active listening and dealing with listening problems during the speech.

- **Presentation aids:** A refined approach to presentation aids is designed to help students choose the right aids for their presentations and tailor those aids to their audience and rhetorical situation.

- **New and updated examples**—drawn from cutting-edge events and designed to keep the book fresh and relevant—include the economic recession, the war in Afghanistan, the release of the iPad, the 2008 elections, the 2010 Academy Awards, and many others.

- **Updated and streamlined illustration program** has been honed to make it as pedagogically effective as possible: more "don't-and-do" examples showcase common pitfalls, such as failing to maintain eye contact when using presentation aids; additional visual metaphors help students understand complex concepts, such as subordination and logical fallacies; and contemporary pop-culture and current-events examples keep students engaged with references to the U.S. Air Guitar Championships, *Iron Man*, Lady Gaga, and more.

- **Expanded end-of-chapter pedagogy** is designed to help students grasp and apply the key concepts from each chapter. In addition to a chapter summary and list of key terms, three new sets of questions offer increasingly sophisticated types of pedagogy, encouraging students to review chapter concepts, think critically about those concepts, and apply them in the real world.

- **Even more full-text sample speeches.** Providing students with the models they need to study and further develop their personal speaking styles, *Speak Up* now offers fourteen full-text sample speeches—two more than in the previous edition. These addresses, from real-life students and professional speakers, offer examples of informative, persuasive, and special-occasion speeches, and include new presentations from Ronald Reagan, Barack Obama, and Shakira.

RESOURCES FOR STUDENTS AND INSTRUCTORS

Resources for Students

For more information on the Student Resources or to learn about package options, please visit the online catalog at bedfordstmartins.com/speakup/catalog.

Free and Open Book Companion Web Site at bedfordstmartins.com/speakup

This Web site provides quick access to our extensive student aids for *Speak Up*, such as self-assessment quizzes for each chapter, speech topic lists and topic research links, research tools (including tutorials on evaluating sources and avoiding plagiarism), and much more. From the *Speak Up* Companion Web site, students can also access a host of useful premium tools within *Speech Central Plus*.

Speech Central Plus

A Bedford/St. Martin's e-library for speech resources. Available at the *Speak Up* Companion Web site, bedfordstmartins.com/speakup, a suite of premium resources offers students even more powerful tools to help them master the concepts and skills of public speaking. Organized within the Companion Web site in the "*Speech Central Plus*" tab, these powerful premium resources include:

- *VideoCentral: Public Speaking*, the largest video collection available for the public speaking course, with over one hundred clips and full-length speeches by real students that show the power of public speaking—and how to harness it.
- *Bedford Speech Outliner 2.0*, a powerful online tool that helps students with the stages of the outlining process, from invention through organization and practice.
- Unique Video Quizzes that pair video clips with content questions, allowing students to see key concepts in action and testing their ability to identify these concepts.
- *Relaxation Audio Download*, designed to help students combat anxiety and visualize success.

Premium access is available on its own or packaged with each new copy of *Speak Up*. To order the book + access code package, use ISBN 978-0-312-60444-8.

CourseSmart e-Book for *Speak Up*
We've partnered with CourseSmart to make this book available as a PDF-style e-book, which offers page-by-page fidelity, highlighting, and notetaking. Students can choose whether to download the e-book and access it from one machine, or to purchase the online version and access it from wherever they are. Visit coursesmart.com for more information, and to order.

Video Theater 3.0 CD-ROM
This CD-ROM offers seven full student speeches—informative, persuasive, special-occasion, and demonstration—with analysis and guidance for each speech, plus twenty professional speech clips. These video examples work not just as models but as powerful teaching tools. For ordering or packaging information, visit bedfordstmartins.com/speakup/catalog.

Outlining and Organizing Your Speech
Merry Buchanan, *University of Central Oklahoma;* ISBN 978-0-312-45202-5

This student workbook provides step-by-step guidance for preparing informative, persuasive, and professional presentations and provides students with the opportunity to practice the critical skills of conducting audience analysis, dealing with communication apprehension, selecting a speech topic and purpose, researching supporting materials, organizing and outlining, developing introductions and conclusions, enhancing language and delivery, and preparing and using presentation aids.

The Essential Guide Series
This series has been designed to give communication instructors greater flexibility and support when designing their communication courses. Each brief booklet begins with a useful overview and then addresses the essential concepts and skills students need.

The Essential Guide to Presentation Software
Allison J. Ainsworth, *Gainesville State College,* and Rob Patterson, *McIntire School of Commerce, University of Virginia;* ISBN 978-0-312-53819-4

The Essential Guide to Rhetoric
William M. Keith, *University of Wisconsin-Milwaukee,* and Christian O. Lundberg, *University of North Carolina-Chapel Hill;* ISBN 978-0-312-47239-9

The Essential Guide to Interpersonal Communication
Dan O'Hair, *University of Kentucky,* and Mary O. Wiemann, Emeritus, *Santa Barbara City College;* ISBN 978-0-312-45195-0

The Essential Guide to Group Communication
Dan O'Hair, *University of Kentucky,* and Mary O. Wiemann, Emeritus, *Santa Barbara City College;* ISBN 978-0-312-45194-3

The Essential Guide to Intercultural Communication
Jennifer Willis-Rivera, *University of Wisconsin, River Falls;* ISBN 978-0-312-55190-2

Media Career Guide: Preparing for Jobs in the 21st Century, Eighth Edition
James Seguin, *Robert Morris University;* ISBN 978-0-312-54260-3
   Practical and student-friendly, this revised guide includes a comprehensive directory of media jobs, practical tips, and career guidance for students considering a major in communication studies and mass media.

Research and Documentation in the Electronic Age, Fifth Edition
Diana Hacker, *Prince George's Community College,* and Barbara Fister, *Gustavus Adolphus College;* ISBN 978-0-312-56672-2
   This handy booklet covers everything students need for college research assignments at the library and on the Internet, including advice for finding and evaluating Internet sources.

Resources for Instructors
For more information or to order or download the Instructor Resources, please visit the online catalog at bedfordstmartins.com/speakup/catalog.

Instructor's Resource Manual
Nancy Fraleigh, *Fresno City College,* Steve Vrooman, *Texas Lutheran University,* Chrys Egan, *Salisbury University*

This comprehensive manual is a valuable resource for new and experienced instructors alike. It offers extensive advice on topics such as setting and achieving student learning goals, managing the classroom, working with ESL students, crafting strong syllabi and effective speech assignments, and evaluating speeches. A special section in Part I gives instructors advice for using an illustrated text in their classrooms. In addition, each chapter of the main text is broken down into detailed outlines, lecture suggestions, student discussion items, and activities that can be used in class or assigned as take-home projects. Download or request an examination copy at bedfordstmartins.com/speakup/catalog.

Print and Electronic Test Bank

Douglas M. Fraleigh, *California State University—Fresno,* Nancy Fraleigh, *Fresno City College*

Speak Up offers a complete testing program, available in print and for Windows and Macintosh environments. Each chapter includes multiple-choice, true/false, and fill-in-the-blank exercises, as well as essay questions.

Content for Course Management Systems

Instructors can access content for course management systems such as WebCT and Blackboard. Visit bedfordstmartins.com/cms for more information.

Microsoft PowerPoint Slides

Each PowerPoint overview—one for each of the nineteen chapters in the text—provides support for the key concepts in each chapter for use in the classroom. All illustrations from the print text are included in these PowerPoint slides. Instructors can customize these slides to fit their own needs. The overviews are available for download from the instructor's section of the book's companion site at bedfordstmartins .com/speakup/catalog.

SpeechClass

ISBN 978-0-312-65874-8

Your students are online, all the time—and with *SpeechClass,* they can study for their public speaking course and prepare their speeches whenever they have time, wherever they have Web access. It puts all of our online resources for public speaking, including *VideoCentral: Public*

Speaking, Video Quizzes, the *Bedford Speech Outliner 2.0,* and the *Relaxation Audio Download,* in a convenient single place. Added to that are course tools that can simplify your life: with *SpeechClass,* students never have to ask you what their grade is, where to find the material you want them to have, or how to participate and stay organized. To package *SpeechClass* and *Speak Up,* use ISBN 978-0-312-56933-4.

ESL Students in the Public Speaking Classroom: A Guide for Teachers
Robbin Crabtree and Robert Weissberg, *New Mexico State University;* ISBN 978-0-312-45197-4

As the United States increasingly becomes a nation of non-native speakers, instructors must find new pedagogical tools to aid students for whom English is a second language. This guide specifically addresses the needs of ESL students in the public speaking course and offers instructors valuable advice for helping students deal successfully with the challenges they face.

Video Resources

VideoCentral: Public Speaking
VideoCentral: Public Speaking is the largest video collection available for the public speaking course, with over one hundred clips and full-length speeches by real students that show the power of public speaking—and how to harness it. Free access to this rich resource is available online to instructors who adopt *Speak Up* for their courses. Instructors who adopt *Speak Up* can also get copies of *VideoCentral: Public Speaking* on DVD for use in their classrooms. For more information, please visit bedfordstmartins.com/speakup/catalog.

Professional Speeches
Bedford/St. Martin's is proud to provide a wide range of professional speeches to adopters in DVD and VHS formats, including more than twenty volumes of the esteemed *Great Speeches* series along with other collections of professional speeches, such as *Greatest Speeches of All Time,* Volumes 1 and 2; *Great Speeches: Today's Women; Kennedy and King: Promises and Dreams;* and many more. For more information, please contact your local publisher's representative.

Student Speeches

Volume 1 ISBN 978-0-312-19223-5; Volume 2 ISBN 978-0-312-25610-4; Volume 3 ISBN 978-0-312-39300-7

Three videotapes of student speeches provide students with attainable models for study, analysis, and inspiration. Included are a variety of speeches that fulfill the most common assignments in public speaking—informative and persuasive speeches—by students of varying ability from Texas Tech and the University of Oklahoma.

The Bedford/St. Martin's Video Library

A wide selection of contemporary and historical videos focuses on public speeches and media-related issues. Qualified instructors are eligible to select videos from the resource library upon adoption of the text. Please contact your representative for more information.

ACKNOWLEDGMENTS

We would like to offer special thanks to Bedford/St. Martin's President Joan Feinberg and Editorial Director Denise Wydra for convening the meeting that gave birth to this project, and for seeing it all the way through to completion. Publisher for Communication Erika Gutierrez soon joined this project and since then has done a marvelous job working with us and sharing ideas for *Speak Up*, while Director of Development Erica Appel has been superb in keeping the project on track. Shepherding any textbook from manuscript to production is a daunting task, even more so when working with a brand-new idea that creates new challenges. We appreciate Erika and Erica's enthusiasm and their professionalism, which enabled us to complete the project on time.

We also owe a particular debt of gratitude to Executive Editor Simon Glick, who has been with us on this project on both editions, from conception to completion. Simon's work on *Speak Up* transcends any job description for an executive editor. To us, Simon has been virtually another member of the authorship team. Working with us from conception to design on the artwork, collaborating on ideas for chapter structure and content, and providing limitless optimism and energy for this project during our conference calls, Simon has been a highly valued colleague. It may be our names on the cover, but Simon's finger-prints are on every page. He is without peer as an editor.

It was a pleasure to collaborate with professional artist Peter Arkle on this project. It has been exciting to work on a new concept in higher-education textbook publishing—regular use of illustrations to help teach course concepts. Peter's ability to depict our ideas in pictures was simply amazing. When our own public-speaking students fill out course evaluations, Peter's illustrations are at the top of the list for what students enjoyed about the class.

On this second edition of *Speak Up,* we were honored to work with the extraordinarily talented Developmental Editor Ann Kirby-Payne, who contributed insight, wisdom, humor, and class to everything she did. We especially appreciate her keen sense of examples and pedagogy that would work well in the classroom, and are thrilled that her work is reflected on virtually every page of the book. Ann had an uncanny ability to synthesize the ideas of twenty-plus reviewers into concrete suggestions for improving our second edition. We were also extremely fortunate to work once again with Mae Klinger on the second edition of *Speak Up,* with a much expanded role (and a well-deserved promotion) since her work on the first edition. Mae's work was central to the crafting of this text, focusing on both the overall vision of the book and the specific content. She served as the conduit to our illustrator and managed the development of our ancillary materials.

Designer Jerilyn Bockorick and her team at Nesbitt Graphics did a wonderful job with the design and layout of our book, consistently using their visual and bookmaking skills to blend illustrations and text and achieve truly inspired results. This book will always owe a debt of gratitude to Art Director Lucy Krikorian, whose work with the original design of the book was instrumental in creating a truly *illustrated* speech text.

We are very thankful to the incredible professionals who guided the production of *Speak Up*: Director of Production, Sue Brown; Production Manager, Marilyn Doof; Associate Director, Editorial Production, Elise Kaiser; and Marcia Cohen, who retired during this edition and who was so instrumental in helping make *Speak Up* happen. Managing Editor Shuli Traub made sure that all the diverse efforts needed to create this book were completed on time. Project Editor Jessica

Skrocki Gould expertly guided the process from manuscript through pages; she got us page proofs with great efficiency and helped us with the tricky business of making each page look its best. Picking up where Jessica left off, Senior Production Supervisor Nancy Myers put in the hard and careful work needed to turn hundreds of manuscript pages with more than five hundred illustrations into the finished product, as did Linda Winters, Kalina Hintz, and Diane Kraut, lining up permissions for the book's many sample speeches and speech excerpts.

Beyond producing the book itself, we have been fortunate to work with a crackerjack marketing team. We love working with Marketing Manager Adrienne Petsick, who did an amazing job promoting the first edition of *Speak Up* and is sure to do the same with the second. We also thank Marketing Assistant Alexis Smith for a great job managing the details; Sally Constable for helping develop our marketing and sales message; and Dennis Adams for his brilliant work overseeing Bedford/St. Martin's Humanities Specialists.

We want to thank Nancy Fraleigh of Fresno City College for her expert work revising the *Instructor's Resource Manual* and Test Bank for this book. She built upon the strong foundation created by Steve Vrooman of Texas Lutheran University and Chrys Egan of Salisbury University, who authored the instructor materials for the first edition. Many thanks also to Bruce Sherwin and Linda DeMasi of Publishers Solutions for all their help with the ancillary program.

We are also grateful to the many reviewers and class-testers who gave us feedback on *Speak Up* and helped us make it even better. The input of our colleagues in the public-speaking profession played a central role in our decisions for revision of the second edition, and they offered both validation for what was working and constructive suggestions for improvement. For the second edition, we would like to thank: Toni Black, *University of New Mexico–Valencia;* Sandra K. Bowen, *Fayetteville Technical Community College;* Ferald J. Bryan, *Northern Illinois University;* Gordon Carlson, *University of Illinois at Chicago;* Genevieve M. Dardeau, *University of South Alabama;* Steve Decker, *University of Wisconsin–Waukesha County;* Cori Ellis, *Northwestern University;* Lori Franklin, *Northern New Mexico College;* Stacy Freed, *University of Tennessee at Martin;* Kevin M. Gillen, *Indiana University South Bend;* Cindy Greenberg, *Kingsborough Community College;* Angela M. Holland,

College of Southern Nevada; Chris Kennedy, *Western Wyoming Community College;* Shelly Lutzweiler, *Guilford Technical Community College;* Daniel Mortensen, *Edgewood College;* Maryanna Brannan Richardson, *Forsyth Technical Community College;* Tasha VanHorn, *Citrus College;* B. Jane Varmecky, *Tulsa Community College;* Steven S. Vrooman, *Texas Lutheran University;* Susan M. Wieczorek, *University of Pittsburgh at Johnstown.*

We would like to thank our own speech teachers and forensics coaches for their contributions to our development as public speakers and teachers. We thank our faculty colleagues for their support and understanding as we balance teaching, writing, and other academic responsibilities. We are grateful for the many students and forensics team members who have worked with us to develop and present speeches over the past quarter century, and we hope that our book will help a new generation of students gain public speaking skills and confidence.

The authors' friendship began at the 1977 Governor's Cup Speech and Debate tournament in Sacramento, California. This is our fifth major book project, and it continues to be a privilege and pleasure to write together. Our families have been exceptional at supporting our work and serving as sounding boards for ideas. It seems like only yesterday that our kids, Douglas, Helen, Nate, and Whitney, were encouraging us to stop writing for a while and play or read with them. Now they are away from home at college and work, but still offering their strategic input on illustrations through e-mails. For over twenty-five years, our wives Kirsten and Nancy have encouraged and supported our writing and contributed valuable ideas to our projects. Needless to say, their love and patience has sustained through all our collaborations—none more so than for the edition you now hold. The authors appreciate the opportunity to continue to share ideas and write with one another—something we will do long after *Speak Up* is (hopefully) in its tenth edition.

CONTENTS

THE BASICS OF PUBLIC SPEAKING

GET THE BUTTERFLIES

FLYING IN FORMATION

WORD ASSOCIATION

ANIMAL RIGHTS

FAKE FUR

COUNTERFEIT MONEY

COUNTERFEIT SOFTWARE

IDENTITY THEFT

ORGANIZING AND OUTLINING

LANGUAGE AND DELIVERY

12 LANGUAGE AND STYLE   355

TYPES OF PUBLIC SPEAKING

19 GROUP COMMUNICATION 635

PANEL DISCUSSION

Speak Up

INTRODUCING PUBLIC SPEAKING

"Public speaking is right for you."

Starting in 1999, British celebrity chef Jamie Oliver became a worldwide television fixture. In addition to his culinary expertise, Oliver was renowned for his energetic onscreen speaking style, sometimes incorporating music and special effects into his live cooking demonstrations. This approach made Oliver quite popular—he's had more than a dozen television series—and also wealthy: he is worth millions of British pounds.

Yet with all this success, some would argue that Oliver didn't exert his *biggest* impact until he began speaking out about a different kind of *pounds*. Concerned about the decline in healthy eating and resulting increases in obesity, Oliver used his culinary and presentation skills to educate students and parents about the importance of nutritious meals. In 2005, his television show and social campaign, "Jamie's School Dinners," led the British government to serve better food in schools. And after several more campaigns—including one in the U.S. in 2009—Oliver won the 2010 TED (Technology, Entertainment, and Design) Prize, which allowed him to gain support from a large and influential audience. In his speech accepting the prize, Oliver shared his wish that the audience help create "a strong sustainable movement to educate every child about food, to inspire families to cook again, and to empower people everywhere to fight obesity."[1]

Oliver's story—and many others like it—helps explain why public speaking is a required course in so many colleges and universities. As his story proves, public speaking is a vital skill for anyone seeking to inform, influence, or persuade others. And most professions require abilities in all three areas. For example, as the leader of a team developing a new video game controller, you may have to deliver a presentation to a group of managers updating them on the group's progress. As a leader in a not-for-profit environmental organization, you may need to give a talk during a major fund-raising dinner to influence potential donors to open their wallets. As an account manager for a company that offers strategy consulting services, you may be called on to deliver a persuasive presentation on a new methodology to an important potential customer.

Yet many college graduates enter the work world without any experience in public speaking. As Marilyn Mackes, executive director of the National Association of Colleges and Employers, noted: "For more than ten years, we've asked employers about key skills, and they have consistently named communication skills as critical, yet have also said that this is something many candidates lack."[2] A public speaking course helps you master skills that will enable you not only to advance in your career but also to excel in other courses (especially your major) *and* make valuable contributions in other areas of your life—such as community service and local politics.

Of course, you may find the thought of giving a speech terrifying. If so, you're not alone. A survey by Whitworth and Cochran[3] found that public speaking is Americans' number-one fear, while another researcher noted that many people find it "even scarier than rattlesnakes."[4] But there's good news: you *can* learn to master public speaking—just as most people learn to read, ride a bicycle, or use the Internet. In our fifty-plus years of teaching public speaking, we've seen students gain confidence and lose their fear of public speaking as they acquire experience with it.

This book walks you through the steps you need to follow in order to create and deliver an effective speech—one that gets a favorable response from your listeners. In the chapters that follow, we explain each step in clear terms and show you how to make smart choices at each stage of the speech preparation process. And we supplement these explanations throughout with illustrations that depict key points and major concepts. Not only are these images interesting and fun, but they will help you grasp and remember the most important concepts in the book.

But before we jump into the process of preparing and delivering an effective speech, we will take a few moments to explore the field of public speaking itself. In this chapter, we take a closer look at the benefits of studying public speaking. We also survey the rich tradition of public speaking and consider highlights of contemporary trends in the study of public speaking.

WHAT IS PUBLIC SPEAKING?

What is public speaking, exactly? This activity has several characteristics that distinguish it from other types of speech.

YOU ARE A PUBLIC SPEAKER WHEN

Public speaking features communication between a speaker and an audience. In public speaking, the speaker does most of the talking, while the audience primarily listens. However, that does not mean audience members don't respond to what they're hearing. Audience members may smile, frown, or look puzzled. Talented speakers recognize these signals and modify their message if needed—for example, clarifying a point when they notice confused expressions on their listeners' faces. Audience members might even respond with more than just silent facial expressions. For instance, they may applaud the speaker or shout out words of encouragement and appreciation if they're pleased with or excited by the speaker's message. Or they may boo or heckle the speaker if they disagree with or disapprove of the message. However, in public speaking, even the most energetic interjections are usually brief. For the majority of the speech, the speaker "has the floor."

Public speaking is audience centered. In public speaking, the presenter chooses his or her message with the audience's interests and needs in mind. Good speakers consider what topic would be appropriate for their audience on a particular occasion. They also

YOU ARE NOT A PUBLIC SPEAKER WHEN

develop their message in a way that their audience will find interesting and understandable.

For example, suppose you recently got a job as a product developer at a furniture company. You've asked to meet with members of your company's management team to discuss a new line of dorm furniture that you'd like to launch. At the meeting, you want to persuade your listeners to approve funding for a proposed line. In preparing your speech, you think about what members of the management team care about most: the company's profitability—its ability to increase revenues while reducing costs. So you develop explanations for how the proposed campaign will enhance profitability ("This new line will increase sales 10 percent over the next two quarters while cutting our expenses 5 percent—leading to a 6 percent increase in profitability"). You make sure to avoid sales-style language, such as "This new design is bold and provocative," because you know that such language will hold little interest for your business-oriented listeners.

Public speaking emphasizes the spoken word. Any speaker can supplement his or her speech with pictures, charts, videotapes, handouts, objects, or even a live demonstration. However, public speakers devote most of their time to *speaking* to their audience. The spoken word plays the central role in their delivery, though speakers use gestures, posture, voice intonation, eye contact, other types of body language, and even presentation aids to heighten the impact of their words.

Public speaking is usually a prepared presentation. Few public speakers simply walk up to the lectern or podium and make up their talk as they go. The best speakers choose their topic in advance, carefully consider what they might say about that topic, and then select the best ideas for the audience they will be addressing. They organize those ideas, choose their words carefully, and practice delivering the speech before the big day. Even people who suspect that they may be called on to deliver an impromptu speech—for example, at a community-service awards dinner—know how to quickly piece together a few comments as they step to the front of the room.

WHY STUDY PUBLIC SPEAKING?

As you make your way through life—completing your degree, advancing in your career, establishing yourself in a neighborhood or community—you will sometimes find yourself in situations in which you need to express your ideas to others. By studying and practicing public speaking, you can learn to deliver effective presentations in each of these contexts. Public speaking skills give you the power to share your ideas and bring about needed change in the world around you.

Public speaking skills can also come in handy in everyday situations. As you become more comfortable with public speaking, you will find yourself more confident about asking a question at a meeting or speaking up when hanging out with new coworkers. And you will be equipped to speak on the fly if you are asked to give a toast, accept an award, or make a presentation at the last minute.

Using Public Speaking as a Student

Of course, you'll need to start practicing your public speaking skills to get through this class. But the skills you acquire by working your way through this book will also help you as you complete your degree and participate in additional educational opportunities throughout your life. Those later opportunities may include adult-education workshops, other higher-education degrees, or professional development courses. Instructors in all types of courses often ask students to stand up on the first day of class and introduce themselves as well as explain what they hope to get from the class.

Many instructors also require students to deliver oral presentations on research projects and other coursework. Students with strong public speaking skills can share their findings more effectively than those with a limited background in presenting speeches. Think about other students you know who have given oral presentations in your classes; most likely, you've noticed that those who give thoughtfully crafted and skillfully delivered presentations make a better impression on the instructor *and* the rest of the class. Equally important, the information they offer is probably more useful to listeners than information delivered by less skilled speakers.

Public speaking skills also enhance your ability to participate in campus activities. If you belong to an organization or a club, team, sorority, or fraternity, you may want to speak out at a group meeting or represent your group before the student senate or other campus organizations. When you present an effective speech to these audiences, you boost your chances of achieving your goal—whether it's persuading your sorority to take up a new social cause or convincing the student senate to fund a campus job fair related to your major.

Using Public Speaking in Your Career

A knack for public speaking is one of the most important assets you can possess in the workplace. Jean Gatz, a professional speaker and workplace consultant, notes that verbal skills "are essential in every work environment" and that knowing how to listen (another skill taught in public speaking courses) is "equally important."[5] According to the National Association of Colleges and Employers 2009 Job

Outlook Survey, communication skills outrank all other qualities that employers seek in potential job candidates.[6] Employees themselves agree that communication skills are important. In the survey "Making the Grade? What American Workers Think Should Be Done to Improve Education," 87 percent of the 1,014 U.S. adult workers surveyed rated communication skills as very important for performing their jobs.[7]

No matter which career path you choose, you'll almost certainly need public speaking skills. Consider these examples:

- A police officer faces an angry crowd on the verge of violence. The officer talks calmly and rationally to the group, defusing the tension and preventing a brawl.

- A nurse wants to explain to her hospital's management team why high patient loads and long work hours justify the nurses' union strike threat. By making her case persuasively, she builds support for the union's position, and the two parties forge a contract agreement without a strike.

- An accountant has the opportunity to explain recent changes in tax law to a group of investors. Impressed by the speech's clarity and the accountant's expertise, several audience members decide to become clients.

- An elementary schoolteacher faces a roomful of parents who are skeptical about a new math curriculum, which differs markedly from how they learned math in "the good old days." The teacher clearly and energetically presents research results defending the curriculum, and the parents happily accept the new method.

Using Public Speaking in Your Community

Beyond work or school, you may wear many different hats in your community. For example, you might be active in service organizations, athletic leagues, clubs, religious groups, or political committees. If you're a parent, you may find yourself taking on leadership roles in your children's schools, sports teams, clubs, or other activities. You may also decide to get involved in a social cause that you feel passionate about. In each of these endeavors, public speaking skills can help you. For example, Tammy Duckworth, a veteran wounded in Iraq, returned home from combat and decided to run for Congress. She and ten other post–September 11 veterans ran for the House in 2006. They needed to deliver campaign speeches not only discussing the Iraq war but also explaining their stances on health care, gas prices, and the economy.[8] Although Duckworth did not win that election, she made an impression. She was asked to speak at the 2008 Democratic National Convention, and in 2009 she was appointed assistant secretary for public and intergovernmental affairs at the U.S. Department of Veterans Affairs.

To participate in and contribute to your community, you will sometimes need to speak out. You may actively seek out opportunities to lead, or you may be encouraged to take leadership roles. Or, as a group member, you may simply have a point you want to share. In addition, you will occasionally be asked to speak in less formal situations—for example, offering a wedding toast or presenting an award to a friend or colleague who is retiring. In each of these cases, the skills you learn in a public speaking class will help you ensure that others hear and respect your views.

PUBLIC SPEAKING: A GREAT TRADITION

For centuries, people around the world have studied the art and practice of public speaking and used public address to inform, influence, and persuade others.

As far back as the fifth century B.C.E., all adult male citizens in the Greek city-state of Athens had a right to speak out in the assembly and vote on proposals relating to civic matters. Sometimes as many as six thousand citizens attended these meetings.[9] Indeed, the ancient Greeks were the first people to think formally about rhetoric as well as teach it as a subject. A century later, the Greek scholar Aristotle wrote *Rhetoric*, a systematic analysis of the art and practice of public speaking. Many of Aristotle's ideas influence the study of public speaking even today. Later, in first-century B.C.E. Rome, senators vehemently debated the issues of the day. Cicero, a Roman politician, was a renowned orator and a prolific writer on rhetoric, the craft of public speaking. Another noteworthy Roman rhetorician, Quintilian, emphasized the ideal of an ethical orator—the good person speaking well.

Yet the tradition of public speaking was not limited to Greece and Rome. From the time of Confucius in the fifth century B.C.E. until the end of the third century B.C.E., China enjoyed an intellectual climate whose energy rivaled that of ancient Greece.[10] Scholars traveling throughout China passionately advocated a variety of systems of political and economic philosophy. In fifteenth-century western Africa, traveling storytellers recited parables and humorous stories, while in northeastern Africa, Islamic scholars embarked on lecture tours attended by large crowds.[11] On feast days in one African kingdom (near present-day Mali), it was traditional for a bard to dress in a bird's-head mask and deliver a speech encouraging the king to live up to his predecessors' high standards.[12] Native Americans prized oratory, too; indeed, many of them deemed oratorical ability a more important leadership quality than even bravery in battle.[13]

The tradition of public speaking flourished in colonial America as well. During the Great Awakening of the 1730s and 1740s, preachers sought to revive religious zeal, which had been waning in the colonies. George Whitefield traveled through the colonies and drew large crowds with his dynamic open-air sermons.[14] He preached in fields because churches weren't large enough to accommodate his listeners.[15] Jonathan Edwards's well-known 1741 sermon "Sinners in the Hands of an Angry God" impelled worshippers in Enfield, Massachusetts (now Connecticut), to shriek and moan as Edwards described "the God that holds you over the pit of hell, much as one holds a spider."[16] Fervent preaching was not limited to men: more than one hundred evangelical women preached from the time of the Great Awakening to the early nineteenth century.[17]

Of course, the American Revolution presented numerous opportunities to demonstrate the power of oratory. Colonists took to the streets to passionately decry new taxes. Then they launched the famous Boston Tea Party, in which they dressed as Mohawk Indians, boarded three ships in Boston Harbor, and hurled the vessels' cargoes of tea overboard.

Later, political leaders in each of the states energetically debated the merits of ratifying the U.S. Constitution and the Bill of Rights. In the nineteenth century, public speaking became a hallmark of American society. Through public address, Americans freely debated political issues, expanded their knowledge, and even entertained one another. Political debates drew particularly large and enthusiastic crowds, such as the debates between Abraham Lincoln and Stephen Douglas, candidates for a U.S. Senate seat from Illinois in 1858. More than fifteen thousand people gathered to hear the contenders in Freeport, Illinois—a town with just five thousand residents.[18]

The antislavery movement spurred additional use of public speaking to drive major social change. Frederick Douglass, a former slave who moved audiences with his discussion of life under slavery, counted among the most compelling antislavery speakers. Women also actively participated in the American Anti-Slavery Society, holding

PUBLIC SPEAKING: AN ENDURING LEGACY

offices and delivering public lectures. Consider Angelina Grimké—an eloquent orator who won audience members' commitment to the antislavery cause with graphic descriptions of slave abuse she had witnessed while growing up in South Carolina. Other women—such as Elizabeth Cady Stanton, Susan B. Anthony, and Lucy Stone—took leadership roles in the women's suffrage movement, which also arose around this time. These able orators used fiery speeches to convince Americans that women deserved the right to cast a ballot at the polls—a radical notion at the time.[19]

During the twentieth century, public address continued to play a key role in American Society. After World War I, President Woodrow Wilson traveled through the United States advocating the League of Nations, while Republican leaders rushed to the same tour stops and presented the opposite viewpoint.[20] In 1963, a whopping 250,000 people gathered near the Lincoln Memorial in Washington, D.C., to hear Martin Luther King Jr. deliver his "I Have a Dream" speech,[21] an address that instantly excited the imaginations of people around the world. In a similar vein, the Million Man (Washington, D.C., 1995) and the Million Woman (Philadelphia, 1997) marches culminated in public speeches by activists on the issues closest to their hearts, including job creation, human rights, and respect for African Americans.[22] And in the past few years, tens of thousands of "Promise Keepers" have crowded into football stadiums to hear speakers address issues of family and religion.

Today, people seem to communicate more through e-mail, blogs, videoconferences, smartphones, and cell phones than they do through public address. Nevertheless, public speaking still counts among the most potent leadership tools around. Presidents continue to deliver weekly radio addresses to the American public, advocate policy initiatives at joint sessions of Congress, and travel thousands of miles overseas to address international audiences. Just as Ronald Reagan spoke at the Brandenburg Gate in Berlin to challenge Russian leader Mikhail Gorbachev to "tear down this wall!" in 1987, Barack Obama addressed about thirty thousand people near the ancient Prague Castle in the now free Czech Republic in 2009 to advocate an end to "the most dangerous legacy of the Cold War," nuclear weapons. Technological innovations continue to create new channels of communication, but they have not replaced the powerful impact of public speaking.

PUBLIC SPEAKING: A DYNAMIC DISCIPLINE

Clearly, public speaking has a long history, and many of the principles taught by ancient scholars such as Aristotle are still relevant today. However, it's also a dynamic discipline that has evolved to reflect changes in society. In this section, we highlight several of these major changes: new ways of depicting the public speaking process, greater awareness of audiences' cultural diversity, new emphasis on the importance of critical thinking in preparing a speech, and increasing attention to ethics in public address.

From Linear to Transactional: Evolving Views of the Public Speaking Process

At the dawn of the modern communication disciplines, scholars viewed all forms of communication—including public speaking—as a linear process. In their view, a speech was a one-way flow of ideas from speaker to audience. That is, the speaker "injected" listeners with his or her ideas, much as a doctor injects a patient with a vaccine or antibiotic.

A MODEL OF COMMUNICATION

WE ARE ALL CHANNELS

This linear process involves several key elements. Specifically, a person with an idea to express is the **source**, and the ideas that he or she conveys to the audience constitute the **message**. The source **encodes** the message, meaning that he or she chooses **verbal** and **nonverbal symbols** to express the ideas. Verbal symbols are the words that the source uses to convey an idea; nonverbal symbols are the means of making a point without the use of words, such as hand gestures, movement, and facial expressions.

The source communicates the encoded message through a **channel**, the medium of delivery. For example, to deliver their message, speakers could simply use their voices to address a small group, rely on a microphone or the broadcast airwaves to give a speech to a huge crowd, or even post a speech online for later viewing from faraway places.

In the linear model, sources communicate their messages to one or more **receivers**, who try to make sense of the messages by decoding. To **decode**, receivers process the source's verbal and nonverbal symbols and form their own perception of the message's meaning.

Noise (also called **interference**) is a phenomenon that disrupts communication between source and receiver. Noise may be caused by external sources (for example, when a speech is drowned out by a fleet of jets roaring overhead). But noise can also originate internally—within the source or his or her listeners. For instance, a student giving an oral presentation in class might forget key elements in her speech if she is preoccupied with a recent argument with a coworker. Meanwhile, several members of her audience might have difficulty focusing on her message if they, too, are distracted by their own thoughts and concerns.

Scholars today no longer view communication as a one-way transmission of messages from source to receiver. Instead, they consider communication—including public speaking—to be transactional. A **transaction** is a communicative exchange in which all participants continuously send *and* receive messages.[23] For example, suppose you're about to deliver a speech. As you organize your notes at the lectern, you notice a man in the front row of your audience yawning. In this case, the man is both a receiver of your message and a sender of his own message: "I hope you're not planning to talk for two hours."

Participants in a public speaking transaction can also send and receive messages by providing **feedback** in the form of verbal or nonverbal responses. An audience member who shouts "That's right!" in response to a compelling point in a speech is giving feedback. People listening to a speech can also provide nonverbal feedback. For example, an audience member leans forward to express interest, nods vigorously to show agreement, folds her arms to signal disagreement, or adopts a puzzled look to convey confusion.

In the transactional model of communication, the participants in a public speaking exchange seek to create **shared meaning**—a common understanding with little confusion and few misinterpretations.[24] Good public speakers don't merely try to get their point of view across to their audience. Instead, they strive to improve their own knowledge, seek understanding, and develop agreements when they communicate with others.[25]

For example, suppose an audience member nods when the speaker says, "Our nation faces an identity theft crisis." The speaker must assume the role of *receiver* and decode the message behind that nod. The nod may mean "I agree," or it could mean "Well, duh, we all know that. Move on!" To better decode the message, a speaker may look for additional cues, such as signs of understanding or boredom on the faces of other audience members. Suppose the speaker determines that the nod conveyed agreement that identity theft is a serious problem. He or she might respond by saying, "Since we agree that identity theft has reached epidemic proportions, let's take a look at how we can prevent it." This speaker and his or her audience have created shared meaning.

SHARED MEANING

Awareness of Audiences' Cultural Diversity

Most effective and ethical public speakers today take into account the cultural backgrounds of their listeners. By **culture**, we mean the values, traditions, and rules for living that are passed from generation to generation.[26] Culture is learned, and it influences all aspects of a person's life, including religious practices, use of language, food choices, dress, and ways of communicating with others.

In the United States, public speakers have increasingly needed to consider the range of cultures represented by their audience members as American society has grown more culturally diverse.

In the words of Arnoldo Ramos, who was born in Costa Rica and is now executive director of the Council of Latino Agencies, the United States is a nation where everyone comes from somewhere else.[27] As of 2007, about one-fourth of the children under age ten in the United States have parents who were born in another country.[28] And increasingly, the birthplace of U.S. residents born abroad is a nation in Asia or Latin America, such as Mexico, the Philippines, China, or India.[29] This trend is exemplified by a list of the most common surnames of home buyers: Rodriguez, Garcia, and Hernandez have joined Smith and Johnson in the top ten, and Nguyen is number fourteen.[30] And this trend is not limited to "gateway" states such as California, New York, and Florida: Nguyen is also the fourth most frequent name among Nebraska home buyers.[31]

Communication scholars have recognized the importance of understanding and relating to persons from diverse cultures. Myron Lustig and Jolene Koester note that it is no longer likely that your clients, customers, coworkers, or neighbors have the same values, customs, or first language as you do. Your career success and personal satisfaction will increasingly depend on how well you can communicate with persons from other cultures.[32]

The most effective public speakers are sensitive to their audience members' cultural backgrounds. For example, they avoid biased language and ethnic jokes. They also adapt their delivery to acknowledge their awareness of different cultural norms regarding communication. For example, audience members from one particular culture might interpret extensive eye contact as rude or disrespectful, while individuals from another culture might welcome it. Savvy speakers take pains to identify the cultural norms of their audience and customize their presentation accordingly.

An audience member's culture not only influences how he or she perceives a speaker's behavior but also affects the person's **worldview**—the "lens" through which he or she sees and interprets

CONFLICTING WORLDVIEW PROBLEM #2

DIFFERENT WORLDVIEWS

reality. And worldview in turn influences how listeners respond to a speaker's message. For example, suppose your audience members' culture maintains a worldview that says, "It's not polite to challenge a speaker's claims." In this case, your listeners may decline to ask questions during or after your speech, since (to their thinking) asking questions may come across as being challenging and therefore disrespectful to you. But without questions, you don't have the feedback you need to assess whether your listeners have understood you.

Listeners' worldviews can also affect how they respond to a speaker's words during a presentation. For instance, the debate over United States immigration policy in 2006 aptly revealed how a person's worldview can influence his or her interpretation of—and therefore response to—a speaker's message. In 2006, the U.S. House of Representatives passed a bill intended to make illegal residence and the assisting of such efforts felony offenses, and to provide stiff fines for employers who hired illegal immigrants.[33] The Senate Judiciary Committee countered with a proposal to bolster security at the U.S./Mexico border, create a "guest worker" program for immigrants, and allow immigrants already in the United States to pay a fine and earn eventual citizenship.[34]

Americans were deeply divided over which policy was better, owing to their vastly different worldviews on who should be entitled to work and to obtain citizenship in the United States. To some people, the fact that immigrants were in the United States illegally was all the justification needed for stiffer criminal penalties and denial of the opportunity to earn citizenship. As one proponent of that viewpoint stated, "Giving amnesty to illegal aliens would be similar to catching a man driving a stolen car and then allowing him to keep the car and providing him with a lifetime supply of gas."[35] To other people, immigrants' work ethic and family values warranted a less restrictive approach. An advocate of this viewpoint stated, "They work, they pay taxes, they live here, they get married and have children here, they shop here, and they worship in local churches and are an asset to local economies."[36]

Where do you stand on the immigration policy debate? It depends on your worldview. More important, where does your *audience* stand on the topic that you're discussing in your speech? By understanding your listeners' worldviews, you can more easily gauge their likely reaction to your speech—and craft an appropriate and effective message.

Emphasis on Critical Thinking

In addition to encouraging greater attention to cultural awareness, scholars of public speaking have begun emphasizing the importance of critical thinking skills for speakers who are preparing presentations. **Critical thinking** refers to the analysis and evaluation of ideas based on reliability, truth, and accuracy. When you are engaged in critical thinking, you carefully evaluate the evidence and reasoning presented in the message.[37] You are also open-minded about your own ideas and assumptions, and subject them to the same analysis that you apply to others' viewpoints.[38]

Before you present ideas to an audience, you should feel confident that those ideas are reasonable. Rather than assuming that your beliefs are true, suspend judgment and consider other perspectives. For example, suppose you drive a car to campus and often have trouble finding a parking spot. You decide to propose a solution to the campus authorities: demolish an old building on campus and replace it with a parking structure. Historical preservation advocates, environmentalists, and campus parking officials may well have alternative viewpoints. To use your critical thinking skills in preparing to present your proposal, you would carefully consider the perspective of each of these groups, and then modify your opinions if other ideas made sense.

In exercising your critical thinking skills, you would also evaluate the probable truth of a claim you're making. Anybody can make a claim, but not all claims are based on careful analysis. For example, let's say you're researching the environmental impact of building a

THIS IS CRITICAL THINKING

* CONSIDER DIVERSE PERSPECTIVES
(SOME PEOPLE ENJOY MARCHING)

* RESEARCH
(LOOK FOR SURPRISES)

* EVALUATE EACH POSSIBILITY
(DON'T JUST OBSESS ABOUT HAVING TO CUT YOUR HAIR)

* KEEP AN OPEN MIND
(THE MORE IDEAS YOU LET IN, THE STRONGER YOUR OWN
IDEAS WILL BE WHEN THEY COME OUT)

100 REASONS TO JOIN THE ARMY

NATIONAL SERVICE NO WAY!

MANDATORY NATIONAL SERVICE
PRO   CON

ARMY LIFE

GOOD POINT!

new parking garage on campus. In this case, the views of a scientist who has studied the issue are more likely to be accurate than are unsupported opinions presented by an ill-informed person in an angry letter to the editor of the local newspaper.

A Focus on Free and Ethical Communication

Public speaking also involves careful consideration of the rights and responsibilities that come into play when individuals are free to express their ideas in a public forum. **Freedom of expression**—the right to share one's ideas and opinions free from censorship—is vital in a democratic society, where self-governance depends on both the free flow of information and open debate.

While you are guaranteed the right to express your ideas freely, as a public speaker you also have a responsibility to express your ideas ethically. **Ethics** refers to a set of beliefs shared by a group about what behaviors are correct or incorrect. Protecting freedom of expression and encouraging the ethical use of that right are increasingly important concerns in the field of public discourse. The principles endorsed by the National Communication Association include the following:

- "We advocate truthfulness, accuracy, honesty, and reason as essential to the integrity of communication."
- "We endorse freedom of expression, diversity of perspective, and tolerance of dissent to achieve the informed and responsible decision making fundamental to a civil society."[39]

Concerns about free expression and ethics are not a new consideration in public speaking. In the first century C.E., the Roman rhetorician Quintilian argued that parents and teachers should strive to produce "the good person speaking well." That is, communicators should be virtuous, moral, and public spirited, in addition to being effective orators.[40] Today, as unethical communication has increased in the United States, people have stepped up their demands for ethical public speaking. Americans are tired of politicians, lawyers, and multimillionaire chief executive officers who have lied blatantly to the public. And they have had their fill of journalists who have fabricated news stories in the hopes of winning awards. According to one-third of adults responding to a 2005 Gallup Poll, people don't even consider doctors and members of the clergy as having high credibility.[41]

Consequently, ethics have begun playing an increasingly prominent role in the study of communication, to say nothing of other disciplines. As it turns out, there's far more to public speaking than just presenting your message in a way that induces your audience to agree with you and take the actions you have advocated. You must also treat your listeners ethically. That means telling the truth, helping your audience make a well-informed decision about your topic, avoiding manipulative reasoning, and incorporating research materials properly in your speech. We say more about ethical public speaking in Chapter 3.

CHAPTER REVIEW

"Public
speaking is
right for you."

In this chapter, we introduced the field of public speaking. Key elements of public speaking are communication between speaker and audience, a focus on the audience by the speaker, an emphasis on the spoken word, and a prepared presentation. We also examined the benefits of mastering public speaking—on the job, in the classroom, in your community, and in everyday situations.

Next, we turned to the rich tradition of public speaking, citing examples from across time (including antiquity) and from around the world (such as ancient Greece and Rome, China, Africa, and the United States).

We also examined the ways in which public speaking has evolved as a discipline to reflect changes in society. We provided examples of several contemporary developments in the field: new ways of viewing the public speaking process, an emphasis on understanding your audience's cultural background, the usefulness of critical thinking when you're planning your speech, and the importance of protecting freedom of expression and making ethical use of that freedom.

Key Terms

source *20*
message *20*
encode *20*
verbal symbol *20*
nonverbal symbol *20*
channel *20*
receiver *20*
decode *20*
noise (interference) *20*

transaction *21*
feedback *21*
shared meaning *21*
culture *23*
worldview *25*
critical thinking *27*
freedom of expression *29*
ethics *29*

Review Questions

1. Describe the four basic characteristics that distinguish public speaking from other forms of communication.

2. Name and explain three ways in which becoming a competent public speaker can have a positive impact on your life and career.

3. Describe the great tradition of public speaking. Offer some specific examples of rhetoric playing a role in world events.

4. What is the transactional model of communication? How does it differ from linear models?

5. Why is it important to consider culture when analyzing an audience?

6. In what ways can you employ critical thinking in a public speaking situation?

7. Why is it important for speakers to behave ethically?

Critical Thinking Questions

1. In what ways might becoming a more effective and confident speaker affect your life? How could it impact your performance in classes? Help you in your career? Enable you to make a difference in your community?

2. Name one person whom you believe to be an effective public speaker. What are the main characteristics that make him or her effective?

3. What kinds of public speaking situations are you exposed to on a daily basis? What kind of feedback do you provide to the speaker? How might this feedback affect the speaker's message?

4. Consider your public speaking class as an audience. In what ways is the group alike? In what ways is it diverse?

5. Have you ever gotten the sense that a speaker was not being totally honest with his or her audience? What made you think that the speaker was behaving unethically?

Activities

1. Watch a video or listen to an audio recording of a famous speech, and consider it in light of the four primary characteristics of public speaking. What makes this speech significant, noteworthy, or important? In what ways does it fulfill the four characteristics of public speaking?

2. Watch a video clip from a live-broadcast public address, such as the State of the Union Address, and compare it with a clip of a cable news political pundit, such as Keith Olbermann, Bill O'Reilly, Rush Limbaugh, or Rachel Maddow. Can both clips be considered examples of public speaking? Why or why not? How does the channel of communication used affect each speaker's message and delivery? Would the political pundit have to adjust his or her message or delivery if he or she were in front of the same audience as the speaker giving the public address?

3. Watch a video of a political debate. Based on the ideas presented by each participant, what assumptions do they seem to be making about the worldview of their audience members?

Go to **bedfordstmartins.com/speakup**, where you'll find helpful study materials, videos, and speech-building tools.

DEVELOPING YOUR FIRST SPEECH

2

"Preparation and perseverance are the keys to a successful speech."

On August 28, 1963, tens of thousands of Americans traveled huge distances to join the March on Washington for Jobs and Freedom. Gathering at the Lincoln Memorial, they sang civil rights songs and hymns and listened to speeches advocating support of civil rights.[1] After nearly three hours, the final orator stood at the lectern, with the Lincoln Memorial in the background, and addressed an audience that had expanded to about 250,000 people.[2]

The speaker, Martin Luther King Jr., told the audience "I have a dream . . . a dream big enough to include all Americans."[3] The dream that King shared—one in which people would "not be judged by the color of their skin but by the content of their character"—had his listeners cheering and weeping with emotion as he concluded his address. Covered by major television networks and newspapers, the speech captured the imaginations of people around the world. And in the aftermath of the March on Washington, Congress passed civil rights legislation that banned discrimination in public facilities, in laws or practices pertaining to voting rights, and by employers.

King's "I Have a Dream" speech has won renown among speech scholars as the greatest oral presentation of the twentieth century. A gifted public speaker, King won his first oratorical contest when he was just fifteen years old.[4] Yet he still diligently prepared for the March on Washington speech, putting more care into it than any of his previous public addresses.[5] Indeed, he typically invested much time in speech preparation, writing multiple drafts of his Nobel Peace Prize acceptance speech and spending as many as fifteen hours preparing a typical Sunday sermon.[6]

The careful attention that King gave to preparing his addresses illustrates an important lesson that can benefit all public speakers, whether they have experience or are new to public speaking: *preparation and perseverance are the keys to a successful speech.* We have found that students who have a well-organized plan for speech preparation, and who devote enough time to following that plan, become more effective speakers than those who rely solely on natural talent and confidence.

In this chapter, we provide a preview of the speech preparation process. We begin by discussing the importance of preparation. Next, we cover the five major issues you should keep in mind while preparing

YOU ARE NOT PREPARED WHEN...

You waited until the last minute.

You focused on length, not quality.

a public address. Finally, we lay out steps you can follow to deliver a successful speech early in the term and offer tips for minimizing speech anxiety. In Chapters 15–19, we offer additional guidance for preparing major speech assignments, including informative or persuasive speeches, talks for special occasions, and group presentations.

WHY PREPARE?

For beginning speakers, preparation is crucial. The more rigorously you prepare your speech, the more likely you'll avoid three common problems that inexperienced public speakers typically encounter:

- *Leaving too little time for planning and practicing.* Students who wait until the last minute to develop their speeches usually deliver weaker addresses than their better-prepared classmates. Why? If you put off your assignment until just before the due date, you can't plan or practice your presentation. And without a plan or sufficient practice, you risk losing track of your thoughts while delivering your speech.

- *Focusing on length rather than quality.* Beginners sometimes focus more on meeting time requirements than on developing their ideas. They write down the first thoughts that come to mind or simply insert chunks of researched material. They don't consider what information might be most interesting, useful, or convincing to their listeners, nor do they try to organize their ideas in a way that their audience can easily follow. And the result? A disjointed, lackluster presentation.

- *Failing to follow the assignment.* A speech may impress a classroom full of beginning speakers if it's delivered well and includes interesting details.

CAREFULLY "FILED" ASSIGNMENT DESCRIPTION

You did not follow the assignment.

Yet it will not succeed if it fails to meet your instructor's assignment regarding such matters as which topics are acceptable, how the speech should be organized, and how many sources are required. Make sure to clarify such expectations before preparing your speech.

Fortunately, you don't have to succumb to these challenges. This chapter introduces steps of the speechmaking process that will help you avoid these stumbling blocks and deliver a successful speech.

THE CLASSICAL APPROACH TO SPEECH PREPARATION

The speech preparation process that we outline in this book is based on principles of rhetoric that ancient Greeks conceptualized. Cicero (106–43 B.C.E.)—a Roman lawyer, a politician, and one of history's most famed orators—elaborated on these concepts. Public speakers have been learning about these ideas for the past 2,400 years.

In his treatise *De inventione*, Cicero maintained that effective speakers attend to five key matters while preparing a speech: invention,

CLASSICAL CANONS OF RHETORIC

εὕρεσις — INVENTION

τάξις — ARRANGEMENT

λέξις — STYLE

μνήμη — MEMORY

ὑπόκρισις — DELIVERY

arrangement, style, memory, and delivery. Contemporary scholars refer to these five concepts as the **classical canons of rhetoric**. These five canons form the basis of speech preparation to this day. Here, we take a closer look at each one.

- **Invention** is the generation of ideas for use in a speech, including both the speaker's own thoughts on the topic and ideas from other sources. Speakers generate a large number of ideas for their speeches and then choose those that will best serve their purpose in an ethical manner. Talented speakers select the best ideas for a particular speech based on their analysis of their audience, their choice of topic and purpose, and the research they conduct and evidence they gather.

- **Arrangement** refers to structuring ideas to convey them effectively to an audience; today, we refer to this as *organization*. Most speeches have three main parts: an introduction, a body, and a conclusion, with the body serving as the core of the speech. Effective speakers arrange the ideas in the speech body based on the goals they hope to accomplish by delivering the speech. For example, in a persuasive speech, the three main points might explain a problem, analyze the cause of the problem, and offer the solution.

- **Style** is the choice of language that will best express a speaker's ideas to the audience. Through effective style, speakers state their ideas clearly, make their ideas memorable, and avoid bias.

- **Memory** (also known as *preparation*) is somewhat analogous to practice and refers to the work that speakers do to remain in command of their material when they present a speech.[7] This canon originally emphasized techniques for learning speeches by heart and creating mental stockpiles of words and phrases that speakers could inject into presentations where appropriate.[8] In contemporary settings, most experienced speakers don't recite speeches by rote memory; instead, they rely on extemporaneous notes. Such notes remind speakers of the key ideas in their speech but enable speakers to develop these ideas conversationally.

- **Delivery** refers to the speaker's use of his or her voice and body during the actual presentation of a speech. A strong delivery—one in which the speaker's voice, gestures, eye contact, and movements are appropriate for the audience and the setting—can make a powerful impression. Chapter 13 covers delivery skills in detail.

The five canons—invention, arrangement, style, memory, and delivery—inform the steps you will follow to prepare and deliver an effective speech.

PREPARING AND DELIVERING YOUR FIRST SPEECH

It's happened: you've just begun this course, and already your instructor has assigned your first speech. Often, this first assignment is designed to be an icebreaker—a speech introducing a classmate, for example, or talking about yourself. Such assignments are usually focused on giving students an opportunity to speak in front of the class in a low-pressure situation and a chance to get to know one another a little better. Other instructors may begin with a more substantive assignment, such as a three- to five-minute speech describing a hero in your community or an artifact that is significant to your culture. In either case, because the speech comes early in the term, you will not be expected to be familiar with all of the concepts in this book. However, your professor will have covered some of these topics and will expect to see you apply them in your presentation.

The remainder of this chapter offers a quick guide to preparing and delivering your first assigned speech. By following each of these steps, you should be able to pull together a workable speech and deliver it on the appointed day. You should refer to your assignment description or ask your instructor which of these steps you will be responsible for, and emphasize them in your preparation. If you want to know more about any of these steps, use the table on the facing page to find the corresponding chapter where each step is discussed in more detail.

ICEBREAKER ASSIGNMENTS

If you want to know more about	Go to
analyzing your audience	Ch. 5
selecting a topic for your speech	Ch. 6, pp. 175–80
determining your speech's purpose	Ch. 6, pp. 180–87
creating a thesis statement	Ch. 6, pp. 189–91
generating supporting materials	Ch. 8
selecting main and supporting points	Ch. 9, pp. 268–77
organizing the body of your speech	Ch. 9, pp. 277–87
outlining the body of your speech	Ch. 11
organizing and outlining the introduction and conclusion	Ch. 10

(continued)

(continued)

If you want to know more about	Go to
incorporating transitions	Ch. 9, pp. 288–90; Ch. 11, p. 333
considering word choice	Ch. 12
incorporating presentation aids	Ch. 14
practicing your speech	Ch. 13, pp. 388–96
delivering your speech	Ch. 13

Analyze Your Audience

 To help ensure that your speech is effective, start by thinking about the audience. **Audience analysis** is the process of learning about an audience's interests and backgrounds in order to create a speech that meets their needs. Learn about the audience members (or make educated guesses) before you select a topic and choose the ideas you will use to develop your topic. By understanding your audience members, you can boost your chances of selecting a speech topic that will appeal to them.

At this early point in the course, you may not have had the opportunity to conduct a detailed, formal analysis of your audience. However, you have probably spoken with classmates and learned about their interests and backgrounds. You may also have heard them share information about themselves, particularly if your instructor had the students in the course introduce themselves to the entire class or to another classmate on the first day. In addition, you and the other students will likely have shared experiences in class and at your college or university. Use your knowledge of these shared experiences to anticipate your listeners' attitudes and interests.

If you feel you need to do more to analyze your audience, here are some questions you could ask several classmates:

- Are there popular sports teams, activities, and traditions on campus? Unpopular experiences such as scarce parking or difficulty in signing up for required classes?
- Are the students in our class interested in politics? Do they share any common viewpoints on political issues?
- Are many of our classmates first-year students? Seniors? Do most of them live on campus or commute? Are most working to finance their education?
- What are the cultural backgrounds of the people taking this class?

Jot down responses to these questions as well as your own thoughts about topics that may interest your classmates.

Select Your Topic

Your **topic** is the subject you will address in your speech. The topic for your first speech will depend on the assignment your instructor has given you. Typical assignments include informing the class about an interesting issue you studied in another course, telling the class about a pet peeve, or sharing a cultural tradition with your audience.

To choose a topic, list as many possibilities as you can and then use your audience analysis to select one that you think would appeal most to your listeners. Your topic should also interest you. When you personally care about the topic, you'll be more willing to invest energy in preparing and practicing the speech. And you'll convey

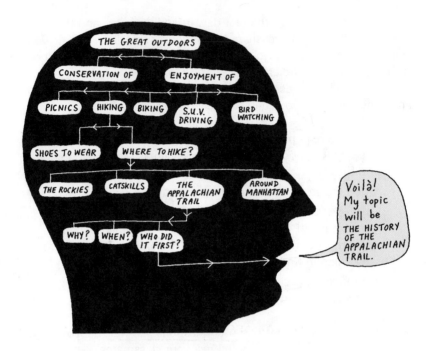

your interest in the topic while delivering your speech, which will further engage your audience.

Make sure to avoid overused topics—such as bad cafeteria food, steroids in sports, or the "art" of making a perfect peanut butter and jelly sandwich. Every instructor has a list of "reruns" that he or she would prefer not to watch again. If you choose a topic that is often presented in student speeches—for example, abortion or legalization of marijuana—you must make sure to take a fresh perspective or approach. If you have any doubts whatsoever whether your topic is appropriate, be sure to check with your instructor.

Finally, consider ways to narrow your topic. Most topics are too broad to cover in a five- or ten-minute presentation. For example, it would be impossible to tell your audience everything there is to know about your major, your culture, or your favorite sport in a single speech. Select one or more *aspects* of your topic that you think will most interest your audience and that you can also cover in the available time for your speech. For example, instead of trying to describe your entire culture, you might focus your topic on how your family or neighborhood celebrates a particular holiday.

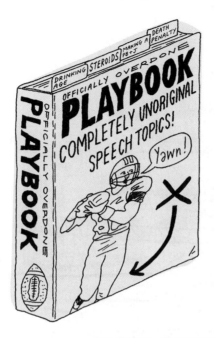

AVOID OVERUSED TOPICS

Determine Your Speech's Rhetorical Purpose

Every speech must have a **rhetorical purpose**—a primary goal for the speech. The rhetorical purpose is the reason why a speaker is giving a particular speech. For example, do you want to help listeners understand a process or become more aware of a problem? Persuade your audience to support a cause? Mark a special occasion, such as a graduation, memorial service, or wedding? Inspire audience members and move them emotionally? Provide a lighthearted and entertaining—yet worthwhile—look at your topic? Speeches typically have one of the following objectives:

- *Informing*: increasing your audience's understanding or awareness of your subject.
- *Persuading*: trying to influence your audience's beliefs or actions with respect to your subject.
- *Marking a special occasion*: speaking at events, such as graduations, memorial services, weddings, awards ceremonies, and holiday commemorations.

Clarifying your rhetorical purpose helps you shape the content of your speech. The ideas you ultimately develop and the information you present must support the purpose you've defined. For many classroom speeches, your instructor may specify a rhetorical purpose. If he or she does not, determine the purpose yourself. How? Decide whether you want your audience members to understand, believe, feel, or do something in particular about your topic after they listen to your speech. For instance, if you're giving a speech about an accomplished leader and you want your listeners to feel reverence and awe for what this person has accomplished, your rhetorical purpose would be to mark a special occasion related to the person and thus inspire and move audience members.

Create a Thesis Statement

Once you've selected your topic and identified your rhetorical purpose, draft a thesis statement for your speech. The **thesis statement** (sometimes called the *central idea* or *topic statement*) is a single sentence that sums up your speech's main message and reflects your narrowed topic and rhetorical purpose. Basically, the thesis statement should convey your speech's bottom line, enabling audience members to understand the essence of your overall speech message. Here are some examples of thesis statements:

- "Today I will inform you about how the New Year is celebrated in my culture."
- "Today I will describe a vegan diet and explain its health benefits."
- "Today it is my great pleasure to introduce an honored speaker at graduation."
- "We gather today to celebrate the life of an important scientific pioneer."
- "Tonight I hope to entertain you with a humorous look at online shopping."

Determine Your Main Points

Main points are the major ideas you will emphasize in your presentation. By calling attention to these points, you help your audience understand and remember the most important ideas from your speech. When speakers fail to do so, their listeners have difficulty following and retaining a speech's message.

Even as you select and narrow your topic, you may already begin getting ideas for main points. Researching your topic can generate additional possibilities. To identify your main points, think about which ideas would be most interesting to your audience and would best help listeners understand your thinking about the topic you've chosen.

Each main point you select must also support your thesis statement. Otherwise, your audience may conclude that you're straying off course, or they may lose interest or become confused.

Generate Supporting Materials

Once you've selected your main points, generate **supporting materials**—information that bolsters and fleshes out the claims made in each of those points. There are several types of supporting materials, including examples, definitions, testimony, statistics, narratives, and analogies. You can generate some of these materials internally by brainstorming and externally by conducting research.

Brainstorming is the process of quickly listing every idea that comes to mind, without evaluating its merits, in order to develop a substantial list of ideas. To brainstorm potential supporting materials, ask yourself questions such as "What do I know about my topic?" "What do I think is most important or interesting about this topic?" List all the responses to these questions that come to mind. Your goal is to create a diverse list of many possible ideas, not to make a final decision about which ones you will use. Therefore, write down all ideas that come to mind.

Research is the process of gathering information from libraries, quality online sources, and interviews with sources who are knowledgeable about your topic. Through research, you obtain information from experts that will enhance your understanding of the topic and strengthen your speech's credibility. Even if your instructor requires less research for your first speech than for later assignments, you should still do a little research to answer any questions you have about your topic area.

As you research, be sure to record, copy, or print any useful information you unearth. Write down what the source of the information says word-for-word, so that you can accurately quote it if you decide to use the information in your speech.

For each research source you consult, be sure to write down the **bibliographic information**, noting the following items so that you can incorporate them into your outline and your speech:

- The author—the writer or sponsoring organization of a book, an article, or an electronic database entry.
- The author's qualifications to write or speak on the subject—his or her job title; relevant education or job experience; or academic or institutional affiliation.
- The name of the source— the title of a book; the title of an article and the name of the periodical or newspaper it ran in; or the name of a person you interviewed.
- Publication date—the copyright date for a book you used; publication date of a periodical or newspaper you

SELECTING THE BEST IDEAS

researched; date you accessed a Web site; or date you conducted an interview.

- The page(s) on which you found relevant information in a printed source or the URL of an online source.

After brainstorming and researching supporting materials for your main points, select the *best* materials from all the ideas you've collected. Again, choose supporting materials that would most interest your listeners and help them grasp what you're saying about your topic.

Organize and Outline the Body of Your Speech

A speech should be well organized, meaning that your ideas are structured in a way that enables the audience to follow your message easily. To organize your speech, draft an **outline**. Your outline contains the text of your speech in complete sentences or briefer phrases (depending on what your instructor prefers).

A speech outline has three major parts: the introduction, the body, and the conclusion. The **body** is the core of your speech and is where you present your main message about your topic. For this reason, we recommend outlining the body of your speech before

ALWAYS BUILD THE BODY FIRST—IT'S THE CORE OF YOUR SPEECH (AND YOUR SNOWMAN)

outlining the introduction, even though the body follows the intro-duction when you actually deliver the speech.

To create a full-sentence outline for the body of your speech, first express each of the main points you've selected as a single sentence that states a key idea you're planning to emphasize. Then number each main point with a roman numeral. It is common to have be-tween two and five main points, although your instructor may ask you to develop a single main point in your first speech.

Next, create subpoints from the supporting materials you have gath-ered through brainstorming and research. **Subpoints** explain, prove, or expand on your main points. In your outline, indicate each subpoint with a capital letter, and indent each under its corresponding main point.

An important principle of outlining is **subordination**. Each main point must relate to your specific purpose, and each subpoint must relate to the main point that it supports. If you include additional sup-porting material under any subpoint, it must relate to that subpoint. Note also that you must use at least two subpoints for each point, if you have subdivisions at all. Here's a generic example of how sub-ordination might look in a typical outline:

    I. Main Point 1
       A. Subpoint
       B. Subpoint
          1. Sub-subpoint
          2. Sub-subpoint
    II. Main Point 2

Outline Your Introduction and Conclusion

The **introduction** to your speech serves several vital purposes, each of which is the basis for one major section of the introduction, as shown in the following list (your instructor may require a specific combination or order of these elements):

I. *Attention-getter*. Start your speech with a brief story, quotation, striking fact or statistic, or humorous incident that grabs listeners' attention while also hinting at what your speech will cover.

II. *Thesis statement*. In a single sentence, convey the topic and purpose of your speech.

III. *Show the audience "what's in it for them."* In one or two sentences, summarize why audience members should listen to your speech. Will you provide information they need to know? Information they will want to share with friends and family?

IV. *Establish your credibility*. To show that you are a believable source of information on your topic, indicate any relevant expertise, experience, or education that you have.

THE CLINCHER LEAVES YOUR AUDIENCE WITH A VIVID MEMORY OF YOUR SPEECH

V. *Preview your main points.* To help the audience understand where you will be going in your speech, list each main point using no more than one sentence per point.

The **conclusion** of your speech summarizes what you have said and leaves the audience with a memorable impression of your presentation. There are two main parts to a conclusion:

I. *Summary of your main points*—a brief recap of the major points you made during your speech.
II. *Clincher*—a closing sentence or paragraph that leaves your audience with a vivid memory of your speech. A clincher may be related to the introduction (for example, supplying a happy ending to a story you began in the attention-getter). Or it may consist of a statement or quotation that characterizes the content of your speech.

Incorporate Transitions

Once you've outlined the body, introduction, and conclusion, you will want to create transitions to connect the parts of your speech. A **transition** is a sentence that indicates you are moving from one idea to another. Transitions are especially helpful in the following places:

- between the introduction and your first main point
- between each main point
- between the final main point and the conclusion

Here are some examples of transitions:

- "First, let's talk about . . ." (*transition from introduction to first main point*)
- "Now that we've considered . . . , let's move on to . . ." (*transition between two main points*)
- "This completes our discussion of . . ." (*transition from final main point to conclusion*)

Consider Your Word Choice

Reread your entire outline, this time carefully considering the language you will use to express your ideas. Effective **word choice** (also called **diction**) can help make your speech much more memorable and engaging for listeners. When preparing your speech, select words that your audience will understand, use precise terms to express your ideas, and choose language that makes your speech come alive. Focus on simplifying your sentences—remember, audiences cannot reread parts of your speech if they become confused. Finally, be sure to avoid biased language that may hurt others or damage your credibility.

Consider Presentation Aids

A **presentation aid** is anything (in addition to your speech) that your audience members can see or hear that helps them understand and re-member your message. Traditional aids include actual objects (for example, a physical model of DNA), video and au-dio recordings (such as a short clip of several birds and their calls), drawings, photographs, charts, maps, and graphs. PowerPoint presentations or other elec-tronic slide shows are also common aids. Some instructors may allow or even require aids for your first speech.

To get the most from your presentation aids, make sure each one supports your point. For example, if you want your audience to appreci-ate the differences between bird calls, an audio recording that clearly demonstrates those differences would be entirely relevant. Also take care that audio aids are loud and clear and that visual aids are uncluttered and large enough for your audience to see from all points in the room. The key point to remember is that presentation aids should support your spoken presenta-tion, not overshadow it.

Practice Your Speech

After outlining your speech, considering word choice, and creating any presentation aids, make sure to practice your speech. With practice, you'll feel more confident about your presentation—and more comfortable talking in front of your classmates. Becoming more comfortable through practice will allow you to work on the **extemporaneous delivery** of your speech—that is, your ability to deliver your speech smoothly and confidently from your outline without reading from it. To do this, practice delivering your speech from your outline at least four or five times, until the content starts to feel familiar. Then condense your outline into a set of briefer notes. Using these notes, try delivering the speech in a more conversational way, explaining the main points and subpoints in your own words, without reading word-for-word. If you have time, condense your outline even further to a list of your main points and the titles or summaries of the subpoints supporting each main point. This will be the outline you use when actually presenting your speech. Consider documenting your speaking outline on a series of index cards, recording one main point and the title or summary of each subpoint on each card. Alternatively, you could write the speaking outline on a small number of 8.5 x 11 inch pieces of paper, in large type.

Deliver Your Speech

The moment has come: you're watching a classmate wrap up her speech, and you're next in line. As you approach the lectern and start delivering your speech, keep the following guidelines in mind:

- *Project your voice.* Speak loudly and slowly enough that your audience can easily hear what you are saying.
- *Maintain an even rate of speaking.* Many speakers tend to rush through a speech, particularly if they are nervous. Speak at a rate that enables you to pronounce the words clearly and allows the audience to follow your speech.
- *Convey interest in your topic.* Maintain energy and variety in your speaking voice, so that you build audience enthusiasm for your speech.
- *Maintain eye contact.* Try to make eye contact with people in each section of the room during the course of your presentation.

Each speech you deliver is a learning experience. Your instructor (and perhaps your classmates) will offer feedback after your presentations. Use these suggestions to prepare future speeches; you'll soon see your public speaking skills improve.

OVERCOMING SPEECH ANXIETY

As you follow the steps for preparing your first speech, you may begin experiencing some nervousness about delivering your talk. If so, you're not alone. Many people feel nervous (at the very least) before they speak in public, even professionals who know their subject well.[9] The symptoms of **speech anxiety**—the worry or fear that some people experience before giving a talk (also called **stage fright**)—can take a wide variety of forms. Some people experience the stereotypical sensation of "butterflies in the stomach," as well as sweaty palms and a dry mouth. Others endure nausea, hyperventilation, and downright panic.

A little nervousness can actually be a good thing when you're giving a speech: it helps focus your attention. But in its extreme forms, speech anxiety can prevent you from speaking clearly or keeping your train of thought while delivering your presentation. Though speech anxiety is quite common, you *can* learn to manage it. As one seasoned public speaker put it, "You may not be able to get rid of the butterflies, but you can at least get them flying information." The following strategies can help you combat speech anxiety.

GET THE BUTTERFLIES FLYING IN FORMATION

Select a Topic You Know and Enjoy

If you know your subject well, you'll find researching and planning your speech relatively easy, which leaves you more time to practice your delivery. And with more practice, you'll be better prepared and more relaxed in front of your audience. When you're familiar with your topic, you'll also notice that it's easier to explain the topic naturally, as you would in a conversation with a friend. And when you select a subject that you also enjoy, your interest adds enthusiasm to your speaking voice, which engages your audience even more.

Start Preparing Early

Resist any temptation to procrastinate in preparing your speech. Select a topic as soon as possible after receiving an assignment. Also complete an outline of your speech well before the day you're scheduled to present it. Drafting an outline mitigates anxiety because it shows you

	8	9	10	11	12	13
	PICK TOPIC ✓ ~~DOGS-CATS~~ PETS✓	RESEARCH Who keeps records?	RESEARCH Survey? Visit vet?✓ online?	RESEARCH Rules✓ Library✓	READ ✓	Buy onions — Make outline
14 STOP PROCRAST- INATING!	**15** Lilly's birthday PRACTICE	**16** REVISE✓ MoRE ✓ PRACTICE	**17** YET MORE PRACTICE + GET HAIRCUT	**18** REST + RELAXATION	**19** THE BIG DAY	**20** Ha ha ha! You did it!!!

EARLY PREPARATION IS KEY

that you've at least established the basics for your presentation. It also gives you time to develop the full speech and "test drive" it with trusted friends, family members, or teachers to get their ideas for fine-tuning it.

Take Care of Yourself

Get a good night's sleep before a speech. And avoid excessive sugar and caffeinated beverages the morning of your presentation—these will only get you hyped up even more. If you don't feel much like eating on the day of your speech, consume a light meal before you deliver your presentation. Then reward yourself with a favorite feast when it's all over.

Also budget your time in the days leading up to your speech. It's hard to get sufficient sleep, prepare nutritious meals, and practice your presentation if you have to work six hours, study for a test, and write a ten-page paper the day before you deliver your speech. Having too much to do in too little time intensifies anxiety. To avoid this scenario, look at the syllabi for all your courses early in the semester to see when major assignments are due. Consider other commitments as well, such as job, family, and community responsibilities. Then plan your time so that the days leading up to your speech are as relaxed as possible.

Visualize Success

Researchers have found that visualizing success reduces anxiety for public speaking students.[10] With **visualization**, you imagine yourself scoring a resounding success, such as presenting your speech without a hitch and winning enthusiastic applause from an appreciative audience. Make your visualization as specific as possible. For example, imagine yourself striding confidently to the front of the room. Watch as you present your speech to the audience in the same way you would converse with a friend—natural and relaxed. Visualize the audience nodding in agreement with a key point, smiling when an idea hits home, and laughing at your jokes. Listen to the thundering applause as you wrap up your speech. The power of positive thinking is no mere cliché. When you visualize success, you can ease your anxiety—if not eradicate it entirely.

Use Relaxation Techniques

When you're suffering from speech anxiety, your muscles tense up, and your mind swarms with negative thoughts. You know you should relax. But who can chill out on command? **Relaxation strategies**—techniques that reduce muscle tension and negative thoughts—can help. For many people, exercise is a powerful relaxation strategy. It helps you expend energy before you tackle preparing your speech, and it leaves you relaxed and limber on the day of your presentation. It's also renowned for clearing your mind. But exercising doesn't necessarily mean heading for the nearest gym to lift weights or take a Pilates class. All you have to do is practice tightening and releasing your muscles—wherever you are at the moment. Breathe in as you tighten a group of muscles, and then exhale as you release the tension. Consider progressing from your neck muscles down to your feet. You can use this and other relaxation techniques even as you're waiting to deliver your speech.

Here's another relaxation strategy: budget some time for an activity that you enjoy—reading, watching a movie (comedies are great for relaxation), listening to music, gardening—before the day of your speech. If you simply don't have time for such activities, imagine yourself in a situation or setting that you find peaceful and serene—whether it's sitting silently atop a mountain, strolling along a beach during a gorgeous sunset, or enjoying some other scene that you find restful.

Volunteer to Speak First

Many public speakers experience more anxiety shortly before their presentation than during the actual speech.[11] If this describes you and you're going to be one of several speakers in a class or program, ask to speak first—or as early as possible in the lineup. That way, you'll have less time to work up a debilitating level of worry.

CHAPTER REVIEW

"Preparation and perseverance are the keys to a successful speech."

The most successful presentations in history, such as Martin Luther King's "I Have a Dream" speech, usually derive from careful thought, planning, and preparation. Both beginning and more experienced speakers should remember this lesson—even a first-time speaker can give a much stronger presentation by taking a bit of extra time and effort.

In this chapter, we emphasized the importance of preparing for public speaking. First, we introduced the five classical canons of rhetoric, a set of guidelines that continue to inform the way many speech instructors teach speech preparation today.

Next, we presented a step-by-step process for preparing your first speech. It's important to note that preparing a speech is a craft comprising a set of specific skills that you can master. The main steps are analyzing the audience; selecting a topic; determining the rhetorical purpose; creating a thesis statement; developing main and supporting points; organizing and outlining the body, introduction, conclusion, and transitions; considering word choice and presentation aids; and practicing and delivering the speech. By making good choices at each step of the speech preparation process, you improve your chances of delivering a successful presentation.

In this chapter, we also outlined some basic techniques to help you overcome your speech anxiety by emphasizing the idea that you can channel your nervousness to help you become a better speaker. To help you "get the butterflies flying in formation," we suggest that you select a topic that you know and enjoy, and that you give yourself adequate time to prepare and practice your speech. Also strive to take care of yourself by balancing responsibilities with personal needs, such as getting enough rest, relaxation, and exercise. To keep a positive outlook, try visualizing success and practicing relaxation techniques. Finally, ease your nervousness on the day of the speech by volunteering to go first.

Key Terms

classical canons of rhetoric *39*
invention *39*
arrangement *39*
style *39*
memory (preparation) *39*
delivery *40*
audience analysis *42*
topic *43*
rhetorical purpose *45*
thesis statement *46*
main points *47*
supporting materials *48*
brainstorming *48*
research *48*

bibliographic information *49*
outline *50*
body *50*
subpoints *51*
subordination *51*
introduction *51*
conclusion *53*
transition *53*
word choice (diction) *54*
presentation aid *55*
extemporaneous delivery *56*
speech anxiety (stage fright) *57*
visualization *61*
relaxation strategies *62*

Review Questions

1. What are three common mistakes that inexperienced speakers make when preparing a speech?
2. Name and define each of the five classical canons of rhetoric.
3. What is audience analysis, and why is it important?
4. Explain what is meant by rhetorical purpose. What are the three basic rhetorical purposes that speeches can serve?
5. What is a thesis statement, and how does it differ from a speech topic?
6. What are supporting materials, and how do they help a speaker develop main points?
7. Define *main points* and *subpoints*, and explain the principle of subordination.

8. What are presentation aids, and how can a speaker make sure that they support his or her message?

9. What is extemporaneous delivery, and why is it generally the best approach for speakers?

10. List three guidelines for effective delivery.

11. Name and explain five techniques that can help you overcome speech anxiety.

Critical Thinking Questions

1. How would you analyze your public speaking classmates as an audience? Consider the backgrounds and interests of your classmates. What are some of their shared experiences? How could you use this information to adapt a speech to your classmates?

2. Have you ever felt that a speaker was not making his or her case well? What made you think so? What could the speaker have done better?

3. How would the research and supporting materials you would use in a persuasive speech differ from those you would use in a special-occasion speech?

4. When you see a speaker who is obviously feeling nervous, how can you as an audience member help put him or her at ease? Can thinking about your experience as an audience member help you feel less nervous as a speaker?

Activities

1. Consider a speech that impressed you—an on-air editorial, for example, or a campaign speech from a candidate you respect. Download a copy of the text (most news sources and candidate Web sites make such text available), and then outline the speech. How well did the speaker structure the speech? Can you identify the thesis statement? The main points? The subpoints? Supporting materials?

2. Think back on any awards programs you like to watch (for example, the Oscars, Grammys, ESPYs, or Video Music Awards) and the ways in which different winners approach their acceptance speeches. Is it obvious when a winner has prepared a speech beforehand? Is it obvious when he or she has not? Have any speakers made comments that you thought were inappropriate for that type of event?

3. Go online and research famous speeches, such as Martin Luther King Jr.'s "I Have a Dream" (1963); George W. Bush's remarks in memory of the *Columbia* astronauts (2003); Sojourner Truth's "Ain't I a Woman?" (1851); or Margaret Chase Smith's "Declaration of Conscience" (1950). Can you identify the rhetorical purpose of each speech? (Note: Each of these speeches can be accessed at American Rhetoric, americanrhetoric.com.)

Go to **bedfordstmartins.com/speakup,** where you'll find helpful study materials, videos, and speech-building tools.

SPEECH ETHICS 3

"Strive to be an ethical public speaker."

All of us face difficult choices throughout our lives. For example, imagine that your romantic partner recently modeled a new, expensive sweater, saying, "I just love this fabric. What do you think? Do I look good in this?" You find the sweater downright ugly, but you know (from experience) that if you answer honestly, you will hurt your loved one's feelings and perhaps even start a fight. Yet you also feel uncomfortable telling a lie. So you hesitate, wondering what exactly to say.

Some of these difficult decisions may have much more significant consequences. Consider Joe, a college student on a scholarship with solid grades and a reputation for integrity. Joe is preparing a speech that he'll need to deliver in his public speaking class at the end of the week. The speech is important because he cares about public speaking and because he needs to maintain a B+ average to keep his scholarship. He's done some research on his topic already and has found some excellent supporting materials, which he has documented diligently. But he still needs to do more work, and he plans to wrap up his research the night before his speech. That evening, his car breaks down on the way to the library. By the time he gets the car towed to a garage and returns home, he has run out of time to do the rest of the research he needs to finish developing his speech. Panicked, he jumps on the Internet and soon finds the text for a great speech related to his topic. He really likes the language in the speech and doesn't think he could get the information across as well in his own words, so he considers cutting and pasting a few paragraphs from the speech into his own outline. He knows this would amount to plagiarism, but he tells himself, "It would just be this once; I don't have time to put the text into my own words, and if I don't do it, my scholarship could be on the line." The scenario with your romantic partner's sweater and the story about Joe demonstrate the difficulty posed by ethical dilemmas—situations in which the right decision isn't immediately clear.

In public speaking, **ethics**—rules and values that a group defines to guide conduct and distinguish between right and wrong—can come into play during every stage of the process. For example, as you research and write your speech, you must make decisions about what information you'll include in your presentation and how that information will influence your audience. As you deliver your speech, you have to make choices about the language and tone of voice you use, and how those aspects of your presentation will affect your listeners. In this chapter, we examine the responsibilities of both speakers and their audiences.

CODES OF ETHICS: ABSOLUTE, SITUATIONAL, AND CULTURALLY RELATIVE

How do people make ethical choices? Some adopt a code of behavior they commit to using consistently. These individuals are demonstrating **ethical absolutism**—the belief that people should exhibit the same behavior in all situations. For instance, you would be using ethical absolutism if you decided to tell your romantic partner how you really felt about the sweater. In this case, your code of ethics might contain a principle saying, "People should always tell the truth, even if doing so hurts loved ones."

Other people use **situational ethics**—which hold that correct behavior can vary depending on the situation at hand. Joe, for example, would be (inappropriately) using situational ethics if he decided that under the extenuating circumstances, it would be okay for him to plagiarize "just this one time."

Whether you tend to see ethical decisions in absolute or situational terms, there are some generalizations that apply in most situations. For example, most societies believe that it's more ethical to tell the truth than to lie. In the context of public speaking, most people believe that lying is wrong. They see it as an ethical violation, not to mention (in some circumstances) a possible violation of the law.

Yet some of these same individuals might think little or nothing of intentionally exaggerating their qualifications during a job interview—especially if they believe that "everybody does it and gets away with it." Thus, many people use a blend of approaches to making ethics-related choices. In truth, most people are not strictly absolutists; even

SOMETIMES WE LOOK TO OUR LEADERS AS MODELS OF ETHICAL BEHAVIOR. SOMETIMES WE CAN BE DISAPPOINTED.

those who generally follow a strict ethical code may sometimes face dilemmas that compel them to engage in situational ethics, and all of us face such situations at some point in our lives.

In this book, we do not presume to tell you what your ethical system must be; we do insist, however, that you always strive to make the most ethical choice. To help you with such choices, in this chapter we expose you to the kinds of communication-related ethical dilemmas that speakers and audience members sometimes face, and we explore behaviors most people consider unethical. As you'll discover, one guiding principle that can help you make ethical choices is that of respect for other people—treating others in ways you would want to be treated, as well as avoiding treating them in ways you would *not* want to be treated. For instance, if you would resent a public speaker who had withheld important information in order to persuade you to take a particular action, you shouldn't exhibit that same behavior in your own speeches.

Ethics can also vary across societies, making them **culturally relative.** For example, in some cultures, people consider knowledge to be something that is owned collectively rather than by individuals.

In cultures with strong oral and narrative traditions, for example, stories are passed from one generation to another and are shared as general cultural knowledge. In such cultures, people don't consider working together or paraphrasing without attribution to be cheating or any other form of unethical behavior. When discussing ethics in this book, we reflect a Western cultural perspective, which holds that individuals do own the knowledge they create. This perspective informs the academic guidelines and honor codes that are stated explicitly by most colleges and universities in the United States—indeed, you will often find these guidelines cited in your instructors' syllabi. Thus, we require proper citation and attribution of sources for all speeches.

As you approach the following sections about ethics and public speaking, consider your own approach to making ethical decisions while developing and delivering presentations. What are your beliefs regarding proper behavior in general and in public speaking in particular? Do you always honor these beliefs strictly—or only in certain situations? To help you answer these questions, let's consider some of the ethical issues you may confront in public speaking. These include communicating truthfully, crediting others' work, using sound reasoning, and behaving ethically when you're listening to someone else give a speech. Though making ethical choices in public speaking situations can sometimes be difficult, this chapter will help you develop a responsible system for doing so. The key word here is *responsibility*; whenever you give a speech, you wield power—over what your listeners think, how they feel, and what actions they end up taking. You're thus responsible for your audience's well-being. And making sound ethical decisions as you develop and deliver your speech constitutes one important way to shoulder that responsibility. The following sections offer guidelines for exhibiting ethically responsible behavior in public speaking.

LEGAL SPEECH, ETHICAL SPEECH

As we connect ethics and public speaking, it is worth observing that many people in the United States often confuse (sometimes intentionally) **ethical speech** with **legally protected speech.** While these

It's perfectly **LEGAL** for me to describe my speech as **ORGANIC** (as it does contain some organic material).

It's **ETHICAL** for me to describe my speech as 5% **ORGANIC** (as that's all the organic material it contains).

two concepts sometimes overlap—that is, what you say is both legal and ethically responsible to your audience—they are most definitely *not* the same. Ethical speech refers to incorporating ethical decision making into how you engage the public speaking process *and* ultimately what you say. It means that you follow guidelines for telling the truth and avoid misleading an audience—because such actions are ethical and *the right thing to do*.

Focusing on legally protected speech, by contrast, refers to using the law as your boundary for what you may say *and* how you say it. Thus, with this approach, you would make decisions about telling the truth or withholding information based on whether there is a legal requirement to make a certain action or a legal consequence for violating the rules. When you rely on legal guidelines for acceptable speech, your decision-making calculus has nothing to do with ethics—it is only driven by what is technically within legal rules. If you (unethically) use legal protection as your guiding principle for speaking, you can technically stay within the bounds of what is lawful but still speak unethically.

It's vital to note that far more types of speech are technically legal than are strictly ethical. In the United States, the First Amendment to the Constitution mandates "freedom of speech," and this freedom allows for a vast range of legally protected statements. In fact, there are relatively few exceptions, and these are typically handled in narrow terms such as slander (intentional falsehood about another person), fighting words (words meant to provoke a violent response), and obscenity (hard-core, sexually explicit expression). Political speech—expression that relates to political discourse—is the most legally protected and privileged form of expression under the First Amendment. However, just because something is political speech (or any form of legally protected speech) doesn't mean that it is ethically responsible. For example, in a speech at the Conservative Political Action Conference in March 2007, columnist Ann Coulter referred to Democratic presidential candidate John Edwards with a homophobic sexual epithet. As political speech, her comments were fully protected by the law, but that does not make her speech ethically responsible.

Be certain you understand the distinction between ethical and legal speech when crafting your own presentations—and remember that when you consider ethics here, you are doing more than just what is legally required—you are doing what is morally correct for your situation.

COMMUNICATING TRUTHFULLY

The most basic ethical guideline for public speaking is this: *tell your audience the truth.* How do you feel when someone has lied to you or intentionally misled you? If you're like most people, you resent it and feel manipulated by it. Audience members who discover that a speaker has deceived them seldom believe anything that person said—and they rarely do what he or she asks of them. They also remember being lied to. A known liar will have trouble ever convincing future listeners of his or her credibility or trustworthiness.

That being said, the words *truth* and *truthfully* are fairly subjective and elude precise definition. It is easier to describe truth in public speaking by examining what is *not* truth.

Lying

Public speakers who lie are intentionally seeking to deceive their audience. Why do people lie when giving a presentation? Some fear what their listeners would do if they knew the truth; they don't trust their audience to react in a supportive or understanding way. For example, an older student once fabricated his identity as a military veteran for a speech he gave in which he demonstrated gun-safety tips. He suggested that he had gone into the army straight out of high school and had received training in the use of many firearms. He told this lie because he believed that it would give him more credibility in his audience's eyes. Yet the audience might have accepted his suggestions anyway; after all, a safety certification course is a worthy credential in itself. By lying about his background, he risked losing his listeners' trust if they ever learned of his deception.

Half-Truths

When a speaker reveals only part of the truth and then mixes it with a lie, he or she is telling a **half-truth**. In practice, a half-truth has the same damaging impact as a lie: it deceives the audience. Consider the example of a corporate manager who is required to explain to the board of directors why her company has lost so many top executives in recent months. In her presentation, she says that many departing executives had simply elected to take early retirement or had accepted positions at other companies—normal occurrences in business. The part of her answer regarding accepting positions at other firms was true. But the part of her answer regarding early retirement was a half-truth. As it turned out, two of the executives who chose to retire early did so as part of a legal settlement related to accusations of accounting malpractice.

False Inference

When a speaker presents information that leads listeners to an incorrect conclusion, that speaker has caused a **false inference**. Speakers who commit this ethical breach intentionally drop hints designed to make their audience believe something that isn't true. For example, in a presentation titled "UFOs, Extraterrestrials, and the Supernatural," a student described a series of events that occurred in a midwestern town: an increase in the number of babies with birth defects, a rise in the rate of kidnapping, and a jump in the amount of farmland seized by the federal government. This student did not say outright that there was a government conspiracy to conceal the presence of aliens and UFOs, or a plot to cross-breed aliens and humans. However, he clearly intended his audience to draw this inference from his presentation. In reality, the increase in birth defects amounted to exactly one—from six to seven. The increase in kidnapping was actually a statewide statistic, caused by a change in laws about divorce and child custody. And the government seizure of land had happened—but only for the construction of a highway overpass. The speaker had arranged his facts in such a way that his audience would conclude that the government was trying to conceal the presence of aliens.

False inferences can also occur accidentally, like when a speaker gathers insufficient data and therefore unknowingly presents an incomplete understanding of the speech topic to the audience. Accidental false inference isn't unethical, but it prevents you from conveying accurate information to your audience. Thus, it damages the effectiveness of your speech. To avoid an accidental *or* a deliberate false inference, avoid overgeneralized claims based on statistical findings. And always explain to your audience what the statistics mean and how they were derived.

Taking evidence out of context is another form of false inference. Here, the speaker shares a source's data or statements without explaining how they relate to the original situation. The speaker uses these facts or words *selectively* to support an argument. For example, in a speech about the propensity of pit bulls to attack people, a student once quoted an animal-behavior expert out of context to imply a genetic predisposition toward attack: "[T]here is an observable tendency in the genetic makeup of pit bulls to viciously attack humans. . . ." The student did *not* explain to her audience that the quotation came from this longer statement:

> Some have argued that there is an observable tendency in the genetic makeup of pit bulls to viciously attack humans. But surely this is not the case. While it is true that *some* pit bulls have attacked *some* humans, there is no research to definitively prove a genetic tendency to attack humans. More study of this is needed.

OUT—OF—CONTEXT EVIDENCE

"... ~~Some have argued that~~ there is an observable tendency in the genetic makeup of pit bulls to viciously attack humans. ~~But surely this is not the case. While it is true that some pit bulls have attacked some humans, there is no research to definitively prove a genetic tendency to attack humans.~~ More ~~study of this is needed...~~"

"... Some have argued that there is an observable tendency in the genetic makeup of pit bulls to viciously attack humans. But surely this is not the case. While it is true that *some* pit bulls have attacked *some* humans, there is no research to definitively prove a genetic tendency to attack humans. More study of this is needed..."

Philosophers—and cheating romantic partners—have long argued about whether keeping silent about something is the same thing as lying about it. Thus, **omission** is another source of false inference. Here, presenters mislead the audience not by what they say but by what is left unsaid. For example, in a presentation about on-campus drug use, a student government representative was asked about the extent of drug use and abuse in her campus dormitory. In response, she merely smiled and moved on to another question. Her silence implied that there was no drug problem in her dormitory, but in fact, her dorm had the worst record for on-campus substance abuse. If silence about a topic will mislead your audience, and if you are aware of this likelihood but withhold information anyway, you have acted unethically through omission. Such actions suggest that you view your listeners as consumers of information and take an unethical and cynical *caveat emptor* (let the buyer beware) approach to public speaking.

To communicate truthfully and therefore ethically, never lie, never tell half-truths, and never cause false inferences—whether by taking evidence out of context or by omitting pertinent information. There are always alternatives to these behaviors. For example, if you fear that the truth may weaken your argument, then you need to do further research and think about your topic. There are at least two sides to every issue, as well as multiple solutions and perspectives to consider. If you fear what the audience might think if they knew the truth, consider the opposite: how will they react if they learn you have deceived them? In most situations, listeners will react to a lie much more negatively than to an unwelcome truth.

ACKNOWLEDGING THE WORK OF OTHERS

Researching a speech topic exposes you to a wealth of interesting facts, information, and ideas—many of which you will want to include in your presentation. But finding these materials also raises some questions: Should you include a particular piece of information in your presentation? If so, how should you use it? And how will you acknowledge its source?

Listeners—and especially speech instructors—want speakers to demonstrate their own ideas and thinking during a presentation. At the same time, all of us recognize that most speeches can be enhanced by research and examples from outside sources. The question is, how should you reconcile these objectives? To do so, you must use a blend of materials that demonstrates your own ideas and also ethically incorporates and acknowledges the original ideas of others. This approach is honest for you and fair to your listeners and sources.

Imagine coming across an article or a published essay addressing the same topic as your speech—as Joe did when he was rushing to complete his speech preparation. Maybe you admire the way the authors have worded their prose. Would there be a problem if you incorporated a few lines from the article word-for-word into the text of your speech without citing the quotations? What about taking a preponderance of the ideas from the publication and making them your own by rewording them but not attributing them to the author? Would that be unethical? The answer to both questions is an unequivocal "Yes!"

Presenting another person's words or ideas as if they were your own is called **plagiarism,** and it is always unethical. If you plagiarize, you mislead your audience by misrepresenting the source of the material you've used. Equally important, when you plagiarize, you are stealing the ideas and words of another person.

Though plagiarism is wrong, people sometimes have difficulty discerning the line between plagiarism and appropriate use of researched material. To illustrate why, let's consider plagiarism in two contexts: quoting from a source and paraphrasing the work of others.

Quoting from a Source

Suppose a student named Larissa gave a speech informing her audience about the history of drive-in movie theaters. She had drawn her inspiration from a magazine article she saw in an airport while traveling home from school for the holidays. She thought the topic was unusual enough to make an interesting presentation, and she later shared the idea with her instructor, who approved the choice of topic.

When trying to research the topic, however, Larissa could find little or no material beyond the magazine article she had found in the airport. Panic set in as the day for her in-class speech approached. In desperation, Larissa decided that no one in her class could have known about the article because it was published in a magazine called *Nevada Horizons*, sold only in the greater Las Vegas area, and because Larissa attended college at the University of Michigan—in Ann Arbor. Rationalizing her actions, she took the article and used nearly all of it verbatim as her speech.

It turned out that the magazine article had appeared simultaneously in several different publications, including a large national newspaper. As fate would have it, Larissa's instructor had read the article in the newspaper. Larissa earned an F in the class and was suspended from school.

Clearly, what Larissa did constituted plagiarism. But suppose that she had taken only one-third, one-half, or even just a few lines from the story and represented the material as her own. Would any of these scenarios still constitute plagiarism? Yes. Whether she lifted five pages or one page or only a single sentence, she would still be stealing the original author's words and ideas. By analogy, whether you steal one or two eggs—or an entire dozen—will matter little to a shop owner. Either way, you stole the eggs.

Plagiarism is particularly common among students who research their speech topics online. The temptation to lift and use text from a Web site can be overwhelming, but doing so without attribution is stealing. Students also face the danger of unintentional plagiarism when they copy a quotation from a source and paste it into their notes without writing down the citation information; when they return to their notes later, they may not remember that they had copied and pasted the material as opposed to writing it themselves.

Most of the direct quotations you use in a speech will be short—a line or two, or at most, a paragraph. To avoid plagiarism, you must attribute the quote to its source. How should you cite the source? If Larissa had used just several quotes from the magazine article, she might have attributed this material in the following way:

> As Roberta Gonzales wrote in the June 19 issue of *Nevada Horizons* (p. D4), "The growth and popularity of drive-in theaters tracked with the affordability of automobiles for a larger and younger population of drivers."

The first part of this sentence is the attribution. Note that the page number is mentioned. In delivering your speech, it's okay not to cite the page numbers of all your sources. However, we strongly suggest that you document a complete citation on your speech outline or text. That way, anyone (including your instructor) who wants to check your facts can easily do so. Before preparing your speech, make sure to check with your instructor to find out if he or she has additional expectations for proper attribution.

Paraphrasing the Work of Others

Suppose Larissa never lifted the text from the magazine article verbatim. Instead, she used **paraphrasing**—restating the original author's ideas in her own words. Would this constitute plagiarism?

This is where the rules defining plagiarism are a bit less clear. Is it stealing if you use your own words but not necessarily your own ideas? Your teachers will not expect you to be an authority on every speech topic you address; you *will* have to research your subject matter. This may cause you to wonder: "How could it be plagiarism if I'm paraphrasing someone else's words or ideas? After all, these are *my* words!"

Students at the college level regularly struggle with this challenge. To resolve the dilemma, consider this simple rule of thumb: if you're using most or all of the original material, simply rearranged and restated in your own words, you're still taking another person's ideas and presenting them as your own. This isn't the same as directly copying without attribution, but it is wrong on several fronts. For one thing, you're not generating your own ideas and opinions about your topic—so you're not meeting your instructor's expectations. For another, you're being unfair to the person whose ideas you're presenting as your own.

The safest bet is always to acknowledge the original source of any material you use in your speech, whether you are directly quoting or paraphrasing. And avoid paraphrasing large portions of an original source or another work in its entirety. For example, if Larissa had paraphrased some ideas from the magazine article, she could have mentioned the author and source of her material in this way:

> According to Roberta Gonzales, writing in the June 19 issue of *Nevada Horizons* on page D4, drive-in theaters tended to grow in popularity with Americans who were increasingly able to afford and enjoy the freedom of automobiles. This was especially true of younger drivers, who yearned for freedom of mobility and a common place to meet and socialize outside the scrutiny of mom and dad.

In this case, Larissa would have appropriately paraphrased the material and given proper credit to the original source.

Common Knowledge

There are limited situations—known as common knowledge—in which you can use information from a source without giving a direct citation. **Common knowledge** information is widely known and disseminated in many sources. For example, you may not need to cite the fact that France presented the Statue of Liberty to the United States in 1886, but you might need to cite a source if you wanted to give statistics such as the statue's total weight (125 tons), the weight of the statue's concrete foundation (27,000 tons), or the distance the statue's torch sways in the wind (5 inches).[1] Be sure to check with your instructor on guidelines for common knowledge. But most importantly, remember the following: if you are in any doubt, include the citation.

USING SOUND REASONING

Every public speaker has a responsibility to provide well-reasoned support for his or her points. **Fallacious reasoning** is faulty (and thus unsound) reasoning, in which the link between a claim and its supporting material is weak. Unfortunately, fallacious reasoning is all too common in speeches, even if it's often unintentional. But when public speakers *intentionally* misuse logic to deceive their audience, their actions are profoundly unethical. In this section, we address four ways in which a speaker might misuse logic: *hasty generalization*, *post hoc fallacy*, *personal attack*, and *bandwagoning*. We discuss these and other logical fallacies in more depth in Chapter 17, Methods of Persuasion.

Hasty Generalization

A speaker who intentionally generalizes about all members of a group from information based on a limited part of the group is making a **hasty generalization**.

   For example, a student once suggested in his speech that all fruits and vegetables grown in California should be taken off the market because of a number of reported cases of E. coli infection. Although he generalized about all fruits and vegetables grown in the Golden

HASTY GENERALIZATION

...across the nation fruits and vegetables of all shapes and colors are being rounded up. In a press conference this afternoon the secretary of agriculture warned that since E. coli was found in Californian broccoli, none of them can be trusted. "It could be lurking anywhere. All produce is suspect," he said.

State, the information on which he based his statement applied only to a type of broccoli that had been grown in Monterey County, in the central part of the state.

The speaker was correct about the need to take broccoli grown in that particular area off the market, but he intentionally overgeneralized about all fruits and vegetables produced in California. Before making such a claim, this student should have researched other types of vegetables (and other types of broccoli) grown in Monterey and across the state. And he should have avoided mentioning fruit entirely—there was no indication that the E. coli problem affected it.

Post Hoc (After the Fact) Fallacy

A **post hoc fallacy** occurs when a speaker wrongly identifies the cause of one event as the event that immediately preceded it. (The Latin phrase *post hoc* literally means "after this.") Here, the speaker's line of reasoning goes something like this: "Event B happened after event A; therefore, event B was caused by event A."

For instance, in a speech about notorious murders, a student described the killing of a famous man by one of his children. The student reported that the man had recently remarried after divorcing his

POST HOC FALLACY

MONDAY MORNING:	TUESDAY MORNING:	TUESDAY AFTERNOON:
Cool!	Even Cooler!	Of course: EAGLES WIN SUPER BOWL + STOCK MARKET GOES UP = EAGLES CONTROL WALL STREET.

wife of twenty-five years. The student then suggested that "the divorce caused the man's son to commit the murder—because a child's anger over divorce is known to be a cause of aberrant behavior." If the student had used this reasoning along with other evidence (such as findings from a psychiatrist's examination of the son), he would *not* have committed this fallacy. But because he offered no other evidence, he misled his audience, especially given that the "child" in question—the son—was an adult at the time of the murder. This speaker could not credibly claim that the divorce, in itself, caused the murder.

Personal Attacks

You big DOG HATER!

Ha, you're a CAT HATER!

Some speakers try to compensate for weak arguments by making **personal attacks**—also known as *ad hominem* attacks—on their opponents. (In Latin, *ad hominem* means "to the man.") In a campaign speech, for example, one candidate for student body president referred to her rival as a "tree-hugging environmental whack job." Her goal? To stir up listeners' bias against outspoken environmentalists on campus. The speaker used these words to persuade the audience to reject the other candidate as an extremist. This tactic was unethical because she supplied no evidence to support her claims, and those claims were not relevant to her opponent's qualifications for serving as student body president.

Bandwagoning

BANDWAGONING

As an additional consideration, avoid using reasoning that implies an argument must be true because most people believe it is. Originally labeled the ***ad populum* fallacy**, today it is more commonly known as **bandwagoning** because it implies that the sheer number of people behind a point makes the point more persuasive and invites the audience to rhetorically "jump on the bandwagon" and go along with the conclusion. Bandwagoning is especially common in advertising and marketing. When a fast-food restaurant proclaims "billions served," it is implying that because so many people eat the same fast food, the food must be worth consuming, *and* that the audience for this message should do the same! Likewise, when a news-

paper ad for a new movie trumpets: "Last week more people watched this movie than any other movie in America!" it suggests that the film must be worth paying for because so many other people have paid for it.

Yet it is important to note that some arguments may be both true *and* commonly believed or followed. Although many people buying into an argument does not make that argument true, the fact that many people believe it does not prove that the argument is *false* either. Bandwagoning creates an unethical fallacy only when the speaker relies on the effect as the primary means of proving the point instead of using other objective forms of evidence or logical explanations to convince an audience.

BEING AN ETHICAL LISTENER

So far, we've focused our discussion of ethics on speakers' responsibilities. But audience members also have a responsibility to demonstrate ethical behavior. The qualities that characterize what we call an

ethical audience include courtesy, open-mindedness, and a willingness to hold a speaker accountable for his or her statements. When you're listening to someone who's giving a speech, consider the following guidelines for exhibiting ethical behavior.

Show Courtesy

The old adage about treating others as you expect to be treated applies just as much in public speaking as in all other areas of life. When someone else is delivering a presentation, extend to him or her the courtesy you would appreciate if you were speaking. Courteous behavior includes focusing your attention on the speaker as soon as he or she begins the presentation. Stop any activities that may distract you or the speaker, such as reading a newspaper, working on a class assignment, texting your friends, or chatting with the person sitting next to you. Let the speaker see that you are paying attention.

Demonstrate an Open Mind

Avoid prejudging the speech or speaker. Even if you have a strongly held belief on the topic or you dislike the speaker, look for parts of the message—or aspects of the speaker—that signal common ground. And consider the fact that you might hear something that changes your mind—or that broadens your perspective on the speech topic.

Hold the Speaker Accountable

Prejudging a speech or speaker is clearly unethical. But mindlessly swallowing what the person says in his or her presentation can be equally damaging. To avoid this damage, you need to hold the presenter accountable for his or her claims. How can you do so? If time is available at the end of the speech, ask questions that prompt the speaker to explain or defend statements that you think require additional evidence. If your instructor allows time for a longer exchange, don't hesitate to honestly (and respectfully) express your response to the speech. Convey questions and opinions politely, focus on the content of the speech itself, and scrupulously avoid attacking the speaker's character. For example, say, "Can you tell us more about how you arrived at those figures?" not "You obviously didn't care enough to do a thorough job in your research." In offering feedback to the speaker on his or her presentation, frame your comments or suggestions constructively—that is, in ways that can help the person build his or her public speaking skills. Avoid destructive feedback, which only diminishes the presenter and denigrates his or her speech.

CHAPTER REVIEW

“Strive to
be an ethical
public speaker.”

As you saw in Joe's story at the beginning of this chapter, public speaking can present numerous ethical challenges—dilemmas that make it difficult to determine what constitutes right and wrong behavior. This chapter has focused on those challenges—from speakers' as well as listeners' perspectives. Whether you strive to communicate truthfully, use and acknowledge others' work, employ sound reasoning, or be an ethical listener, there's one theme that crosses all these ethical concerns: how can you best show respect for others? People have different ways of deciding what constitutes ethical behavior in public speaking. But by asking yourself if an action you're considering taking would demonstrate respect for others, you can more easily make the right—and ethical—choice. When you demonstrate respect for your audience by exhibiting ethical behavior, you win listeners' trust and boost your chances of getting your message across. And when you show respect for speakers as an audience member, you help them deliver more effective presentations. Everyone benefits when presenters *and* listeners attend to speech ethics.

Key Terms

ethics *70*
ethical absolutism *71*
situational ethics *71*
culturally relative *72*
ethical speech *73*
legally protected speech *73*
half-truth *76*
false inference *77*
taking evidence out of context *78*
omission *80*
plagiarism *82*

paraphrasing *84*
common knowledge *86*
fallacious reasoning *86*
hasty generalization *86*
post hoc fallacy *87*
personal attacks (*ad hominem* attacks) *88*
ad populum fallacy (bandwagoning) *89*
ethical audience *91*

Review Questions

1. Define *ethics*, and explain the difference between ethical absolutism and situational ethics.
2. What ethical responsibilities does the speaker have in a public speaking situation?
3. What rules govern legally protected speech? How do they differ from the rules governing ethical speech? Which category is broader, and why?
4. Describe three ways in which a speaker can present untruthful information.
5. Define *plagiarism*, and explain the importance of properly citing your sources.
6. How is a paraphrase different from a quote? How are they similar?
7. Name and describe four types of unsound logic covered in this chapter.
8. What are the ethical responsibilities of the audience in a public speaking situation?

Critical Thinking Questions

1. As an audience member, have you ever felt that a speaker was intentionally misleading you? What gave you this feeling? How might you have verified his or her facts?
2. How does the failure to properly acknowledge a source in a speech affect the speaker's credibility?
3. The "shark" drawing on page 76 does not include false inference or evidence out of context. What do you think the shark or person would say in those situations?
4. Give a real or hypothetical example of each logical fallacy discussed in this chapter. Which of these do you think are most common in the media today?
5. Name a practice on your campus that is legal but not necessarily ethical. Can you name a practice that is ethical but not legal?

Activities

1. Look for a recent survey, poll, or study conducted by a credible organization. Then look up coverage of the poll online to see how it is covered in different news sources and blogs. Can you find any fallacious reasoning in the ways in which the data is presented by different writers? If so, please provide several examples.

2. Review your school's policies on plagiarism. How clear is the definition of plagiarism? Do you think that the guidelines provide clear rules for citing others' work? What is the punishment for stealing someone else's words or ideas?

3. Listen to a few of the twentieth century's greatest speeches (you can find most of them at americanrhetoric.com). Do they all stand up to ethical scrutiny? Does the Internet—which allows for instant fact checking and counterargument—make modern public figures more or less careful about what they say?

Go to **bedfordstmartins.com/speakup**, where you'll find helpful study materials, videos, and speech-building tools.

LISTENING SKILLS

4

"Listening is a vital skill in public speaking and beyond."

Jason was psyched. While preparing an informative speech on the ways young people use the Internet, he focused on the popularity of Twitter. An active Twitter user, Jason found the topic fascinating and looked forward to developing the speech. To learn more about the habits of other students using Twitter, he conducted six face-to-face interviews with classmates from his speech course. He felt pleased with the amount of information his classmates were sharing during the interviews. But when Jason later reviewed his interview notes, he realized they were a bit sparse.

With time running out, Jason finished developing the presentation using the few insights he could pull from his notes. On the day of his speech, Jason proudly presented his claims about young people's use of Twitter and their opinions about the service. As he spoke, he felt confident and comfortable talking in front of his class. All that changed, however, during the question-and-answer period after the speech. Judging from the questions his classmates were throwing at him, few—if any—of his fellow students agreed with his observations about student Twitter users. Feeling confused and blindsided, Jason wondered how things could have gone so wrong.

Jason's unpleasant experience reveals the importance of listening in public speaking. Unfortunately for him, he missed two opportunities to listen. When he was interviewing his classmates, he failed to pay enough attention to take detailed notes. Later, when he reviewed his notes and saw that they were sparse, he couldn't remember many details from the actual interviews—further suggesting that he hadn't listened carefully during the conversations. Jason also failed to listen to his audience as he was delivering his speech. If he had paid careful attention to his classmates while he was talking, he may have detected both auditory and visual signs that they disagreed with his claims: one or two of his listeners may have muttered sarcastic comments, such as "Yeah, right" or "Is he kidding?" And several of them may have been shaking their heads or rolling their eyes. By failing to listen carefully while researching *and* delivering his speech, Jason never connected with his audience members and lost credibility with them.

As Jason's story reveals, listening is a vital skill for public speakers at all stages of the speech preparation process. Yet many novice speakers find this idea surprising. After all, it's the *audience* who has to listen, right? To be sure, audiences can be good listeners by respectfully and carefully attending to the speaker's message. But speakers have many opportunities to practice good listening skills while preparing and delivering a presentation. Think about it: You interview people to research your speech. You practice your presentation in front of trusted friends or family members and listen to their feedback. And you deliver your speech, paying attention to your audience's responses to decide whether you need to adjust your voice, your volume, your pacing, or some other aspect of your delivery. Fail to listen at any of these stages and you risk ignoring important information that you need to present the most effective speech possible.

Research further affirms the importance of listening—versus merely hearing—for both public speakers and their audiences because listening and hearing are two different activities. For example, several studies have suggested that people can miss virtually all the content of oral messages when they only hear, rather than listen (imagine the

Who needs to demonstrate good listening here?

A: THE AUDIENCE?   B: THE SPEAKER?   C: BOTH?

droning teacher's voice in Charles Schulz's *Peanuts* cartoons).[1] **Hearing** means merely receiving messages in a passive way. **Listening**, on the other hand, means actively paying attention to what you're hearing; it involves both processing the message to decide on its meaning and remembering what you've heard and understood.

For example, suppose you're interviewing Mel, a pet owner, for an informative speech about health insurance for pets. When you ask for his opinion on this type of insurance, Mel says, "Don't get me wrong; I think people should do what's best for their pets." After a pause, his voice gets a bit louder, his eyes widen, and he says, "But that insurance is expensive!" If you only *heard* Mel's response (but didn't really listen), you would probably conclude that *Mel thinks the insurance is expensive.* But if you actually *listened* to Mel by paying attention to his words *and* other delivery cues, such as an agitated facial expression and a loud voice, you would realize that Mel has especially strong feelings about the high cost of pet health insurance. You might even conclude that Mel is unwilling to purchase it even if he thinks it beneficial for his beloved pet. Your listening might then lead you to ask further questions to learn more about Mel's views on the subject.

If you're less skilled at listening than at hearing, you're not alone—many people have similar difficulty. Yet you *can* learn how to strengthen your listening skills, and this chapter offers helpful guidelines. In the pages that follow, we explore the importance of listening in public speaking, examine the process of listening, and then consider the causes behind ineffective listening behaviors. We then offer suggestions for listening effectively that you can put into practice as both a speaker *and* an audience member.

ADAPTING TO THE AUDIENCE

WORDS (TONE, VOLUME, CLARITY), YAWNING NOISES, GROANS, LAUGHTER, CHEERS, SIGHING, CRYING, APPLAUSE, CELL PHONE RINGTONES, etc.

LISTEN WITH YOUR EARS...
... AND YOUR EYES

FACIAL EXPRESSIONS, EYE CONTACT, ATTITUDE, STYLE, GESTURES, BODY LANGUAGE, APPEARANCE, VISUAL AIDS, SPECIAL EFFECTS, LIGHTING (AND STUNTS?), etc.

WHY LISTEN?

As we've seen, listening is a crucial skill for both speakers and audience members. How you listen as a speaker—while preparing and delivering a speech—can have a powerful impact on the quality of your presentation and your ability to connect with your audience. How you listen as an audience member can strongly affect your ability to absorb the information the speaker is imparting to you. Equally important, improving your listening skills as both a speaker and an audience member will help you interpret and use more of what you hear from others in a wide variety of situations—not just in your public speaking course. For example, you'll be better able to evaluate and make decisions about a political candidate who is delivering a public address. You'll be better positioned to interpret and respond to a neighbor who stands up at a town meeting and argues for an increase in the special-education budget. And if *you're* the one standing up at a town meeting to advocate a change in the budget, you'll be more likely to sense confusion or disagreement among your neighbors and adapt your delivery as needed to win their attention and support.

THE LISTENING PROCESS

Effective listening is made up of two steps: *processing* (actively thinking about what you've heard and observed) and *retaining* (remembering what you've heard).

Processing What You've Heard

When you engage in **processing**, you actively think about a message you're receiving from someone else—not only the words but also the nonverbal cues. For example, suppose you're a small-business owner who's meeting with Jeff, a salesperson for eLogic, a business-software developer. You want to decide whether eLogic's software for tracking and fulfilling orders is right for your business. As Jeff describes the product, you do more than just listen to his words. You also consider the implications of what he is saying, how using the software will affect your bottom line, and whether Jeff represents a reputable company. You then mull over questions such as: "Can my business afford this investment? Will I need to provide extensive training to help my workers learn the new software? Are there other programs that

PROCESSING A MESSAGE

would deliver similar advantages but are easier and cheaper to use?" By weighing these matters—that is, by processing the information in your mind and possibly through jotting down notes—you stand a better chance of making a smart decision for your business.

Retaining What You've Processed

The more carefully you process what you're hearing, the more you will engage your powers of **retention**—your ability to remember what you've heard. In fact, in a ten-year study of listening patterns, one of the authors of this textbook found that poor retention of a speech was directly related to audience attentiveness during the presentation.[2] This study also found that individuals with poor attention habits remembered only a fraction (25 percent or less) of what was said in a speech. Worse, what they *could* recall was often inaccurate or confused with something else they had in mind at the time of the presentation. Among people who fail to process what they're hearing, the ability to accurately recall what they hear decays over just three to six hours after the original communication.

The study also revealed a recurring pattern of attentiveness in people who did not listen well. At the beginning of a presentation, poor listeners tended to pay little attention. Their attention quickly improved as the presentation continued—perhaps because they realized they *should* have been paying attention—but then just as quickly fell to a very low level, only to rebound near the end of the speech. Clearly, the sporadic levels of attention made it much harder for these listeners to process messages; no wonder, then, that they retained very little.

To further see the connection between processing and retention, consider your own listening behavior as a student. How much information do you retain if you pay little attention to your instructors in class? If you take notes during lectures, how accurate are they? How much do you remember from lectures in which you did not process what you were hearing? There's no doubt about it: the more carefully you process messages, the more likely you'll remember what you heard—and retain it accurately.

THE ATTENTIVENESS CURVE

TIME OF SPEECH

THE CULPRITS BEHIND POOR LISTENING

What causes ineffective listening—especially in public speaking situations? The culprits include specific behaviors: unprocessed note taking, nonlistening, interruptive listening, agenda-driven listening, argumentative listening, and nervous listening. Later in this chapter we also discuss defeated listening and superficial listening.

Unprocessed Note Taking

While researching your speech, you may decide to take notes during interviews. And while listening to a speech, you might take notes based on what you're hearing. People who engage in **unprocessed note taking** in these sorts of situations take word-for-word notes without thinking about what they're writing down. That is, they listen *only* to take notes—not to process what they're hearing and writing.

The words they hear enter their consciousness and just as quickly exit, deposited in their notebooks or on their laptops. Unprocessed note takers usually have trouble remembering what was said in an interview, a lecture, or a speech. And they miss opportunities to ask clarifying questions or to comment in informed, thoughtful ways. Not surprisingly, unprocessed note taking greatly hampers retention, since it skips the processing stage of listening.

Nonlistening

People who engage in **nonlistening** simply do not pay attention to what they're hearing. For example, if you're overly interested in your own questions during an interview, you won't be attuned to what the interviewee has to say in response. In a lecture, you are likely to engage in nonlistening if you are more focused on your own thoughts about the subject than on what the speaker has to say. Not surprisingly, nonlistening prevents you from processing another person's message—and therefore keeps you from retaining it.

Interruptive Listening

With **interruptive listening**, one person consistently interrupts another. You've probably seen or heard instances of interruptive audience members, shouting things like "Yeah, right!" or blurting out questions before the speaker is ready to entertain them. Speakers can also be interruptive listeners. For example, a speaker might see an audience member raise her hand; instead of recognizing her and listening to her question, the speaker rudely cuts her off mid-sentence and finishes the question for her. Speakers who do this are likely to miss certain aspects of the question or comment. Worse, they often come across as rude and arrogant, thus losing the respect of audience members.

Agenda-Driven Listening

Public speakers who focus solely on the mechanics of their presentation may demonstrate **agenda-driven listening**. This listening challenge applies primarily to a speaker giving a presentation who also has to accommodate questions and comments from audience members. For example, as audience members raise questions and offer comments during your speech, you think only about your next point. Perhaps you scan your notes while a listener asks a question or you provide monosyllabic and overly brief responses—revealing that you're not really listening to your audience. Not surprisingly, this behavior can annoy audience members and damage your credibility.

Argumentative Listening

People who feel in conflict with individuals they are listening to may display **argumentative listening**—listening to only as much as they need to fuel their own arguments. Argumentative listening can also afflict speakers who feel personally attacked by audience members during question-and-answer sessions. Because they hear only part of what a questioner has asked, they can't respond to the question in a thoughtful, informed way. And that hurts their credibility.

You can also fall victim to argumentative listening during an interview if you disagree with the interviewee's opinions or ideas. Here, you may focus more on your own views and miss out on everything the other person has to say.

Nervous Listening

People who fall victim to **nervous listening** feel compelled to talk through silences because they're uncomfortable with a lapse in the conversation. This occurs often in interpersonal situations. For example, imagine that you've just met an attractive person and you've tried to strike up a conversation with him. When he takes a long moment to respond to a question, you start filling in the silence with nervous chatter—making it even more difficult for him to respond.

In the realm of public speaking, nervous listening can cause just as much havoc. If an interview subject takes a long time to answer a question, a nervous listener might ask more questions or blurt out a string of comments; the interviewee would never have any opportunity to answer, and the interviewer would end up with incomplete research. Or imagine giving a speech introduction in which you ask a provocative question in an attempt to engage the audience. If no one in the room responds to your question, you might get thrown off and feel compelled to say something—anything—to get the speech moving again. You might fill in the silence with a random joke or comment, only to see confused or annoyed looks on your listeners' faces.

Nervous listening—in any context—can damage your ability to gather and interpret information that you need to deliver an effective speech. If you feel twinges of nervousness, collect yourself and wait a few beats before continuing.

BECOMING A BETTER LISTENER

Despite the many different behaviors constituting ineffective listening, you *can* overcome the challenges through practice and attention to a few details. In this section, we offer suggestions for improving your listening skills through **interactive listening**. In interactive listening, you filter out distractions, focus on what the other person or people have said, and communicate that you've paid attention.

Filter Out Distractions

There are potentially countless distractions in any speaking situation, both external and internal. *External distractions* could be anything from street noise, a flashy visual aid left up during an entire presentation, or chattering audience members. *Internal distractions*, often referred to as **internal noise**, are any thoughts that make it hard for you to concentrate—for example, worrying about how well you're doing in class or about other pressing assignments, thinking about a movie from the night before, or pondering aspects of your personal life. If you are an audience member, filtering out distractions means focusing on the speaker and the message while avoiding other elements or activities that could draw your attention, such as gazing around the room, studying for another class, or surfing online. As a speaker, filtering distractions during presentations or question-and-answer sessions means focusing on reactions or questions from audience members rather than looking ahead to your next point. While conducting interview research, filtering distractions means focusing on the question that you've just asked and the interviewee's response rather than looking ahead to your next questions or thinking about unrelated topics.

Focus on the Speaker

In any listening situation, keep your mind on what the speaker is saying, not on what you may be about to hear or what you're going to say next. Ask yourself, "What does this statement that I've just heard mean? Do I agree or disagree with it? Do I have questions or comments of my own about it—or even a different point of view? How might other people think or feel about this comment or issue?"

Show That You Are Listening

As a responsible listener, you should show the speaker that you are listening. How? Use a combination of nonverbal and verbal cues. Look at the other person while he or she is speaking *and* as you are responding. Indicate nonverbally—perhaps with alert posture and a smile or nod of your head—that you are paying attention.

When the opportunity presents itself, you can also verbally communicate that you are listening. As an audience member, you can ask thoughtful questions during a question-and-answer session or even applaud appropriately at a rousing portion of the speech. As a speaker, paraphrase questions asked by audience members to show that you understand and to allow them to correct any misinterpretation. And in interview situations, maintain eye contact and be ready to move into new lines of questioning based on your interviewee's responses.

MAXIMIZING YOUR AUDIENCE'S LISTENING

Despite your best efforts, you may occasionally find yourself delivering a speech to audience members who do not listen well. For example, while doing **audience surveillance**—paying attention to an audience's nonverbal and verbal responses while you give a speech—you may notice some audience members who *act* as if they are listening but who you can tell are not. The good news is that there are several strategies you can use to help your audience members listen more effectively to your speech. In this section, we outline several steps that you, as a speaker, can take to both anticipate and deal with audience listening challenges.

Anticipate Ineffective Listening Before Your Speech

Advance preparation is key to ensuring that your audience will truly listen to your message. Be sure to consider your audience's needs as well as outside factors, and plan your speech accordingly.

Consider Your Listeners' Attention and Energy Levels. People listening to a speech at 8:30 on a Monday morning will likely have a limited attention span. Many may be tired from the weekend and may not have adjusted to the new week. Therefore, avoid delivering a long speech with no audience interaction during such times. Instead, give a concise presentation and allot time for active listener participation.

Assess Your Audience's Knowledge and Abilities. If your audience members know little about the subject of your speech, they may become confused when faced with unknown jargon or too many technical details. To avoid that, explain concepts and define key terms. Also, consider any barriers to understanding, such as whether everyone in your audience has a similar capacity with the English language or whether anyone has problems with hearing. Then adjust your word choice or volume level as needed.

Front- and Back-Load Your Main Message. Listeners tend to pay the most attention just after the beginning of the speech and just before the end. For this reason, plan your speech ahead of time in the following way: front-load your main message—that is, present it early

HAMMER HOME YOUR MAIN MESSAGE AT THE BEGINNING AND AT THE END in your speech. Then use your conclusion to give listeners another opportunity to process and retain your message.

Use Presentation Aids Strategically.

Presentation aids can help you capture audience attention and thereby encourage listening. Therefore, plan to space these aids throughout your speech to maintain interest. Also, don't incorporate a given presentation aid until you want your audience to see or hear it. When you are finished with it, put it away, outside your listeners' view or hearing range.

Encourage Active Listening during Your Speech

When you are ready to give your speech, be sure to pay attention to what you see among your audience. Practice audience surveillance, pay particular attention to if and how they are listening to you, and be prepared to make adjustments as you go.

Tailor Your Delivery.

As you deliver your speech, pay attention to factors that affect your audience's ability to listen: voice, volume, fluency, projection, rate, and timing. Speaking too quietly can inhibit listening, as may poor fluency, fast delivery, or

DEALING WITH ARGUMENTATIVE LISTENERS

excessive pausing. Be sure to maintain eye contact with your audience and avoid obtrusive gestures or turning your back on the group while adjusting a visual aid.

Watch Out for Argumentative Listeners. As discussed earlier in this chapter, argumentative listeners will attend to only as much of your presentation as they need to build up their own case against it. To improve your chances of keeping their attention, acknowledge their viewpoints early in your speech ("I know that many of you believe that plastic surgery merely for cosmetic purposes is perfectly harmless") and repeatedly press your main message throughout the presentation.

Watch Out for Defeated Listeners. You might also notice a few audience members who you can tell have tuned you out. Such **defeated listening** often occurs when listeners feel overwhelmed by your message and find it too difficult to follow. Defeated listening is a particular challenge for speakers who deliver presentations that may be technical or detailed and perhaps beyond the easy comprehension of individuals in the audience. Defeated audience members might indicate their feelings by avoiding eye contact or by working on something else while you speak.

You can prevent defeated listening by pausing occasionally during your speech to ask the audience questions—whether they understand what has been said so far, for example, or if they can think of an example or application of what you have just said. By doing so, you can test their comprehension and processing while assessing whether they are really following along. If you cannot engage them here, back up and repeat your message, using simpler language and different examples.

Watch Out for Superficial Listeners. Audience members who pretend to pay attention but who are in fact distracted by internal or external noise (such as wandering thoughts, cell phones, newspapers, or conversation) are engaged in **superficial listening**. To prevent it, request that people turn off cell phones and resist checking for messages on handheld devices or laptops during the presentation. Also, be sure to use direct eye contact with people who you sense are listening superficially (they will pay more attention if they see that you are watching them), and go ahead and ask them questions—or invite them to ask you some.

LISTENING WHEN YOU ARE IN THE AUDIENCE

When you're an audience member, listening not only helps you retain the speaker's message but also enables you to provide the speaker with an informed **speech critique**—written or oral feedback offered after a presentation. Critiquing is an essential component of pub-

lic speaking classes because it helps speakers learn from their experiences. Your instructor will likely specify what you should cover in a critique. The following guidelines can give you additional guidance.

- *Take notes.* While listening to a presentation, jot down your thoughts about the speaker's delivery and message. By recording your impressions as you form them, you'll be able to access your thoughts when it comes time to offer your critique.

- *Identify main points.* As you take notes, begin to distinguish what you think are the speaker's main points—these are the two or three most important ideas that the speaker wants you to remember (speechwriters sometimes call these "takeaways" or the "take-home message"). You can identify main points by listening carefully to the introduction; most speakers will preview main points during that part of the speech. You can also listen for signaling language in the transitions of the speech. Finally, speakers often restate their main points during the speech's conclusion.

- *Consider the speech's objectives.* To provide **constructive criticism**—feedback a speaker can use to improve his or her skills—strive to understand what the presenter is trying to accomplish. Identify the speech's general rhetorical purpose—to inform, persuade, or mark a special occasion— as well as the speech's specific purpose. Next, evaluate how well the speaker achieves his or her goal.

- *Support your feedback with examples.* Offering an overly general comment such as "good eye contact" or "work on your organization" is not particularly useful to a speaker. Support generalizations like these with specific examples, such as "You made eye contact with people on every side of the room" or "You had a good preview, but I found the organization of your main points difficult to follow." Specific comments help speakers know which behaviors to do more of during their next speech and which to avoid.

- *Be ethical.* Be courteous in your critique and treat the speaker the same way you hope and expect to be treated when it's your turn to receive feedback. During the speech, avoid prejudging the speaker or topic. Think critically about the message you're hearing. And make sure that you hold the speaker accountable for his or her words. If you are offended by or disagree with something in the speech, tell the person while providing your critique. But do so courteously, and avoid making your comment sound like a personal attack. Explain why you disagree, and offer examples.

CHAPTER REVIEW

> "Listening is a vital skill in public speaking and beyond."

Because most humans come into this world with the capacity to hear, we too often take this particular sense for granted, assuming (falsely) that merely possessing the ability to receive audio stimuli makes us capable of understanding the sounds and words we encounter. In truth, hearing noises, sounds, and words is not the same thing as listening to them. *Hearing* refers to passively receiving these stimuli; *listening* refers to how one processes and understands them. This is particularly relevant where public speaking is concerned because both speakers and audience members must develop good listening skills. It is important to note that listening is not limited to words only or even sound; tone of voice, rate of speech, and such visual cues as body language and gestures also convey a tremendous amount of information that you as a listener can use to understand a message.

To make the transition from hearing to listening, it is important to understand that true listening takes place when a person pays attention to a message and then processes that message, coming to his or her own conclusions and thereby also engaging the capacity for retention—remembering the message. Research has shown that inattentive listeners typically follow a consistent pattern of attention: they pay little attention at the beginning of a presentation, then their attention improves quickly and falls again, only to rise once more at the speech's conclusion.

There are a host of culprits that lead to unsuccessful listening, including unprocessed note taking, nonlistening, interruptive listening, agenda-driven listening, argumentative listening, and nervous listening. In this chapter, we have explored how the listening process works, what causes ineffective listening, and how to improve your listening skills both as a speaker and as an audience member. Listening is vital not only for developing and delivering a successful speech but also for observing and critiquing a presentation, and happily it is a skill that can be learned. Techniques for doing so include filtering out distractions, focusing on the speaker, and showing that you're listening.

As a speaker, you can anticipate ineffective listening before your speech and plan accordingly, and maximize listening during your speech by tailoring your message and watching out for argumentative, defeated, and superficial listeners.

As an audience member, make sure to take notes and identify the speaker's main points. And when giving feedback, make sure to offer constructive criticism by considering the speech's objectives, supporting your feedback with examples, and always keeping appropriate ethical guidelines in mind.

Key Terms

hearing *100*
listening *100*
processing *102*
retention *103*
unprocessed note
    taking *104*
nonlistening *106*
interruptive listening *106*
agenda-driven listening *107*

argumentative listening *108*
nervous listening *108*
interactive listening *109*
internal noise *109*
audience surveillance *112*
defeated listening *115*
superficial listening *116*
speech critique *116*
constructive criticism *117*

Review Questions

1. What is listening? How does it differ from hearing?
2. What two steps make up the listening process? Explain each one.

3. Detail four of the six culprits behind poor listening.

4. What is interactive listening? Describe three methods for improving your listening skills through interactive listening.

5. Explain four ways you can prepare in advance to enhance the way your audience listens to your speech.

6. As a speaker, what do you need to look for to determine if your audience is listening? If they're not, how can you reengage them?

7. Explain three guidelines for listening when you are in the audience.

Critical Thinking Questions

1. Reflect on your own listening skills. How well do you process information as you listen? How well do you retain a speaker's message? What are some techniques you can employ to improve each of these?

2. Give three reasons why our culture might negatively affect our ability to listen. How can we counteract each of these?

3. Consider the attentiveness curve presented on page 104. Do you recognize this pattern in your own behavior during lectures? How can you combat the pattern as both an audience member and a student? As a speaker, how might your knowledge of this pattern influence the way you choose to organize and deliver your speech?

4. How would you distinguish the ways you can anticipate ineffective listening before you speak from the techniques you might use to deal with ineffective listening once you are speaking?

5. How can good listening skills help you give a constructive critique to a classmate?

Activities

1. Test your listening skills by watching a monologue from a late-night talk show. After viewing it once, write down a summary of the monologue, then watch it again with notes in hand and see how much you remembered. You can try doing the same activity with a

cooking program. If you try both variations on this activity, are the outcomes any different? If so, what is different and why?

2. For one class period, try viewing your public speaking instructor as a speaker trying to keep an audience (the class) engaged in effective listening. What are the strategies he or she uses to keep the audience listening? To reduce ineffective listening? To adapt to nonverbal cues while scanning the audience? How could your instructor be more effective in encouraging effective listening?

3. During one of your other classes, observe how students around you are listening to the teacher lecture. What behaviors do you observe? Does the teacher appear to be aware of them, and if so, how is he or she compensating for them during the lecture?

Go to **bedfordstmartins.com/speakup**, where you'll find helpful study materials, videos, and speech-building tools.

5

AUDIENCE ANALYSIS

"Let the audience drive your message." You're standing with a crowd on the street, waiting for a speech from a woman who has decided to run for a seat in Congress. You heard her speak last week at your college, where she tried to rally student support for her candidacy, and you found her presentation quite convincing. You're now excited to vote for her because she seems to care; she appears quite well informed; and, as someone who cares about education, she would do much to benefit students like you.

Today this candidate is addressing a larger group of voters, many of whom are students from your campus. Soon after she begins her speech, however, you find yourself feeling annoyed and restless. She seems to be covering the exact same topics she addressed during last week's speech, and she's even using some of the same gestures. You exchange glances with several of your dormmates who were at the speech the previous week. They roll their eyes, and a few of them wander off. But even as members of the crowd walk away or shift their weight restlessly, the speaker plows forward with her talk without making any adjustments to her delivery style or content. She seems oblivious to the fact that she has lost much of her audience's attention. Apparently, she failed to analyze her audience both while developing her speech and while delivering it.

Perhaps you have experienced generic speeches—canned presentations delivered in exactly the same way every time, no matter the audience or setting. When a speaker just "phones in" a speech, listeners usually react with boredom, irritation, and lack of attention. The audience members lose—because they stop listening and miss out on any valuable information the speaker is sharing. The presenter loses—because he or she gets a reputation for being insensitive or dull.

By contrast, speakers who tailor their message to their listeners create enormous value for their audience *and* themselves.

- First, listeners become much more interested in and attentive to the speech.
- Second, listeners experience positive feelings toward the speaker when he or she has made an effort to understand listener concerns.
- Third, listeners open their minds to the speech message because it targets their specific needs, interests, and values.

The skills of analyzing your audience are also used far beyond the realm of public speaking. Most of us intuitively practice these skills during our daily interactions with others. For example, suppose

A WELL-TAILORED EXCUSE (ALMOST)

Sorry but I have to ask for an extension.

Why?

Well... er... My dog was sick and I had to rush him to the vet...

What was wrong with him?

Well... when they opened him up in surgery they found his stomach was full of homework...

you want to ask your instructor for an extension on an assignment that you know you can't finish by the deadline. You might develop a casual and straightforward approach if your professor interacts comfortably with students and has granted extensions to other students in a previous semester. On the other hand, you'd probably take a very different and more careful approach if your professor tends to be formal and distant or is known to be unsympathetic to excuses.

Even in everyday conversation, we continually shape our messages as we focus awareness on the people we're talking to; therefore, it's not surprising that this skill is highly important in the context of public speaking. To learn about your audience before developing your speech, you will need to gather various kinds of information about your listeners.

In this chapter, we organize the types of information you will need to gather into the following categories: situational characteristics, demographics, common ground, prior exposure, and audience disposition. We also provide some tips for gathering these details, as well as suggestions for what to do if you discover halfway through a speech that you've misread your audience.

SIZE MATTERS

UNDERSTANDING SITUATIONAL CHARACTERISTICS

Situational characteristics are factors in a specific speech setting that you can observe or discover *before* you give the speech. They include audience size, time, location (forum), and audience mobility.

Size

Audience size is simply the number of people who will be present for your speech. In a classroom setting, the size of your audience will be obvious. But in the world beyond school, this information may not be so apparent. For example, if the leader of a charitable organization asks you to give a speech at an awards dinner, you would need to ask how many people will be attending: Seven to ten people? Twenty-five to thirty? Three hundred? A thousand?

When it comes to speech presentations and audience, *size matters*—that is, the number of audience members affects how you'll craft *and* deliver your message. The smaller the group, the greater the opportunity for you to interact with your audience—for example, through question-and-answer sessions. With small audiences, you can also communicate a more detailed and specific message because you're tailoring it to the needs of just a few people. Conversely, the larger the audience, the less opportunity you have for interaction. Therefore, you'll have to work harder to anticipate your listeners' questions and craft a more generally accessible message.

Consider the example of Jeanine, a marketing representative for a software company. Jeanine's boss asked her to visit several cities and deliver big sales presentations—what the boss described as "dog and pony shows"—for a revolutionary new software product designed to create striking visual presentations. Up to that point, Jeanine had only presented the product to small groups of five to seven people in intimate boardroom settings. In contrast, the dog and pony shows would be in large hotel ballrooms, and her audiences would range from three to five hundred prospective customers.

As she prepared for the first presentation, Jeanine realized that unlike her previous experiences, she simply would not be able to answer every audience member's question as it cropped up; if she did, she'd never get through the presentation. Nor would she have time for a lengthy question-and-answer period. With this in mind, she decided to incorporate some of the more likely audience questions into her presentation.

Jeanine also realized that among audience members, there would be great variety in knowledge about computers. So she decided to cover technical issues by "teaching to the middle": rather than pitching her speech to the few listeners who would be extremely computer savvy, or slowing things down for the few who knew very little about technology, she focused her content for the large group in the middle. That way, she could feel confident that her talk would be accessible to the largest portion of her audience.

Time

Time is an important aspect of any presentation you deliver, both in terms of the time allotted for the speech and your listeners' own time rhythms in the day. Thus, you will want to consider two aspects of timing: presentation time and body clock.

Presentation time is the length of time you have to deliver your presentation. Is it one minute? Five minutes? Twenty minutes? As long as you wish? The answer should shape how you prepare and deliver your speech.

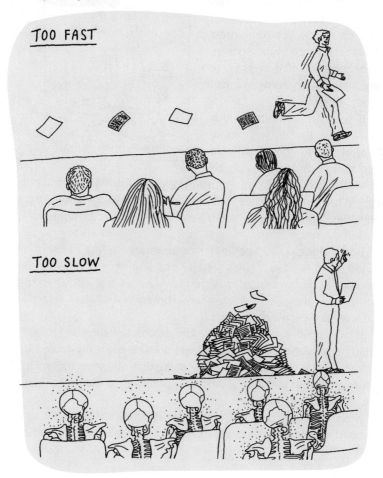

For example, when your presentation time is short, you have to make tough choices about what to include and what to leave out. Remember, though, that some of the most powerful, persuasive messages—television ads—are just fifteen to thirty seconds long, yet they convey extensive information and can strongly influence an audience's behavior. To exert the most impact in a very short speech, carefully reduce your message to something your audience can quickly digest.

NOT CONSIDERING BODY CLOCK

If your presentation time is relatively long, you'll have more opportunity to develop your main points. But you'll also be more at risk of digressing—or veering away from your central message. With long speeches, concentrate on sticking closely to your main message. That way, you'll keep your audience members—and yourself—focused.

Body clock—also known as **chronemics**—refers to the time of day or the day of the week when your audience members will be listening to your presentation. If you have a choice about when to give your presentation, which days and times would you select—and which would you avoid?

If you sought to avoid 8:30 on a Monday morning, you'd be making a wise choice. Many students are still mentally rooted in the weekend and will have difficulty focusing on your speech. Similar distractions abound for people close to lunchtime, at the end of the day, or at the end of the week.

Nevertheless, you can still deliver an effective speech at such times. For example, you might include more humor or anecdotal references to

CONSIDERING BODY CLOCK

OK, I can tell you guys are hungry, so just another two quick points...

Rrrumble, rumble!

engage your audience, or with your teacher's approval, you might open by asking direct questions of some audience members, which heightens their attentiveness. Finally, you could simply shorten your speech to match your audience's attention span.

One of the authors of this book was once invited to give a presentation to a group of lawyers at 3:00 P.M. on a Tuesday. The twenty-five minute speech—about effective negotiating strategies—was part of an all-day conference. Unfortunately, the conference schedule lagged, and the presenter realized that he would have to speak much later, at 4:30 that afternoon. Since his listeners' attention span would be minimal at that time, he quickly reframed the speech: five minutes of simple tips plus a quick question-and-answer period. Invigorated by the concise and lively presentation, the lawyers were fully engaged and asked spirited questions at the conclusion of the speech.

Location

Location, also known as **forum**, is the setting where your audience will listen to your speech. Speech locations vary widely—from classrooms and auditoriums to conference rooms and outdoor venues. And each type strongly influences how you deliver your speech.

Consider the following true story. Joe, a high school junior, was running for student-body president. Each candidate had to deliver a campaign speech at an afternoon rally. The location of the rally was the recently completed high school quad, a sunken plaza built about eight feet below the foundations of four surrounding brick buildings. This design produced some rather spectacular acoustics when sound within the plaza was projected against the brick buildings.

Joe spoke first at the rally. Concerned that the huge crowd would not be able to hear him, he had decided to speak with a microphone. But he didn't realize that the plaza design would amplify his voice anyway. When he spoke into the microphone, the sound was so loud that his listeners grimaced and groaned. Because of his inattention to location, Joe's speech was literally too painful to hear!

Joe failed to consider the acoustics of his speech location. In addition to acoustical problems, locations can present other challenges, such as availability of audiovisual equipment (are there electrical outlets for your audiovisual aids, or should you bring handheld visual aids?), lines of sight (will your listeners be able to see your visual aids?), and lighting (is it adequate?).

NOT TAKING FORUM INTO ACCOUNT

How can you anticipate and address location challenges? Go to the place where you'll deliver your speech. Stand there and imagine yourself giving the presentation. Now position yourself where the audience will be and imagine listening to the speech. Will all your listeners be able to see and hear you?

If Joe had taken stock of the forum for his speech ahead of time, he might not have elected to use a microphone. Given the size of the forum, he might also have decided to walk from behind the podium and make himself more accessible to his audience so that listeners could hear *and* see him better.

Mobility

Different speech settings may have different implications for your audience's mobility—the degree to which listeners move around during a speech. For example, if you're giving a presentation in a classroom, lecture hall, or conference room, you will likely have a **stationary audience**—listeners will be relatively motionless (sitting or standing) and captive as you're talking. If you are delivering a presentation at an exhibitor's booth at a sales conference, on a town common, or on a city sidewalk, you'll probably have a **mobile audience**—strolling by, stopping for a moment to listen to you, or drifting off to get on with their day.

TAKING FORUM INTO ACCOUNT

ATTRACTING A MOBILE AUDIENCE

It slices, it dices...

If you're making a presentation in a college classroom, you know that you will have a stationary audience because your listeners are captive; their grades depend in part on their class attendance and participation. Don't fall into the trap, though, of taking a stationary audience for granted. Surely you have experienced lecturers who do exactly that; knowing that their audience must remain present sometimes misleads teachers into assuming that they don't have to work as hard to capture their audience's attention. Veteran teachers know they should work just as hard to keep the attention of such an audience.

Capturing the attention of a mobile audience is clearly more challenging than capturing that of a stationary one. To do so, take a hint from the salespeople who make their livings at conventions and county fairs selling everything from rugs and hot tubs to produce and kitchenware. These vendors contend with an entirely mobile audience, so they must draw an audience's attention quickly and magnetically. For example, a seasoned vendor might try to sell a fruit and vegetable knife by arranging colorful, pre-cut fruit in pleasing shapes, such as a flower or windmill. She might also make the speech interactive—stopping passersby and encouraging them to "test-drive the knife, have some fruit, watch a little slice and dice!" You can adapt these effective techniques to your own presentations by offering fun (and maybe edible!) visual aids and making your presentation interactive—either by inviting audience members to come over or by asking invitational questions that fit with your overall message (just make sure that the questions are appropriate to the speech setting and aren't invasive or personal).

INCORPORATING DEMOGRAPHICS

In addition to considering situational characteristics, you also need to take demographics into account. **Demographics** refers to certain characteristics of your listeners—for example, age, gender, sexual orientation, race, ethnicity, religious orientation, socioeconomic background, and political affiliation. By assessing your audience members' demographics, you can better anticipate their beliefs about your topic, their willingness to listen to your message, and their likely responses. In this section, we examine demographic characteristics you should consider while developing and delivering your speeches.

Age

Age can affect how audience members respond to your message. For example, a presentation on safe snowboarding would not likely interest most retired persons. But it may hold great appeal for athletic students in their late teens and early twenties.

Naturally, when you're speaking to a large group of diverse listeners, their ages may vary considerably. How can you consider age when targeting these varied listeners? Try tailoring your supporting materials (such as examples and quotations) to the needs of different age groups within your audience. For instance, older listeners may not understand references to the popular musical groups or late-night comedy shows that younger people tend to appreciate. And younger

listeners might not get references to classic film stars like Greta Garbo or Cary Grant or even early rock stars such as Elvis Presley. For younger listeners, you might also try to avoid referring to events that took place before they were born unless you place the events in context for them.

Gender Composition

The **gender composition** of your audience—*mixed* (male and female) or *single gender* (all female or all male)—affects how your listeners will respond to your speech. Some stories, illustrations, or examples might resonate better with one gender grouping than another.

Car sellers, for example, pay close attention to differences in buying patterns between genders. In recent years, marketers in the automotive industry observed that more women were buying cars, and that sales pitches aimed at men did not work so effectively with female customers. Minh, a former student of ours and an automotive salesperson, told a story that shed light on this development. In Minh's experience, effectively selling Volvo station wagons to men and women required two very different approaches.[1] To appeal to men, Minh emphasized the cars' turbocharged engines, high-performance tires, and special detailing. To capture women's interest, he stressed features related to safety, reliability, and fuel economy. While Minh aimed the same broad message at all shoppers: "You'll want to buy this wonderful car," he tailored the specifics of the message to each gender.

While consideration of gender is a valid component of audience analysis, you must never assume you know about an individual audience member's views based on gender; the views of countless men and women cut against the grain of traditional ideas of **gender stereotypes**—oversimplified and often distorted views of what it means to be male or female. Likewise, ethical speakers never resort to **sexist language**, or language with a bias for or against a given gender.

Sexual Orientation

Another demographic characteristic that has become increasingly important to consider and acknowledge is the **sexual orientation** of your audience members. This can include straight men and women as well as gay men, lesbians, bisexuals, and transgendered individuals—or

GLBT for short. Amid the controversy surrounding questions of status and equal protection for GLBT citizens (such as whether their unions should be accorded legal marital status or whether they should be allowed to serve openly in the military), it is obvious that not everyone in the United States feels comfortable with or accepting of people based on differences in sexual orientation.

Given this environment, some might quibble with or object to acknowledging the GLBT demographic, but we strongly believe that acknowledging members of the GLBT community is not only a smart and strategic move for a speaker, but also an ethical responsibility. Statistics vary, but estimates have often suggested that gay or lesbian people (only two parts of the GLBT designation) account for between 5 and 10 percent of our population.[2] Since speakers have a responsibility to all members of their audiences—not simply those in the dominant majority—ignoring GLBT listeners means excluding a substantial portion of an audience from the discussion, and potentially alienating that portion.

Acknowledging a difference in sexual orientation can be accomplished both overtly and passively, depending on what is appropriate for your speech and your situation. Open and overt acknowledgment of these differences might be accomplished by including examples or illustrations that reference GLBTs as well as straight people. So, for example, a speech on conflict in relationships might include examples of gay or lesbian couples in the same breath with examples of heterosexual couples. Likewise, a speech that deals with parenting could include the story of two fathers raising a child, along with examples featuring a mother and father, or a single parent.

You can offer passive acknowledgment of the GLBTs (and do so sensitively) through inclusive word choice when referencing sexual or relational orientation. For example, instead of only speaking of "married couples" or a "wife searching for a husband" (or vice versa), you might refer to "loving partners" or "individuals looking for a long-term commitment." Inclusive word choice invites everyone in the audience to share in the speech while avoiding language that privileges one form of sexual orientation over another.

Race and Ethnicity

In the United States today, the population is far more racially and ethnically diverse than in previous eras. With this increased diversity, your audience members are likely to come from a wide variety of racial and ethnic origins. In preparing and delivering your speech, you need to be sensitive to your listeners' diverse backgrounds and speak to their varied interests. But at the same time, you must not generalize about particular races or ethnicities. For example, all Americans of white European descent don't necessarily feel the same way about affirmative action. Neither do all Americans of African descent.

Still, **race**—common heritage based on genetically shared physical characteristics of people in a group—*can* affect how listeners respond to a speaker's message. This is especially true in situations in which racial issues are sensitive, affecting people throughout their lives.

Ethnicity—cultural background that is usually associated with shared religion, national origin, and language—is another important demographic aspect to consider, as it can shape beliefs, attitudes, and values of audience members. A student named Gunther learned this lesson the hard way. Gunther gave a presentation to members of his campus's student-run Middle Eastern Society and spoke to an audience he had been informed consisted of students who had fled from Iraq shortly after the U.S. invasion in 2003. Attempting to show courtesy, Gunther addressed his listeners as "Iraqis."

Only later did Gunther learn that his audience had been made up of Assyrians who had been living in Iraq. Although Assyria no longer exists as an independent nation, there are millions of people who continue to identify themselves as Assyrian. They speak a common language, share religious beliefs, and have their own distinctive traditions and customs. While many of the Assyrians in Gunther's audience realized his mislabeling of them as Iraqis was unintentional, they still took offense at being categorized with an ethnic group with whom they did not identify. They (rightly) concluded that Gunther hadn't cared enough to find out about their actual backgrounds. Offended and annoyed, many of Gunther's listeners didn't bother to listen to much of his presentation.

Religious Orientation

Religious orientation—a person's set of religious beliefs—is another demographic characteristic that can influence how people respond to your speech. In the United States alone, there are as many as twenty-three hundred religious identifications—including Baha'is,

Buddhists, Christians, Confucians, Hindus, Jews, Muslims, and Zoroastrians, to name just a few.

For some people, religious orientation strongly shapes their views on a wide range of issues—including but not limited to gay marriage, abortion, and men's and women's roles in family life and society. Moreover, some of the larger religions have numerous subdivisions, whose adherents possess conflicting beliefs about specific issues. For example, Anglicans and Roman Catholics share common elements in the celebration of the Eucharist, but they are widely divided over issues such as allegiance to the papacy or the admission of women to the priesthood. Likewise, Muslims don't all necessarily agree about every issue, and Reform and Orthodox Jews certainly part ways over several issues. Thus, like any other demographic characteristic, religious orientation does not preordain (pardon the pun) an audience's reaction to a given message, yet it can still exert great influence. Presenters who craft their speeches accordingly stand a better chance of connecting with their listeners.

Consider the example of the late Pope John Paul II's address to the state of Israel at the Yad Vashem Holocaust Memorial in March 2000. The pontiff knew that many Jews thought that his predecessors had been indifferent to Jewish suffering during the Holocaust. Demonstrating his sensitivity to their feelings, the pope repeatedly used Old Testament passages to describe suffering and awareness of human evil. In addition, he firmly condemned any act of hatred, any persecution, and all displays of anti-Semitism directed at Jews by Christians, at any time and in any place.

Why did the pope make this last point about Christian anti-Semitism when speaking about the Holocaust? For some Jews, the roots of anti-Semitism extend back to a period called the Inquisition, in which Jews suffered at the hands of the Catholic church. In addition, since World War II, there has arisen much controversy about the role of the Catholic church and particularly Pope Pius XII (pope from 1939 to 1958) in the Holocaust; some supporters claim that Pius's actions led to the saving of the lives of thousands of European Jews, while critics claim that the church (with Pius as its leader) was either too silent about the Holocaust or possibly aided the Nazis.[3] Pope John Paul II understood that these concerns might shape Jewish listeners' perceptions of his qualifications to speak at Yad Vashem. By analyzing his audience's religious orientation, the pope gained valuable insight into how best to construct his speech. At the ceremony itself, he was visibly moved as he laid a wreath at a granite slab that covered the remains of unidentified Jewish victims of the death camps and then ceremoniously lit an eternal flame. The pope then gave a heartfelt speech sharing some of his own memories of the fate of his Jewish friends in Poland during the war and decrying the Nazi atrocities. Because John Paul II was aware of the situation and especially his audience members' likely religious concerns, he gave an effective speech that connected with and moved his audience members, including several Holocaust survivors.

Socioeconomic Background

Related to but distinct from questions surrounding demographic characteristics such as race, religion, and political affiliation are those that concern the social and economic background of an audience member or group. **Socioeconomic status** is a measure of where individuals stand in terms of financial resources, education, and occupation in relation to other individuals. As a speaker, it's important to consider your audience's socioeconomic status and how it might influence their individual and collective concerns. The socioeconomic background of an audience member or group may strongly influence the way they receive your message.

Financial Resources. It is likely that people who come from wealth and privilege will have different life experiences from those who are poor and have fewer resources and options. For this reason, a person who has always been financially comfortable may have very different concerns than a person who is struggling financially. A speech extolling the benefits of clipping grocery-store coupons, for example, might be of more interest to a lower-income group than it is to a very affluent group. Conversely, a speech on stock market investing might fail to capture the attention of students with little or no money to invest.

Negotiating your path through assumptions about socioeconomic status can be tricky business: labels like "rich," "poor," and "middle class" are relative terms that carry little real meaning. You can, however, analyze your audience to get an idea of their collective economic status. For example, in a speech focused on whether it was ethical and appropriate for regents of the state university system to increase student tuition, Eleanor considered the fact that many of her classmates came from community colleges before transferring to the four-year state university; that many of them worked to pay for all or part of their tuition; and that because of work obligations, many were compelled to attend classes part-time and thus would likely take five or six years to get through school. Based on this evidence, Eleanor concluded that these aspects of her audience's background would definitely figure in to their attitudes about the cost of education and what they would be willing to spend for it.

Education and Occupation. Your audience's occupation and level of education can also influence their reaction to your speech. For example, suppose many of your listeners are already familiar—through formal education or life experience—with the facts you plan to present in your speech. If you're aware of this familiarity before-hand, you'll know that you won't have to provide extensive background information and explanations in your speech. But if your audience is unlikely to have had exposure to your topic through formal schooling or life experience, you'll need to provide more explanation and examples to help them understand your presentation.

Consider the story of Roy, a civil engineer responsible for civic projects, such as building new bridges and highways. To get approval for his projects, Roy often made presentations about zoning issues to a civilian commission. When doing careful analysis of his audience's educational backgrounds, Roy realized that the commission members actually knew very little about the necessary zoning issues. They lacked formal training in zoning, and because they served only brief two-year terms, no one ever served long enough to acquire extensive knowledge about the relevant issues. Roy therefore kept his speeches simple, explaining or avoiding technical terms. To help his listeners decide how to vote, he explained how issues currently before them compared with issues on which they had voted in the past.

Listeners who lack background in your subject might also benefit from presentation aids that clarify the points you're making. Carefully repeating your main points can also help your audience members understand your presentation by giving them time to absorb and process the information.

Political Affiliation

In some respects, **political affiliation**—a person's political beliefs and positions—is the most difficult of the demographic characteristics to pin down. Traditional labels like "liberal" or "conservative" and "Republican" or "Democrat" elude specific meaning and are so broad as to be relatively useless in predicting a person's views on every issue. "Conservative," for example, may refer to *fiscal conservatism* (belief in balanced budgets and reduced taxes), *law and order conservatism* (belief in the need for a stronger criminal justice system), *defense conservatism* (belief in the necessity for a strong defense and military preparedness), or *social conservatism* (positions on controversial social issues like abortion or the right to die, often informed by religious perspectives). Members of your audience who identify themselves as conservative won't all necessarily hold the same beliefs about each of these dimensions of conservatism. Likewise, membership in a political party does not guarantee that someone will vote for a specific candidate or respond to a speaker's message in a predictable manner.

Nevertheless, knowing your listeners' political orientation—as well as their views on specific political issues—can help you determine how to craft your speech. In a highly polarized political climate, attention to your listeners' political orientation becomes especially crucial to making a successful presentation.

Putting the Demographic Pieces Together

Great public speakers use their knowledge of their listeners' demographic characteristics to understand the people they are addressing—and to make their messages more effective. Every audience is unique; by identifying characteristics that many of your listeners share, you

PUTTING THE PIECES TOGETHER FOR MY SPEECH TO THE COLLEGE ACTIVISM TASK FORCE

AGE 16–25

EDUCATIONAL BACKGROUND: HIGH SCHOOL AND/OR COLLEGE

START SPEECH WITH QUOTE BY MAHATMA GANDHI?

POLITICAL AFFILIATION —UNKNOWN, BUT VERY INVOLVED IN ACTIVISM gain insight into how they might respond to your message. You can then incorporate these insights as you develop your speech and frame your message for the audience.

For example, Jackie, a fifty-two-year-old medical doctor, was asked to give a speech about safe-sex practices. Her goal? To convince her listeners that safe-sex practices decrease the likelihood of unwanted pregnancy and sexually transmitted disease. Her audiences? A group of teenagers in a facility for runaways, and a group of middle-income, working-class parents at a school meeting.

Jackie knew she would need to craft her message differently for each audience. The teenagers, all runaways, were suspicious of authority figures, especially older individuals who wanted to lecture them on their behavior. In her speech to the teens, Jackie avoided calling attention to the age difference between herself and her listeners. She also took care not to lecture them. Instead, she invited them to share their experiences, which made them feel understood. And just as importantly, Jackie avoided scare tactics, because she wisely realized that her young listeners had already been exposed to threats and intimidation that had prompted some of them to run away in the first place.

By contrast, in Jackie's speech to the middle-income parents, she worked hard to build trust immediately. She wanted them to see her not only as a doctor but as an adult woman and a mother. She made pointed references to raising her own daughter and talked about the difficulties of parenthood. She knew that some of the parents in her audience didn't want to acknowledge that their children were sexually active, so she avoided saying things that would make her listeners intensely uncomfortable, such as "You need to make sure that your child does not become pregnant or come down with a sexually transmitted disease." Instead, she cited recent statistics detailing the transmission rate of deadly diseases among youths who did not follow safe-sex practices.

SEEKING COMMON GROUND

Another way to analyze your audience is to look for **common ground**—beliefs, values, and experiences that you share with your listeners. Consider Jay, a student at a commuter school who gave a persuasive presentation to convince his listeners to use mass transit instead of driving to school. Like many of his listeners, Jay had spent his first year of college driving to school every day—getting caught in traffic, having trouble finding parking, and arriving late for classes. As he presented his arguments, Jay shared his own experiences with driving because he knew that many of his listeners faced these same challenges. And he knew that by establishing this common ground, he would gain credibility with his listeners.

In some cases, you can communicate your perception of common ground nonverbally. For example, a candidate for national political office dons a cowboy hat while delivering a speech to voters in Texas or a sports cap from a local team. Of course, merely putting on a hat doesn't necessarily mean that you share actual common ground with your audience. Use this technique only if you feel a genuine sense of shared identity with your listeners. And then reinforce that authenticity by referring to the common ground verbally during your speech.

IDENTIFYING PRIOR EXPOSURE

Do you remember hearing your parents or teachers giving you a lecture you had heard before—and finding yourself completely unconvinced because their points were not even persuasive the first time? Or perhaps you've heard a sales pitch or an ad slogan that seemed lame the first time you heard it, and only more so every subsequent time? This can be a problem for public speakers too—as a student named Henry discovered when giving the fourth of five speeches required of him in an advanced speech class. His fourth speech was a prepared, persuasive presentation that critiqued the existence of global warming. In making this speech, Henry picked up where he had left off with his second speech (given earlier in the semester), an informative speech explaining how people uncritically accepted what they learned from television news media. In the second speech, Henry had used global warming as one of the examples of "stories that television media push on people." In that same speech, he offered explanations of things the "media ignored" about global warming and how audiences "just accepted them." At the time, his class audience was impressed by his speaking ability but fairly critical of his points about global warming. When he revisited the issue in the fourth speech, he repeated the same criticisms of global warming—and was later surprised to learn that the audience was not in agreement with anything he said. The mistake he made was *not* in taking an unpopular position about global warming; it was instead in ignoring the audience's reaction to what he had said the first time and simply repeating the same arguments for the same audience a second time.

POOR ASSESSMENT OF PRIOR EXPOSURE

Hello girls and boys. Today I would like to show you this exciting new music playing machine... Er, I said, I would like to show you th... Are you listening?

Analyzing your audience also includes gauging listeners' **prior exposure**—the extent to which they have already heard your message. The degree of this prior exposure should guide you either to include particular points in your speech or to craft something entirely new. How can you determine whether your audience has had prior exposure to your topic—and then use that information to shape your presentation? Ask yourself the following questions:

Has My Audience Heard This Message Before? If your answer is "No," your listeners have had zero prior exposure and will have no preconceived notions about or positions on your message. You can craft your message as you want, but you may have to explain all relevant issues and concepts in basic terms. If your answer is "Yes," your audience has had prior exposure. Move on to the second question.

Has My Audience Responded Positively to the Message? If the goal of an earlier speech on your same topic was persuasion, consider whether the audience members actually took the actions or adopted the beliefs that the speaker advocated. If the purpose of that earlier speech was to inform, determine whether the audience members became interested in the subject and understood the information the speaker presented.

If you answer "Yes"—your audience responded positively to the message in the past—then use the new speech to reinforce the previous message, add any pertinent new information, and motivate your audience to take action (if you are giving a persuasive speech).

If you answer "No"—your audience did not respond positively to the message in the past—then avoid the approach used in the previous presentation. Now, proceed to the third question.

Why Did the Previous Message Fail? Assess what went wrong the last time your audience heard the message. Then use the resulting insights to tailor a more successful approach. In the case of Henry's speech, it would have benefited him to ask his classmates why they disagreed with his position in his second speech. Perhaps he would have discovered that some of them questioned his knowledge of science, some of them only knew about climate change from what they had heard on television, and some may have even found him a bit arrogant. Knowing the answers to this question would have given Henry other options for his fourth speech.

Additionally, if your audience has had a major change in perspective since the previous presentation, consider whether you need to adjust your message to accommodate listeners' new viewpoints. In 2009, flush from their major gains in the presidential and congressional elections, Democrats in the United States Congress set their sights on meeting President Obama's challenge to reform health care. This reform was heavily debated in the 2008 presidential campaign, and Democrats assumed public support for Obama would translate into support for their efforts to reform health care. But by the end of summer 2009, some members of Congress returning to their states and districts found themselves confronted by angry constituents critical of their approach to health-care reform. Health care, which had worked well as a campaign issue just a year earlier, had quickly become a political minefield.

What happened? The reasons behind the public's changing attitude toward health care are vast and wide ranging. The economic meltdown of late 2008, and the subsequent government bailouts of a number of large banks, insurance companies, and automakers, left many people concerned about growing deficits and increases in taxes and government spending. As the economic slump continued, voters on both sides of the issue were beginning to worry about the cost and effectiveness of an expensive federal health-care program. Meanwhile, opponents of health-care legislation—including politicians as well as television and radio pundits—were delivering their own message of outrage over the growth of the federal government. Congressional Democrats had failed to ask themselves whether anything had changed for voters since their prior exposure to the message. As a result, they underestimated this shift in public sentiment about health care.

IDENTIFYING AUDIENCE DISPOSITION

Finally, complete your audience analysis by assessing listeners' **disposition**—their likely attitude toward your message. In most situations, audiences can be divided into one of three groups: sympathetic, hostile, and neutral.

A **sympathetic audience** already holds you in high personal esteem or agrees with your message and will therefore respond favorably to your speech. For example, imagine that you are giving a speech advocating gun control to an audience made up of American Medical Association members—in this case, surgeons who work in emergency rooms, oftentimes on victims of gun violence. More than likely, you will have found a sympathetic audience.

In contrast, a **hostile audience** opposes your message or you personally and will therefore resist listening to your speech. Imagine, for example, that you are giving the same speech advocating gun control, but this time you are a speaker at a convention of the National Rifle Association (NRA). The audience in this instance would likely be hostile to your message, since the NRA strongly opposes restrictions on gun ownership.

A third type of audience is the **neutral audience**, which has neither negative nor positive opinions about you or your message. Listeners may be neutral for several reasons. Some may be apathetic and simply not interested in you or your ideas. Others may be very interested in hearing you talk but lack strong feelings about your topic. The key thing to remember about neutral audiences is that depending on how you deliver your speech, they can tip toward supporting your message or opposing you. To extend the earlier example, imagine that you are now giving the same speech on gun control, but on this occasion your audience is a meeting of the American Bar Association, an organization for lawyers. The membership of this association has mixed attitudes about gun control and would likely be considered a neutral audience.

As with the other elements of audience analysis, gauging your listeners' disposition can help you figure out how to craft your speech. For example, suppose you'll be facing a uniformly hostile audience. In this case, you should probably define realistic goals for your speech. Though you may not be able to persuade your listeners to follow a course of action you recommend, you might succeed in getting them to reevaluate their opposition to your message or to you personally. Thus, seek incremental or small changes, as opposed to a complete turnaround in attitudes.

An excellent example of this is when Senator Edward (Ted) Kennedy was invited to speak in October 1983 at Liberty Baptist College, a conservative Christian school established by the Reverend

Jerry Falwell. Kennedy, a well-known liberal lawmaker, agreed to speak at the school, though he knew that he would face a hostile audience. For his speech, Kennedy addressed the emotionally charged subject of separating church and state. His speech, entitled "Truth and Tolerance in America," focused on the appropriate place for religion in discourse about politics. In a speech that at times found common ground with Baptists and Reverend Falwell himself, Kennedy carefully but clearly celebrated and encouraged religious groups to enter political discourse where moral and ethical questions were concerned, while encouraging them to avoid name-calling or disparaging those who disagreed. It is unlikely Kennedy convinced many in the audience to change their minds about contentious issues like abortion—but he did make incremental gains with the audience on a personal level, as audience members respected his courage for addressing them and appreciated the lengths to which he had gone to find some commonality with the audience.[4]

If you're addressing a sympathetic audience, you don't need to bother investing a lot of time and energy in trying to convince listeners that your ideas have merit or that you're a credible speaker. Instead, push for more commitment from them: rather than simply asking your audience members to agree with you, urge them to act on your message.

If you'll be facing a neutral audience, determine whether your listeners' neutrality stems from apathy, disinterest, or a lack of firm conviction about you or the issue you are addressing. Then figure out how to overcome these forces of neutrality and get your listeners to support you—not oppose you.

Note, though, that many audiences don't fit neatly into just one dispositional group. In most cases, some listeners in a particular audience will be hostile, others sympathetic, and still others neutral. You'll need to tread carefully to deliver the most effective speech possible. If most of the people in your audience are neutral, a small percentage are sympathetic, and the remaining few are hostile and very vocal, what should you do? Expend just enough effort to silence the hostile listeners. Make an equally modest effort to motivate your sympathetic listeners to act on your message. And devote the lion's share of your energy to reaching your neutral listeners—and persuading them to take your side.

GATHERING INFORMATION ABOUT YOUR AUDIENCE

Thus far, this chapter has reviewed the types of information you will need to analyze your audience. Here, we examine three techniques you can use to obtain that information: surveying, interviewing, and observing.

Surveying Your Audience

A **survey** is a set of written questions that you ask your audience to answer in advance of your speech. Surveys allow you to ask your future audience members direct questions about topics related to your speech. If the audience is small—let's say thirty or less—try to survey all of them. If it is larger, you may want to survey a smaller, representative sample.

There are three general types of questions you may want to ask in a survey: fixed-response, scaled, and open-ended questions.

Fixed-response questions—such as true/false, multiple-choice, or select-all-that-apply questions—give your respondents a set of specific answers to choose from.

Fixed-response questions are useful for gaining concrete insight into an audience's experience with or views on a topic. For example, if Megan, a student, wanted to give an informative speech on why visiting the dentist is a good idea (because she herself has always been afraid of the dentist!), she could ask fixed-response questions to find out if audience members have any experience with dental care or even to learn about potential for common ground—maybe some audience members are also nervous about dentist visits.

Scaled questions measure the intensity of feelings on a given issue by offering a range of fixed responses. The ranges vary; they can take the form of a numerical scale—for example, from one (lowest) to ten (highest)—or a list of options, including "strongly agree," "agree," "neutral," "disagree," or "strongly disagree."

Determining the intensity of your audience's feelings about a topic can help you determine their prior exposure and disposition. For her speech on visiting the dentist, Megan sought to discover the extent to

Megan Dambrowski's <u>DENTAL SURVEY</u>

1. Have you ever been a patient at a dentist's office?
   YES ☐   NO ☐

2. In the past, why have you gone to the dentist?
   (CIRCLE AS MANY AS NECESSARY)
   A: REGULAR CHECK-UP   B: SPECIFIC PROCEDURE (e.g., cleaning)
   C: SPECIFIC PROBLEM (e.g., cracked filling)

3. Have you ever been given an anesthetic at a
   dentist's office?   YES ☐   NO ☐

4. Please respond to the following statement by circling the
   answer that best reflects your feelings:
   "I am nervous about visiting the dentist."

   STRONGLY AGREE —————————— I am terrified of the dentist.
   AGREE —————————— I get nervous when I visit the dentist.
   NEUTRAL —————————— I am neither nervous nor excited.
   DISAGREE —————————— I don't mind going to the dentist.
   STRONGLY DISAGREE — Whoopee, it's time to go to the dentist!

5. When you are going to have dental treatment, how important
   is it to you that you experience no pain? PLEASE ANSWER
   ON A SCALE OF 1 TO 10, WITH "1" REPRESENTING "NOT
   IMPORTANT AT ALL" AND "10" REPRESENTING "VERY IMPORTANT."

   1   2   3   4   5   6   7   8   9   10

6. Describe any problems you may have had during recent
   visits to the dentist (e.g., pain, discomfort, etc.).
   _____
   _____
   _____

   THANKS   Megan

157

which pain influenced people's attitudes about visiting the dentist. If her classmates were very frightened by the prospect of pain, she could focus her points on advances in dental anesthesia and new teeth-cleaning technologies that lessen uncomfortable scraping.

Open-ended questions invite respondents to write an answer of their choosing rather than offering a limited set of responses. For such a question, Megan might ask respondents to describe any problems they have had with dentists.

Open-ended questions can help you identify issues that you might otherwise not have considered or covered in your other questions. So if Megan wanted to know the range of dental problems her audience members had experienced, she could best find out through an open-ended question.

Open-ended questions also allow respondents to communicate in their own words. In fixed-response questions, perhaps none of the options accurately describe the views of a specific audience member; open-ended questions allow each person to state an individual, nuanced answer.

Interviewing Your Audience

In addition to distributing surveys, you may want to **interview** audience members. Ideally you will do so in person, but you can also conduct interviews over the phone or even via e-mail or IM. Interviews allow you to interact through conversation, learning facts and hearing stories you can't get through a survey. Interviews also allow you to get to know members of your audience before you speak; this can serve as a great icebreaker, especially if you don't know the people you will be addressing. Finally, you may find it more practical to interview a few audience members than distributing a survey to a large group.

If you use interviews, carefully consider to whom you talk. It would be easiest to talk to audience members you already know, and if the group has a leader, it would be logical to interview him or her. But your audience may have diverse backgrounds and interests, in which case you should try to interview a range of audience members.

When conducting interviews, ask the same sorts of fixed-response, scaled, and open-ended questions that are used in surveys. It is often a good idea to use fixed-response or scaled questions to get an overall impression of your interviewee's views on a topic, and then ask open-ended questions to gain more insight. During your interview, make sure to put into practice your listening skills, by paying attention and always being respectful. Make sure to prepare your questions ahead of time, show up at the interview location as scheduled, observe appropriate grooming habits, be friendly, and make sure to thank your subject after the interview is over; after all, he or she is helping you out with your presentation!

Surveys and interviews are two effective methods of obtaining information about your audience. But you may not always have the chance to communicate with audience members before you speak. If this is the case, you will need to rely on less direct methods to learn about your audience.

Considering and Observing Your Audience

Along with surveys and interviews, you can always learn about your audience by considering or observing its members. Ask yourself why your audience will be attending the speech. If your talk will occur during a class, you have a captive audience, your status as a student provides you with obvious common ground, and you share some background with your audience in the academic discipline of the course. If you are a member of the College Republicans asked to participate in a debate at the College Democrats club, you would likely find a hostile audience. Those attending would be there voluntarily and thus be free to leave at any time. Nevertheless, politics would be a major interest to your audience, and the fact that both you and your audience participate in political clubs on campus would give you some common ground.

Finally, consider seeking out literature about your audience members. If they belong to an organization, they may have pamphlets or brochures that they distribute, or there may be newspaper or magazine articles or even books written about them.

SITUATIONAL AUDIENCE ANALYSIS

Occasionally in your speaking experience you may find that you have done everything you are supposed to do in terms of tailoring your presentation to your expected audience, only to arrive at your speech opportunity to discover that the audience you are facing is not quite the audience you expected. At other times you may notice that the audience does not seem to be following along while you are delivering a message, or that listeners seem to disagree strongly with your main points. The following suggestions will help you analyze the audience *in the moment*—a skill known as **situational audience analysis**.

If the audience ends up being different from the one you expected, avoid communicating your surprise—audience members will likely interpret your comments to suggest that you are not prepared. Take a quick look at your outline and check whether the examples you have chosen make sense with this new audience. If the audience is smaller than you expected, consider jettisoning a portion of your outline and making time for questions and answers. Also, quickly consider whether your assumptions about common ground, prior exposure, or disposition of audience still apply. Finally, consider your presentation aids. Do they make sense for the new audience configuration? Because it would be difficult to create new visual aids at this point, you may decide to get rid of some if the new audience is already informed about the topic. Or you may want to provide more explanation for certain aids if the new audience is less informed.

And because communication is a transaction between you and your audience, during your delivery your audience will be sending you messages as well. What if you are delivering your speech and your audience seems confused, lost, or hostile? Try to read the mood of your audience members and adjust your delivery appropriately. If listeners seem confused, slow down, leave out some of the specifics or technical concepts, and instead explain a few of your points in more detail; humor might also lighten the mood and get listeners on your side. Or if listeners seem bored or unengaged, consider inviting audience questions or spice up your delivery by adding enthusiasm and varying your tone of voice—either approach will allow you to increase audience interest.

You may notice from your listeners' body language, their gestures, or even their voices that they are opposed to your position. In this situation, you can always flash a sincere smile or use a comforting tone of voice. You may want to reconsider common ground with the audience and your audience's prior exposure to your message. If you can see another element of common ground you share with audience members, you may wish to incorporate that into your speech. Likewise, if the new audience seems to have less prior exposure to your message than you anticipated, you may want to discard some of the points from your outline. If there is more prior exposure—coupled with a slightly more hostile disposition—emphasize points of common ground even more strongly.

CHAPTER REVIEW

"Let the audience drive your message."

In this chapter, you discovered five ways to analyze your audience: assess situational characteristics, consider demographics, identify common ground, gauge prior exposure, and anticipate your audience's disposition. You also found suggestions for gathering information on these elements of audience analysis. Finally, you learned that exceptional speakers analyze their audience while they're preparing a speech *and* while they're delivering it if necessary to retain their audience's attention and support.

Given the fact that audience-driven presentations are consistently the most effective, we strongly encourage you to analyze your audience in advance of your presentation, and then to use that analysis as a tool to shape your main points, your supporting material, and even your delivery and the ways you use your time and visual aids. Yet it is important to recognize that audience analysis is an ongoing process—a process worth reexamining as you develop the topic and speech message and hone the final product into a speech. It may even be the case that the audience slightly changes on the day of your delivery. Don't be afraid to alter things in your speech if assumptions you made about the audience are no longer accurate. Being flexible and open to that possibility will help you craft and deliver a speech message that is targeted to the specific audience you address.

Key Terms

situational characteristic *127*

audience size *127*

presentation time *129*

body clock (chronemics) *130*

location (forum) *131*

stationary audience *133*

mobile audience *133*

demographics *135*

age *135*

gender composition *137*

gender stereotype *138*

sexist language *138*

sexual orientation *138*

race *140*

ethnicity *140*

religious orientation *141*

socioeconomic status *144*

political affiliation *146*

common ground *149*

prior exposure *151*

disposition *153*

sympathetic audience *153*

hostile audience *154*

neutral audience *154*

survey *156*

fixed-response question *156*

scaled question *156*

open-ended question *158*

interview *158*

situational audience
   analysis *160*

Review Questions

1. Describe the following situational characteristics as they relate to audiences: size, time, location, and mobility.

2. Explain what demographics are, and note seven demographic characteristics that a speaker can consider when analyzing an audience.

3. What areas of common ground can a speaker focus on when addressing a diverse audience?

4. Define *prior exposure,* and explain why it is important.

5. Identify and describe three types of audiences in terms of audience disposition.

6. Name and describe three tools a speaker can use to gather information about his or her audience.

7. Explain the nature of situational audience analysis.

Critical Thinking Questions

1. When a speaker makes assumptions about you based on your age, gender, or race, or on some other demographic characteristic, how do you react? Is it fair for a speaker to draw conclusions about you based on such factors? How can you as a speaker use demographic information appropriately?

2. Have you ever been in a situation in which you found yourself at odds with other audience members? How can you as an audience member convey your attitude toward what a speaker is saying when you are in the minority among the crowd?

3. If your classmates are to be your primary audience for your speech, how can you use your class time to perform informal audience analysis? How might the timing of your speeches over the course of the semester affect your knowledge of your audience?

4. What kinds of situational adjustments do you make in everyday conversation? How can you apply these strategies to a speech?

Activities

1. Stephen Colbert performs on *The Colbert Report* nightly before an eager audience of fans from the "Colbert Nation." Check out an episode online or on TV, and note how the audience reacts to Colbert's political satire. Compare it to the audience reaction to his opening roast of President George W. Bush at the 2006

Washington Correspondents' Dinner (you can find it on YouTube). How do the audiences differ? Why might jokes that would be well received by Colbert's regular studio audience fall flat at this white-tie event? What situational factors might make even Colbert's fans stifle their laughter?

2. Make a list of the demographic groups to which you belong, in terms of age, gender, sexual orientation, race or ethnicity, religious orientation, socioeconomic background, and political affiliation. If a speaker were to address you based only on one of these demographic characteristics, how would you react?

3. Next time you are in a crowd—on the bus, at the mall, in a coffee shop, or in class—take a look at the people around you. If you had to address that crowd as a speaker, what common ground could you find? What beliefs, values, or experiences might you share with the members of that crowd?

Go to **bedfordstmartins.com/speakup**, where you'll find helpful study materials, videos, and speech-building tools.

SELECTING YOUR TOPIC

6

> "Use your topic to focus the message."

The first major assignment in Sam's public speaking class was to "prepare a speech on a topic of interest to you and your audience." Her first thought was, "How do I know which topic to pick?" Many different possibilities came to mind, but how should she decide which one would make the best choice? The course had barely started, and already she felt overwhelmed.

But when Sam thought more about her situation, she realized that, in a sense, she actually chose topics many times every day. When she wanted to start a conversation with a friend, a family member, or the student standing behind her in a long line at the bookstore, she needed to figure out what to talk about. In these situations, she tried to select subjects that interested herself *and* the other person. And usually these topics led to satisfying conversations.

With this in mind, Sam considered several topics for her speech. Sam knew what topics interested *her*, and most of them centered on music. She spent her spare time playing lead guitar and singing for a punk rock band, so one topic she considered was "starting your own band." But although two classmates participated in the school's marching band, most did not even play an instrument. Another possibility was explaining the history of punk rock. However, most class members did not listen to any punk bands, and their musical tastes were quite diverse—including hip-hop, country, rock, alternative, gospel, Latin, and jazz.

Despite the varied musical tastes of Sam's audience, they had one experience in common. Nearly everybody had illegally downloaded music from the Internet. Although Sam's band was trying to build its fan base and therefore celebrated when people downloaded songs from its Web site, other artists were not so generous. One of Sam's friends had been sued by the Recording Industry Association of America for allegedly downloading ten songs illegally, and had been forced to pay $3,500 to settle the case. Sam had also read that a Boston student had recently been ordered to pay $67,500 for downloading and distributing thirty songs on a file-sharing network. And on her own campus, the administration had recently warned students that they could be disciplined if they used college-provided Internet access to participate in such activities. Illegal file sharing would be a topic that was interesting to Sam and highly relevant to her audience.

As Sam's experience shows, you can find a good topic for your speech if you put your mind to it, even if you are initially unsure about which topic to choose. In this chapter, we present a process for selecting and refining your topic—including developing a list of possibilities, choosing the most promising one from the list, and narrowing that topic so that it meets your speech's objectives and can be covered in the time available for your presentation.

DEVELOPING A SET OF POTENTIAL TOPICS

Possible speech topics are as varied as human experience. For example, your topic could be lighthearted or serious, address ancient history or current events, or relate to professional interests or a recreational activity—and that's just the beginning. Here are some topics we've seen students select over the past several years:

airplane "black boxes"	Iranian elections
augmented reality	life on other planets
Cleopatra	Mary Magdalene
electric cars	my dog Max
good bacteria	nanotechnology
Great Wall of China	Peruvian civilizations
health insurance reform	recession-proof jobs
helicopter parents	smart power grids
history of toilets	twenty-first-century houses
Hmong weddings	Xhosa narratives
Iditarod dogsled race	zebras

Often it is the speaker's responsibility to select a topic, though in some instances you may be assigned a topic by your instructor, your employer, or those who have invited you to speak. When you are called on to choose your own topic, there is a process you should follow to select the best topic for your speech. The first step is to develop a diverse set of possibilities using these strategies: research, brainstorming, word association, and mind mapping.

Research

Research is often an effective way to begin your topic selection process. General newsmagazines or newspapers are good sources for subjects because they include articles on current events, science, geography and culture, famous people, and the arts. These resources will provide ideas for speeches on topics that are new to most audience members, or offer new perspectives on topic areas that may be familiar to the audience. This can help you avoid repeating a message that many of your classmates have already heard. For example, you might discover recent research findings that would provide you with an original perspective on a topic of interest.[1]

Many libraries keep recent periodicals and newspapers in easily accessible locations. An increasing number of these sources also have Web sites where you can find much of the same information, along with links to related materials. It is also possible to conduct an Internet search for speech topics, *but beware!* As we noted in Chapter 3, it is not ethical to plagiarize a speech. If these sites contain links to actual speeches, you may not copy all or part of a speech (or use it after changing some of the words) and represent it as your own work.

The ideas that you generate through research serve not only as potential speech topics themselves; they can also serve as starting points for other topic selection strategies, including brainstorming, word association, and mind mapping.

Brainstorming

Through **brainstorming**, you list every idea that comes to mind, without evaluating its merits. Your goal is to develop a sizable list of topics quickly; later you will consider which one would be best. Do not censor any idea at this point in time—just let your thoughts flow.

To brainstorm, consider your interests and experiences, issues you care about, organizations you belong to, people you admire, events you find significant, places you have been, and lessons about life you have found important. Think about favorites in each of these categories. For example, what is your favorite use of spare time? The most interesting course you have ever taken? The best organization you've ever belonged to? By focusing on questions like these, you will soon build up a good list of potential topics.

Word Association

Another strategy for generating ideas is word association. To use **word association**, start by listing one potential topic (as you do when

BRAINSTORMING (AKA: FISHING FOR IDEAS)

brainstorming). Then write whatever comes to mind when you think about that first idea. The second idea may suggest yet a third one, and so on. Write each new thought next to the previous idea. Word association (as well as mind mapping, which we discuss next) enables your mind to function somewhat like a search engine. Your brain (rather than the World Wide Web) is your database, and when you write down a word or phrase, your mind "searches" for other terms that you associate with the original idea. If you use word association for every topic idea you generated while brainstorming, your set of options will grow even more.

If you have done research for topic ideas, a current news story may also suggest a variety of topics through word association. For example, a story about the nomination of a new Supreme Court justice could result in the following topic sequence: the Constitution, the

WORD ASSOCIATION

Founding Fathers, Benjamin Franklin, electricity, solar energy. With this technique, even a topic that would not be a good choice may lead you to an appropriate one. Consider what Mike, a public speaking student, experienced. His assignment was to deliver a speech on "a tip for college success." One of Mike's ideas was "my football coach," an unlikely topic for this assignment. But he associated his coach's name with the coach's favorite saying: "Success comes when preparation meets opportunity." That quotation formed the basis for Mike's excellent speech on study habits.

Mind Mapping

To use **mind mapping**, write down a word or phrase in the middle of a large piece of blank paper, and then surround it with words and images representing other ideas that come to you.

Here are some tips for mind mapping:

- Use images—sketches, doodles, symbols—in addition to words.
- Start with a word or sketch at the center of the page, then work outward.
- Print rather than write in script. Lowercase letters make terms more memorable.
- Use colors to indicate associations and make ideas stand out.
- Use arrows or other visual devices to illustrate links between different ideas.
- Don't get stuck on one concept. If you run out of ideas, move on to a new theme.
- Jot down ideas as they occur, wherever they fit on the paper.
- Be creative and have fun with the experience.[2]

The use of multiple colors, pictures, and symbols to create a mind map stimulates your thinking process.[3] You use both sides of your brain and generate more—and more creative—topic ideas.

THIS IS MIND MAPPING

POTENTIAL SPEECH TOPIC #1: QUESTIONING THE QUESTION MARK— WHY IS IT THAT SHAPE?

A MIND → A MAP

WHO INVENTED THE QUESTION MARK?

WHAT ARE THOSE BUMPY BRAIN BITS CALLED? ?????

WHO INVENTED INVENTION?

LOOK AT OTHER TYPES OF MAPS

WHO INVENTED MIND MAPPING?

MIND MAPPING

START HERE

ANOTHER MAP

MONTANA — NORTH DAKOTA
— SOUTH DAKOTA
IDAHO   WYOMING — NEBRASKA
UTAH   COLORADO

WHAT IF ALL THE STATES WERE SQUARE?

CONVOLUTIONS (NOT CRENELLATIONS → THOSE ARE ON CASTLES)

CEREBRUM

No.

MESENCEPHALON

FRONTAL LOBE

← THIS PART OF THE BRAIN IS SHAPED LIKE A BIRD

PONS

MEDULLA OBLONGATA

SPINAL CORD

I AM A BIRD BRAIN!

DO BIRDS' BRAINS CONTAIN THIS BIRD-SHAPED BIT?

PIXEL USA

POTENTIAL SPEECH TOPIC #3:

SQUARE V. WIGGLY: WHY THE STATES ARE SHAPED THE WAY THEY ARE

POTENTIAL SPEECH TOPIC #2: BIRD—BRAINED OR NOT? HOW SMART ARE BIRDS?

SELECTING THE BEST TOPIC

You've generated a list of topics through one or more of the techniques described so far. Now you need to select the best one. To make your choice, consider the assignment, your audience, your knowledge and interests, and the context for your speech. And once you have selected a topic, stick with it. The following guidelines can help you pick the one best topic from the list of possibilities you've generated.

Consider the Assignment

As a student of public speaking, it's important that the topic you select meets your instructor's criteria for the assignment. For example, in most

CONSIDER THE ASSIGNMENT

classroom speeches, your instructor will require references to research. In such cases, you need to make sure that appropriate research sources are available for the topic you select. A humorous speech about your experiences as a food server, horror stories about your ex-roommates, or a demonstration of how you make your favorite fruit salad would probably fail to meet your instructor's criteria for the assignment.

In some cases, a specific topic might be assigned. For example, a history instructor may require an oral report on ancient China, or a biology professor may assign a debate on global warming. On the job, your manager may ask you to prepare a sales presentation on a new product or speak to a group of concerned citizens about a proposed new housing development on agricultural lands. In life, you do not always get a choice of topics; nevertheless, it remains your responsibility to research the subject well and prepare an interesting presentation for the audience.

Even if you have some latitude in choosing a topic, your instructor may have a list of topics that should be avoided. Certain topics crop up in public speaking classes every semester, such as capital punishment, abortion, the drinking age, steroids in sports, and marijuana. Rather than selecting an obvious and overused topic, you would be better off trying to *get ahead of the curve* when choosing a topic. For example, rather than talking about an existing social networking site, consider researching how new technology will change social networking.

Consider Your Audience

Your audience members will devote valuable time to listening to your speech. In return, you owe them a presentation that they will find interesting and important.

Based on your preliminary audience analysis (see Chapter 5), determine your listeners' priorities and backgrounds. The topic you select should meet one or more of these criteria:

- It will interest your audience.
- It's something your listeners need to know about—for their own or society's benefit.
- It will likely inspire, entertain, or emotionally move your audience.

CHOOSE A TOPIC THAT APPEALS TO AS MANY AUDIENCE MEMBERS AS POSSIBLE

BREAKFAST
(NARROWER)

LUNCH
(NARROWER)

BRUNCH
(BROADER)

Consider Your Own Knowledge and Interests

Among all the potential topics you've accumulated, which ones are you most interested in and knowledgeable about? When you choose a topic you're familiar with and passionate about, you'll give a more fluent and enthusiastic presentation. One of our students captivated his audience with a speech on Legos (though his classmates had not played with toys for years) because his enthusiasm for the subject was so infectious. Conversely, a student who appeared totally uninterested in her topic of job interviews failed to connect with her listeners, even though the subject was highly relevant to them.

Your listeners are also more likely to believe your claims if they know you have experience with the subject area. One student discovered firsthand the perils of selecting a topic she knew little about. Although she had no children or child-care experience, she chose to talk about why day-care centers are better than in-home day-care providers. Because of her inexperience, she made some assumptions that didn't line up with the experience of some parents in the class: she based her cost figures on national averages, which differed markedly from the local community's, and maintained (without providing proof) that in-home day-care providers typically have no background in child development. Since these claims were inconsistent with the experiences of class members who had children, she had to defer to more knowledgeable classmates during a question-and-answer session. By the time she sat down, she had lost most of her credibility on this topic.

Finally, by selecting a topic you're familiar with, you streamline the research process. You can focus on researching information that supplements the facts you already know rather than gathering general background information.

Consider the Speech Context

The **context** of your speech is the occasion, surrounding environment, and situation in which you will deliver your presentation. These factors often make one topic choice better than another.

For example, if you are asked to speak at an awards banquet for a campus organization to which you belong, the audience will expect an upbeat speech on a topic related to that organization. A speech on more serious ideas, such as the need for changes in higher education, would be better saved for a more formal occasion.

Situational characteristics—such as audience size and mobility, as well as the time of day and physical setting of your speech—should also influence your topic choice. For instance, suppose you need to play an audio snippet to present a certain topic effectively. In this case, you would not choose that topic if you will be making your speech in a large, noisy location, where listeners would have difficulty hearing the clip.

Choose a Topic and Stick to It

Once you've selected an appropriate topic from your list of possibilities, stick with it. In our experience, students who agonize over their topic selection for days or waver back and forth among several different possibilities lose valuable speech preparation time.

To support this suggestion, an analysis of more than one thousand speech diaries maintained by public speaking students revealed a consistent difference between strong speeches and weaker ones: the topic selection process. The more successful speakers carefully considered their topic choice but chose a topic promptly and then stayed with it, investing the bulk of their time in preparation. Less successful speakers spent days trying to settle on an acceptable topic.[4]

REFINING YOUR TOPIC

Once you have selected a topic, you must refine it—that is, you must decide how you want your speech to affect your audience (your rhetorical purpose). Then you narrow your topic to achieve that effect.

Decide Your Rhetorical Purpose

Your intended effect on the audience constitutes your **rhetorical purpose**. In a public speaking class, your purpose will often be assigned for each speech. Outside the classroom, your purpose may be assigned (for example, by your employer) or dictated by the context of a special occasion (such as a wedding, memorial service, or roast). For other speeches, the choice of purpose will be left to you. The scenario that follows shows how one public speaking student might go about deciding her rhetorical purpose.

Amber's instructor allowed students in her class to select their own topic and purpose for their first speech. Amber chose her major, theater arts, as her topic. She then considered a variety of purposes:

- *Informing.* When your purpose is **informative**, the message is educational, and your objective is to increase the audience's understanding or awareness of your subject. For example, Amber could tell her audience about the courses taken by theater arts majors.

- *Persuading.* When your purpose is **persuasive**, you seek to convince audience members to consider or adopt a new position or belief, strengthen an existing position or belief, or take a particular action. For instance, Amber might try to persuade her audience to attend a play put on by the theater arts department.

- *Marking a special occasion.* When your purpose is to **mark a special occasion**, you seek to

honor an occasion by entertaining, inspiring, or emotionally moving your audience. To illustrate, Amber could
amuse her audience by roasting her favorite director or
move listeners by providing a tribute to a drama professor
at a retirement dinner.

Each of these options would result in a speech that related to
theater arts on campus in some way. However, the rhetorical purpose
of each would be different—to inform, to persuade, or to mark a
special occasion. Therefore, each would have a different effect on
Amber's audience.

Narrow Your Topic

Once you've determined your rhetorical purpose, think about which
aspects of your topic you want to cover in your speech—in other
words, how will you narrow your topic so that you fulfill your rhetorical
purpose? You can't cover all aspects of the topic in a single speech, so
you need to decide which aspects to focus on.

Narrowing your topic is vital for several reasons. First, it allows
you to fit your speech into the available time. Whether you are
speaking in a classroom or in your community, it is inconsiderate to
take more than the time allocated for your presentation. Audiences
may stop listening if you exceed the time limit. Also, resist any urge
to speak fast or to cover each idea sketchily in order to say everything you had planned. Audiences don't respond well to those
tactics, either.

Second, narrowing your topic helps you focus your speech. This
is an especially important step for new speakers, who often select
overly broad topics. When giving a speech on a specific sport, such
as cricket, a novice speaker might try to cover the equipment
required, the rules, techniques for playing well, and maybe even the
sport's history—way too much for the speaker to cover or the listeners to remember.

Conversely, one of the best sports speeches we have heard
succeeded because the speaker effectively narrowed the topic of

tennis. She focused on four interesting professional tennis personalities. And the points she covered—such as the classic 1973 "Battle of the Sexes" match between Billie Jean King and Bobby Riggs—captivated her audience. Even listeners who were not tennis fans or had not yet been born when that match took place enjoyed and remembered the speech.

How should you narrow your topic? Many of the same techniques you used to select your topic can also help you narrow it.

Remember Your Audience. Ask yourself whether the aspects of your topic will be interesting or important to your listeners. Kendra, a student who wanted to deliver a speech about figure skating, surveyed her classmates and found that few were interested in a speech about how to skate. However, most of the class planned to watch the Winter Olympics on television. Kendra then narrowed her topic with the Olympics viewers in mind and chose to explain how her classmates could score the skating events while watching at home.

Draw on Your Interests and Expertise. Your special expertise or unique perspective on an aspect of your subject area can help you narrow the topic. Consider Caesar, a student who had attended school in both Mexico and the United States. He selected high-stakes testing (tests where failure has serious consequences, such as the inability to graduate or be promoted) as his speech topic, and narrowed that topic based on his own educational experiences. He compared the tests that U.S. students take with the tests students needed to take in Mexico. His listeners were interested to learn that some of the same controversies that have swirled around testing in the United States have also emerged in Mexico.

CHOOSE A TOPIC THAT GETS
YOU INTO THE SPEECH

Review Your Rhetorical Purpose. Try to narrow your topic to an aspect appropriate for your rhetorical purpose. For example, suppose you wanted to do a speech about sleep. A focus on sleep disorders and sleep science could make a good informative topic. A speech extolling the benefits of getting eight hours of sleep a night would be a good emphasis for a persuasive speech. And a speech honoring the director of your university's sleep research center would make a good special-occasion speech.

Evaluate the Situation. You can also use situational characteristics to help narrow your topic. For example, one student, Michelle, was interested in entomology (the study of insects), so she chose bugs as her topic. Initially, she considered narrowing her topic to the use of insects to determine the time of death of a murder victim. But she rejected that idea when she remembered that she would be delivering her speech shortly after lunch—when listeners might be especially squeamish. Ultimately, she (wisely) narrowed her topic to interesting facts about bees, including how they make honey—a perfect after-lunch focus.

DRAFTING YOUR SPECIFIC PURPOSE STATEMENT

After you've identified your rhetorical purpose and narrowed your topic, your next step is to determine your **specific purpose**—the objective of your speech—and express it in a concise phrase.

To write your specific purpose, start with a phrase expressing your rhetorical purpose ("to inform," "to persuade," or "to mark a special occasion"). Then follow those words with language indicating what you want to accomplish in your speech. For example:

- "To inform my audience about the events at a Portuguese festa."
- "To persuade my audience members to drink milk produced by our state's dairy farms."
- "To honor Captain Chesley B. "Sully" Sullenberger for safely landing Flight 1549 in the Hudson River."

THE SPECIFIC PURPOSE FOCUSES SPEECH DEVELOPMENT

Hey, pardner! What about the ones with stripes?

Just ignore them. They're INAPPROPRIATE, pardner.

You can use your specific purpose to guide which ideas you should develop in your speech. When selecting ideas, choose those that help you accomplish your specific purpose, and exclude those ideas that are not relevant. Thus, like the sideline on a football field, your specific purpose indicates which ideas are "out of bounds," given your speech's objective.

DRAFTING YOUR THESIS STATEMENT

Once you have determined your specific purpose, create your **thesis statement**—a single sentence that captures the overall message you

YOUR THESIS STATEMENT MUST BE ONE SENTENCE

 WRONG

The dog ate my homework, then my special fella broke up with me, then my grandmother died and I had to go to the funeral. After that my computer crashed and my car broke down on the way here and then the doctor called and said I had iron-poor blood. For all these reasons I should not be penalized for turning in this assignment late.

CORRECT

Due to unforeseen and serious circumstances, I should not be penalized for turning in this assignment late.

want to convey in your speech. This statement conveys the "bottom line" of your speech—the ultimate message that all the facts and ideas in your speech support. As long as your audience members can remember your thesis statement, they should be able to recall the essence of your speech.

In this book, we use the term *thesis* to mean the main position of any type of speech. Some speech instructors may prefer using the term *thesis statement* when a speaker is advocating a position in a persuasive speech and the term *topic statement* when a speaker intends to inform or mark a special occasion. Your instructor will let you know if he or she prefers this alternative usage.

Here are some examples of thesis statements:

- "The Hmong New Year includes many culturally distinctive features."
- "Our college makes significant accommodations for students who are called into military service."
- "A weeklong meatless diet can show you the path to a healthier lifestyle."
- "You should sign up for a service-learning course."
- "The Duke University women's basketball team has much to celebrate at this year's awards banquet."

Here are some guidelines for ensuring that your thesis statement conveys your purpose and topic to the audience efficiently and accurately:

- *Keep it to one sentence.* Make sure that your thesis consists of a single sentence that states the bottom line of your speech.
- *Express your intentions.* Ensure that your thesis clearly conveys what you hope your audience will know, do, or feel after listening to your speech. Listeners can better follow your message if they know what to expect.

- *Be consistent with your specific purpose.* Since your specific purpose guides how you research and prepare your speech, make sure that your thesis communicates the same idea as your specific purpose statement. That way, you'll avoid the all-too-common problem of presenting a thesis in your speech introduction that differs from the content of the body of your speech.

CHAPTER REVIEW

> "Use your topic to focus the message."

As Sam's story revealed, selecting a topic for your speech can seem overwhelming at first. But the systematic approach described in this chapter can help you move past any feelings of frustration or confusion. In this chapter, we focused on the importance of carefully considering the topic for your speech, emphasizing that your topic should fit with your own interests as well as those of your audience members. We explained how to develop a set of potential topics and then pick the best one based on an understanding of the assignment, your audience, your knowledge and interests, and the context of your speech. We then explained how to refine your topic by determining your rhetorical purpose and narrowing your topic to the most relevant aspects, given the time available for your speech.

Next you discovered how to write your specific purpose statement, a phrase starting with your rhetorical purpose and indicating what you hope to accomplish in your speech. You also saw how to create a thesis or topic statement, one sentence indicating what your speech is about. These two statements help you develop your speech as well as communicate the essence of your topic to your audience.

Key Terms

research *170*
brainstorming *171*
word association *171*
mind mapping *174*
context *179*
rhetorical purpose *180*

informative purpose *181*
persuasive purpose *181*
marking a special
   occasion *181*
specific purpose *188*
thesis statement *189*

Review Questions

1. Name and describe four techniques for generating speech topics.
2. Name four basic considerations speakers should keep in mind when choosing a topic.
3. Explain how you can narrow the speech topic by considering your rhetorical purpose.
4. What is the specific purpose of a speech?
5. Describe three characteristics of a thesis statement.
6. Compare and contrast the specific purpose and thesis of a speech.

Critical Thinking Questions

1. How do the topics you generate when you use a term to begin mind mapping or word association differ from the results you would get if you put that same term into a search engine? What are the benefits of writing possible topics on paper and drawing on your own thoughts, ideas, and knowledge? What are the benefits of accessing the nearly endless topics available on the Internet?
2. Why is it ethical to search for speech topics on the Internet but unethical to use all or part of a speech that you found on the Internet as your own?

3. What role should audience analysis, discussed in Chapter 5, play in selecting a topic for a speech?

4. How would your topic selection differ if you were delivering a speech to a club or team to which you belong rather than to students in a public speaking class?

Activities

1. Read through the op-ed pages in a national newspaper or the commentary in a newsmagazine. How successful are the topics in catching your interest? How do you think columnists come up with their topics? Are they always about current events?

2. Now look at each column you found in Question 1. Can you identify the thesis statement in each?

3. Discuss potential topics with other students in your public speaking class. Which topics are already familiar to students? Which topics are likely to be familiar to your instructor? For the topics that are familiar, discuss ways that they could be narrowed to present new and original perspectives to the audience.

Go to **bedfordstmartins.com/speakup**, where you'll find helpful study materials, videos, and speech-building tools.

7

RESEARCHING YOUR SPEECH

"It is not a fact until you prove it to the audience."

When Katie, Mandeep, and Sherri learned that the police in their town were shooting crows that gathered atop the local courthouse, they were appalled. The students called the police department to complain, and the chief explained that the practice was warranted because the crows were a public nuisance: they were noisy and annoying, they left droppings that posed a health risk, and they made it impossible to keep the courthouse steps clean. The crows had to go, the chief said, and other solutions were just too expensive.

Unconvinced by the police chief's explanation, the three students decided to actively oppose the shooting. After gathering signatures on petitions and presenting them to city officials, they were invited to speak about the subject at a city council meeting. The police chief would also attend to present her side of the issue.

Katie and her friends knew that the city council meeting was a make-or-break opportunity and that they must be prepared to respond to the police chief's claims. So they decided to find out whether the crows indeed constituted a health hazard, whether other towns had found alternatives to shooting, and how effective and costly these alternatives were.

In other words, these three students set out to *research* their presentation so that they could convince the city council to stop the practice of shooting crows.

WHY RESEARCH?

Researching materials for your speech offers you several important benefits. For one thing, research helps you learn more about your topic before you select and develop your main points. Equally important, it enables you to gather **evidence**—information from credible

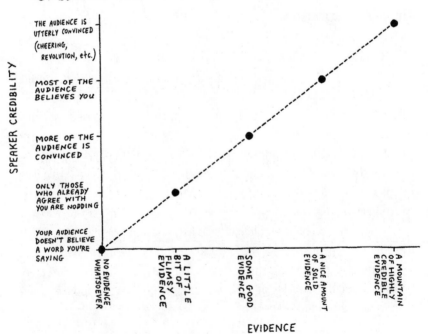

CREDIBLE SPEAKERS PROVIDE STRONG EVIDENCE

research sources that you can use to support your claims. If audience members are uncertain about a point you are making (or if they disagree with you), evidence may convince them to accept that point.[1] If they accept that the source of your evidence is trustworthy and better informed than they are, they are more likely to agree with your claim, even if they would not accept your opinion alone.

When you are informed about your topic and provide compelling evidence, you also gain **credibility** as a speaker—the perception on the part of your audience that you are qualified to speak on the topic in question.[2] Audience members will see that you are well prepared

CREDIBLE EVIDENCE CONVINCES AUDIENCES

and more likely to know what you are talking about because you have taken the time to research.

In this chapter, you'll discover valuable guidelines for researching your speech—including how to approach the research process, and how to find, evaluate, and use evidence in your speeches.

CREATING A RESEARCH PLAN

Good researchers develop a strategy for finding and keeping track of the information they need. Gaining experience, they improve on that strategy throughout their lifetime, particularly as new technologies change the nature of research. What follows are steps to help you formulate a **research plan**—a strategy for finding and keeping track of information to use in your speech.

Inventory Your Research Needs

Begin by deciding your **research objectives**—the goals you need to accomplish with your research. Your knowledge of the topic will influence your goals. If you don't know a lot about the subject, begin with general research to learn more about the basics. On the other hand, if you know your topic well—for example, you already have a good idea of your thesis and even some of your main points— you might want to use research to learn more about specific aspects of your

RESEARCH WORKS BEST

topic. When determining which aspects of your topic to research further, consider your rhetorical purpose and your instructor's research requirements. Finally, before moving ahead with your research, make a list of the subject matter you need to research and the questions you need to answer. This will help you stay focused on your research objectives.

Find the Sources You Need

Once you have determined your research objectives, consider where you can find the information you need.

First, remember that finding specific sources is not always an exact science. Although there are many tools to help you find excellent support materials, it can be helpful to think of the process as a mystery or a treasure hunt: there's great stuff out there on your topic just waiting for you, and it's your job to find it.

Your school or community libraries are two great places to start your search. If you have access to people with expertise on your topic, you may also want to set up an interview or two. Although the Internet can be a useful source of information, remember that there are greater risks in using Web sites than other types of sources. And it's always advisable to mix Internet research with research from other sources.

We strongly recommend that you consult with a research librarian at your school or local library. **Research librarians** are career professionals who are hired to assist students and faculty with their research. They are experts at tracking down hard-to-find

WHEN YOU HAVE A PLAN

information and thus can be amazingly helpful and knowledgeable about the resources available on your topic. More often than not, they will point you in the best direction for finding the most useful and credible sources.

You will also need to consider what types of sources will best meet your research needs:

- *Books* tend to provide extended and broad analysis of the topics they cover. They are one of the best sources to consult to access *synthetic* thinking on your topic because book authors often combine information from diverse sources along with their own analysis or critical judgments.

TYPES OF KEYWORDS FOR SEARCHES

SUBJECT: "IDENTITY THEFT"

BROAD TERM:	NARROW TERM:	SYNONYM:
"fraud"	"Dumpster diving"	"identity fraud"

- *Journal articles*, by contrast, are often peer reviewed and typically provide expert analysis of a subject designed for insiders.
- *Newspapers* can provide you with a "first draft of history"—that is, what people said about events just as those events were happening.
- *Recent newspapers* and *quality online sources* can provide you with up-to-the-minute information.
- An *interview* can be a great idea if an on-campus or local person is an expert on your topic.

Develop a list of potential research sources by researching library indexes (often available online), searching on the Internet, and considering credible people to interview. When searching library indexes, make a list of **keywords**—words or terms related to your topic as well as synonyms of those words. If you do not find what you are looking for under the keywords you have chosen, be persistent; try using broader, narrower, or related terms until you come upon useful sources.

Keep Track of Your Sources

One of the most important (and unappreciated) steps in the speech preparation process is maintaining complete and accurate records of your research sources. When you prepare your speech outline, your instructor will expect you to properly cite the sources of all the research you will use in your presentation. Not only is citation of evidence important to your credibility as a speaker, but it is a major grading criteria for many instructors. If you have lost track of the sources of your evidence or have incomplete citations, it will be very difficult to go back and find this information later.

Therefore, it is essential that you obtain full citations as you gather evidence for your speech. The **citation** contains information about the author of your evidence and where your evidence can be found. It is the academic equivalent of a map to your source. When a source is cited properly, it should be easy for another person to find the original source, whether it is in the library or online. It should also clearly demonstrate why your source is well qualified to discuss the

MAINTAIN ACCURATE RECORDS OF YOUR SOURCES

topic. Your instructor will have a citation format that you need to follow. Be sure that you understand what information is required for each type of source that you research. The following information is typically needed:

- the name of the author and his or her credentials
- the title of the article or book chapter if the work appears in a newspaper, in a periodical, in an anthology, or online
- the source (name of the book, magazine, or newspaper)
- the date of the publication
- the volume number (for periodicals)
- the publisher and city of publication (for books)
- the page number where the evidence appears
- the URL for Internet sources

You also need a reliable system for matching each citation to the evidence that you obtain. Whether you copy down evidence on paper or note cards, photocopy it, print it off a computer, or save it to a computer file, it is crucial that you, *at the same time*, record all of the citation information and place it with the evidence. One of the most common mistakes our students make is to assume that the URL that appears at the bottom of the page when Internet evidence is printed out is sufficient for a citation. *It is not sufficient!* You also need to find and record the name of the author of the information, his or her credentials, and the date of the information.

EVALUATING A SOURCE'S CREDIBILITY

No matter where you gather evidence for your speech (library, Internet, or interviews), you must select the most credible sources possible. Why? When you use **credible sources**—sources that can be reasonably trusted to be accurate and objective—you can be most confident that the facts you present are valid. Using credible sources increases the likelihood that the audience will accept your claims.[3]

To evaluate the credibility of a given source, examine four distinguishing characteristics: expertise, objectivity, observational capacity, and recency.

Expertise

Expertise is the possession of knowledge necessary to offer reliable facts or opinions about the topic in question. An expert source has education, experience, and a solid reputation in his or her field. For example, a nutrition professor would likely have expertise on the question of whether eating red meat is healthy, while a seasoned backpacker would have expertise on how to prepare for a long hiking trip. Likewise, you can look for expertise in printed or online sources by evaluating whether the authors or sponsoring organizations are well established and well informed in the areas about which they are writing.

Objectivity

Sources who demonstrate **objectivity** have no bias—prejudice or partisanship—that would prevent them from making an impartial judgment on your speech's topic. People can be biased for several reasons. Some have economic self-interest, or the desire to make money, so they may slant facts or explanations to make certain alternatives seem more attractive. Other biased people may need to please superiors—for example, a government worker who defends poorly conceived government policies. Still others have what's called ego investment: they're so wrapped up in a pet theory or cause that they lose their ability to evaluate it with an open mind.

Needless to say, you should avoid evidence from biased sources. If you use biased evidence, audience members will be unlikely to accept the point you are trying to prove.[4] Furthermore, if you use biased information, you cannot be confident that you have met your ethical duty to present truthful facts to the audience.

Observational Capacity

A person who has **observational capacity** is able to witness a situation for himself or herself. For example, a person who lived through the earthquake in Haiti, or who witnessed the effects of the troop surge in Afghanistan, would have more credibility than those who watched these events unfold on television. Sources with training and experience also make more credible observers. Thus, a person with expertise in child development would learn more by watching children respond to a violent video game than would a member of the general public.

OBSERVATIONAL CAPACITY: MORE AND LESS

Recency

Credible sources are also characterized by **recency**, or timeliness. Generally, newer evidence is more reliable than older evidence, because many aspects of life change constantly. For instance, in July 2009, a reputable health organization predicted that the H1N1 (swine flu) virus could infect 20 to 40 percent of all Americans.[5] Five months later, a study led by a Harvard public health researcher projected that the swine flu pandemic could be "the mildest pandemic on record."[6] Health experts also expressed concern that complacency could set in; if this was correct, then evidence from the end of the flu season could show yet a different outcome.

Because ongoing change is a reality, recent evidence is likely more accurate than older evidence. If you have a choice between pieces of evidence from two equally credible sources—one from three months ago, the other from several years ago—you should generally select the more recent evidence.

Of course, some evidence is classic and endures to this day. For example, though the teachings of Confucius are ancient, they command more respect today than the precepts of many contemporary philosophers. And the ideas of Machiavelli are still pertinent to the subject of international relations, even though they are almost five hundred years old. To decide whether evidence is outdated, ask yourself, "Has the claim made by my source become doubtful or false because of changing circumstances since the claim was made?"

With these criteria for source credibility in mind, let's now look closely at three major strategies for researching your speech: using a library, searching the Internet, and interviewing experts in your topic.

CONDUCTING LIBRARY RESEARCH

Libraries remain one of the best resources for researching your speech. Despite the Internet's increasing popularity as a research tool, the library still offers you convenient access to the broadest range of *credible* sources. In addition, libraries allow you access to strong evidence and credible sources that are not available on Web sites. And last but not least, no search engine has been able to match the experience and expertise of professional librarians in guiding you to the best material on your topic.

Local and school libraries house a wealth of information sources, including books, periodicals, newspapers, reference works, and government documents.

Books

Books are one of the best systems that humans have ever developed for storing and conveying information; they have important advantages as information sources and are often the best place to start your research. Books have been the primary tools for sharing and storing ideas throughout human history (for example, a surviving part of the Egyptian *Book of the Dead*, written on papyrus, dates from the sixteenth century B.C.E.), and many of today's books contain thousands of years of accumulated human knowledge. Most books are easily portable, and you don't have to plug books in or log on to use them. Books never crash, seize up, or shut down because of a low battery or power outage. And it's easier to read a book on a plane, in a park, or in the bathtub than it is to use any other information source.

In addition, many books are written by people with extensive expertise in their subject—though of course you should always check each author's credentials using the four criteria described earlier.

Books are longer than most other information resources, and thus they are likely to provide more in-depth information on your topic, along with more analysis and consideration of a wide range of ideas on the subject. Additionally, most books—especially scholarly books—are vetted before publication. The vetting process involves having the content reviewed and edited by other experts in the field to ensure the book's credibility.

To find books related to your topic, start by searching your library's electronic catalog by subject. Such catalogs are usually available online, allowing remote access; you can also search online catalogs by author name and book title. After entering your search terms, you'll see a list of links specifying relevant book titles. By clicking on these links, you can find bibliographic information as well as details on where in the library the books are located and whether certain titles have been checked out or are available in the stacks.

Finally, here's a tip followed by some expert library users. After you find some books on your topic in a library's catalog, go into the library stacks and locate the books you have identified. But don't just pull the books you found and leave; instead, browse through some of the books *nearby* on the shelves. Because libraries organize nonfiction books by topic—usually using the Library of Congress or Dewey Decimal systems—the nearby books are likely to have similar coverage but also touch on some different but related areas. These nearby books might point you to aspects of your topic you haven't yet considered.

Periodicals

Periodicals are publications that appear at regular intervals—for example, weekly, monthly, quarterly, or annually. They include scholarly journals and news and topical-interest magazines. Often the most credible information on your speech topic will come from articles in scholarly journals, generally written by people with expertise on a subject. Articles in such journals are subjected to **peer review**—that is, an editor decides to publish only articles that are approved by other experts in the field and that meet the publication's other requirements. In contrast, newsmagazines are particularly helpful for speeches on current events.

The following strategies will help you locate appropriate periodicals.

Consult General Periodical Indexes. General periodical indexes list articles on a wide variety of topics. Traditionally, these resources were available in bound volumes. Now, most college and public libraries have subscriptions to online indexes.

Online indexes are particularly helpful because they include **full-text sources**—links to the complete texts of the articles in question. When they do not provide the full text, indexes often supply an **abstract**, or a summary of the article's contents. The abstract can help you assess whether the article would be useful for your speech.

ONLINE INDEXES OFFER THE BEST OF BOTH WORLDS: THE QUALITY OF LIBRARY MATERIALS AND THE SPEED OF THE INTERNET.

The *Readers' Guide to Periodical Literature* is a general index familiar to many people. It includes numerous magazines popular with the general public. However, other general indexes contain more useful references for college speeches. Typically, these indexes are online, offer access to several thousand journals (many of which are peer reviewed), and cover a wide spectrum of academic disciplines. These indexes also provide other helpful utilities, such as the proper citation formats for the articles you find.

GENERAL PERIODICAL INDEXES ONLINE

Academic Search Premier	Over 8,000 periodicals indexed, including over 4,600 full-text journals (3,600 peer reviewed). Covers a wide variety of academic disciplines.
Expanded Academic ASAP	Includes over 4,300 indexed journals, of which 3,000 are peer reviewed and 2,500 are full text. Diverse academic concentrations included.
InfoTrac College Edition	Full-text articles from almost 6,000 scholarly and popular periodicals available. Also includes *New York Times* articles.
JSTOR (Journal Storage)	Archive of over 1,600 titles, including 1,000+ scholarly journals in arts, humanities, social sciences, and science. Also includes conference proceedings, monographs, and manuscripts. Allows full-text searches and provides scanned articles.
LexisNexis Academic	Full-text documents from more than 6,000 sources, including print, broadcast, and online media. Emphasis is on news, business, and legal topics.

Use Specialized Periodical Indexes. Specialized periodical indexes focus on specific subject areas and are increasingly available online.

SPECIALIZED PERIODICAL INDEXES

AGRICOLA (Agriculture)	*Historical Abstracts*
Art Full Text	*Humanities Index*
Biological Abstracts	*MEDLINE* (Medical journals)
Communication Abstracts	*Music Index*
Criminal Justice Abstracts	*Nursing Resource Center*
EconLit	*Philosopher's Index*
ERIC (Education)	*PsycArticles*
Food Science and Tech Abstracts	*Science Direct*
Gender Watch	*Social Sciences Index*

Ask Your Reference Librarian for Help. If you've found a citation in a general or specialized periodical index for an article that looks promising but you can't find the periodical, ask the reference librarian to assist you. If the library doesn't have the periodical in question, the librarian can probably get the article that you need through interlibrary loan. He or she can also help you navigate the Internet to find articles listed in indexes.

Newspapers

Newspapers are another useful source, especially when you need very current information. Newspapers are sometimes said to provide a "first draft of history" because their articles represent journalists' views of current events as those events are unfolding. Many college libraries have indexes for articles published in major national newspapers, such as the *New York Times, Washington Post, Christian Science Monitor*, and *Wall Street Journal*. Your library may also have indexes for your local newspaper and papers from large cities in your region. Most newspapers now have Web sites, and some are exclusively online (in April 2009, for example, the *Christian Science Monitor* became an online daily newspaper with a weekly print edition). Many of these sites allow you to search for articles. This can be particularly helpful if you want to focus on news from a specific region—for example, coverage of the auto industry in Detroit newspapers. *Editorials on File* reprints editorials from newspapers across the United States and Canada, which offer diverse perspectives on current issues.

General newspaper indexes include *ProQuest Newsstand Complete*, the *Gale Group National Newspaper Index*, *News-Bank*, and *LexisNexis Academic*; many such indexes provide links to full-text articles. More specialized indexes, such as *Ethnic NewsWatch* and the *Alternative Press Index*, also cover a wide variety of newspapers.

Reference Works

Reference works are compilations of background information on major topic areas. They are helpful for doing exploratory research on your subject area or discovering a specific fact (such as the number of people with Internet access worldwide or the capital of Kazakhstan). However, other sources—such as books and scholarly journals—provide more in-depth information about your topic. Reference works are increasingly available in both printed and online form in your library.

There are several major categories of reference works. Most include general works that cover a comprehensive range of topics as well as specialized works that focus on a single subject (for example, philosophy or art) in more detail. **Encyclopedias** offer relatively brief entries providing background information on a wide range of alphabetized topics. **Dictionaries** offer definitions, pronunciation guides, and sometimes etymologies for words, while **quotation books** offer famous or notable quotations on a variety of subjects. **Atlases** provide maps, charts, and tables relating to different geographic regions. Finally, **yearbooks**—such as the *Statistical Abstract of the United States*—are updated annually and contain statistics and other facts about social, political, and economic topics.

Government Documents

If your topic relates to government activities, laws, or regulations, government documents can provide useful information for your speech. Document authors may be experts, but beware of documents motivated by political objectives. To find government documents, use the following resources:

- *Catalog of U.S. Government Publications* (catalog.gpo.gov) provides citations to federal publications, congressional hearings, and committee reports. Records for over 500,000 publications are included, and a number of them can be accessed online. Congressional hearings can be particularly good research sources because they are generally held before major federal legislation is adopted, and experts on both sides of the issue are likely to testify.

- *GPO Access* (www.gpoaccess.gov) contains links to congressional hearings and reports plus the *Congressional Record*, which covers all debates in the House and Senate. Legislators often add news articles, reports, and other documentation to the *Record*. *GPO Access* also includes links to Supreme Court opinions, oral arguments before the Court, and opinions of lower federal courts, as well as information issued by the executive branch of the federal government.

- *CQ Electronic Library* features information from *Congressional Quarterly*, which provides nonpartisan reporting on Congress and politics. *CQ Weekly* provides information about bills pending in Congress and articles about major issues confronting the federal government, while *CQ Researcher Online* provides extended reports on major news issues.

USING THE INTERNET

The **Internet** has become the go-to research option for many college students. The Pew Research Center's survey "The Internet Goes to College" found that 73 percent of college students said that they use the Internet more than the library, whereas only 9 percent reported using the library more when searching for information.[7] These research habits can be hazardous to the typical student's academic progress. A recent study found that higher grades are associated with more frequent use of the library.[8]

Whereas libraries emphasize quality research sources, searching the Web can be a bit like sending an untrained dog out to retrieve the morning newspaper. He might come back with the paper, but he could just as easily end up digging in your flower bed or eating a neighbor's chicken. Put another way, you can't always be certain that your search will generate the information you need. By understanding the benefits *and* limitations of Internet research, you can get the most from this tool.

Benefits of Internet Research

Internet research allows you convenient access to information on nearly any topic without leaving your desk. Even better, many

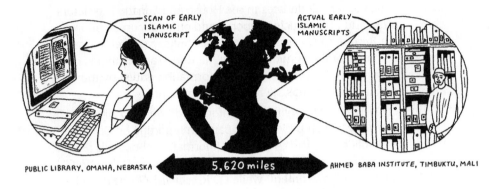

SCAN OF EARLY ISLAMIC MANUSCRIPT

ACTUAL EARLY ISLAMIC MANUSCRIPTS

PUBLIC LIBRARY, OMAHA, NEBRASKA   5,620 miles   AHMED BABA INSTITUTE, TIMBUKTU, MALI

libraries offer you access to full-text periodical and newspaper indexes from remote locations; such indexes are among the most useful available online, and we recommend that you focus on them when the convenience of researching from your own computer is important. In terms of reliable information online, we also recommend researching the "invisible Web" (covered later in this chapter), which is more likely than the standard Internet to offer credible sources.

The Internet also offers speed—enabling you to track down a news report or a research finding almost instantly, from anywhere in the world. Finally, this research tool puts an immense volume of information at your fingertips. In 2003, Peter Lyman and Hal Varian of the University of California, Berkeley, School of Information estimated that the **World Wide Web** contained about 170 *trillion* bytes of information on its surface, which is seventeen times the size of the print collections in the Library of Congress.[9] And the size of the Internet continues to expand rapidly.[10] With careful searching online, you may be able to find quality information that simply does not exist in your own library.

Disadvantages of Internet Research

Despite the Web's vastness, most of the world's knowledge is still contained in printed works. Authorities in many fields publish their works primarily in books and scholarly journals. And many of these works are copyrighted, so they won't likely be available on Web sites that a typical online search engine will lead you to. If they are available, you may need to pay a fee to access them.

Moreover, you can't assume that information you find online is credible, since most of it is not vetted in the same way that books and periodicals are. There are literally millions of **Web sites** created by individuals, advocacy groups, clubs, and businesses that may contain incorrect or biased information.[11] And as anyone with a free blog, a Facebook page, or an ISP knows, it's a snap for anyone to publish as much and as often as desired in the online world.

As a consequence, many of the Internet sources found by students do not have the quality that is expected by their instructors. Professor Wendy Lerner Lym of Austin Community College compares Internet research to fast food: sources can be quickly obtained, but they are not good for your academic health.[12] Research has confirmed the low quality of many sources found on the Web. For example, a team headed by Professor Chuanfu Chen of Wuhan University, China, recently evaluated 2,814 Web pages found through keyword searches on Google, Yahoo!, and AltaVista on such topics as genetically modified foods. The researchers concluded that 11 percent of the Web sites were very weak and 45 percent were weak. Only 11 percent were rated as excellent or good.[13]

Some students have been taught to evaluate the quality of a Web site by assessing its URL's (or Web address's) **top-level domain** (for instance, .com designating a company, .org designating an organization, or .edu designating an educational institution). However, Web sites may opt to register as .com, .net, or .org without restriction.[14]

BE CAREFUL WITH INTERNET RESEARCH:
YOU NEVER KNOW WHAT YOU'LL GET.

DANGERS OF INTERNET RESEARCH

Furthermore, a Web site's name does not necessarily indicate its credibility. For example, a site such as "tobaccotruths.org" may look like it was created by research scientists with impeccable credentials—but it could actually have been created by public relations specialists funded by the tobacco industry; similarly, a professional, polished design provides no guarantee of a site's credibility. Of course, many .com sites include nonobjective information, as companies try to promote their products or services, but even sites with .gov or .edu might not be fully credible: for example, government agencies are unlikely to criticize their own programs, and some .edu URLs offer students' personal sites.

Evaluating the Credibility of Online Sources

Evaluating the credibility of Web sites can be particularly difficult. Many sites fail to identify authors or the dates of publication, and even sites that indicate authorship may provide no information on authors' credentials. And, of course, many articles are posted online without expert reviewing or editing.

Thus, it's essential that you develop guidelines for evaluating the credibility of all sites you're considering using. For example, if a Web site provides the name but not the qualifications of an author, research that author further—either online or in periodical indexes such as the *Academic Search Premier*—to see if he or she has published in scholarly journals. For online documents that don't indicate an author, try to determine what organization sponsored the site, and then assess that organization's credibility through further research.

BE CAREFUL—SOME ONLINE SOURCES ARE CREDIBLE...
... AND SOME ARE NOT!

How can you learn about a sponsoring organization? Robert Berkman, a faculty member of the graduate media-studies program at the New School University, suggests reviewing the organization's stated purpose to gain insight into its objectivity or bias. Also research the credentials of any listed directors or board members of the organization. Consider whether they may have any political or economic interest that compromises their objectivity.[15]

The Virtual Chase, a Web site established to teach legal professionals about online research, offers the following additional guidelines for assessing the credibility of Internet information.[16]

- *How credible are the Web sites linked to and from this site?* If the linked sites are credible, the site in question is more likely to be credible.

- *Does another credible source provide information similar to that found on the site you're evaluating?* If so, that's a good sign of credibility.

- *Does the site weigh arguments for both sides of an issue?* If so, this suggests objectivity—a key criteria for credibility.

- *Is there advertising on the site?* If so, evaluate whether the site's creator(s) may have an economic incentive to offer content that pleases the advertiser.

CREDIBLE

I'm happy to provide you with a list of other sources.

Several other sites will verify those facts for you.

I always like to look at both sides of an argument.

You don't see pages of advertising in textbooks, do you?

ALLEGEDLY is a particularly beautiful word.

SLEAZY

What do you mean by OTHER sources?!? I'm the one and only and don't you forget it!

Verify? Whatever. I'm unique. Of course no one else knows the stuff I know...

I bought the last wise guy that disagreed with me a nice pair of concrete shoes.

Big Al's, BROUGHT TO YOU BY FAST WILLY'S BURGER 'N' SHAKE JOINT (HOME OF THE WHO'S YA DADDY MEGA BURGER), is never influenced by advertisers.

Big Al never denigrates those sad morons with no brains that dare to disagree with him.

E.PROF.COM

BIG AL'S .COM

- *Is the site's word choice professional?* A source is more likely to be suspect when it uses biased language (see Chapter 12) or denigrates those with opposing viewpoints.

Searching the World Wide Web

How do you conduct an effective search for information online? Two tools—search engines and Web directories—can help.

Search engines are specialized programs (sometimes called "spiders" or "crawlers") that continually visit Web pages and index what they find. To use one, you enter specific search terms, and the engine searches millions of Web pages to find the best matches for the terms you have entered.[17] The program then displays the results

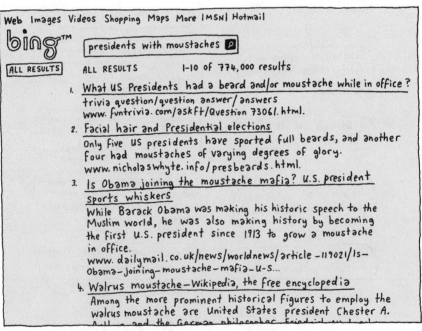

RESULTS FROM A SEARCH ENGINE

of your search as a list of Web pages. These pages are represented as live links accompanied by brief information about each site's contents.

All search engines sort results in an effort to make them more useful. Some engines organize the results by listing them according to specific criteria—such as how frequently your search terms are used, whether search terms occur near each other, or whether search terms appear in the title or near the top of a page.[18] Other engines list sites based on how many other sites link to them. But beware—a search engine may prioritize sponsored sites. If so, carefully consider the sponsor's credibility. Regardless of which search engine you use, start with the first ten or twenty sites listed in your results: they are more likely to contain useful information. Still, you may find other useful sites on subsequent results pages.

ADVANCED SEARCH OPTIONS FROM A SEARCH ENGINE

Another type of search engine is a **metasearch engine**, which searches several different search engines at once. A metasearch engine may find more of the available Internet resources than any single engine, but it requires simple search requests that all the search engines involved can understand. Also, according to librarians at the University of California, Berkeley, metasearch engines tend to look through smaller search engines and highly commercial ones—suggesting that you may end up with information that's not only limited but also biased.[19] In fact, some critics note that advertisers or media outlets may pay metasearch engines to prioritize their links in the results for certain searches. Thus, be extra careful when evaluating metasearch results.

Which search engine is best for you? Try several and compare their features and functionality. You can also check online for reviews

POPULAR SEARCH ENGINES

Search Engine	Features
Google (www.google.com)	Probably indexes more Web pages than any other engine. Prioritizes a site if other popular sites link to it. Google Scholar searches academic literature.
Yahoo! (www.search.yahoo.com)	Indexes a huge number of Web pages and combines results with sites from Yahoo! directory.
Bing (www.bing.com)	Microsoft's new search engine. Bing includes links to news, visual searches, and local databases. Search Builder allows user to prioritize factors that select search results.
Ask (www.ask.com)	Results ranked by subject-specific popularity. Ask attempts to determine which sites are linked by experts; it also suggests narrower topics.

POPULAR METASEARCH ENGINES

Metasearch Engine	Features
Clusty (www.clusty.com)	Queries directories and search engines, including Ask, Bing, and Open Directory. "Clusters" search results into categories.
Dogpile (www.dogpile.com)	Queries Google, Yahoo!, Bing, Ask, and directories. Best of Breed icon lists each search engine's top-ranked sites.
Info (www.info.com)	Queries Google, Yahoo!, Bing, Ask, LookSmart, and Open Directory. Offers results from single search engines.

POPULAR WEB DIRECTORIES

Directory	Features
ipl2 (Internet Public Library 2) (www.ipl.org)	New site hosted by colleges with information science programs, it is a merger of resources from the Librarians' Internet Index and the Internet Public Library.
Infomine (www.infomine.ucr.edu)	Built by university librarians. Focuses on resources relevant to college students and faculty.
Google (directory.google.com) Yahoo! (dir.yahoo.com)	Each offers a directory in addition to its search engine tools.

of engines that highlight key features and provide updates as more features become available.

Many search engines also offer **advanced search**, which provides commands for making searches more precise. For example, you can search for Web sites containing all your search terms, containing a particular phrase, or *not* containing certain words (this last function can help you narrow your results considerably). Advanced search also allows you to limit your search by date of posting, language, country, file format, or domain. It also allows you to conduct a "safe" search that eliminates sites with pornographic or explicit content.

Web directories are compiled by human editors who review Web sites and index them into subject categories and subcategories. Because editors read each page, evaluate its quality, and place it in an appropriate category, you are more likely to find quality sources with this resource. Search engines, on the other hand, can cover more Web sites than a human being could possibly cover in the same amount of time.[20] Because search engines and Web directories have different strengths, it is helpful to use both in your research. Some of the top Web directories are listed on page 225.

Hybrid search engines combine directories and search engines in one. For example,

Yahoo! allows you to search its directory of sites that have been visited and evaluated by editors. Alternatively, Yahoo! lets you search the Web and obtain links to sites that have not been evaluated (along with sites included in the directory).

The Invisible Web

The **invisible Web** consists of information that is available online but that can't be accessed by standard search engines. This invisible (or "deep") Web contains 400 to 550 times the information found on the surface Web.[21] Some of this information is stored in databases that can only be reached with specialized search tools. For example, to search a college or university's library resources online, users must often first enter a login or password to gain access; this password procedure makes it impossible for traditional engines or directories to search these resources.

Other examples of online information considered part of the invisible Web are breaking news reports, exchanges posted in an Internet chat group, or data generated by scientific monitoring equipment, along with streamed audio or video content.[22]

But how do you locate this information? These tips can help:

- *Include "database" as one of your keywords when using a search engine.* If you use the search words "global warming" and "database," your results will likely include databases where you can find quality information.

- *Use advanced search features.* Google and other engines now allow you to search formats such as Excel, PowerPoint, and Rich Text.[23]

- *Use search tools that emphasize finding resources on the invisible Web.* For example, try Complete Planet (aip.completeplanet.com), GoshMe (goshme.com), Library Spot (libraryspot.com), and OAIster (oaister.org).

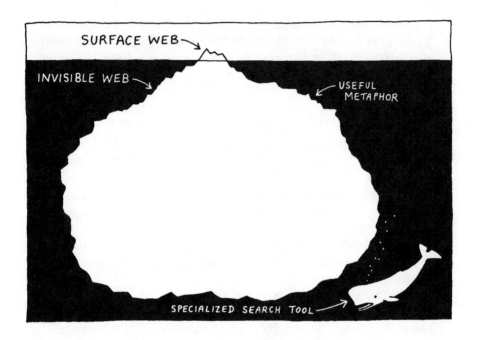

INTERVIEWING SOURCES

In addition to conducting library and online research, you can interview experts in the field to learn about your topic. When you conduct an interview, you can talk to your source about the questions or issues most important to you; you are not limited to whatever your source has written. To get the most from interviews, follow the steps discussed in this section.

Prepare for Your Interview

First, determine what you want to find out through an interview. Are there any questions you are having difficulty answering through library and Internet research? Are there any individuals who, if interviewed, would add credibility to your speech?

Next, decide whom to interview. The person you talk with should be an expert on the subject; on most topics, a roommate or relative would not be the best source of evidence. If your school has a department focused on your subject, ask the chair or another knowledgeable person to recommend faculty who would make good interview subjects for your speech.

Off-campus sources such as high-ranking members of political organizations, government agencies, businesses, nonprofit entities, and community groups or clubs can also prove useful. Many of these individuals are "people-persons" who will appreciate the opportunity to talk about their areas of expertise. If the person whom you would like to interview is too busy, he or she may give you a lead about another potential subject.

Students who have not researched their speech in advance sometimes rely on friends, family members, or neighbors for interviews because they can be found at the last minute. Although these sources may be able to provide lay testimony on some topics, they are generally not the type of credible research sources that instructors will expect. Check with your instructor in advance before using this type of interview to obtain evidence.

Set Up Your Interview

If possible, contact in person those people you would like to interview. (It's far easier for busy people to say no to an interview request via e-mail or over the telephone than face-to-face.) Identify yourself, explain that you're preparing a speech, and describe what you hope to learn from the interview. Be prepared to answer any questions the interviewee may have, such as wanting to know more specific information about you or about the speech you're researching. Finally, be willing to accommodate the person's schedule.

Plan Your Interview Questions

Once you have set up your interview, decide what you want to ask the person you will interview. Prepare focused questions that he or she is in a unique position to answer, rather than general questions you could easily address through your own research.

If you want the interviewee to elaborate or provide examples, formulate open-ended questions that require more than a "yes" or "no" response. For example, instead of saying, "Do you approve of the latest ruling in this case?" ask "What are your thoughts about the latest ruling in this case?"

You might also plan to ask the interviewee a candid question, one that you think he or she would prefer to avoid. But be sure to phrase such a question professionally. Coming across as needlessly confrontational will only put your interviewee on the defensive and may cause him or her to clam up.

For more information on types of questions to ask during an interview, see Chapter 5.

Conduct the Interview

Arrive on time for your interview, and dress professionally unless the occasion warrants different attire (for example, an interview on a farm). When you arrive, greet your interviewee and introduce yourself if you have not already met.

Keep these considerations in mind during the interview:

- *Start with friendly, easy-to-answer questions.* Straightforward questions allow you to establish rapport before you pose more difficult questions. If the interviewee has a limited amount of time, however, move on to your most important questions quickly.
- *Stay focused.* If the interviewee digresses, politely steer the discussion back to the topic.

- *Maintain eye contact.* Though you may occasionally need to look down at your questions or to take notes, keep the interview conversational and relaxed through frequent eye contact.

- *Be open to new information.* If new and valuable ideas come up, don't feel forced to stick to your planned questions. Feel free to deviate from them to explore the new information.

- *Listen carefully.* To ensure you're hearing your subject's actual answers, paraphrase key responses back to the person.

- *Tape the interview if your subject gives permission.* Recording an interview secretly is a serious breach of ethics.

Evaluate Your Notes

Immediately after the interview, check your notes to see whether you wrote down all the responses you may want to use in your speech. If you did not get everything in your notes, write down the person's answers while the interview is still fresh in your mind. If you cannot remember an answer accurately, contact the interviewee again to clarify his or her response rather than guessing. For any answers you want to use in your speech, run them by the interviewee to make sure you're quoting or paraphrasing him or her accurately. And no matter what, send a thank-you note to the person.

PRESENTING EVIDENCE IN YOUR SPEECHES

You've gathered credible evidence for your speech from library and Internet research as well as interviewing. Now, how do you actually present that evidence during your speech? Here are several important considerations:

- *Document all your sources*, and provide a complete citation for each one in your speech outline. Check with your instructor to determine what format is required.

- *Cite each source in your speech at the time you present evidence.* Before you quote or paraphrase a piece of evidence, identify the author, his or her credentials, and the publication if applicable. For example, "In an interview on May 18, 2009, Janna Wirch, a longtime ornithologist, maintained that crow droppings do not constitute a health hazard." Here's another example: "In an article published last Thursday on the Concerned Citizens' Web site, author Paul Dunn, the group's director, wrote that violent crime has decreased 3 percent over the past year." In citing Internet sources, specify the date of the source's publication if available. Otherwise, cite the date you visited the Web site.

- *Paraphrase responsibly.* If you are **paraphrasing** evidence (stating it in your own words rather than word-for-word from your source), be sure to accurately represent the author's intent. It is unethical to present evidence using **power wording**—that is, to reword evidence in a way that better supports your claim but that misrepresents the source's point of view.

HONEST WORDING:

A recent survey shows that 1 in 10 American Internet-using adults have gone to an online dating Web site.

POWER WORDING:

EVERY DAY is Valentine's day on the Web, with a WHOPPING 1 in 10 American Internet users LOOKING FOR LOVE online.

CHAPTER REVIEW

"It is not a fact until you prove it to the audience."

Katie, Mandeep, and Sherri, whom we met at the beginning of this chapter, have numerous possible strategies for researching their presentation on crow shooting, which they will deliver at the upcoming city council meeting. You can use these same strategies for researching your own speeches. In this chapter, you learned that providing evidence for the claims in your speech can help make your presentation more convincing and can make you more credible as a speaker. To gather evidence, you were advised to research your speech topic, first by creating a search strategy.

Next, you were encouraged to focus on credible sources, especially those found at the library and those that have undergone peer review, and learned that it is imperative to carefully assess the credibility of Web sites because they can be created without any checks on content.

You discovered tips for collecting evidence from libraries, the Internet, and interviews, as well as for evaluating the credibility of each source based on four key criteria: expertise, objectivity, observational capacity, and recency. These criteria mean that credible sources should be knowledgeable on the topic, able to analyze the topic in an unbiased manner, and be in a position to observe or study the topic. Generally speaking, more recent evidence is more credible than older evidence.

You also learned how to present evidence during your speech. When you do so, you begin by citing the source (author, qualifications, title of information resource, and date), and then you present a word-for-word quotation or accurate paraphrase.

Key Terms

evidence *196*
credibility *197*
research plan *198*

research objective *198*
research librarian *199*
keyword *201*

Review Questions

1. What are two key benefits of doing research for your speech?
2. Outline the three main steps involved in creating a research plan.
3. Why is it important to copy down complete citation information for a source at the time you obtain it?
4. What four key characteristics determine a source's credibility?
5. What advantages do libraries offer over the Internet?
6. Describe the advantages and disadvantages of Internet research.
7. Name four different Internet search tools, and describe the differences among them.
8. Explain the steps involved in conducting a useful interview.
9. What is the proper way to cite evidence in a speech outline and during a speech?

Critical Thinking Questions

1. How do peer review, vetting, and editing affect the quality of information presented in a book or journal? How can you determine whether information that you find online has been through these processes?

2. How can you determine the credibility of information presented on a Web site? Are there any red flags that immediately make you question a site's integrity? What characteristics are likely to make you trust an Internet source?

3. Imagine you have been assigned to speak on a controversial topic. How would you go about choosing potential interviewees? What kinds of questions would you ask your interviewees? How would you use the information gleaned in interviews to bolster your thesis ethically?

Activities

1. Go to the campus library and locate a book on a topic that you are considering for a speech. Then try the process discussed on pages 208–209 to find other books on your topic. Did you find additional useful information in these books?

2. Use an index for scholarly sources, such as *Academic Search Premier* or *JSTOR*, to find three articles on a topic you are considering for a speech. Then find three Web sites that cover that topic. Compare the credibility of the authors of the scholarly sources with that of the online sources, as well as the content of the information.

3. Use diverse Internet search tools (including search engines, metasearch engines, and directories) to search for the same keyword or phrase. How do the results differ?

4. Watch an episode of a news personality program such as *The O'Reilly Factor*, *The Rachel Maddow Show*, *Glenn Beck*, or *Countdown with Keith Olbermann*. Do the hosts of these programs (or others who speak on these shows) offer evidence to support the claims they make? What claims are made without evidence? What type of person would be a credible source of information about these claims?

Go to **bedfordstmartins.com/speakup**, where you'll find helpful study materials, videos, and speech-building tools.

USING SUPPORTING MATERIALS FOR YOUR SPEECH

8

> "The sum of the parts determines the success of the whole speech."

Graciela was a member of her college's varsity tennis team, so for her informative speech topic, she chose to focus on Title IX— the federal law prohibiting sex discrimination by educational institutions that receive federal aid. As she began her research, one of the first things Graciela discovered is that there are three ways a school can demonstrate compliance with Title IX. Graciela's first feeling was relief: the assignment called for an eight- to ten-minute speech, and it would take at least six to explain the ways a college could comply. She was more than halfway done!

Then Graciela reconsidered. Of all the points that she could make about this important and sometimes controversial law, would the details about compliance be the most important and interesting aspects to share with her audience? She decided to do more research about how Title IX issues were handled at *her* school. And she found a tremendous amount of material: articles in the school newspaper about the impact of Title IX when it was first applied on campus, stories from athletes about their experiences on the college's first women's teams, and even a copy of the program from the first women's tennis tournament ever held on campus.

Now Graciela had ideas and evidence that would be much more relevant and interesting to her classmates. By going the extra mile to find engaging support, she had the materials she needed to create sound support for her main points.

As we note in Chapter 2 and throughout the book, every speech offers a limited number of main points. **Supporting materials** are the different types of information that you use to develop and support your main points. You discover these materials as you research your speech; they then become the building blocks that you use to construct a successful speech.

Selecting the best supporting materials for your main points is a key step in the speech preparation process, similar to choosing the right mix of ingredients for a special meal you'll be preparing. In an excellent speech, the supporting materials fit together to help your listeners better understand your message, to capture their interest, and to convince them that you've done your research and are informed about your topic.

Consider a class period in which you learned a lot about a subject, a political argument you found persuasive, or a movie that kept

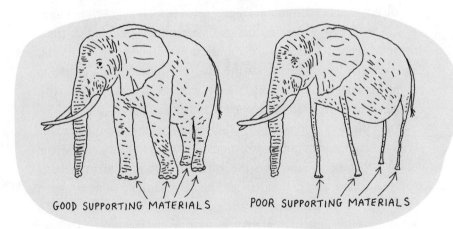

GOOD SUPPORTING MATERIALS   POOR SUPPORTING MATERIALS

you glued to your seat for hours. Chances are good that the teacher used understandable language and examples that clarified the concepts and made the subject seem relevant. The person making the political argument likely offered convincing proof of his or her claims and touched your emotions in a way that you remembered at the voting booth. And the movie probably combined an interesting story with memorable characters and an exciting plot. With the right supporting materials, you can craft a speech that has an equally strong impact on your audience.

In this chapter, we show you why supporting materials are important, what supporting materials you can use, and how to present supporting materials more effectively.

WHY USE SUPPORTING MATERIALS?

Supporting materials strengthen your speech in many ways. They build audience interest in your topic and help the audience understand your

SUPPORT IS IMPORTANT

ideas. In addition, they convince the audience that your points have merit and breathe life into your speech.

Building Audience Interest

If you want audience members to actively listen to your speech—and ignore everything else in the meantime—you must motivate them to focus on what you're saying. By selecting supporting materials that appeal to your listeners' interests, you sweeten the odds that they will pay attention to you. For example, suppose your school is located in the Midwest region of the United States and you're developing a speech on emergency preparedness. In this case, you might put together supporting materials that focus on preparing for tornadoes—common events in the Midwest—rather than hurricanes or earthquakes.

And by including supporting materials that surprise audience members, make them laugh, or touch their emotions, you increase the chances that they will listen to what you are saying.

SELECT SUPPORTING MATERIALS THAT RELATE TO THE AUDIENCE

Enhancing Audience Understanding

If you're presenting information that's new to your listeners, they may have difficulty understanding your topic. For instance, let's say you're preparing a speech on string theory that you'll present to an audience of mostly liberal-arts students. In this case, supporting materials such as definitions could help your audience members understand the meaning of technical terms such as *superstring*. And brief, accessible examples could help them grasp the basic concepts behind your topic and help them form mental images of a superstring.

ENHANCING AUDIENCE UNDERSTANDING

Winning Audience Agreement

You can't expect your listeners to unthinkingly embrace all the claims you make in your speech. Rather, audience members may be skeptical of a point if they've never heard it before, if it strikes them as counterintuitive, or if it contradicts their worldview. Supporting materials help convince your audience that your claims merit their consideration. If you quote an expert, present a demonstration, or provide examples to illustrate your point, you give your audience reasons to agree with you.

Evoking Audience Emotion

Factual information greatly enhances any speech. However, you'll capture more of your audience members' attention and interest if you also touch their emotions. For example, an effective speaker may use humor to warm up her listeners or give them a mental break from a slew of sobering statistics. The right supporting materials can also stimulate listeners' empathy, anger, or commitment.

TYPES OF SUPPORTING MATERIALS

There are many types of supporting materials from which to choose to develop your main points. Here, we take a closer look at some of the more common types: examples, definitions, testimony, statistics, narratives, and analogies.

Examples

Examples are samples or instances that support or illustrate a general claim. In everyday conversation, you probably use examples frequently. To illustrate, suppose you tell a friend that parking is difficult on your campus, then you point out that you couldn't find a spot three times last week and your roommate had to drive around for thirty minutes to find a space. In this case, you are using examples to support your claim that parking is difficult.

Brief examples are a set of short instances (usually a single sentence) used to support or illustrate your claim. The following excerpt shows how brief examples can be used to support the claim that Americans' privacy is at risk:

- Data brokers can sell records of your marriages and divorces, lawsuits, and old addresses, as well as the names, addresses, and phone numbers of your relatives and neighbors.[1]
- In one survey, 38 percent of companies reported that they reviewed the content of their employees' e-mail in 2009.[2]
- Diverse U.S. cities have implemented video surveillance, and the market for this technology is expected to grow from $6.6 billion in 2005 to $11.9 billion in 2011.[3]

You can also use **extended examples** to illustrate a point. An extended example provides details about the instance being used, giving your audience a deeper and richer picture of your point. This extended example describes the experience of a police sergeant and SWAT team member, who learned about employer monitoring of text messages the hard way:

EXAMPLES OF THREATS TO PRIVACY

Sergeant Jeff Quon was provided a pager by his employer, the Ontario (California) Police Department. The lieutenant in charge of administering the pagers told Quon that he would not audit his pager use, but that Quon would be responsible for overage fees. Quon paid these charges several times, and the department did not monitor his pager use for eight months. Then, without warning, the police chief required that the messages be audited. An internal affairs investigation found that Quon had sent personal messages, a number of which were sexually explicit. Sergeant Quon sued the department on the grounds that his 4th Amendment rights were violated. The U.S. Supreme Court ruled that in this case, his rights were not violated.[4]

Definitions

When you introduce new information to audience members, you may well use terms unfamiliar to them. If you don't take time to define these terms, your listeners may have difficulty understanding your message—which can leave them frustrated.

For example, suppose you're preparing an informative speech on the Persian Empire, and you want to explain that the Persians practiced a religion called Zoroastrianism. This term will likely be new to your audience, so you'll need to define it. There are several different types of definitions you could use:

A **dictionary definition** provides the meaning of a term as presented in a dictionary. You might use a general dictionary or, if available, a more specialized one for your topic. For example, according to

Cambridge Dictionaries Online, Zoroastrianism is "a religion which developed in ancient Iran, and is based on the idea that there is a continuous fight between a god who represents good and one who represents evil."[5]

An **expert definition** comes from a person who is a credible source of information on your topic. For example:

According to Mary Boyce, Professor of Iranian Studies at the University of London, in *Zoroastrians: Their Religious Beliefs and Practices*, 1979, Zoroastrians believe that "there is a

According to my dictionary, the DEFINITION of DEFINITION is "an act of determining; a statement expressing the essential nature of something" or "a statement of the meaning of a word or word group or a sign or symbol" or "a product of defining" or "the action or process of defining" or "the action or the power of describing, explaining, or making definite and clear" or "clarity of visual presentation: distinctness of outline or detail..."

MERRIAM–WEBSTER'S COLLEGIATE DICTIONARY, 11TH EDITION, 2003

supreme God who is the creator; that an evil power exists which is opposed to him, and not under his control," [that this god] "created this world for a purpose," [and that the world in its present state will have an end that] "will be heralded by the coming of a cosmic Saviour, who will help to bring it about."[6]

An **etymological definition** explains the linguistic origin of the term. This type of definition is appropriate when the origin is interesting or will help the audience understand the term. For example: "Zoroastrianism has been so named in the West because its prophet, Zarathustra, was known to the ancient Greeks as Zoroaster.[7] Zoroastrians believe that Ahura Mazda (God) revealed the truth through Zarathustra."

A **functional definition** explains how something is used or what it does. For instance, a speaker might define Zoroastrianism in terms of how it is practiced by its followers:

According to the Ontario Consultants on Religious Tolerance, March 24, 2005, Zoroastrian worship includes prayers and symbolic ceremonies. The rituals are conducted before a sacred fire. [Practitioners] regard fire as a symbol of their God.

Members are dedicated to a three-fold practice, as shown in their motto: Good Thoughts, Good Works, Good Deeds.[8]

Testimony

Testimony consists of information provided by other people. Typically, you will find testimony from the sources you research at the library, online, or through interviews.

Expert testimony consists of statements made by credible sources who have professional or other in-depth knowledge of a topic. As with any source, you must carefully assess any expert testimony and be sure that expert sources have specialized knowledge of the topic, objectivity, and observational capacity. Testimony from expert sources is likely to increase audience members' acceptance of your claims. Thus, you should try to use expert testimony when you are asserting claims that the audience may not accept.

A second type of testimony is **lay testimony**, which consists of statements made by persons with no special expertise in the subject they are discussing. Because they lack expertise, lay sources should generally not be used to prove factual claims in a speech. This type of testimony is *not* a substitute for evidence. For example, testimony from lay persons would not credibly prove that a low-carbohydrate diet improves people's health or that the U.S. economy has been helped or hurt by the outsourcing of jobs. However, lay testimony can help you show how a typical person has been affected by your topic. Thus, you could quote lay sources to explain their particular experiences with a low-carbohydrate diet or to discuss how they were affected when their jobs were moved overseas.

Statistics

Statistics are information (or data) presented in numerical form. They can help you quantify points you're making in your speech and help your audience understand how often certain types of situations occur. While supporting materials such as examples or anecdotes help the audience understand a single instance, statistics can help you show the big picture regarding multiple instances or instances over time of the situation you are discussing.

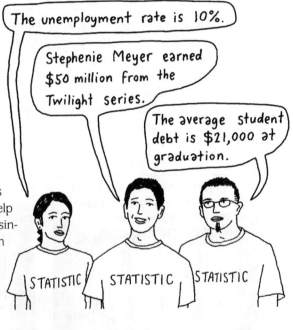

For example, in a speech on the rising costs of a college education, you might present an example of a single student who struggled to afford $1,000 for books and supplies in 2009. Then you could use statistics to argue that this cost is typical:

> The College Board reports that the average cost of books and other course materials at four year public colleges in 2009–10 is $1,122.[9]

Though useful, statistics also have disadvantages. Specifically, as your use of statistics increases, so does the chance that your audience members will perceive your topic as overly complicated.[10] A long string of statistics may also bore or confuse your listeners if they're struggling to figure out what "all those numbers" mean. To present statistics in a way that helps your audience understand the information *and* remain interested in your speech, apply these guidelines:

- *Limit the number of statistics you present.* Of all the possible statistics you could offer your audience, select the best few.
- *Use visual aids to explain your statistics.* For example, you could use a bar graph to illustrate increases in textbook costs, tuition, and overall cost of living over the past eighteen years.
- *Establish context.* Explain what the statistics imply for your listeners. For instance, "What does a 6.5% annual increase mean? The average price for books and supplies is now $1,100, and the average tuition at four-year public colleges and universities is over $7,000. At the rates of increase I've just presented to you, books and supplies will cost over $1,500, and tuition will rise to $9,600, in just five years."

PROVIDE CONTEXT FOR STATISTICS

Narratives

Narratives are anecdotes (brief stories) or somewhat longer accounts that can be used to support your main points. Narratives stimulate your listeners' interest because humans (by our very nature) love a good story.[11]

Here is a medium-length anecdote offered by a student in his speech about how the city of Los Angeles improved water quality in the Los Angeles River:

On March 6, a writer for the *Los Angeles Times* filled an aquarium with water taken from the Los Angeles River. Two goldfish, Little Ed and Little Antonia, were plopped into the tank, to see if they could survive in the river water. One month later, the fish were still going strong. You can follow

THIS IS AN ANECDOTE

the fish's progress on a Web cam on the newspaper's Web site, and the fish even have their own page on MySpace.[12]

In a speech on healthier living, a presenter used the following somewhat longer narrative to show how it is possible to improve your health through lifestyle changes:

Arkansas governor Mike Huckabee knew he had a problem when he sat down at a staff meeting and his chair collapsed. Soon after this, he was diagnosed with type-2 diabetes and was told by his doctor that unless he changed his lifestyle, he

THIS IS A NARRATIVE

had ten years to live. So the governor began what he called a "twelve-stop program" to stop unhealthy habits. First he walked. Then he ran, working his way up to the Little Rock Marathon. He exchanged junk food for a healthy diet. He dropped 110 pounds and no longer needs diabetes medication. He also spearheaded a Healthy Arkansas Initiative in his home state and joined with former President Clinton and the American Heart Association in a campaign against childhood obesity.[13]

Stories like these are great for capturing audience attention or for illustrating a point. Consider incorporating such stories as attention-getters or when you want to show how concepts play out in the real world. And you can always use a quick anecdote—lasting no more than five or ten seconds—to reenergize an audience after tackling complex or technical material.

Narratives and anecdotes are like lay testimony in that they can effectively build audience interest or illustrate a concept; however, anecdotal evidence is no substitute for credible proof. Stories of a relative who smoked two packs of cigarettes a day and lived to the ripe age of ninety-eight, or a roommate who partied every night and still maintained a 3.8 grade point average, do not prove that such behaviors are safe for the population as a whole.

Analogies

An **analogy** is a comparison based on similarities between two phenomena, one that's familiar to the audience and one that is less familiar. Analogies can be **literal**, meaning that two entities in the same category are compared. For example, a speaker might compare Sarah Palin to Ronald Reagan, punk rock to hip-hop, or German policy on wind energy to a similar policy in the United States. Analogies can also be **figurative**, which means that the two entities are not in the same category, but the characteristics of one (which is familiar to the audience) can help the audience understand the characteristics of another (which is unfamiliar). This type of comparison helps listeners use their existing knowledge to absorb new information.[14]

Here's how one speaker used a figurative analogy to help his listeners understand how a jellyfish-like sea creature known as a siphonophore emits a red glow to lure its prey:

> According to Steven Haddock of the Monterey Bay Aquarium Research Institute, in a July 7, 2005, article on the CNN.com *Science & Space* Web site:
>
> > The tiny lure mechanism [is] something like a Tootsie Pop. In the core of the lure, the blue green light is emitted. It is covered by a red material, so when the

light is triggered, it passes through this red surface. The wavelength of the light is converted, and looks orangey-red on the outside.[15]

When you are preparing a speech, one effective approach is to provide analogies that draw on concepts you heard in speeches your classmates have delivered. That way, you'll know that your audience members already understand those concepts, and you'll demonstrate goodwill to show that you have learned from your classmates' speeches. Additional good sources of analogies are familiar sights and traditions on your campus, or aspects of college life that your listeners can all relate to.

GUIDELINES FOR USING SUPPORTING MATERIALS

Recall that supporting materials serve a variety of purposes in your speech—building audience interest, helping the audience understand,

and proving facts to the audience. In the Internet era, it is not difficult to find mass quantities of information on your topic in a short amount of time. It is not as easy to select the best supporting materials out of all the information you have found. How can you be sure to select the most effective supporting materials? The following guidelines can help.

Choose the Most Credible Proof

Give priority to supporting materials that are backed by credible evidence. Whether you are relying on examples, testimony, statistics, or other types of support, these materials will be most effective when they are proven. For example, in a speech on the hazards of texting while driving, the statement that the average "eyes off the road time" for sending a text message is equivalent to "traveling the length of a football field at 55 mph without looking at the roadway" is a compelling analogy. But it will be a much more believable one if you identify the author of the study: the Virginia Tech Transportation Institute.[16] If you merely asserted this fact without proof, or attributed it to a Web site of uncertain authorship, the analogy would be much less convincing.

Use a Variety of Supporting Materials

In the previous section, you learned about a number of different types of supporting materials. To get the best results, you should use a

REPETITIVE TYPE OF SUPPORT

DIVERSE TYPES OF SUPPORT

variety of these types to support your main points. If you use the same type of supporting material over and over, your effectiveness will be reduced as fatigue sets in with your audience.

For instance, one funny personal example might pull listeners into your speech, a well-chosen analogy can help your audience understand a key point, and a startling statistic can convince audience members that a problem you're describing is serious. By contrast, a speech that mainly uses one type of support—be it personal examples, analogies, or statistics—will quickly lose listeners' interest.

Appeal to Different Learning Styles

Select supporting materials that appeal to different audience members' learning styles. *Active learners* learn best by "doing something active" with the material being presented, while *reflective learners* "prefer to think about it."[17] *Visual learners*, by contrast, tend to "remember best what they see," while *verbal learners* tend to "get more out of words—written and spoken explanations."[18]

LEARNING STYLES

To appeal to this range of learning styles, use a combination of supporting materials throughout your speech. For instance, to clarify a point for verbal learners, you could use a spoken definition along with a vivid analogy; to appeal to visual learners, you can also incorporate visual aids (see Chapter 14). One study found that students retained 26 percent of what they heard and 30 percent of what they saw, but those totals increased to 50 percent for information that they heard *and* saw.[19] And asking thought-provoking questions or providing opportunities to think about a concept can help reflective learners.

To appeal to diverse learning styles in a speech on abstract art, for example, you might begin by defining abstract art and comparing it to other art forms, such as nineteenth-century African masks and traditional Japanese prints. You might then present a few pictures of abstract art pieces (perhaps alongside some non-abstract pieces) and then ask the question, "Which pieces are examples of abstract art?" (See Chapter 10 for a discussion of rhetorical questions.)

To appeal to active learners, you can give audience members a chance to do something with your supporting materials. For instance, after using a narrative to help her listeners understand how bees fly, one student invited audience members to manipulate their arms to simulate the motion of bees' wings.

Avoid Long Lists

People usually find it difficult to understand and remember long strings of facts, examples, or statistics, especially when they are not presented with any elaboration. Consider this excerpt from a speech entitled "My Hometown":

> There are great restaurants in my town. You can get Chinese food, Italian food, Mexican food, and Ethiopian food. There are lots of places to go. You can go to the

lake, the amusement park, the movies, or the ballgame. If you like to exercise, try our running trails, swimming pools, and bicycling paths.

If this speaker followed this pattern for five minutes or more, his presentation would quickly become tedious and forgettable.

To avoid this scenario, select a smaller number of supporting materials (most should take between fifteen and thirty seconds to present), and focus on the materials that *best* develop your main points. The "My Hometown" speech could have been more effective if the speaker had concentrated on the most noteworthy aspects of the town and expanded on them. By focusing on a notable hometown restaurant, for instance, the speaker could use examples, and even testimony and analogies, to get audience members to almost see themselves dining in that restaurant and feel as if they could actually taste the food.

Consider Your Audience

Your audience members' knowledge and interests can be exceptionally useful in helping you choose the best possible supporting materials. For example, suppose you want to persuade your listeners to volunteer for community service. If your audience consists of many future teachers, you might offer examples and narratives about service opportunities with young children. Or if many of your listeners enjoy outdoor activities, your supporting materials could relate more to environmental service.

Respect the Available Time

Select supporting materials that you can comfortably fit into the time you have available for your speech. In a five- to ten-minute speech, for instance, you wouldn't have time to use supporting materials that each take one minute or more to present—no matter how interesting and relevant they might be. To illustrate, suppose you were preparing a seven-minute speech about ecotourism in Central America. You may feel strongly tempted to relate a four-minute narrative about the life lessons you learned while traveling throughout Central America, but this narrative would eat up over half of the time allotted for your speech. You would need to either streamline the narrative or replace it with a shorter but equally effective one.

CHAPTER REVIEW

"The sum of the parts determines the success of the whole speech."

As the story about Graciela's speech on Title IX illustrated at the beginning of this chapter, the right supporting materials can help you build credibility with your audience and enhance your listeners' understanding of and interest in your topic. To choose the best supporting materials, you can start by understanding the many forms they take—such as examples, definitions, testimony, statistics, narratives, and analogies. You can then apply important guidelines, such as using a variety of types of supporting materials, avoiding long lists of information, considering your audience's interests, and ensuring that your supporting materials don't consume too much of the time available for your presentation. When you use supporting materials, it is important to use a variety of different types of materials so that you can appeal to different learning styles: active, reflective, visual, and verbal.

Key Terms

supporting materials *238*
example *243*
brief example *243*
extended example *243*
dictionary definition *244*
expert definition *245*
etymological definition *246*
functional definition *246*

testimony *247*
expert testimony *247*
lay testimony *247*
statistics *248*
narrative *250*
analogy *253*
literal analogy *253*
figurative analogy *253*

Review Questions

1. Name four purposes of using supporting materials.
2. Name six types of supporting materials. Provide an example of each type of supporting material that you could use in a speech on the topic of your choice.

3. Why is it important to select supporting materials that are backed by credible evidence?

4. Name four or more guidelines for using supporting materials in a speech.

Critical Thinking Questions

1. What are a speaker's ethical obligations when presenting statistical information? How could failing to provide solid context for statistics mislead audiences?

2. Narratives and anecdotes are often used to evoke an emotional response. What other types of supporting materials might tap audience members' emotions? Could expert testimony support an emotional appeal? Could statistics generate an emotional response?

3. Think of a time that one of your instructors explained a subject effectively. What supporting materials did he or she use to help the class understand the topic? What supporting materials did he or she use to build interest in the subject?

4. Consider the nature of television advertisements during political campaigns. Some offer personal narratives—stories about a candidate's life. Do you think these ads present enough evidence to allow you to cast an informed vote? What other kinds of evidence would you require before making a voting decision?

Activities

1. Review a newsmagazine article or another source that presents statistics to support points it makes. How well do the statistics support the author's thesis? Does the author provide appropriate context for the statistics?

2. Review the evidence sources cited in the text of Chapter 8, and then look at the endnotes for this chapter in the back of the

book. What types of sources did the authors use to back up the points they raise? What kinds of supporting materials are included in this chapter that do not require citations to research? Would the chapter work as well if only one or the other type of supporting material was presented?

3. What does it mean to say that the lure-mechanism-as-Tootsie-Pop analogy on pages 253–254 is figurative? Select a topic that is familiar to you but that may not be as familiar to others in your class. Develop a figurative analogy that could help your classmates better understand an aspect of your topic.

Go to **bedfordstmartins.com/speakup**, where you'll find helpful study materials, videos, and speech-building tools.

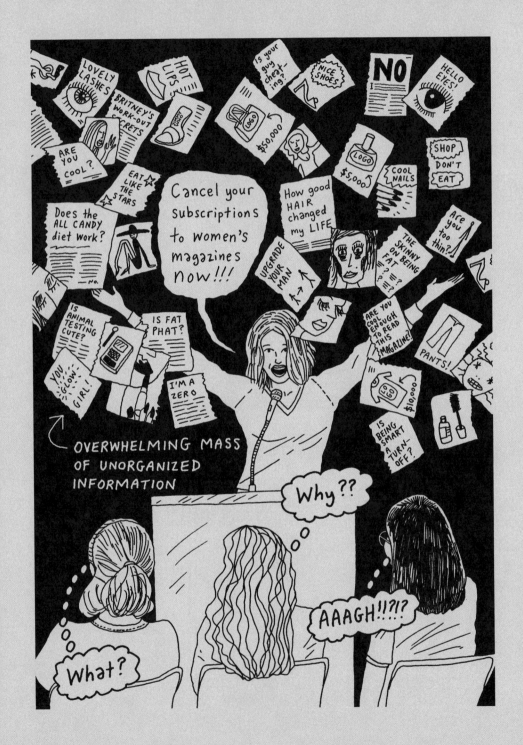

ORGANIZING YOUR SPEECH

9

> "Good organization makes the message clear."

Carly stood at the lectern and announced to her audience that her speech would be about magazines targeted at women and teenage girls. She showed her listeners several magazine advertisements featuring gaunt models and explained how listeners could help friends struggling with anorexia or bulimia. One of the ads was for cosmetics, and Carly presented evidence supporting the claim that the testing of cosmetics harms animals. Carly also presented several magazine articles with titles she considered inane—such as "What His Kitchen Tells You about Him" and "Are You a Bella or a Hermione?" She then contrasted these articles with pieces from more serious magazines.

Carly concluded her speech with a plea for audience members to cancel their subscriptions to women's magazines. Then she sat down, feeling confident that she had scored a success with her audience.

During the evaluation of her speech, however, many of her classmates said that they had trouble following her presentation. Some admitted that they found her ideas downright confusing. Surprised and upset by their feedback, Carly didn't realize that she had made an all-too-common mistake: failing to organize her speech clearly.

Carly's story reveals the importance of organization in developing a successful speech. When you organize your ideas clearly, you help your audience see how the different ideas in your presentation fit together, which allows them to better comprehend your message.[1] They know what to listen for because your organization provides cues to indicate the main ideas. And they don't have to devote their mental energy to figuring out your main points and how all the details in your speech relate to those points.

Good organization is particularly important in oral communication because listeners don't have the luxury of reviewing printed information to understand your message. By contrast, someone who's reading a printed message—whether in a book, a magazine, or online—can go back and reread the text if they're confused. Thus, when giving a speech, you must take special care to help the audience follow your ideas.

When you organize your speech clearly, you also enhance your credibility. Effective organization shows that you have taken the time to prepare your talk.[2]

Organizing a speech is not merely a matter of applying an arbitrary set of rules. Rather, a well-organized presentation imposes order on the set of points that you present in your speech by showing the relationships *between* ideas. Thus, the organizational pattern you

select can communicate important information to the audience: What are the most important ideas? Why do you believe that each idea has merit? What evidence are you providing to back up your claims?

In this chapter, we focus on organizing the **body** of your speech—the part where you present your main points and support them with examples, narratives, testimony, and other materials. To organize a speech effectively, you must learn to group your ideas into a sequence that your audience can easily follow. In the following pages, we explore ways to select your main points and structure your supporting materials. We also examine common patterns for arranging main points, and present some organizing language that you can use to make your speech structure clear to your audience.

SELECTING YOUR MAIN POINTS

The body of your speech should be structured around your **main points**—those few ideas that are most important for your listeners to remember. The body also contains **supporting points**—materials designed to prove or substantiate your main points. A speech body organized around main points and corresponding supporting points helps listeners make sense out of the details of your presentation. By contrast, if you present randomly ordered ideas about your topic (as Carly did), your audience will have trouble determining what is most important and understanding the information you're presenting. Even a five-minute speech requires careful organization, since it can contain fifty or more sentences.

How should you select your main points? The following guidelines can help.

Consider Your Purpose

Make sure that every main point you select relates to the specific purpose of your speech. Consider the following two sets of main points for a speech advocating collective licensing of music file sharing as a solution to illegal music downloading. (With collective licensing, Internet service providers would pay a fee to the music industry; in return, users could legally download music files.)

FIRST SET OF MAIN POINTS
I. The history of peer-to-peer file sharing
II. Background on copyright law
III. Collective licensing of file sharing is the best solution for artists and consumers.

SECOND SET OF MAIN POINTS
I. Current copyright enforcement against music file sharing singles out individuals and is thus inequitable to consumers.
II. Current copyright enforcement fails to stop most illegal file sharing and is thus unfair to performing artists.
III. Collective licensing of music file sharing serves both artists and consumers.

In the first set, main points I and II are not arguments for replacing the current system of copyright enforcement with collective licensing. Thus, they do not relate to the speaker's specific purpose, which isn't addressed until main point III. In the second set, however, each main point relates to the specific purpose: the first two points show flaws in the current system of copyright enforcement, and the third shows how collective licensing would be a better alternative.

Take Your Audience into Account

Out of the many relevant main points that you might use to develop your topic, which ones will prove *most* interesting to your audience? Which ones will provide your listeners with the most useful information to *them*?

AUDIENCE ANALYSIS

Consider the following two sets of main points for a speech on backpacking tips.

FIRST SET OF MAIN POINTS
I. Choosing the right backpack
II. Remembering the essential equipment
III. Packing your backpack strategically

SECOND SET OF MAIN POINTS
I. Coping with extreme elevation changes
II. Selecting light, nutritious food for weeklong trips
III. Choosing optimal equipment for subzero temperatures

Both sets of main points contain information that fits the topic of "backpacking tips." Thus, they fit the first guideline for main points: they relate to the specific purpose of the speech. However, the question of which set is better depends on the audience. The first set contains basic information that would be appropriate for novice backpackers. The second set contains information that would be more useful for experienced backpackers who are contemplating challenging trips.

Select an Appropriate Number of Main Points

In most situations, effective speeches present two to five main points. In our experience, student speeches typically contain three main points. However, there is no rule that you must have three. You may also have two, four, or five main points if that number gives you the most logical organization of ideas.

Still, most audiences have trouble remembering more than three points. Also, it is unlikely that you will have enough time to develop that many points. Here are a few suggestions for whittling down your main points to a manageable number.

- See whether any of your main points are related. Can two or more main points be combined into a single broader category?
- Review your audience analysis. Are there any points that can be excluded because they will be less likely to resonate with your audience?
- Evaluate which points are the most important to developing your topic or thesis. Exclude the point(s) that are less essential.

If you find that you have only one main point, consider making that point the topic or thesis of your speech. Then organize the information you plan to use to support that point into two to five key ideas, which will become your main points.

CHOOSING THE APPROPRIATE NUMBER OF MAIN POINTS

ORGANIZING YOUR SUPPORTING MATERIALS

Once you select your main points, you need to develop (explain and prove) each one with supporting materials. Supporting materials enable your audience to understand your main points and help prove why you think those main points are valid. In Chapter 8, we discussed a number of different types of supporting materials that you can use, such as examples, definitions, and statistics. Now we consider how you can organize these supporting materials to help audience members follow your speech.

Subordination and Coordination

The principle of subordination is the key to a well-organized speech. Using **subordination** means creating a hierarchy of points and their supporting materials in your speech. Thus, main points are the most important (or highest) level of subordination, and supporting materials used to develop a main point (called **subpoints**) are subordinate to that main point. (There should be at least two subpoints to support each main point.) In the same way, materials that support subpoints are called **sub-subpoints**, and these sub-subpoints are subordinate to the corresponding subpoint. A well-organized speech also features

coordination. Each main point is coordinate with other main points—
that is, they are at the same level of significance—just as subpoints
are coordinate with other subpoints, and so on.

Sound confusing? It isn't, really. To see how subordination and
coordination work, compare the subpoints (indicated by capital letters)
supporting each main point (signaled by roman numerals) in this
outline for an informative speech on filmmaking in India:

I. Culture plays an important role in Indian filmmaking.
   A. Indian moviemakers developed a style of their own by
      the 1950s, based on the teachings of *Natya Shastra*
      (*Science of Theater*), a 1,000-year-old Hindu book. Enter-
      tainment was to embody nine essences: love, hate, sorrow,
      disgust, joy, compassion, pity, pride, and courage.[3]

B. In Indian culture, women are expected to be closely tied to their families. Thus, female stars are often chaperoned by their mothers, who sit at the edge of the set.[4]

II. There are differences between Indian-made films and films made in the United States.

A. In India, films need not follow the linear, scripted story line that is popular in Western movies. Of any one hundred films made in India, about three will have scripts prepared in advance, according to screenwriter Anjum Rajabali.[5]

B. Many Indian films do not address serious social issues. Director Shyam Bengal notes that mass cinema "is nothing more than a series of continuing sensations. New pictures are made to imitate whatever was most successful previously in order to mop up the largest audience."[6]

Notice that both subpoints for main point I pertain to the subject of the main point: the role of culture in Indian filmmaking. These subpoints are *subordinate* to main point I. Next, consider main point II. Subpoint IIA supports that main point; however, subpoint IIB does not because it fails to explain why U.S.-made and Indian-made films are different. You can probably think of many American-made films that also have little serious content. Because subpoint IIB is not relevant to the idea that U.S.- and Indian-made films are different, it is not subordinate. Therefore, the speaker should not include it under main point II.

SUBORDINATION!

MAIN POINT

SUBPOINTS

SUB-SUBPOINTS

A, B, AND C ARE SUBPOINTS

I. Leonardo da Vinci's art had many impacts.

   A. Leonardo's artistic technique was unprecedented.

   B. Leonardo's technique influenced future artists.

   C. Leonardo's art has generated many controversies.

1, 2, AND 3 ARE SUB-SUBPOINTS

C. Leonardo's art has generated many controversies.

   1. Who was the model for the *Mona Lisa*?

   2. Who is to the right of Jesus in *The Last Supper*?

   3. Is the *Vitruvian Man* a geometrical algorithm?

When a Subpoint Doesn't Fit

In developing a speech, you may discover that some of the supporting materials you researched do not relate to any of the main points you selected. Nevertheless, you believe that these materials would improve your speech. What should you do?

One option is to reword the main point to encompass the additional information. In the first example that follows, the main point is that healthy eating is important for college students. Note in this example how subpoint B focuses on getting exercise, not on healthy eating. Thus, it does not relate to the main point. In the second example, the speaker has rewritten the main point to make both subpoints subordinate.

FIRST EXAMPLE

I. Healthy eating is essential for college students.
   A. Limiting fried foods, whole milk, and sweetened drinks help you avoid the "freshman fifteen."
   B. Participating in intramural sports and walking to campus help you stay fit.

SECOND EXAMPLE

I. *A healthy lifestyle* is essential for college students.
   A. Limiting fried foods, whole milk, and sweetened drinks help you avoid the "freshman fifteen."
   B. Participating in intramural sports and walking to campus help you stay fit.

A second option is to create an additional main point to include the supporting material in question. If you use this option, be sure that you have enough supporting materials to develop the new main point. Also, ensure that the new main point relates to your topic or thesis statement.

ARRANGING YOUR MAIN POINTS

How do you decide the structure in which you'll present your main points during your speech? Familiarize yourself with common patterns of organization and then select the pattern that best suits your speech. In this section, we take a closer look at these patterns.

Spatial Pattern

In a **spatial pattern**, the main points represent important aspects of your topic that can be thought of as adjacent to one another in location or geography. This approach is effective with speech topics that can be broken down into specific parts that relate to each other spatially. You take the audience from one part to the next—much as a museum guide ushers a group from exhibit to exhibit, or as an anatomy professor chooses to lecture about the parts of the human skeleton from head to toe. For example, you could use a spatial pattern to discuss prehistoric cultures that existed around the world:

I. Early *Europeans* adapted to the Ice Age and competed with fellow carnivores for prey.

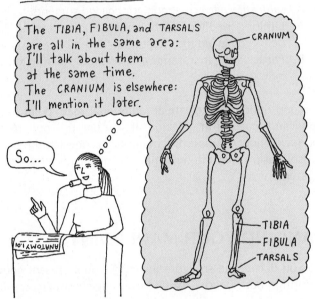

II. Prehistoric *Thais* lived in dense forests.

III. *Australian Aborigines* were the world's first known food processors.

Temporal Pattern

In a **temporal (chronological) pattern**, you present the information in time-based sequence, from beginning to end. Each main point covers a particular point in the chronology. If you are discussing a subject that follows a sequence, such as a historical event or a process, this pattern can help your audience keep track of what you're saying. For instance, a speech discussing the decline and rebound of bald eagles in the lower forty-eight states could use a temporal pattern:

I. In 1963, the bald eagle had nearly disappeared from the lower forty-eight states.

II. In 1972, the pesticide DDT was banned in the United States.

III. During the next twenty years, governments and individual
citizens took steps to protect bald eagles.
IV. By 1995, the bald eagle had made a remarkable comeback.

Causal Pattern

If your speech is explaining a cause-and-effect relationship, a **causal pattern** will help your audience understand the link between particular events and their outcomes. There are two ways to organize main points when you use this pattern. First, if several major causes exist for the situation or phenomenon you are discussing, each main point can cover one of the causes. Second, if there is a chain of events between cause and effect, each main point can become one link in the chain from cause to effect. So to explain why e-commerce has grown in significance, you might use the following chain of causation:

I. Internet use grew rapidly in the 1990s.
II. Businesses took advantage of this new channel of communication by marketing products online.
III. Consumers have increasingly chosen to shop online because of the convenience.

Comparison Pattern

A **comparison pattern** organizes the speech around major similarities and differences between two events, objects, or situations. Each main point discusses an important similarity or difference. This pattern can help your audience learn about a new subject by comparing it to a subject with which they are familiar. To illustrate, you might compare newly discovered planets outside our solar system with the planets in our own system:

I. The orbits of planets outside our solar system often differ from our planets' paths.
II. The size and composition of planets outside our solar system are most likely to resemble Jupiter's.
III. Many planets outside our solar system have moons, as our planets do.
IV. Some planets outside our solar system are in a "habitable zone," as Earth is.

THIS IS A COMPARISON PATTERN

DORM LIFE

Ladida...

I. College food services will cook for you.

II. You are not responsible for paying bills.

III. You need to get along with your roommates.

APARTMENT LIFE

INSTANT MAC + CHEESE

ELECTRIC CO. FINAL DEMAND!

TERMINATION NOTICE

HIP HOP HITS

COUNTRY CLASSICS

I. Your own cooking will replace college food services.

II. You and your roommates will become responsible for sharing the bills.

III. You will still need to get along with your roommates.

Problem-Cause-Solution Pattern

Consider using a **problem-cause-solution pattern** if you want to ask your audience to take specific action or support a particular policy on an issue. With this pattern, your first main point argues that one or more problems exist. Your second main point covers the cause(s) of the problem. And your third main point develops your proposed solution, which mitigates or eliminates the cause(s). A problem-cause-solution format could help you organize a speech encouraging expanded use of solar energy, as shown in the following example outline:

  I. Fossil fuel energy sources hurt our environment and our pocketbooks.
  II. Current energy policies encourage fossil fuel use.

THIS IS A PROBLEM—CAUSE—SOLUTION PATTERN

THESIS

Buy a hybrid car.

AIR POLLUTION IS A SERIOUS PROBLEM.

COUGH! COUGH!

FUEL-INEFFICIENT VEHICLES ARE A MAJOR CAUSE OF POLLUTION.

Move!

Eek!

A SWITCH TO HYBRID CARS WOULD DECREASE POLLUTION.

GOOD MORNING.

III. Expanded tax credits for solar technology would promote clean, inexpensive energy.

Criteria-Application Pattern

A **criteria-application pattern** proposes standards for making a judgment about a topic and then applies those standards to a related topic. This pattern accommodates two main points. The first main point establishes the *criteria* (or standards) that you believe listeners should use to make a judgment about a topic. The second main point is the application of those criteria to your speech topic.

One type of speech in which this pattern works well is the "hero" speech (explaining why a person is a hero in his or her community or culture). To use this pattern, you could first advocate criteria for heroism. Then you might show why a specific person is a hero based on those criteria. Here is how one student used this approach in a speech about her cousin, Kyle:

I. If a person overcomes serious hardship while maintaining an optimistic attitude, he or she is a hero.

II. My six-year-old cousin Kyle is a hero because he has maintained a positive outlook on life despite his parents' marital troubles and his father's cancer.

Narrative Pattern

With a **narrative pattern**, you organize your speech as a story, using characters and a plot to convey your message. You still have a thesis, but you support the thesis with a story rather than a set of explicit main points. The story should have a plot and build to a climax that communicates the main idea of your speech to listeners. Audi-

CRITERIA–APPLICATION PATTERN

THE CRITERIA:

A dog has four legs, fur, a tail, and barks.

THE SUBJECT WITH CRITERIA APPLIED:

TAIL
FUR
WOOF!
BARKS
FOUR LEGS

CONCLUSION:

This is a dog.

ence members should be able to determine your thesis intuitively from the story and see how the story demonstrates the validity of the thesis.

For example, suppose you want to persuade your audience that smoking should be prohibited. Your narrative could tell the story of a friend, a relative, or a person who you learned about through your research who smoked and died of cancer. You would need to be confident that your audience members were familiar with the scientific evidence linking tobacco to health risks. You'd also have to count on them to understand from the details of your story that you were advocating a ban on cigarettes.

Here is an example of how you could organize a narrative speech on this topic, and how it would compare to a speech using the problem-cause-solution pattern:

Narrative	Problem-Cause-Solution
Introduction	*Introduction*
Aunt Amanda was my favorite aunt. She always had time to talk to me, and although she was fifty-six when I was seventeen, she understood what it was like to be a teenager. She never attended college, but she kept telling me that I would be the first person in our family to get a degree.	I. Provide attention-getter (endearing story about Aunt Amanda). II. State thesis: cigarettes should be prohibited. III. Establish credibility. IV. Connect with the audience. V. Give preview.
Body	*Body*
I. I called Aunt Amanda when I got an A on my first college essay. She tearfully told me that she had been diagnosed with lung cancer and did not have long to live.	I. Cigarette smoking is hazardous to your health. **(Problem)**
II. Aunt Amanda had been a heavy smoker since she was my age. The models in magazine and television ads seemed so glamorous when they smoked. So, my aunt started smoking, and although she tried to quit several times, she never could.	II. Tobacco company advertising hooks new smokers. **(Cause)**
III. Aunt Amanda got so mad at me when I got caught smoking at school. She said that if it were up to her, smoking would be outlawed like any other dangerous drug. She told me that it was not as glamorous as those ads make it seem, and that once you get started, it is almost impossible to stop.	III. The federal government should prohibit the sale of cigarettes. **(Solution)**

(continued on next page)

(continued)

Narrative	Problem-Cause-Solution
Conclusion	*Conclusion*
I. Now my Aunt Amanda will never see me graduate from college. I miss her so much. But I will always be thankful that she encouraged me to go to college.	I. Provide summary.
II. And I am even more thankful for her lifesaving message: "Smoking kills like any other dangerous drug, and there ought to be a law against this hazardous product."	II. End with clincher: smoking killed my Aunt Amanda, but if we outlaw cigarettes, other families will be spared the loss I have felt.

Categorical Pattern

Another option for organization is a **categorical (topical) pattern**. This pattern is effective when you have a diverse set of main points to support the thesis of your speech. Each main point emphasizes an important aspect of your topic that you want the audience to understand. For example, Jodie was presenting an after-dinner speech poking fun at the practice of holiday gift giving. She used a categorical pattern as follows:

I. Gift wrap and gift bags generate four million tons of waste.
II. Holiday shopping is a major source of anxiety.
III. Half of all Americans admit to regifting the gifts they receive.
IV. Charitable donations are a worthwhile alternative to gift buying.

USING ORGANIZING WORDS AND SENTENCES

As the person who has developed your speech, you will know what your main points are, when you are moving from one point to the next, and what part of the speech you are delivering at any point in time. However, without assistance from you, your audience members will have difficulty keeping track of your organization. To see how difficult this task is, watch a speech with two or three classmates and have each person try to outline the speaker's main points. Unless the speech is very well organized, chances are good that you will each have different perceptions of what the main points were.

To make the structure of your speech easy for audience members to follow, you need to insert organizing words, phrases, and sentences throughout your presentation. These words, phrases, and sentences offer the audience clear signals that will help them to identify your main points and navigate your supporting information. The primary types of organizing language include transitions, signposts, and internal previews and summaries.

Transitions

A **transition** is a sentence that indicates you are moving from one part of your speech to the next. A transition usually includes an indication that you have completed one idea and are about to present a new one. Here are some examples of transitions:

- So that is what archaeologists say about the significance of the year 2012 to the classic Maya; now I will present the viewpoint of contemporary Mayan elders.
- Now that you have learned about wildlife sanctuaries in Belize, let me describe Mayan archaeological sites you can visit.

Be sure that your transition introduces a new point *while also* signaling the end of the previous point. Students often have trouble creating transitions that achieve both tasks, as shown by these two failed attempts:

- What do contemporary Mayan elders say about the year 2012?
- Let me describe some Mayan archaeological sites you can visit.

THERE ARE TWO PARTS TO A TRANSITION

JUST LAUNCHING INTO A NEW IDEA WITHOUT GETTING CLOSURE ON THE OLD ONE CAN BE CONFUSING AND ISN'T REALLY A TRANSITION.

Ugh, why's it not moving?

OLD IDEA

NEW IDEA → Let me describe how to safely tow a trailer.

PART ONE: REFERENCE THE PREVIOUS IDEA.

PART TWO: INTRODUCE THE NEW IDEA.

Now that you have learned how to install a hitch to a vehicle,

let me describe how to safely tow a trailer.

Neither of these sentences would make a good transition. The first one only asks a question pertaining to the main point to follow (contemporary Mayan elders' thoughts about the year 2012). It does not help the audience see that the speaker has finished with the main point about archaeologists' take on the significance of 2012 to the classic Maya and is moving on to discuss contemporary Mayan elders' thoughts about it. The second sentence only notes the subject of the next main point (archaeological sites), without signaling that the speaker has wrapped up the previous point (wildlife sanctuaries).

Signposts

Signposts are words or phrases within sentences that help your audience understand your speech's structure. Signposts in a speech serve the same function as their counterparts on a road. Highway signs tell drivers what direction they're traveling in and how the roads are organized. In a similar vein, speech signposts inform audiences about the direction and organization of a presentation.

You can use signposts to show that you are at a specific place in your speech (for example, "to preview my main ideas," or "my third point is," or "in summary"). You can also use signposts to indicate that you are about to cite research ("according to") or to indicate that a key point is coming ("if you remember one idea from this speech, I hope it will be that . . ."). You can also use signposts to help your audience understand the structure of your subpoints. For example, in a persuasive speech advocating educational reform, you might have a main point on the causes of poor student performance. You could then write your subpoints with signposts, as follows:

- *One cause* of educational failure is inadequate funding of public schools.
- *Another cause* is educators' low expectations for students.
- *An additional cause* of our schools' failure is that athletics receive higher priority than academics.

SIGNPOSTS

On the road...

In a speech...

Internal Previews and Internal Summaries

In crafting your speech, you may have selected a main point that needs several different points of support or requires considerable detail to develop. To help the audience follow your explanation of such a complex main point, you may want to use an **internal preview**—a short list of the ideas that will follow. Or to help the audience remember what you have just said about the main point, you might use an **internal summary**—a quick review of what you just said about that main point.

For example, in an informative speech on test strategies, suppose that one main point covers test preparation. You might state your main point, followed by an *internal preview*, as shown here:

> Test taking requires good planning and healthy living. *The four steps for test preparation that I will cover are: plan your study time in advance, follow your study schedule, get a good night's sleep, and eat a healthy breakfast.*

In a persuasive speech on campaign finance reform, you might follow a main point on possible solutions with an *internal summary*, as follows:

> *To review my proposed solutions: First, the government should require that all federal elections be publicly funded. Second, an independent commission should be established to enforce campaign financing laws. Finally, you too can be part of the solution by refusing to vote for candidates who accept large contributions.*

CHAPTER REVIEW

"Good organization makes the message clear."

In this chapter, we focused on the importance of a well-organized speech and presented strategies for organizing the body of your speech. Good organization helps your audience understand your message and enhances your credibility as a speaker. Remember the following principles when you organize the body of your speech: Select an appropriate number of main points. Arrange your main points in a pattern that will best convey your ideas to the audience. Organize supporting materials to back up each main point. And use organizing words and sentences to help the audience keep track of where you are in a speech.

Key Terms

body *268*
main point *268*
supporting point *268*
subordination *272*
subpoint *272*
sub-subpoint *272*
coordination *273*
spatial pattern *277*
temporal pattern *278*
causal pattern *279*

comparison pattern *280*
problem-cause-solution
   pattern *282*
criteria-application pattern *283*
narrative pattern *284*
categorical pattern *286*
transition *288*
signpost *290*
internal preview *292*
internal summary *292*

Review Questions

1. What three main factors should a speaker consider when selecting his or her main points?

2. Explain the importance of subordination and coordination when organizing supporting materials.

3. Name and describe eight organizational patterns that you can use to arrange the main points of your speech.

4. Describe transitions, signposts, and internal previews and summaries, and explain how these types of organizing language help speakers indicate the structure of their speech to the audience.

Critical Thinking Questions

1. In what ways does organizing a speech resemble organizing a piece of written work? How does it differ? Are there any organizational tools that a writer can use that a speaker cannot? Does a speaker have any options that a writer does not?

2. What kind of organizational patterns do you think are most common in public speaking? Is there one kind of pattern that you think can work for almost any speech?

3. Visit a Web site such as American Rhetoric (americanrhetoric.com) or Gifts of Speech (gos.sbc.edu) and select a speech. How could you revise the main points or add organizing language to make the speech's structure more apparent to the audience?

4. In the illustration on page 287, the speaker dons a large hat whenever he makes a main point. While this is clearly an exaggeration, might a speaker use nonverbal cues or presentation aids to help the audience navigate his or her speech? Would such tools work if the speech itself did not make proper use of organizing language?

Activities

1. Think about Carly's speech about women's magazines, described at the beginning of the chapter. If you were to reorganize her speech, how would you do it?

2. Consider the newscaster illustration on page 292. With that image in mind, watch a broadcast of a nightly newscast and jot down the different types of transitions, internal previews, and internal summaries that are used by the news anchor. What purpose do they serve? Would you use the same tools in a speech? Why or why not?

3. Working individually or in groups, select four organizational patterns. Then choose a topic area and write three to five main points on the topic that fit each pattern.

4. Read the narrative and problem-cause-solution speech outlines presented on pages 285–86. Can you envision using one of the other organizational patterns described in the chapter to organize a speech on this topic? Write an outline showing how you would do it.

Go to **bedfordstmartins.com/speakup**, where you'll find helpful study materials, videos, and speech-building tools.

INTRODUCTIONS AND CONCLUSIONS

10

"Strong introductions create audience interest; strong conclusions create lasting impressions."

You've finally had time to break away from your schoolwork and go see the latest James Bond movie. You're sitting in the theater, munching popcorn as the curtains open, the lights dim, and the film's opening sequence starts to roll. Every element of that sequence—the music, the visuals, the credits for the movie's title and cast—conveys information about the picture and heightens your desire to see more.

For the next two hours, you're transported into an exciting world. And at the end of the movie, you're left with the lasting sense that you've had a great time. The final close-ups of Bond's face, the swelling of the classic James Bond theme, and the sweeping views of gorgeous scenery as the camera pans back—all of these elements combine to conclude your experience on a satisfying note.

Just as a movie's opening and closing elements powerfully influence the quality of your theater experience, your speech's introduction and conclusion play crucial roles in your audience's reception of your message. An effective introduction builds audience interest, orients audience members to the speech, and establishes your credibility as a speaker, while a strong conclusion leaves them with an enduring impression of your speech.

Your next step after planning the body of your speech is to prepare the introduction and conclusion. Although these elements are shorter than the body, they're just as crucial. After all, you won't get your message across unless your audience is eager to listen. And you want your audience to remember your presentation long after it ends—so they can put into action the information you've imparted to them. In this chapter, we show you how to craft memorable beginnings and endings to your presentations.

INTRODUCING YOUR SPEECH

Buckle up. I'm about to take you for a ride on a verbal roller coaster...

In public speaking, as in many other situations in life, first impressions are vital. Your introduction creates a first impression of you as a speaker *and* of your message. Scholars have recognized the importance of the introduction for as long as people have discussed speechmaking: Cicero included the introduction as one of six essential parts of a speech,[1] and contemporary scholars note that the introduction is a key opportunity for the speaker to build a bond with the audience.[2]

A good introduction thus accomplishes a number of important purposes. Specifically, it

- gains your audience's attention
- signals the topic and purpose of your speech
- conveys the importance of the topic for your audience
- establishes your credibility
- previews the main points of your speech

Your introduction must accomplish all this in a brief period of time. For example, in a five- to ten-minute speech, the introduction should take up no more than one minute. With these kinds of time constraints, there's no doubt about it: your introduction needs to be efficient *and* effective. Let's look more closely at each of the objectives your introduction must achieve.

Gain Your Audience's Attention

Begin your speech with an **attention-getter**—material intended to capture the audience's interest at the start of a speech. People listening to a presentation may have other things on their minds (for example, a problem at home, a distracting sound coming from the next room, worries about an upcoming test or paper). You need to help your listeners redirect their focus from these other matters to you and your message. Otherwise, they won't absorb or remember the information you convey in your speech.

How do you craft an effective attention-getter? The following guidelines can help.

Tell a Story or Anecdote. Most people love a good story, so opening with one can be a compelling yet comfortable way to begin your speech. If you start your speech with a story, be sure that it relates to your message, takes up an appropriate amount of time, and comes across as believable. Avoid making up a story to open your speech unless you note that you are offering a hypothetical example.

Here is how one student used an anecdote to begin a speech about reforming the No Child Left Behind education law:

> *Time* magazine, May 2, 2005, reported that in the Utah War of 1857–58, President Buchanan sent thousands of federal troops into the territory to install a non-Mormon governor.

The people of Utah did not respond well. They spooked the federal livestock, burned federal wagons, and incinerated over 300,000 tons of military provisions. Nearly 150 years later, the Utah legislature sent another message to Washington by becoming the first state to pass a bill that gives schools options for ignoring the No Child Left Behind Act.

Notice how the anecdote about Utah in the 1850s grabs the audience's attention by relating a dramatic, almost over-the-top, historical incident in vivid language and startling detail. The story also relates to the speech's topic because in both cases, the state of Utah rebels against a federal mandate.

Offer a Striking or Provocative Statement. A compelling fact or idea pertaining to your topic can immediately pull the audience into your speech. For example, you might present a surprising statistic or make an ironic statement to defy your listeners' expectations about what they'll hear during your speech. This approach works only if you present a fact or idea that's new, ironic, or counterintuitive to your audience. You are also likely to be more effective if you incorporate vivid language into your striking or provocative statement.

Consider Vaclav Havel, who addressed the people of the former Czechoslovakia when he became their president on New Year's Day 1990. From 1948 until 1989, Czechoslovakia had been under Communist rule. Havel, a Czech playwright and dissident, had been imprisoned and had his works banned in the 1970s and 1980s. Havel was a leader of the 1989 nonviolent Velvet Revolution, which led to his selection as the first popularly elected president in more than forty years in a nation long under the thumb of corrupt, authoritarian Communist leaders. Note how Havel offered a striking statement that differentiated him from his unelected predecessors, who had controlled the Czech media and propagandized the government's achievements.

> My dear fellow citizens, for forty years on this day you heard from my predecessors the same thing in a number of variations: how our country is flourishing, how many millions of tons of steel we produce, how happy we all are, how we trust our government, and what bright prospects lie ahead of us. I assume you did not propose me for this office so that I, too, should lie to you.[3]

Build Suspense. Consider increasing audience curiosity and anticipation before you reveal your topic. For example, "What will be one of the biggest problems in the next ten years?" or "One of the most exotic vacation spots in the world is unknown to 98 percent of American tourists."

Here's how one student built curiosity in her listeners' minds during the introduction of a speech on rising gas prices:

> Would you like to spend less money on gasoline? I have a solution that does not require drilling in Alaska or importing more oil from the Middle East. You will not need to spend $20,000 on a new hybrid car. My solution does not require an act of Congress; you can apply it yourself on your way home from school.

After this suspenseful introductory statement, the student went on to give ten driving tips that she claimed could improve fuel economy by 20 percent or more.

Let Listeners Know You're One of Them. Consider highlighting similarities or shared interests between you and the audience. When listeners believe that a speaker is like them, they tend to see him or her as more credible—something that encourages them to pay close attention to the speech. However, to make this type of attention-getter effective, be sure to assert *genuine* common ground. Otherwise, you won't win your audience's confidence.

Here's how one student highlighted common ground in a speech about the importance of understanding the federal government's new food pyramid:

> When I surveyed our class, I discovered that over 70 percent of you agreed with the statement "I try to eat a healthy diet." Like many of you, I have been on a diet more than once, and I do my best to eat my fruits and vegetables. To help us make good dietary decisions, the federal government has created a new food pyramid that contains some useful information but that is also more complicated. The old, familiar pyramid with six basic food groups has been replaced by twelve pyramids containing multicolor regions,

supplemented by online calculators. If we can learn
to decode it, the new pyramid can help all of us eat
more healthily.

Former secretary of state Condoleezza Rice used a similar strategy in a
speech at Sciences Politiques, one of the top universities in France:

> The founders of both the French and American Republics
> were inspired by the very same values and by each other.
> They shared the universal values of freedom and democracy
> and human dignity that have inspired men and women
> across the globe for centuries.[4]

Use Humor. Most people enjoy jokes, amusing stories, or other
humorous references. A funny or playful attention-getter can be a great
way to gain audience interest, break the ice, and enhance your credibility. However, not all humor is created equal. If you begin a speech with
humor, the material should relate to your topic. Also, consider your
audience members and choose material they will find amusing. Don't
tell jokes or stories that may offend some or all of your listeners.

Also note that using humor as your attention-getter can be a high-
risk/high-reward approach. If the audience appreciates a joke, your
credibility is liable to increase, you'll feel especially confident, and
your speech will be off to a great start. For example, Texas governor

Ann Richards used humor effectively in the introduction to her keynote address at the 1988 Democratic National Convention:

> Twelve years ago Barbara Jordan, another Texas woman, made the Keynote Address to this convention and two women in 160 years is about par for the course. But if you give us a chance, we can perform. After all, Ginger Rogers did everything that Fred Astaire did. She just did it backwards and in high heels.[5]

Yet it can be deeply deflating when a joke falls flat. If you have trouble telling jokes or remembering punch lines, you may find that a relevant anecdote from your own life is a better source of humor. At one time or another, most people have told a funny story about something that has happened to them; this more personal approach may help you feel more relaxed and conversational. For example, as a commencement speaker at Harvard University in 2007, Microsoft founder Bill Gates poked fun at his own standing as "Harvard's most successful dropout":

> I guess that makes me valedictorian of my own special class. . . . I did the best of everyone who failed. But I also want to be recognized as the guy who got [Microsoft CEO] Steve Ballmer to drop out of business school. I'm a bad influence. That's why I was invited to speak at your graduation. If I had spoken at your orientation, fewer of you might be here today.[6]

Ask a Rhetorical Question. A **rhetorical question**—one that you want listeners to answer in their heads—can capture your audience members' attention because it gets them thinking about your speech topic. For example, to introduce a speech about the Winter Olympics, you could ask, "What's the first sport that comes to mind when you think about the Winter Olympics?" Make sure your rhetorical questions address something of interest to your audience. And avoid overly general questions ("What would you like to learn about winter sports?"); your listeners won't find them as interesting as more focused queries.

RHETORICAL QUESTIONS CAN RISK DISAPPOINTING ANSWERS

Provide a Quotation. A stimulating quotation that illuminates your topic can make an effective attention-getter—especially if you're quoting someone your audience likes and respects or the quotation is thought-provoking or counterintuitive. For example, in a speech about reforming the U.S. auto industry, you might quote a related joke from Conan O'Brien: "In Detroit, a church put an SUV on stage in order to pray for a miracle for the Big Three automakers. And apparently there was a miracle. Someone bought the SUV. At factory price."[7]

You can also quote an expert in the field as an attention-getter. Consider how this speech on the need for college students to improve their sleep patterns begins:

> According to Dr. LeAnne Forquer and her colleagues in
> the Central Michigan University psychology department,

"Adolescents and young adults, including college students, appear to be one of the most sleep-deprived groups in the United States. Individuals in this group require about 9 hours of sleep each night; however, most receive only 7 to 8 hours. This sleep deprivation can have detrimental effects on performance, including driving and academics."[8]

Signal Your Thesis

Once you've riveted your listeners' attention, your next step is to indicate the thesis of your speech. You can use your topic statement for this purpose. Recall from Chapter 6 that your thesis statement is the single sentence that expresses the aspect of the topic you will be emphasizing in your speech; your thesis conveys the speech's "bottom line." Providing this statement early in the speech answers a question in the minds of many audience members—"What will this speech be about?"—and helps focus listeners' attention on your message rather than forcing them to use their mental energy to figure out what your speech is about.

Your thesis statement should clearly convey your topic and purpose in delivering the presentation, further preparing your audience members to listen. It should also be specific and include a signpost that makes it clear that your attention-getter is finished and you are now revealing your topic.

Consider the following example:

ATTENTION-GETTER

I. The tallest mountain in North America. Grizzly bears eating berries just ten feet from the road. Clean, fresh air that you will not find in "the lower forty-eight."

POSSIBLE THESIS STATEMENTS

II. *Vague thesis statement:* All these features can be found in a pristine wilderness environment.
Or

II. *Specific thesis statement:* You can find all these features in Denali National Park, Alaska, and I hope to convince you to visit Denali.

Notice that the specific thesis statement clarifies that the subject of the speech is Denali and that the presenter's purpose is to persuade his audience to go there.

Show Your Audience "What's in It for Them"

Once you have revealed your thesis, you need to generate audience interest and motivate their active listening. Our former colleague Dr. Gail Sorenson referred to this as WIIFM ("whiff-em"), or "What's in It for Me?" Through WIIFM, you clarify why your message is relevant to and important for your listeners.

To accomplish this goal, provide one sentence or a short paragraph that indicates why the audience should take an interest in your topic. Avoid going on and on. Instead, give listeners just enough to whet their appetite. In the body of your speech, you'll go into more detail about how the ideas or suggestions in your presentation will benefit listeners.

Here are some examples of effective WIIFM statements:

- Drunk driving is not just a problem on somebody else's campus. According to the campus police chief, driving-while-intoxicated arrests at this school have soared by 45 percent over the past decade. And that threatens us all.

- I doubt that many of you have lost sleep over the state budget deficit. It did not make my "Top Ten Worries" list, either. But when I found out that our tuition had increased by 27 percent this year as one means of making up the shortfall, I started to worry. And you should, too.

- Today, we will consider the history of the war between the United States and Mexico in 1846 from a Mexican perspective. This will provide you with an alternative to the romanticized version that many of you were taught in your high school history class.

- My survey showed that 77 percent of this class believes that they are spending too much time on school and work at the expense of their social lives. So, instead of focusing on academics today, let's take a brief look at the art of asking someone out on a date.

WHAT'S IN IT FOR ME?

Establish Your Credibility

Your audience members now know what they'll get out of listening to your speech. Next, you need to answer the question, "Why should we listen to *you*? What makes you a credible source on this topic?"

How do you build credibility? The same way your sources of evidence do—by showing that you have relevant experience and education and that you've thoroughly researched the subject area of your speech. You gain even more credibility when your listeners see you as trustworthy and perceive that you have their best interests at heart.

To establish credibility, explain how you have gained knowledge about your topic. Use only one or two sentences, emphasize your most relevant credentials (resist any urge to go over your entire résumé or life history!), and adopt a modest, not superior tone.

A student speaker named Alexandra established her credibility in an informative speech about judging competitive ice skating by emphasizing her own relevant experience. Alexandra was especially qualified to speak on the subject because she had won nearly one hundred awards during her skating career and had also served as a judge at several prestigious skating events in her home state. She might have discussed her many accomplishments in the sport, but instead she established her credibility in this clear, concise, and modest way:

> I have been active in the sport of ice skating since I was six years old and won my fair share of events. I still love skating, so after retiring from competition, I became certified as a judge and have judged at many competitions during the past two years.

With this information, Alexandra left no doubt in her listeners' minds that she was a good source of information on ice skating. She also held their interest: she summarized her experience without providing excessive detail about specific awards or competitions, which would have meant little to her audience.

Preview Your Main Points

A **preview** is a brief statement of the main points you will be developing in the body of your speech. It lets your audience members know what main ideas to expect and helps them visualize the structure of your speech—the sequence of ideas you'll present. Your preview should consist of no more than one sentence per main point.

To differentiate the main points in your preview, include *signposts* (for example, *first*, *next*, and *finally*) to help your audience grasp the structure of your speech. Also, avoid the use of *and* or other connecting words while previewing a single main point.

Consider the following two previews that Alexandra might use in her speech about judging ice skating:

WEAKER PREVIEW

The rules of judging and the ways you can judge, along with the many controversies over Olympic judges, are all interesting aspects of judging competitive skating.

STRONGER PREVIEW

Today, we'll look at *three major topics* about judging competitive ice skating: *first*, we'll look at rules for judging the event, *followed by* tips you can use to score the performances yourself, and *finally*, controversies in the judging at previous Olympics.

Both of these previews offer information about the main points to be developed. However, the first preview is much less explicit. It mentions the three points Alexandra plans to cover, but it runs them together in a single sentence. Thus, it doesn't help the audience understand the structure of the speech. This preview also contains no hints indicating that Alexandra is previewing her main points. This statement could just as easily be an attempt to connect with the audience. By contrast, the strong second preview signals the speech structure clearly, making it easy for Alexandra's audience to recognize exactly what the main points will be and in what sequence she will cover them.

INTRODUCTION

CONCLUDING YOUR SPEECH

While your introduction helps you set the stage for your speech, your conclusion serves another equally important purpose: it helps you sum up the message you developed in the body of your speech and leave a memorable impression in your audience members' minds. Don't use the conclusion to develop new ideas about your topic or further expand on points you've already made. Instead, use it to highlight content that you have already presented. A good conclusion generally takes one minute or less (few sins of a speaker are worse than saying "in conclusion" and then

CONCLUSION

continuing to speak for several more minutes). Your conclusion should start with a transition, summarize your main points, and finish with a clincher—a memorable idea. We examine each of these elements in this section.

Transition to Your Conclusion

After presenting your final main point, insert some transitional language that signals you're ready to wrap up your presentation. For example, a persuasive speech encouraging students to participate in a campus food drive might offer this transition to the conclusion:

> Today, *we have seen* how important it is for every member of this class to participate in our annual campus food drive.

In this example, the use of the phrase *we have seen* signals that you're finished with the main part of your speech and are ready to move on to the next part.

Here's another example of a transition into the conclusion:

> I hope *you have learned more* about the first cultures to inhabit the Americas.

Summarize Your Main Points

The first part of your conclusion is a **summary**, a brief review of your main points. The summary is similar to the preview of your main points that you offered in your introduction, except that here you are reminding the audience of what you said instead of telling them what ideas you'll present. You may summarize in a single compound sentence that covers each main point, or you may restate each main point in a complete sentence. In either case, your goal is to remind the audience of your main ideas one last time. An effective summary helps listeners remember your message by enabling them to put your speech together in their own minds.

Be sure that your summary includes each main point from your speech. That way, you'll break the speech down into manageable

DON'T REGURGITATE YOUR WHOLE SPEECH... SUMMARIZE IT WITH QUICK BULLET POINTS

sections for your audience members and remind them of the presentation's structure.

Here is how Alexandra might summarize her main points during the conclusion of her speech about judging ice skating:

> Today, *we have covered* three major topics about judging competitive ice skating. First, we considered the main rules for judging ice skating. Then, we considered some tips for you to use if you want to score at home. Finally, we considered controversies in the judging at previous Winter Olympics.

Note how Alexandra made a clear reference to each main point and used the past tense to help the audience recognize that she was reviewing her points rather than developing new material.

Finish with a Memorable Clincher

Finish your conclusion with a **clincher**, something that leaves a lasting impression of your speech in your listeners' minds. Once your speech

A GREAT CLINCHER FINISHES YOUR SPEECH WITH A BANG

ends, audience members will have countless demands on their time and attention. To make your presentation memorable, select and word your clincher carefully.

The clincher should take up only about thirty seconds in a five- to ten-minute speech. Rock musicians have been known to smash their guitars at the end of a show in order to leave a lasting impression. We would not recommend such mayhem in a speech, but there are a number of less destructive strategies that you can use to make your speech memorable. Following are several ways to craft a good clincher.

Tie Your Clincher to the Introduction. If you began your speech with a compelling anecdote or example, consider extending it in your clincher. One speech asking audience members to serve as volunteer tutors began with the story of Hector, a twelve-year-old at risk of dropping out of school because he had fallen behind. The presenter effectively touched again on Hector's story in her clincher:

> Remember Hector, the boy who was on the verge of dropping out in sixth grade? Ana, a student at this university, became his tutor and role model. Today, Hector has a B average in high school and has applied to several colleges. There are many more Hectors in our local schools, and your help as a tutor will make sure that there is a happy ending to their stories too.

End with a Striking Sentence or Phrase. There may be a single sentence or phrase that effectively sums up your speech. Advertisers and political campaign managers often use this technique because the words are easy to remember. For example, an advertiser refers to a product as "The One," or a campaign manager describes his candidate as possessing "the right stuff for the job." We do not recommend ending your speech with a trivial phrase or a catchy tune. However, do consider using memorable, relevant phrasing to conclude your speech.

For example, one student used the following clincher to end her informative speech about the mental health benefits of running:

> So, I hope you will remember that running is not just good for your body but also great for your mind.

And a speech about Hmong history effectively concluded with a theme that had been evident in each main point:

> The name Hmong means "free." And no matter what continent we are living on, that is what we will always be—a free people.

Conclude with an Emotional Message. Recall a speech or presentation that ended by touching your emotions. If you're like most people, that speech left more of an impact on you than one merely using cold hard facts. Often, a clincher that delivers an emotional charge makes a speech particularly memorable—especially in a persuasive or commemorative presentation. For example, one student concluded a tribute to a beloved pet in this way:

> My mind flooded with memories: finding him as a tiny kit and nursing him to health with my own hands. He became my best friend. I let him go lovingly, with the same arms that held him fast as a baby. Good-bye, my friend— I'll never forget you.

End with a Story or Anecdote. A story that illustrates the message of your speech can make an effective clincher. Consider the following anecdote about Albert Einstein that a student used as her clincher in a speech advocating greater efforts to raise students' self-esteem and prevent them from dropping out:

> Over one hundred years ago, there was a boy who was considered "backward" by his teachers. They said the boy was mentally slow and adrift forever in his foolish dreams. His

father said that when he asked the headmaster what profession his son should adopt, he was told, "It doesn't matter, he'll never make a success of anything."[9]

Who was that hopeless student? Believe it or not, his name was Albert Einstein. We must never give up on the mind of a child. Educators must convince every student that he or she is valued and capable of learning. Not a single dropout should be acceptable.

CHAPTER REVIEW

> "Strong introductions create audience interest; strong conclusions create lasting impressions."

In this chapter, we provided ideas for crafting effective introductions and conclusions for your speeches. You learned that a good introduction has several purposes—including capturing your audience's attention, indicating your thesis, conveying the importance of your topic for audience members, establishing your credibility, and previewing your main points. And you discovered that an effective conclusion transitions smoothly from the body of your speech, helps your audience remember your main points, and enables you to leave a lasting impression on listeners. There are many strategies to choose from in developing your introduction and conclusion, so you have room to be creative. By tailoring these elements of your speech to your audience and allotting the right amount of time to each, you stand an excellent chance of delivering an effective presentation.

Key Terms

attention-getter *299*
rhetorical question *305*
preview *311*

summary *314*
clincher *315*

Review Questions

1. Briefly explain the five major functions of a good introduction.
2. Describe seven specific strategies you can use to create an attention-getting introduction.
3. What three steps must you take to develop a solid conclusion?
4. Offer four types of memorable clinchers.

Critical Thinking Questions

1. Why is it so important to offer an attention-getting introduction in a speech? In what kinds of public speaking situations do you think it might be preferable to present a less dramatic or entertaining opener?
2. How can you effectively determine if a joke will work or fall flat? How important is audience analysis in using humor to start a speech?
3. What happens if you fail to present a solid conclusion to your speech?

Activities

1. Find transcripts of several speeches or watch the beginning of several speeches on the Internet. Does each speaker begin with an attention-getter? If so, identify which strategy each speaker is using and decide whether it is likely to pull audience members into the speech.
2. Select the speech topic of your choice. Use three different attention-getting strategies to develop possible beginnings for a speech based on the topic.
3. Imagine that you are about to give a speech to a group of total strangers you know little about. How would you use your introduction to establish credibility? How would this differ from the way you would establish credibility to a group you knew you had something in common with—for example, students at your

college, members of your religious faith, or people who participate in the same sport or activity that you do?

4. Think of a particular quotation that you find meaningful or inspiring. Would you be able to build a speech around it following
its use as an attention-getter? How would you develop a speech
based on that quotation?

Go to **bedfordstmartins.com/speakup**, where you'll find helpful
study materials, videos, and speech-building tools.

OUTLINING IS USEFUL (AND FUN)

11

OUTLINING YOUR SPEECH

"A good outline strengthens organization and preparation."

Once you have delivered a few speeches, you will certainly be on your way toward developing better skills. You might even begin getting over any speech anxiety you felt when you gave your first presentation. And, with several speeches under your belt, you may begin to find opportunities to personalize your approach to speech assignments—that is, to develop a style that works best for you. While your public speaking instructor may assign you a speech with a specific purpose (informing, persuading, or marking a special occasion), he or she will often ask you to select the subject matter for your speech and decide how to organize your ideas. By making these kinds of choices yourself, you have the opportunity to put your own stamp on your speeches and to add life and energy to the proceedings.

At the same time, you want to ensure that your presentations are always clear, well organized, and well supported. **Outlining**—organizing

DNA AS METAPHOR FOR SPEECH OUTLINE, BUT IT'S ALSO JUST FINE IF YOU THINK THIS DRAWING LOOKS LIKE TWO PIECES OF TWISTED SCOTCH TAPE WITH SOME IDEAS IN BETWEEN, AS THAT GETS ACROSS ALMOST THE SAME MESSAGE

the content of your speech into a structured form—can help you immensely in doing that. Outlines are valuable tools: they help you lay out the sequence and hierarchy of your ideas so that you can see if your speech flows logically and covers the subject matter adequately. Thus, you can think of an outline as representing the "structural DNA" of your speech. You can also use an outline to practice your delivery and therefore present your speech with confidence and flair. In most speech situations, an outline can help you further polish your skills; even seasoned presenters find outlining highly useful!

THIS IS AN OUTLINE

I. How an outline helps speakers organize their thinking

    A. Shows relationships between ideas

        1. SHOWS IDEAS IN THE ORDER OF PRESENTATION

        2. SHOWS WHICH IDEAS ARE MORE IMPORTANT THAN OTHERS

II. How outlines can improve presentations

THIS IS A MANUSCRIPT, NOT AN OUTLINE

Today, I will discuss the major ways that outlines are especially important tools for public speakers.

First, outlines show relationships between ideas by showing ideas in their presentation order and showing which ideas are the most important.

Second, outlines help improve speakers' presentations

The key function of *all* outlines is to clearly depict the hierarchy of the ideas in your speech—what your main points are and what material supports each of these main points. By using an alphanumeric system of headings (beginning with roman numerals for main points and working down to capital letters, numbers, and so on) and a system of indentation, your outline presents all of your points and evidence and clearly shows how your points are supported. This system makes an outline different from a manuscript or an essay, each of which is organized paragraph by paragraph.

TWO STAGES OF OUTLINING

Imagine that you're about to set off on a car trip to a place you've never been before. There are two steps you would probably take before you set out. First, you'd likely consult a road map or an online mapping site to assess where you'd need to go, how you'd get there, and how long it would take. You'd study the map, committing the general picture to memory and figuring out any tricky portions. Second, you'd work on distilling all that you learned from the detailed map into a very brief set of directions (take this highway to that exit, turn right at second light) that you could quickly glance at while driving.

In much the same way as you'd take these two steps to ensure a safe journey, many speech instructors suggest that you take two steps in outlining your speech. In fact, many instructors require two versions of your outline for each presentation. The first is usually known as a working outline, which functions like a road map to help you prepare your speech. The second is known as a speaking outline, which, like a brief set of directions, provides you with quick and easy-to-follow notes that you can refer

USEFUL

FULL SENTENCES

EVERYTHING
(INCLUDING THE
KITCHEN SINK)

EXPLAINS POINTS IN DETAIL

WORKING OUTLINE

USEFUL

PHRASES OR KEYWORDS

JUST THE BARE
ESSENTIALS

GETS STRAIGHT TO THE POINT

SPEAKING OUTLINE

to without really "taking your eyes off the road"—or, in this case, your audience. In this section, we take a look at these two types of outlines, each of which represents an important step in the development of your presentation. But before we move forward, we wish to emphasize that it's *essential* for you to check with your speech instructor on his or her requirements for outlining in your speech course. Different instructors have different philosophies about and requirements for creating outlines, so be sure that what you do aligns with your instructor's expectations.

The Working Outline

A **working outline** (also referred to as a detailed or preparation outline) is a thorough outline that you use to craft your speech. A working outline should be relatively detailed to include your entire speech, from attention-getter to clincher, with each idea written down in full sentences or detailed phrases (depending on your instructor's preference). If you were to wake up with laryngitis on the day of your speech, another classmate should be able to use your working outline to deliver your speech.

A working outline offers many benefits, both for you and for your instructor. Because it is detailed and formatted in a way that shows the hierarchy of ideas, it helps you assess the content and organization of your speech, ensure that your thesis and main points are well supported, and create smooth transitions between (and connections among) all the points and evidence you present. Your instructor might also wish to review your working outline to evaluate your preparation effort; thus, it should clearly show that you have included all required components, cited research sources properly, developed your ideas in sufficient detail, and organized all of your information thoughtfully. Finally, your working outline can serve as a reference when you *begin* to practice your speech, helping you become familiar with the content. Once you've become more comfortable with the material, you're ready to make the transition to a speaking outline.

FULL SENTENCE:

> The study showed that even a large spider, on a good day, makes only 1.5 mg. of silk.

DETAILED PHRASE:

> Study — large spider on good day makes 1.5 mg. silk

BRIEF PHRASE / KEYWORD:

> Study: Best = 1.5 mg. silk

The Speaking Outline

A **speaking outline** is a shorter outline that expresses your ideas in keywords or brief phrases, rather than in complete sentences or detailed phrases. This is the outline that you will use when you actually deliver your speech. Like the brief set of driving directions we talked about earlier, this brief outline (often written on note cards rather than manuscript paper) provides quick notes that you refer to, rather than read, as you deliver your speech.

The purpose of a speaking outline is to facilitate **extemporaneous delivery**. As we discuss in both Chapter 2 and Chapter 13, extemporaneous delivery requires that you speak with limited notes; you do not attempt to present a speech word-for-word from manuscript or memory. Your limited notes are there for your reference—you can use them as a reminder of what idea comes next. But you trust yourself to deliver the details more spontaneously, so that your speech feels fresh and conversational.

CREATING YOUR WORKING OUTLINE

A working outline consists of three main sections: the introduction, the body, and the conclusion of your speech. (Note: most instructors will recommend that you outline the body of your speech first and then go back to outline the introduction and conclusion of your speech.) As you create your working outline, label each of these three parts in bold so that you can more easily see the speech's structure.

Outlining the Body of Your Speech

You can think of the **body** of your speech as representing the "meat" of your presentation. In the body, you'll present your main points and supporting materials (such as examples, stories, statistics, and testimony from experts). The body thus contains most of the content of your entire speech. How do you effectively outline the body of your presentation? Follow the practices listed in this section.

Use Proper Labeling and Indentation. Start each main point at the left margin of your working outline, and indicate each new main point with a roman numeral. Label your subpoints with capital letters, and indent them in this part of your outline. If you develop a subpoint further with two or more supporting ideas, indicate each of these sub-subpoints with arabic numerals, and indent the sub-subpoints another step beneath the subpoint they support. Typically, you'll want to include between two and four subpoints for each main point, and the same number of sub-subpoints for each subpoint. (In a proper outline, support can never stand alone; in other words, you must *always* include a minimum of two subpoints supporting each main point and two sub-subpoints supporting each subpoint).

Use Full Sentences or Detailed Phrases. In your working outline, you should express your main ideas, subpoints, and sub-subpoints in complete sentences or detailed phrases (each instructor will have his or her own preference for the level of detail required). As noted earlier, your working outline should be detailed enough that another person

IN A WORKING OUTLINE, NEVER LEAVE THE READER GUESSING

could deliver your speech from it. Furthermore, your instructor is likely to require you to turn in a copy of your working outline. If it is too brief, he or she may misinterpret the points you want to make or, even worse, conclude that you haven't put enough effort into preparing your speech.

Check for Subordination. In a well-organized speech, supporting materials show **subordination** to their corresponding main points. Thus, be careful that each subpoint is relevant to the main point it's supposed to support and that each sub-subpoint relates to its corresponding subpoint. How can you tell whether your supporting materials show appropriate subordination to the corresponding point? Complete the following sentence for each of your supporting materials:

"This supports the point I am making because   ."

If you can't come up with a logical way to complete this sentence, you may need to reexamine your supporting materials and find ways to make them more clearly relevant. For example, you might want to move a subpoint to a different place in your outline where the idea fits better. Or you may decide to reword a main point or subpoint so that the supporting material more clearly explains or expands the idea it is meant to support. Finally, you could consider developing a supporting example or explanation into a main point.

SUBORDINATION

Include Full Information for Citations, Quotations, and Other Evidence.

When you use evidence to support a claim, you need to include in your working outline all the information about the source of your **evidence**—the author, his or her qualifications, the source publication or Web page, and the date of publication. And if you are quoting a source, be sure to present the information word-for-word and enclose the information in quotation marks to remind you that you are using someone else's words.

For example, here's how you would outline evidence for a commemorative speech about Cammi Granato, one of the first two women elected to the Hockey Hall of Fame and two-time U.S. Olympic Team captain. In this case, the evidence is used as subpoint A, which supports a main point about the beginnings of Granato's hockey career:

I. Cammi Granato got an early start on her hockey career.
   A. Cammi Granato honed her skills by playing hockey with her brothers. According to Ken Campbell, senior editor for *Hockey News*, in *American Hockey Magazine*, December 1997: "The Granato kids painted lines on the floor, set up nets, and played two on two, Tony and Cammi against Donnie and Robbie. 'Those games got pretty intense,' Tony recalls. 'But Cammi hung right in there and she never backed down. She was one of the most tenacious kids I've ever seen.'"

Insert Transitions. Using **transitions**—words, phrases, or sentences that indicate you are moving from one part of your speech to another—helps you keep on track and makes it easier for listeners to follow along. At minimum, include transitions

- between the introduction and body
- as you move from one main point to the next
- between the body and conclusion

In your outline, indicate a transition by labeling it and placing it in brackets, as shown in the following example:

[TRANSITION   The food and scenery in Belize may be a new adventure, but you will find the language very familiar.]

Outlining Your Introduction

After you've outlined the body of your speech, turn to outlining the **introduction**. In Chapter 10, we identified the five purposes of an introduction: gaining the audience's attention, signaling your thesis, connecting with the audience, establishing your credibility, and previewing your main points. Each of these purposes provides the basis for one part of the introduction. When you have prepared them, insert each one into your working outline. The structure of the introduction should look like the following:

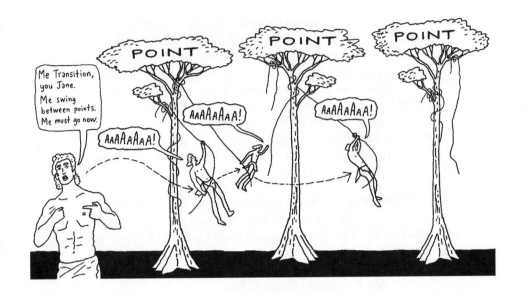

INTRODUCTION

    I. Attention-getter
   II. Topic or thesis statement
  III. Connection with the audience
  IV. Speaker's credibility
   V. Preview of main points

In your working outline, each of these five elements should be expressed in complete sentences or detailed phrases, so that a reader will understand what you are planning to say for each part.

Outlining Your Conclusion

Once you've finished outlining your introduction, do the same for the **conclusion** of your speech. Just as the introduction grabs your listeners' attention, your conclusion should end your speech on a strong note. Start by outlining the two parts of the conclusion that we discussed in Chapter 10: a summary of your main points and a clincher. When you have prepared these two parts, write them down in your outline and indicate each with a roman numeral. The structure of the conclusion should look like this in your working outline (with each part expressed in complete sentences or detailed phrases):

CONCLUSION
I. Summary of main points
II. Clincher

Creating a Bibliography

Your instructor may require you to include a **bibliography**—a list of the sources you cited in your speech—at the end of your outline. A bibliography should not include sources that you discovered during your research but did not quote or use in your speech. Some colleges consider including unused sources in a bibliography academic dishonesty and will take strict disciplinary action against students who commit this kind of wrongdoing.

If a bibliography is required, include a full citation for each source you used in your speech. Your instructor will likely require you to use a particular style for documenting sources in your bibliography; three of the most common are those recommended by the American Psychological Association (APA), the Modern Language Association (MLA), and the *Chicago Manual of Style*. Regardless of which style you use, make sure to follow your instructor's requirements for the bibliography.

A bibliography is *not* a substitute for the proper citation and quotation of evidence in your outline or speech. Even if you place a bibliography at the end of your working outline, it remains your ethical obligation to properly attribute all information that comes from research sources; each time such information is used in your outline or speech, you must identify the source.

Inserting the Title, Specific Purpose, and Thesis

Some instructors may also ask you to write the title, specific purpose, and thesis of your speech at the top of your working outline to guide

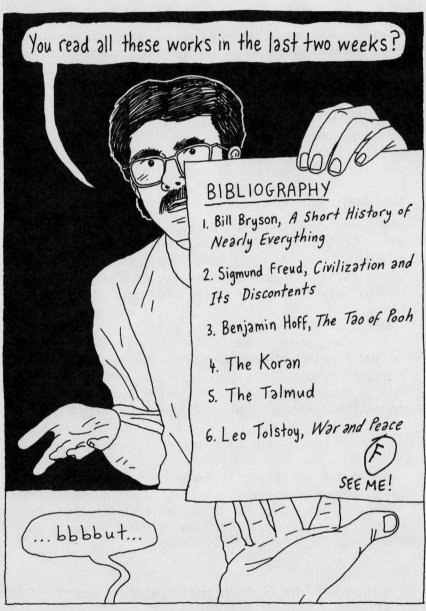

BOGUS BIBLIOGRAPHIES = BIG TROUBLE

the development of your main and supporting points. If your professor has requested this information, indicate the title of your speech, and type or write it out in relatively large or bold type. Indicate your speech's specific purpose and thesis at the left margin, as shown in the following example:

TRANSLOCATION AND ANIMAL INSTINCTS

SPECIFIC PURPOSE To inform my audience about the process of animal translocation and explain the challenges to its success.

THESIS Animal translocation, a process in which human beings relocate a threatened species to a new and, ideally, better habitat, is sometimes a necessary but also challenging process.

A SAMPLE WORKING OUTLINE

Robin McGehee of William Carey College developed a speech titled "A Deadly Mistake," in which she advocated steps for reducing prescription-drug errors. In this section, we show the full-sentence working outline of her speech, with updated evidence, along with annotations highlighting key concepts covered in this chapter.

A DEADLY MISTAKE

SPECIFIC PURPOSE To persuade my audience that prescription-drug errors are a serious health threat in the United States, requiring their personal efforts to reduce the problem, accompanied by new governmental policies. •

• Your instructor may require a written specific purpose statement: the speech itself begins with the introduction.

INTRODUCTION

- Robin begins with an anecdote to gain the audience's attention.
- Source citation for the anecdote.

I. On July 15, 1994, Megan McClave underwent tonsillectomy surgery. Four days later, she was dead. The reason? According to the May 1995 *Ladies Home Journal*, • she died because her pharmacist made a deadly mistake—accidentally filling a prescription for the painkiller Demerol from a bottle of Roxanol, a brand name for the powerful painkiller morphine. Megan followed the directions for taking her prescription and swallowed enough morphine to shut down her entire respiratory system. Everyone makes mistakes, but this was a deadly mistake that could have been avoided.

II. I hope to convince you that prescription-drug errors (PDEs) should be reduced through individual and governmental action. •

- Robin includes the five components of the introduction: attention-getter; thesis; connection with the audience; credibility; and preview.

III. Library and interview research indicate that Megan's tragedy was only the tip of the iceberg.

IV. My research revealed that seven class members currently take one or more prescription drugs and that most of us have friends and loved ones who are taking prescription medications. We are all at serious risk if drug errors are made.

V. To analyze the issue of prescription-drug errors, let's consider the consequences of drug errors, some causes of these errors, and some urgent and immediate solutions.

[TRANSITION   Let's start by analyzing the seriousness of the problem.] •

- Transition from introduction to body.

BODY

I. The costs of drug errors include disease, dollars, and death.

  A. Megan's case is not rare.

    1. A study led by Dr. Florence Bourgeois—a pediatrician at Children's Hospital Boston—and

reported in the October 2009 issue of *Pediatrics* found that over 500,000 children per year seek medical treatment for adverse drug events. •

2. The *Washington Post*, April 25, 2001, reported a study by Rainu Kaushal and colleagues at Boston's Brigham and Women's Hospital: "Hospitalized children experience potentially dangerous medication errors three times as often as adults." •

B. National statistics are startling.

   1. At least 1.5 million preventable injuries are caused by medications in the United States each year, according to the Institute of Medicine's 2007 study *Preventing Medication Errors*.

   2. The same study concluded that these errors resulted in approximately $3.5 billion of additional hospitalization costs each year.

C. Deaths are an even more tragic cost.

   1. According to an Institute of Medicine report, *To Err Is Human: Building a Safer Health System*, 2000, the annual number of lives lost to medication errors exceeds seven thousand—more than the number of Americans who die from workplace injuries each year.

   2. In the April 25, 2001, issue of the *Washington Post*, David Brown provided a tragic example of a nine-month-old girl who died at Children's Hospital in Washington, D.C.: a misplaced decimal point in an order led to her getting ten times the intended dose of morphine.

[TRANSITION   Drug errors are causing needless death and suffering. Why do these deadly mistakes continue?]

• Proper citations to research material used to support a point.

• Subpoints and sub-subpoints are indented properly.

II. The causes of prescription-drug errors are threefold.

A. One cause: lack of reporting requirements. •

● Note the parallel wording of the three main points.

1. According to Michelle Meadows, in *FDA Consumer*, May–June 2003, "Since 1992, the [FDA] has received about 20,000 reports of medication errors. These are voluntary reports, so the number of medication errors that actually occur is thought to be much higher."

2. When drug errors are not reported, we receive no explanation of why or how a pharmacist could confuse medicines, and the pharmacist remains licensed to practice and is able to make more mistakes in the future.

3. We cannot save patients unless we learn from pharmacist mistakes and implement precautionary measures.

B. Another cause: the trust we place in medical professionals. •

● The terms *one*, *another*, and *a third* signpost subpoints on the causes of the problem.

1. People in the health-care professions are among the most trusted individuals in our society.

2. Have we come to trust these human beings too much?

a. Pharmacists, like other workers, may get tired, bored, or distracted.

b. Pharmacists may assume that someone else is ensuring that prescriptions are properly filled.

3. Economic pressures are making pharmacists' jobs even harder.

a. According to *American Druggist* in January 1998, "HMOs, with their eye on the bottom line, pay pharmacists less for each drug they dispense than insurers did in the past."

b. This forces pharmacists to scramble to fill as many prescriptions as possible.

In *Pharmacotherapy*, 2005, Dr. David
Phillips of UC San Diego and colleagues
report that a high prescription workload is
a major cause of medication errors.
   c. William Campbell, dean of the School of
Pharmacy at the University of North
Carolina, calls this situation a "doomsday
machine" (*American Druggist* article).
  C. A third cause: failed communication—noted
by Kevin Doherty, Alissa Segal, and Patrick
McKinney in *Consultant*, February 2004—including
poor handwriting, misinterpreted directions, and
misplaced decimals.

[TRANSITION   There are many causes of drug errors,
but are there solutions? Yes.] •

           • Transition links main points II and III.

III. The solutions to prescription-drug errors depend on
both individual and government efforts.
  A. First, a nationwide drug error reporting system
should be implemented. •

           • The words *first*, *second*, and *third* signpost the three aspects of Robin's solution.

    1. The Institute of Medicine of the National
Academies made this recommendation in
To Err Is Human, 2000: "A nationwide mandatory reporting system should be established
by building upon the current patchwork of
state systems and by standardizing the types
of adverse events and information to be
reported."
    2. As customers of the health-care profession
and citizens of the United States, we should
ask Congress to pass legislation with sufficient funding for every state to implement
a sound reporting system.
  B. Second, computerized prescription systems can
further reduce error—Patricia Wen in the *Boston*

Globe, February 14, 2008, explains that a computerized system at Boston's Brigham and Women's Hospital reduced preventable medication errors by over 55 percent.

   C. Third, I will distribute a wallet-sized card provided by the American Pharmacists Association with reminders of action you can take to reduce the risk of drug error:

      1. Write down the name, dose, and purpose of the drug when it is prescribed.

      2. Introduce yourself to the pharmacist.

      3. Read the prescription label carefully to be certain that you have received the proper drug.

      4. Ask the pharmacist any questions you have, and get a phone number you can call if you have questions later.

      5. Use this card as a quick reference when having a prescription filled, and it may save your life or the life of a loved one.

[TRANSITION In conclusion, I hope that you have become more aware of the prescription-drug-error problem in the United States.]

• Transition from body to conclusion.

CONCLUSION

   I. Today, I described the deadly consequences of prescription-drug errors, focused on some causes of these errors, and presented immediate solutions. The prescription errors that pharmacists are making are serious, but we *can* do much to reduce these deadly mistakes. •

• Efficient summary of main points.

   II. Remember Megan McClave and her family, and how a young life was lost because of a deadly mistake that could have been avoided. If the pharmacist had been more careful, or Megan's family had known the right questions to ask, this girl would be alive today. Are you going to ask these questions the next time you or a loved one needs a prescription filled? Or will you just walk out the door and take your chances? Let's not allow these needless deaths to continue. •

• The clincher refers to the introductory anecdote and leaves the audience with a challenge.

Bibliography

Bourgeois, F., K. Mandl, C. Valim, and M. Shannon. "Pediatric Adverse Drug Events in the Outpatient Setting: An 11-Year National Analysis. *Pediatrics* 124 (October 2009): 1188. •

Brown, D. "Study Looks at Children, Drug Errors." *Washington Post*, April 25, 2001, A19.

Doherty, K., A. Segal, and P. McKinney. "The 10 Most Common Prescribing Errors: Tips on Avoiding the Pitfalls." *Consultant* 44 (February 2004): 173.

Institute of Medicine. *Preventing Medication Errors*. Washington, D.C.: National Academies Press, 2007.

———., *To Err Is Human: Building a Safer Health System.* Washington, D.C.: National Academies Press, 2000.

McLellan, D. "Megan Won't Wake Up." *Ladies Home Journal*, May 1995, 132.

Meadows, M. "Strategies to Reduce Medication Errors." *FDA Consumer*, May–June 2003. http://www.fda.gov/fdac/features/2003/303_meds.html (accessed November 29, 2004).

Phillips, D., et al. "A Spike in Fatal Medication Errors at the Beginning of Each Month," *Pharmacotherapy* 25, no.1 (2005): 1.

Slezak, M. "*Good Housekeeping* Examines Rx Errors." *American Druggist* 215 (January 1998): 19.

Wen, P. "1 in 10 Patients Gets Drug Error." *Boston Globe*, February 14, 2008, A1.

• Full citation of sources in the references section. (Check with your instructor on his or her preferred citation format.)

CREATING YOUR SPEAKING OUTLINE

As noted earlier, your speaking outline is a very brief version of your working outline; it is a set of notes to aid you in extemporaneous delivery of your speech. By limiting these notes to brief words or phrases, you prevent yourself from reading the speech word-for-word, and allow yourself to improvise, choosing fresh words as you speak.

The speaking outline provides useful reminders of your main and supporting points as well as guidelines for organizing them in case you lose track.

To deliver the most effective extemporaneous presentation possible, you'll need to transform your working outline into a speaking outline. You may want to prepare the speaking outline *after* you've practiced your speech several times with your working outline and have become thoroughly familiar with the ideas in your presentation. Then you can use the speaking outline for your final practice sessions and for delivering your speech.

Formatting Your Speaking Outline

Prepare your speaking outline on 5 × 7 inch note cards or on regular 8½ × 11 inch paper. Keep your points brief, using only quick phrases or one or two keywords for each point. The more you've practiced your speech, the more useful the speaking outline will be as a reminder while you're delivering your speech.

Because you'll refer to this outline as needed while giving your presentation, make it easy on the eyes. If you use a word processor to create the outline, double-space and select a large font size. If you handwrite your outline on note cards, write neatly and leave space between each line.

Base your speaking outline on your working outline. Use a similar structure by indenting subordinate points and using roman numerals, capital letters, and numbers. Number each note card or page of your speaking outline—this will help you reassemble the outline quickly if you happen to drop your pages or cards while walking up to the front of the room or delivering your speech.

Note that your instructor may have specific requirements about the form and length of your speaking outline. Check to ensure that your outline meets these requirements.

Elements of Your Speaking Outline

Your speaking outline should be a condensed version of your working outline that retains all of your points, subpoints, and source quotations. Indicate main points and supporting points in no more than a sentence each, and trust yourself to develop these ideas conversationally while delivering your speech. Include the following elements in your extemporaneous outline:

- *Main points.* Write each main point as a brief phrase or as one to three keywords. Stating your main points in similar words or parallel structures will signal to your listeners that these points are important.

- *Subpoints and sub-subpoints.* Write just enough to remind yourself of the key idea.

- *Abbreviations.* To condense your outline, use abbreviations whenever possible. However, as you have probably realized

THE ART OF BEING COMFORTABLE AND ONLY
LOOKING AT YOUR NOTES ONCE IN A WHILE

when going back to study notes you took in class, it is essential
to use abbreviations that you will recognize.

- *Evidence.* When providing evidence for your claims in your
  speaking outline, include necessary citation information and
  consider including word-for-word quotes or evidence from
  the original source.

- *Difficult words.* If you'll be using words that are difficult to
  pronounce or remember, include them in your speaking
  outline. For example, in the sample outline on pages 337–43,
  if the speaker wanted to include complex names of medications, such as "acetazolamide," she would insert pronunciation notes.

- *Transitions.* Include a brief reminder of each transition in
  your speech. These reminders don't need to be word-for-word,
  but make them detailed enough to indicate to your audience that you're done with one idea *and* you're moving on

to the next. Consider using brackets to set your transitions apart from your points.

- *Delivery notes.* In the margin, consider jotting down **delivery reminders** for handling speaking challenges effectively. For example, write "SLOW DOWN!" in places where you tend to rush or "LOOK UP!" if you often read from your notes rather than making eye contact while presenting. Consider writing "KEY POINT" or "EMPHASIS!" to remind yourself to use voice or gestures to highlight an important idea. Try writing "COVER WHEN DONE!" as a reminder for what to do after you've finished using a visual aid. To make reminders stand out, circle them, write them in capital letters, use a different colored ink, or highlight them.

INTRO

LOOK UP — EYE CONTACT

I. Megan McClave anecdote: experienced pharmacist gave her Roxanol (morphine), not Demerol.

II. Reduce PDEs through indiv. + govt. action.

III. Research: Megan = tip of iceberg.

IV. Survey—7 taking PD and most have friends and loved ones taking PD.
ALL AT RISK

EMPHASIS!

V. Consequences, causes, solutions.

PAUSE

A SAMPLE SPEAKING OUTLINE

Here is a speaking outline of Robin McGehee's speech, "A Deadly Mistake." Compare this outline with her working outline (see pages 337–43). Notice how Robin used keywords and abbreviations to condense her ideas. She inserted direct quotations word-for-word and highlighted her evidence in boldface. Finally, she included delivery reminders.

A DEADLY MISTAKE

INTRODUCTION

• All five
parts of the
introduction
are included,
but limited to
keywords.

Look up

I. Megan McClave anecdote: experienced pharmacist gave her Roxanol (morphine), not Demerol. •

• Abbreviate
"prescription-
drug errors"
as *PDEs*.

II. Reduce PDEs through indiv. + govt. action. •

III. Research: Megan = tip of iceberg.

IV. Survey—7 taking PD and most have friends and loved ones taking PD. All at risk.

V. Consequences, causes, solutions.

Pause

• Remember
to include a
transition to
body of speech.

[TRANSITION   Let's start by analyzing problem.] •

BODY

I. Costs = disease, dollars, and death.

A. Megan's case not rare.

• Abbreviate
"adverse drug
events" as
ADEs.

1. Dr. Florence Bourgeois, *Pediatrics*, October 2009, **over 500k children/yr treated for ADEs.** •

2. **"Hospitalized children experience potentially dangerous medication errors three times as often as adults,"** *Washington Post*, April 25, 2001, study by Rainu Kaushal et al. @ Brigham and Women's Hospital. •

• Include
evidence
citations.

B. Natl. stats startling. **1.5 mill inj and $3.5 bill hospital costs,** Institute of Medicine, *Preventing Medication Errors*, 2007.

C. Deaths.

1. **7,000+ deaths annually, > workplace deaths,** Institute of Medicine report, *To Err Is Human*, 2000.

2. **9-month-old girl died at Children's Hospital in D.C.—misplaced decimal point,** *Washington Post*, April 25, 2001.

Slowly

[TRANSITION   Errors cause needless deaths, why do they continue?]

II. Causes of PDEs are threefold.
  A. Lack of reporting requirements.
    1. Reporting limited—**"Since 1992, the [FDA] has received about 20,000 reports of medication errors. These are voluntary reports, so the number of medication errors that actually occur is thought to be much higher,"** Michelle Meadows, *FDA Consumer*, May–June 2003.
    2. No reporting = no improvement.
    3. Learn from mistakes + precautions.
  B. Trust in med. pros. •
    1. Most trusted in society.
    2. Trust too much?
      a. Pharmacists: tired, distracted.
      b. Assume someone else verifying RXs.
    3. Economic pressures.
      a. **HMOs pay less per drug dispensed,** *American Druggist*, January 1998.
      b. Pharms. fill as many RXs as possible. Dr. David Phillips, UCSD, **high workload major cause of med errors,** *Pharmacotherapy*, 2005.
      c. **A "doomsday machine,"** William Campbell, dean of School of Pharmacy at University of North Carolina (*American Druggist*).
  C. Communication errors: **poor handwriting, misinterpreted directions, misplaced decimals,** Doherty, Segal, and McKinney, *Consultant*, February 2004.

• Robin's detailed outline is condensed to keywords with abbreviations. She trusts herself to explain the details.

[TRANSITION   Many causes, but are there solutions? Yes!]

III. Solutions: indiv. and govt. efforts.
  A. Nationwide reporting system.
    1. **"A nationwide mandatory reporting system should be established by building upon the**

current patchwork of state systems and by standardizing the types of adverse events and information to be reported," Institute of Medicine, *To Err Is Human*, 2000.

2. Pressure Congress: legislation with enough $ for reporting system in every state.

Look up

B. Computerized systems. Patricia Wen, *Boston Globe*, February 14, 2008, **reduced preventable med errors 55% at Brigham and Women's Hospital, Boston.** •

• Explanation of subpoints is very brief.

C. Wallet-sized card from Am. Pharmacists Assn.
   1. Write down name, dose, purpose.
   2. Intro. self to pharm.
   3. Read label, check for proper drug.
   4. Ask questions, get phone number.
   5. Use card as reference.

[TRANSITION   In conclusion, hope you are more aware of PDE problem.]

CONCLUSION

 I. Summary: consequences, causes, solutions to PDEs.
II. Remember Megan. Don't let it happen again.

CHAPTER REVIEW

"A good outline strengthens organization and preparation."

In this chapter, we explained the importance of outlining and showed you how to develop and use a working outline and a speaking outline to organize your ideas, practice your presentation, and ultimately deliver an effective speech. A working outline shows the structure of your speech and the hierarchy of your ideas, as well as full quotations for all evidence you'll provide in your speech. This outline also includes notes for transitions and visual aids. Use your working outline to practice your speech until you're thoroughly familiar with it.

Your speaking outline condenses your ideas, using phrases, keywords, and abbreviations, though it should still retain word-for-word quotations from your evidence sources. Speaking outlines are usually prepared on numbered note cards or on pieces of 8½ × 11 inch paper; writing on these outlines must be clear and easy to read for a speaker delivering a presentation. You may want to develop your speaking outline only after you've practiced your speech extensively with your working outline. The speaking outline helps you present your speech conversationally—conveying your ideas in your own words and maintaining eye contact with the audience rather than reading a word-for-word script or reciting your presentation from memory. The speaking outline also serves as a handy reminder if you lose your place while delivering your speech, if you need to quote evidence during your talk, or if you want to remember certain delivery tips (such as adding emphasis to a particular point while presenting your speech).

Key Terms

outlining *323*
working outline *327*
speaking outline *328*
extemporaneous delivery *329*
body *329*
subordination *331*

evidence *332*
transition *333*
introduction *333*
conclusion *334*
bibliography *335*
delivery reminder *347*

Review Questions

1. Explain the differences between a working outline and a speaking outline.
2. How does creating an outline help ensure that your ideas are well supported?
3. Describe the most important guidelines for creating a working outline for a speech's body, introduction, and conclusion.
4. What are the benefits of delivering your speech from a relatively brief speaking outline?
5. Describe the most important guidelines for creating an effective speaking outline.

Critical Thinking Questions

1. If you were to give a speech on the nature of working outlines, what would your main points be? How would they compare to the main points of a speech about the nature of speaking outlines?
2. How can the process of developing a working outline help you be more confident when delivering your final speech?
3. Can you think of a situation in everyday life in which you use subordination? How might you use subordination in a conversation with a friend? In a writing assignment? What does this lead you to believe about the importance of subordination in communication?

Activities

1. Open one of your textbooks from another course and outline a chapter based on the headings, subheadings, and key terms that appear in boldfaced or colored text. Do these elements show a clear hierarchy of ideas? How clear a picture of the chapter does the outline create? Could you summarize the chapter using only the outline?

2. Take a look at both the working outline (pp. 337–43) and the speaking outline (pp. 348–50) for Robin McGehee's speech, "A Deadly Mistake." Could you deliver the speech yourself using her working outline? Why would it be difficult to deliver the speech yourself, right now, using only her speaking outline? What type of preparation could help you deliver her speech from her speaking outline?

Go to **bedfordstmartins.com/speakup**, where you'll find helpful study materials, videos, and speech-building tools.

12

LANGUAGE AND STYLE

"Choose your words carefully."

Marvin was eager to present his speech about law-enforcement techniques in large cities to his public speaking classmates. A civilian volunteer with the local police department, he had forged close bonds with the police officers there and hoped to become a homicide investigator one day. In delivering his speech, Marvin drew on the terminology and style of talking that he had come to know through his experiences at the department. For example, he made frequent references to the "guys on the job" and described what it was like to "deal with perps" and "make collars." At one point in his presentation, he also mentioned how the police "handle certain neighborhoods where residents won't cooperate, even though they say they want police protection." When Marvin sat down after concluding his speech, he felt confident that he had both conveyed his credibility and met his objective: informing the audience about his topic.

Yet the students in Marvin's class had mixed reactions to his talk. Many found him credible because of his volunteer experience and his wide vocabulary of police terms and slang. Others, however, found some of his slang impenetrable. Several audience members resented his use of *guys on the job* instead of *police officers*. Some listeners found the phrase *certain neighborhoods* insensitive because it seemed to be a veiled reference to socioeconomics or race. And members of the audience reacted differently to the word *protection*, with some reminded of the heroic efforts and sacrifice of police officers featured on the nightly news, and others thinking of recent reports of excessive police violence and corruption.

Clearly, Marvin failed to get his message across to many people in his audience—in large part because of his word choice. **Word choice**, or **diction**, requires consideration of audience, occasion, and the nature of one's message when using language for a speech. If Marvin had used the same language in talking to an audience of police officers, he might well have had more success. But his classmates consisted of diverse students who had very different perspectives on law enforcement than police officers have—and who used very different language. Marvin failed because he didn't adapt his word choice to these listeners' expectations. When it comes to giving speeches, your word choice can matter far more than you might think.

Another great example of the importance of word choice can be found in Martin Luther King Jr.'s "I Have a Dream" speech, which we discussed in Chapter 2. When King presented this address on August 28, 1963, at the March on Washington, he didn't give it an official title. Only later did people start calling it the "I Have a Dream" speech. Why has this phrase endured in people's memories? It was an exceptionally powerful expression that encapsulated King's vision of a time and place free from prejudice and discrimination. Nearly forty years after his death, people still experience profound emotion when they recall this expression. If King had calmly used the words *I hope* instead of *I have a dream*, he would have had much less impact on his listeners.

An average speech may contain hundreds or even thousands of words. And every one of them matters. Selected carefully, your words can help you connect with your audience and get your message across clearly. Used thoughtlessly, they may confuse, offend, bore, or annoy your listeners, preventing them from absorbing your message. In this chapter, we examine the importance of choosing the right words for your speeches, and the difference between oral and written language. Then we explain how to use language to present your message clearly, express your ideas effectively, and demonstrate respect for your audience.

THE IMPORTANCE OF LANGUAGE AND WORD CHOICE

Even if you don't think of yourself as much of a reader or a "word" person, you still make thousands of word choices every day: when talking with friends and family, taking notes in class, writing e-mails, making phone calls, and sending text messages. You probably try to

THE POSITIVE POWER OF WORDS

choose your words carefully in each of these situations. After all, you know that your words have a lot of power. They can inform, inspire, and uplift others. But they can also confuse people (for example, if you've used jargon or slang that others might not understand), and they can hurt others (for instance, if you've used biased language).

Your word choice reflects on you as a speaker. In earlier chapters, we introduced the concept of a speaker's *ethos*, or personal credibility, and explained how ethos can influence an audience's perception of the presenter's message. Your words and phrases convey your ethos to your listeners because they say something about you as a person.

How do you use words in ways that clarify your message and enhance your credibility? Along with using appropriate and considerate language, you can explain technical terms and use helpful presentation aids (for clarity) and thus effectively incorporate such terms into your speech (to enhance credibility).

THE NEGATIVE POWER OF WORDS

A student speaker named Gillian applied these practices while delivering an informative presentation about armor plating used during the Ottoman Empire. Gillian showed photographs depicting the armor worn by soldiers and their horses. She also used technical terms in a way that the audience would understand. For instance, at one point she discussed a "gilded copper chanfrein," which she immediately explained was "forehead armor for the horse—like the helmet a soldier might wear." By using the correct technical terminology, Gillian showed authority and gained credibility in the eyes of her audience. And by explaining these terms through devices such as analogy ("like the helmet a soldier might wear"), she made her message accessible without coming across as condescending to her listeners.

...gilded chanfrein.

DIFFERENCES BETWEEN ORAL AND WRITTEN LANGUAGE

You may have noticed that words and sentences can come across quite differently when you hear them spoken aloud, as opposed to when you read them to yourself. In a public speaking context, that difference between spoken and written language is usually even more pronounced. To help you craft better language for your speeches, you should consider three key differences between oral and written language:

- *Oral language is more adaptive.* Writers seldom know exactly who will read their words, or in what context; the best they can do is to take educated guesses and make language choices accordingly. When you speak before a live audience, however, you can get immediate feedback that is virtually impossible for a writer. Thus, you can observe your audience members during your presentation, interact with them, and *respond* to the way they are receiving your message. Because a speech is a live, physical interaction that generates instanta- neous audience feedback, you can adapt to the situation, such

ORAL vs. WRITTEN LANGUAGE

as by extending or simplifying an explanation if listeners seem confused or by choosing clearer or simpler language.

- *Oral language tends to be less formal.* Because writers have the luxury of getting their words down on paper (or on screen) and then going back to make changes, they typically use precise word choice and follow the formal rules of syntax and grammar. This careful use of language aligns well with most readers' expectations. In most speech situations, however, language choice tends toward a somewhat less formal style. Because listeners lack the chance to go back and reread your words, you will usually want to use shorter and less complicated sentences (of course, certain speech situations—such as many political settings—require elevated sentence structure and word choice). In addition, effective oral language is often simpler and less technically precise than written language. Thus, consider incorporating appropriate colloquialisms, conversational tone, and even sentence fragments into your speeches.

- *Oral language incorporates repetition.* Most writing teachers and coaches advise their students to avoid repeating themselves or being *redundant* by covering the same ground more than once. But in speaking situations, repetition can be an especially effective tool because your listeners can't go back and revisit your points—your words are there and then suddenly they are gone. Because most audience members won't take notes (especially outside of a classroom setting), there is nothing for listeners to rely on except their own memory of your words.

As a speaker, you can help your listeners remember your message by intentionally repeating keywords and phrases throughout your presentation. If an audience hears certain words often enough, they will remember them.

DENOTATIVE AND CONNOTATIVE MEANING

In addition to using words to express your message clearly and to enhance your credibility, you need to be aware that words can have two very different kinds of meaning. By understanding these differences, you can select your language more strategically to exert the impact you want. In the sections that follow, we take a close look at this notion of two different meanings: denotative meaning and connotative meaning.

Denotative Meaning

The **denotative meaning** of a word is its exact, literal dictionary definition. When you use a word that has one dictionary definition (and that is not overly technical), you can pretty well expect that your audience will understand what you mean. But many words have several dictionary definitions. In these cases, you may need to take steps to avoid confusion.

Consider the word *run*. According to *Merriam-Webster's Collegiate Dictionary*, *run* has numerous definitions. It can be a verb meaning "to go faster than a walk," a noun meaning "an unbroken course of performance" (such as "a good run of profits this year"), and an adjective meaning "being in a melted state" (for instance, "the butter is run"). Suppose you wanted to use the word *run* in a speech to refer to a successful series of victories by your school's track team. If you said, "We've had a great run this season," your listeners may wonder if you're referring to a specific running race or to a string of victories scored by the team against opponents during the season. In this case, you may want to avoid the risk of confusing your audience by saying, "We've consistently trounced the competition during this season" instead of "We've had a great run this season."

Connotative Meaning

In addition to denotative meanings, many words also have **connotative meanings**—associations that come to mind when people hear or read the word. A word's connotative meanings may bear little or even no resemblance to its denotative meanings. For example, the word *dog*, when used as a noun in a statement about stocks, may connote a poor investment opportunity—yet the literal meaning of the noun *dog* is a specific type of canine.

By using words in your speeches deliberately for their connotative meanings, you can make a powerful impression on your audience. For example, a student named Betty made the following statement in her presentation on the history of hairstyles in the twentieth century: "In the roaring 1920s, the short 'bob' or 'flapper' haircut exploded on to the scene through the rise of silent film star Louise Brooks." When Betty used the verb *exploded*, she triggered the strong, fiery association that most people have with this word. This

DOG   "DOG"

EXPLODED

"EXPLODED"

% OF POPULATION WITH BOB HAIRCUTS

1915 1920 1925 1930 1935
Year

savvy use of the connotations of *exploded* helped Betty make her point far more forcefully than if she had merely said that the bob haircut "became very popular."

On the other hand, careless use of a word that has very different denotative and connotative meanings can backfire and confuse your audience. Consider Albert, a student who made the following statement in an impromptu speech about a school district's refusal to lower the student/teacher ratio for class size in elementary schools: "That kind of decision really demonstrates some bigotry by the school board." The word *bigotry* literally means the state of mind of a person who is intolerantly devoted to his or her personal opinions or prejudices—the meaning that Albert intended in his comment. Unfortunately, many people have come to associate the word *bigotry* with racial prejudice. Albert did not intend a racial connotation—he just wanted to say that he thought the school district was unreasonably wedded to its decision about class size. Unfortunately, many students in Albert's class had experienced the pain of racial prejudice firsthand. Thus, they inferred from Albert's use of *bigotry* that issues of race underlay the school board's decision, which wasn't true. If Albert had analyzed his audience more carefully, he might have known to avoid using the word *bigotry* because of its potentially misleading connotative meaning.

PRESENTING YOUR MESSAGE CLEARLY

You can't get your message across to your audience unless you present it clearly. To make your message as clear as possible, use language that's understandable, concrete, proper, and concise.

Understandable Language

Understandable language consists of words that your listeners find *recognizable*. In most situations, the best ways to ensure that you're using understandable language are to choose words that reflect your audience's language skills and to avoid technical terms beyond your listeners' comprehension. For example, if a cell biologist gave a talk to a roomful of English majors, she would quickly confuse her listeners with terms such as *ribosomal DNA* and *anaerobic cellular metabolism*. Yet those terms could be appropriate in a speech delivered to a group of experts or insiders—for example, when presenting a paper to scientists at a biology conference.

Thus, you need to analyze your audience to determine what language your listeners will recognize. Audience members' educational background can suggest their general vocabulary level. Meanwhile, demographic information and stories about listeners' life experiences can help you predict what language the audience will understand.

Also take care in using **jargon**—specialized or technical words or phrases familiar to people in a specific field or group. Jargon includes technical terms as well as abbreviations, acronyms, slang, and other esoteric expressions. For example, people in the field of telecommunications use jargon extensively—including expressions such as *FTTP* ("fiber to the property"), *3G* ("third-generation telecom networks"), *CapEx* ("capital expenditures"), and *first-tier ops* ("telecom operators with the largest market share").

Here are two simple guidelines for deciding whether to include a particular instance of jargon in a speech:

- *If you can say something in plain language, do so.* Unless you see a pressing reason to use jargon—such as to clarify an important point or bolster your credibility—use widely accessible words.

- *If you do use jargon, explain it.* By clarifying your use of jargon, you can gain whatever advantages it offers while still maintaining your audience's understanding.

For example, a student named Patrick was giving a speech in his public speaking class on safe horseback-riding practices. Most of his fellow students had grown up in the city and had had little exposure to horses. In explaining the steps required to prepare a horse for a trail ride, Patrick said, "Be very careful about how you tack up your horse— that is, how you put the bridle and saddle on." He guessed (correctly) that many of his listeners wouldn't understand the phrase *tack up*. By using the term—which is common among people who ride horseback—he gained credibility as someone familiar with his topic, and by explaining it, he helped his audience understand the information.

Concrete Words

Whenever possible, strive to use concrete words instead of abstract ones. What's the difference? **Concrete words** are specific and suggest exactly what you mean. **Abstract words**, on the other hand, are general and can be confusing and ambiguous for your audience. Consider these four sentences, which range from abstract to concrete:

This past week, Jane arrived in a vehicle. *(abstract)*

Four days ago, Jane arrived in a car. *(less abstract)*

Last Tuesday at noon, Jane arrived in a blue Toyota. *(more concrete)*

Last Tuesday at noon, Jane arrived in a 2001 blue Toyota Corolla. *(most concrete)*

Only the third and fourth sentences convey in specific terms how and when Jane arrived. If this information is relevant to the presentation, these sentences would help the speaker convey more information than the first and second sentences.

This is not to suggest that you should never use more general language. In fact, some situations clearly call for a more general language style. In the language of speechwriters, this is the difference between speaking from "five thousand feet, as opposed to fifty feet." Sometimes you will want to describe a concept or theory from a much bigger perspective (hence the term *five thousand feet*), and thus give the audience the *big picture* or the *grand vision*, invariably using more general language. On occasion, speakers

LANGUAGE FLYING AT 5,000 FEET

Speaking as a swallow, I think it's well worth making the long, long, journey to California every summer...

LANGUAGE FLYING AT 50 FEET

As a member of the species of Petrochelidon pyrrhonota, I always look forward to flying over 12,000 miles from Goya, Corrientes, Argentina, to San Juan Capistrano, California, USA...

may also want to do both, beginning with general concepts (five thousand feet), and then moving toward more specific details (fifty feet). For example, in a 2007 speech before Congress, Kevin M. Brown, chief operating officer of the American Red Cross, used both lofty language and more grounded examples to describe his organization's goals and accomplishments. He began with general language:

> Charities provide an important role in our nation—in communities from coast to coast. For the American Red Cross, our congressional charter mandates our mission: to help our neighbors prevent, prepare for, and respond to disaster.

Brown then followed up with concrete examples:

> Each and every day, our more than seven hundred chapters respond to more than two hundred house fires and other

disasters, in addition to providing first aid, CPR/AED, and other health and safety training programs to more than 11 million individuals each year. Our thirty-five blood regions collect, process, and distribute more than 40 percent of all blood needed in and used in the nation. Our two Service to the Armed Forces Centers annually provide 650,000 emergency communications from 193,000 families to loved ones serving in our nation's armed forces. And our international relief operations respond to an average of thirty international disasters annually.[1]

Proper Use of Words

The audience's understanding of your message will improve if you use words that correctly express the point you want to make. Incorrect word choice can confuse listeners or undermine your credibility. For example, if you were to use the words *recession* and

USE PROPER WORDS

depression interchangeably in a speech on the economy, you would likely lose credibility with any audience members who understood the difference between these two very specific economic terms. At the same time, you might confuse or mislead audience members who didn't understand the distinction. You should also watch out for words that are commonly misused (such as *literally* and *effect*) as well as words that are frequently mispronounced (such as *probably* and *nuclear*).

It's also very easy to fall into the trap of mixing up words that sound alike in a speech. For example, one student delivering a speech on the Seattle music scene of the 1990s accused the late Kurt Cobain of "immortal behavior." The audience laughed, knowing that musicians clearly don't live forever and that the speaker probably meant "immoral behavior." Though this speaker's listeners were amused, the joke was on him: most of his audience members probably lost some respect for him.

Concise Language

Because audience members cannot reread or rehear portions of your speech, they have only one chance to grasp your ideas—during the actual presentation. For this reason, make sure that each of your sentences expresses just one thought. Although long sentences linking different ideas may be understandable in print, they're hard to follow in a speech.

As a rule of thumb, aim to be *concise*; that is, use the fewest words necessary to express an idea. When you outline your speech, focus on making your points in the fewest words possible. Of course, you may occasionally want to add words or phrases to incorporate color, eloquence, wit, or humor into your talk. However, make certain you have a good reason to insert those extra words.

The term for unnecessary words in a presentation is **verbal clutter**, extraneous words that make it hard for the audience to follow your message. Here are three examples:

- "The death penalty cannot deter crime *for the reason that* murderers do not consider the consequences of their actions."

- *"Regardless of the fact that* you disagree with the government's position, you cannot dispute the FCC's ruling."
- "If we are to *make contact* with our bargaining opponents, we have to find a mutually acceptable schedule."

AMOEBA

You could easily revise those sentences to eliminate verbal clutter:

- "The death penalty cannot deter crime *because* murderers do not consider the consequences of their actions."
- *"Although* you disagree with the government's position, you cannot dispute the FCC's ruling."
- "If we are to *meet* with our bargaining opponents, we have to find a mutually acceptable schedule."

EXPRESSING YOUR IDEAS EFFECTIVELY

Words have great power to move an audience, especially when used vividly. Empower your own language through the use of repetition, hypothetical examples, personal anecdotes, vivid language, and figurative language.

Repetition

Repetition—saying a specific word, phrase, or statement more than once—helps you grab your audience's attention and leave listeners with enduring memories of your speech:

At the end of the battle, every soldier was killed. Every soldier.

OVERUSING REPETITION GOOD USE OF REPETITION

This use of repetition draws listeners' attention to the fact that all the soldiers *on both sides of the conflict* died at the end of the battle. It thus drives home a sobering point that the speaker wants to make.

To get the most from repetition, use it sparingly. If you repeat too many statements in your speech, your listeners won't be able to discern the *really* important points in your presentation.

You can also use repetition by returning to a point later in a speech to provide a gentle reminder to your audience. In the following example, a student named Allyson employs this technique in a speech about trekking across Russia:

> When most people think about mountains in Russia, if they know anything, they think about the Urals. These are old mountains, stretching some twelve hundred miles from north to south. The mountains themselves are covered with taigas—large forests that blanket the area. . . .
>
> As I mentioned a few minutes back, these twelve hundred miles of Ural Mountains are an impressive sight, with all sorts of wildlife, including wolves, bears, and many different game birds.

Later in her speech, Allyson again repeated the north-to-south distance ("twelve hundred miles") to emphasize the challenges of backpacking through the vast Ural mountain range.

Finally, you may want to repeat a point through *rewording* it—making the point again but in different words. Rewording is useful when the original point could be confusing, because it gives your audience another option for grasping what you mean. Rewording is similar to the technique you use to explain jargon. Here's one example:

> According to the engineering report, the shuttle booster rockets had systems failure with the cooling system, not to mention serious problems with the outer hatch doors and the manually operated crane. Put another way, there were at least three mechanical problems we know of with this last shuttle mission.

As a speaker, you can help your listeners remember your message by intentionally repeating key words and phrases. As a speaker, you can help your listeners remember your message by intentionally repeating key words and phrases. As a speaker, you can help your listeners remember your message by intentionally repeating key words and phrases. As a speaker...

Rewording works particularly well in those parts of your speech where you enumerate a list or make a technical statement that might be difficult for your audience to follow.

Hypothetical Examples

With technical, complicated messages—as well as policy statements and points in a speech where you particularly want to focus your audience's attention—consider using **hypothetical examples**. These are imagined examples or scenarios that you invite your audience to think about. Hypothetical examples can help your listeners follow a complicated point that you present immediately afterward.

For instance, a student named Blake wanted to inform his audience about the legal test for defamation of character. He introduced his presentation with the following hypothetical example:

Suppose a television news crew was shadowing a paramedic team to record their average day, and the paramedics were called out to a highway accident. Now suppose the camera crew taped the whole rescue, and the reporter talked to a badly injured victim who was sedated with painkillers. Under the influence of the painkillers, the victim said many foolish things, including some unkind words about her employer. Would the news station be justified in broadcasting the whole story—including everything the victim said to the reporter? What would the victim's rights be here, if any? This scenario suggests the difficulty of determining whether defamation of character has taken place.

Personal Anecdotes

Illustrating a concept with *personal anecdotes* (brief stories) can help you further build credibility and reassure your listeners that you're not judging them. Adam, a sophomore in a speech class, used the following personal anecdote in a speech about phobias:

> Phobias come in many different forms—and most, if not all, can be cured with therapy and/or medication. I know this because I've lived with one of these myself. Although you would not know it to look at me today, I once had a horrible fear of flying. Just the thought of getting near a big jet used to give me the shakes. Sweaty palms. The works. It was a real problem. But a half year of therapy—which included taking some flights with someone I really trusted—cured me of the fear.

Adam illustrated one type of phobia in a way that gave him credibility (he spoke from experience). His personal anecdote also helped him demonstrate that he took his subject seriously. And it enabled him to avoid offending audience members who may have struggled with similar fears.

You can achieve similar effects with anecdotes about events that your listeners may have experienced personally. In a speech on credit card debt, a freshman student named Jackie sought common ground through the following anecdote:

> You really have to be careful about these credit cards. You get on somebody's mailing list right after you're out of high school and starting college. Suddenly your mailbox is filled with offers of free credit cards. And they don't have a service charge for the first three months. You can get credit up to five thousand dollars. Just a minimum payment each month. Hasn't that happened to most of you in this room? It happened to me, too. And we all know how fast that credit card debt can pile up!

Vivid Language

Vivid language grabs the attention of your audience with words and phrases that appeal to all the senses—touch, hearing, taste, smell, and sight. The following examples from an autobiographical presentation illustrate the difference between ordinary and vivid word choice. In the first example, Jamie describes his childhood years with his family in relatively uninspiring language:

> I remember those mornings at home only too well. Mom would call us if we overslept. She was downstairs making breakfast, every morning at eight o'clock sharp. My brothers and I would fight to be the first into the bathroom.

Now consider this more vivid version of Jamie's story:

> Mornings were memorable in my house. It was always cold in the room I shared with my brothers. With no curtains on

...the place was thick with the smell of pretzels, stale nachos, and hockey pads that had not been washed for three years.

The back-and-forth tug-of-war between both our teams eventually had an effect on the home crowd. In the closing seconds, they grew quiet — very uncharacteristic for hockey fans. It was so quiet in the place that you could hear the still-sharp blades on our skates as they scraped the worn ice.

Just like you could hear the grunting of the players as they floated and then scrambled inevitably toward the home net. And then there was a loud whack, which came just before the buzzer, and we held our breath as the puck sailed through space and whispered into the net.

our windows, light would stream in, poking us in the eyes before Mom ever called us down for breakfast. The smell of bacon wafting upstairs did the rest. Routinely we shoved one another, forming a line outside the bathroom, knowing Mom would demand to know if we had washed up before coming to the table.

The second version conveys the same basic information as the first. However, it paints a more graphic picture of the scene, with stronger **imagery**—mental impressions—for the audience. We can *see* the bright light. We can also smell the bacon and hear Mom's voice.

To use vivid language, select descriptive words that evoke pictures, smells, textures, sounds, and flavors in your listeners' minds. But use such language sparingly. If you overuse it, it may lose its effect.

Figurative Language: Similes and Metaphors

Similes and metaphors suggest similarities between objects that are not alike. **Similes** make explicit comparisons and contain the words *like* or *as*. Here are three examples (the similes appear in italics):

- His mind works *like an adding machine.*
- After bumping her head, she fell *like a tree.*
- The baby's crying was *as sweet as music* to his ears.

Metaphors make *implicit* comparisons. They suggest connections between objects that are not alike by identifying one object with the other. The comparisons, however, are not meant to be taken literally. Here are three examples:

- My willpower is *my shield against temptation.*
- Her life was *a journey along a path filled with obstacles.*
- Innovation is *the engine that drives our economy.*

Similes and metaphors can add color, vividness, and imagery to your speech. When you use these devices, be sure to use clear and consistent terms so that the images make sense. Mixed metaphors—such as "it's not rocket surgery" or "he nailed that one out of the park"—can conjure images that either don't make sense or are unintentionally funny. Further, overly complicated metaphors can become tiresome in a speech.

Likewise, avoid mixing comparisons—that is, using more than one metaphor or simile at a time. Otherwise, you might produce some unintentionally funny statements. Here's an example of a mixed metaphor:

> Outlawing the possession of marijuana paraphernalia was exactly the *bullet* the House of Representatives needed to *cook* the new drug bill and *drive* it over to the Senate.

When used properly, a metaphor or simile can help your audience understand one idea through its reference to another.[2] A metaphor can also help listeners experience a new idea "in terms that resonate with their past experience."[3]

CHOOSING RESPECTFUL AND UNBIASED LANGUAGE

When you use respectful language in your speeches—words, phrases, and expressions that are courteous and don't reflect bias against other cultures or individuals—you deliver far more effective presentations. Why? Your audience members remain open to your ideas and view you as trustworthy and fair. In this way, you gain immense personal credibility.

By contrast, using **biased language**—word choice that suggests prejudice or preconceptions about other people—erodes your credibility and distracts your audience from listening to your message. For these reasons, avoid language that suggests you're making judgments about your listeners' or someone else's race, ethnicity, gender, sexuality, religion, or mental or physical ability. In the rest of this section, we present ideas for keeping biased language out of your speech.

Avoid Stereotypes

Stereotypes are generalizations based on the false assumption that characteristics displayed by some members of a group are shared by all members of that group. Stereotypes are often based on ethnicity, race, gender, religious beliefs, or sexual orientation. But stereotypes can also be based on a person's economic background, what schools they attended, what region they come from, even things as seemingly innocuous as musical taste or appearance. Stereotypes, especially negative ones, are a form of biased language that put a speaker's credibility at risk.

Stereotyping can come into play when speakers make claims beyond the facts that their evidence proves—by generalizing about their topic. Suppose a presenter offers only a few examples of persons who received jobs through affirmative action policies but who didn't have the skills or experience required for those jobs. The speaker argues that those few examples prove that everyone who benefits from affirmative action is unqualified. The speaker would be making a claim without proof and thus perpetuating a stereotype.

Take special care to use arguments that avoid stereotypes when discussing topics that are loaded with potential for controversy. For example, if you wanted to argue against affirmative action, you could claim that race or gender should play no role in any hiring decisions. Or you could advocate stronger remedies for reducing discrimination in society, thereby acknowledging that discrimination does exist.

Use Gender-Neutral References

Experts in grammar openly advocated the use of the generic *he* as early as 1553,[4] and by 1850, this preference was legally supported (*he* was said to stand for *he* and *she*).[5] By the 1970s, however, modern linguists began questioning the generic use of masculine pronouns because they reinforced gender-based stereotypes.

Using gender-neutral references can be challenging at times. For instance, suppose you keep saying *he or she* in a speech about jobs that can be held by men and women—such as chief executive officer (CEO), nurse, or high school principal. Occasional use of *he or she* is fine, but frequent use could get tedious for your audience. How would *you* react if you heard a speaker say, "A good president keeps his or her meetings organized, listens to his or her employees, and puts his or her company's needs first"? Happily, there are ways to work around any awkwardness with pronouns. Using plurals where appropriate can help: "Good *presidents* keep *their* meetings organized, listen to *their* employees, and put *their* company's needs first." Or, if a singular pronoun is appropriate in your speech, alternate the use of *she* and *he* from paragraph to paragraph or from example to example.

Also avoid gender-specific nouns or noun phrases, such as *poetess*, *chairman*, *congressman*, *cleaning lady*, and *fireman*. Instead, look for **gender-neutral terms**—words that do not suggest a specific gender—such as *poet*, *chair*, *congressional representative*, *cleaner*, and *firefighter*.

Make Appropriate References to Ethnic Groups

To show respect for your audience, use the noun or phrase preferred by a particular ethnic group when you are referring to that group. For example, *African American* is commonly preferred to *black*.

Sometimes people from a group may use more than one name to refer to themselves—for example, *Latino/Latina* and *Chicano/Chicana* or referring to themselves from their country of origin. If you are uncertain about which term to use in such a case, ask friends or classmates who are members of that group which name they prefer.

When ethnicity is relevant to your audience, be sure to refer to ethnic groups correctly. Not all people from Laos are Hmong. A visiting professor from Nigeria is not African American. And people from Puerto Rico or Spain are not Mexican Americans. Moreover, when a word comes from a language that uses different masculine and feminine forms, pay attention to those forms. For example, author Ana Castillo is a Chicana, not a Chicano. Attentiveness to such distinctions during a speech will pay big dividends in the form of appreciation from your listeners.

Steer Clear of Unnecessary References to Ethnicity, Religion, Gender, or Sexuality

When a person's ethnicity, religion, gender, or sexuality is not relevant to a point you are making, there's no need to mention it in

UNNECESSARY REFERENCE

Hank Greenberg, the Jewish first baseman, played on the Tigers from 1930 to 1946.

NEUTRAL REFERENCE

Hank Greenberg, the big-hitting first baseman, played on the Tigers from 1930 to 1946.

USEFUL REFERENCE

Hank Greenberg was a principled man who took his Judaism seriously. In 1934 he refused to play on Yom Kippur, even though the Tigers were fighting for the American League Pennant.

your speech. Including it can only hurt your credibility. For instance, if you say "the *Chinese American* judge," "the *Jewish* baseball player," "the *male* first-grade teacher," or "the *lesbian* CEO," listeners may believe that you find it odd for a judge to be Chinese American, a baseball player to be Jewish, a man to be a first-grade teacher, or a lesbian to run a company. On the other hand, in an informative speech about baseball great Jackie Robinson, you *would* probably want to refer to his African American heritage. Why? Robinson was subjected to many forms of racism and broke the "color barrier" when he joined the Brooklyn Dodgers in 1947. His enduring legacy stems just as much from his experiences as an African American as it does from his talent as a ballplayer. Thus, it would be appropriate and even necessary to acknowledge his race during your speech.

A Note on Appropriate Language and Political Correctness

The notions of "appropriate language" and "political correctness" have made it even more difficult for people to know how to avoid bias in their speeches. What do these terms mean exactly? The idea behind appropriate language is that words have tremendous power to influence the ways that people think of, feel about, and treat each other; thus, it is important to avoid—as often as possible—words that could cause harm or pain to others, especially in terms of a person's or a group's identity.

Some critics, on the other hand, argue that efforts to encourage the use of appropriate language often go too far. Rather than protecting certain vulnerable people from hurtful language, critics argue that these guidelines limit people's precious rights to freedom of expression by establishing strict rules of "political correctness"—written or unwritten codes of conduct requiring language that reflects a politically and socially liberal view.

The best way to avoid the debate over appropriate language and political correctness entirely is to simply support your position on an issue—no matter what it is—with credible evidence and logical reasoning. Otherwise, your listeners will likely perceive you as prejudiced. Saying something like, "We all know that the Americans with Disabilities Act puts an unfair burden on employers" would instantly reveal bias and a lack of thought about your topic. On the other hand, you could build a much stronger case on the difficulties some businesses might encounter in complying with the Americans with Disabilities Act by making careful word choices and offering solid and unbiased evidence, such as compelling examples, credible statistics, and solid expert testimony.

CHAPTER REVIEW

> "Choose your words carefully."

As Marvin's story early in this chapter revealed, your word choice can make or break the effectiveness of your speech. In this chapter, we explained how to use language specifically to clarify your message, captivate your audience, and enhance your credibility. Key practices include understanding the denotative and connotative meanings of words, and evoking those meanings strategically. We also offered ideas for presenting your message clearly—including using understandable language and concrete words, employing words properly, and adopting concise language. And we suggested that to infuse your speech with color and evocative imagery, you can use devices such as repetition, hypothetical examples, personal anecdotes, vivid language, and similes and metaphors. Finally, we addressed the importance of using unbiased language to show respect for your listeners. Suggestions on this front include avoiding stereotypes; using gender-neutral references; referring to ethnic groups properly; and avoiding references to ethnicity, religion, gender, or sexuality that are irrelevant to a point you're making.

Key Terms

word choice (diction) *356*
denotative meaning *362*
connotative meaning *363*
jargon *365*
concrete word *366*
abstract word *366*
verbal clutter *370*
hypothetical example *373*

vivid language *375*
imagery *377*
simile *377*
metaphor *377*
biased language *379*
stereotype *379*
gender-neutral term *380*

Review Questions

1. How does a speaker's choice of words affect his or her credibility?
2. Describe three ways in which oral language differs from written language.
3. Define *denotative meaning* and *connotative meaning*, and describe the differences between the two.
4. What four qualities ensure clear language?
5. Describe four tools you can use to express your ideas more effectively.
6. Explain four steps you can take to ensure that the language you use is unbiased and respectful.

Critical Thinking Questions

1. What role should audience analysis play in choosing language for a speech? How can a speaker choose words that an audience will understand and relate to without appearing to pander to the audience?
2. Is the dictionary your only tool for checking that you understand a word's meaning and have used (and pronounced) it properly? How else can you assess connotative meanings that might be associated with a particular word?

3. Can you think of an instance in which abstract words would be a more appropriate choice than concrete words? What kinds of speeches benefit from this kind of language?

4. What does the term *politically correct* mean to you? Are words like *fireman* and *cleaning lady* merely offensive to some people, or are they inaccurate? Are there any words that would offend you if they came up in a speech? Are there any politically correct terms that bother you? Why or why not?

Activities

1. Imagine that you are writing a speech on a type of new technology that's very familiar to you and your friends: Twitter, for example, or a popular cell phone app. Write a brief list of words that you think would come up in your speech. Would those same words be appropriate in a speech delivered to your grandparents? How would you change or explain the words on your list?

2. Open a dictionary at random and take a look at one particularly long entry. How many different meanings are listed for the word you found? How do the meanings vary? Can you think of any connotative meanings not listed in the dictionary?

3. Find a news article that references a relatively complicated study, a piece of legislation, or a reputable survey. Compare the news article with the original item (which you can usually find through a Web link or search). How different is the language presented in each? What choices has the newswriter made in deciphering the study, legislation, or survey for a more general audience?

Go to **bedfordstmartins.com/speakup**, where you'll find helpful study materials, videos, and speech-building tools.

13

DELIVERING YOUR SPEECH

"How you say something is often as important as what you say."

Hannah, a student in a political science class, just finished delivering an oral presentation of her essay advocating more fiscal conservatism in the federal government. An experienced writer, she had structured her speech clearly and concisely. In just eight minutes, she commented on a wide range of issues—including federal income taxes, entitlement programs, and the national debt. She had carefully outlined her speech and delivered it using a small stack of note cards. And she used several helpful visual aids, such as charts showing government spending on various social programs.

Though Hannah had worked hard to develop a well-organized speech, she received only a B— from her instructor on the presentation. When she asked why, her professor explained that while the content of the speech was excellent, her **delivery**—the combination of verbal and nonverbal communication skills used to present the speech—was less than ideal. The instructor explained that Hannah had spoken too fast and in a monotone, and she had fussed too much with her note cards. In addition, she had turned her back on her audience while pointing to and discussing her visual aids.

Hannah's experience reveals a major lesson for all public speakers: how you say something can be as important as what you say. Why is effective delivery so crucial in public speaking? It helps make your speech compelling and memorable. In an age when audience members may be easily distracted by their many responsibilities, even the most carefully researched and clearly organized talk may not be enough to hold their attention. Speakers today need every advantage they can get to capture—and keep—their listeners' interest. And skillful delivery can give

you that edge. Think about it: in your lifetime, you may have listened to dozens or even hundreds of speeches. Of these, how many did you find truly memorable? And what made them so outstanding? If you're like most people, you'll realize that the best speech you've ever heard not only contained valuable ideas but was also delivered in a way that held your attention and had you remembering the speech long after it was over.

In fact, delivery is what comes to mind for most people when they think about speechmaking. Though audience analysis, research, preparation, and practice all play vital roles in public speaking, it's how you deliver your speech that determines whether you find success with many audience members.

In this chapter, we discuss speech delivery—focusing on the various ways you can present a speech as well as the verbal and nonverbal skills you need to deliver a powerful, evocative, and exciting presentation.

SELECTING THE RIGHT MODE OF DELIVERY

Imagine yourself standing before an audience, preparing to make an address. How will you actually deliver your speech? Will you read from a manuscript? Recite from text that you've memorized? Speak extemporaneously from an outline?

In most classroom settings (as well as many settings outside of class), speaking extemporaneously from an outline will allow you to achieve the best possible results. This delivery mode enables you to adopt a natural, conversational style that audiences appreciate. Yet there are certain situations in which you may want to read from a manuscript or recite your speech word-for-word from memory. Below, we examine each of these three delivery modes in turn, starting with reading from a manuscript.

Reading from a Manuscript

In this delivery mode, you give your speech by reading directly from a **script**—a typed or handwritten document containing the entire text of your speech. As you read, you typically do not deviate from your script or ad-lib.

While most people using this delivery mode read from a printed script, it has become increasingly popular for speakers to use teleprompter devices when addressing large audiences. From the audience's perspective, teleprompters are clear, appearing as small glass screens around the speaker; from the speaker's perspective, however, they display lines of text, which advance in time with the speech. Having more than one teleprompter allows the speaker to appear to shift his or her gaze toward different parts of the audience while continuing to read the text from the prompter. While teleprompters might seem

READING FROM A MANUSCRIPT   MEMORIZING FROM A MANUSCRIPT   SPEAKING FROM AN OUTLINE

ubiquitous—they are used by news anchors, politicians, presenters at award ceremonies, and so on—the technology is not available in most public speaking situations. Thus, for the purposes of our discussion, reading from a script means reading from a printed or handwritten manuscript that the speaker holds in his or her hands.

ONLY SPECIFIC, FORMAL SITUATIONS CALL FOR MANUSCRIPT DELIVERY

Delivery from a script is appropriate in circumstances in which speakers (or speechwriters) need to choose their words very carefully. The word-for-word manuscript delivery ensures that listeners hear *exactly* what you want them to. For example, public speakers often use this mode of delivery in press conferences. Imagine a lawyer approaching the microphone to "make a statement" to the press about his client, a professional athlete accused of wrongdoing. The lawyer reads directly from a carefully prepared manuscript to ensure that his specific words are heard and reported in the news—no deviations and no surprises. By closely controlling his message, he stands a better chance of controlling what journalists say about him or his client—and therefore influencing public perceptions.

Still, reading from a script has its disadvantages. To begin with, the script itself becomes a prop—something you can hide behind as you read. And like other props, it can limit your eye contact with the audience.

In addition, when you read from a script, you tend to speak in more of a monotone rather than sounding as if you're conversing with your listeners. Some listeners may find the resulting impersonal quality dull, while others may even consider this mode condescending. Consider the words of one student: "To tell you the truth, I almost found it insulting. If all [the speaker] wanted to do was read to us, he could have just given us the notes and let us read them ourselves."

Memorizing from a Manuscript

To recite a speech memorized from a script, you learn your script word-for-word and deliver it without looking at any text, notes, or outline. You behave like an actor on the stage or the screen who memorizes dialogue and recites the words in a *performance*. When would you want to deliver a speech by memorizing from a script? Memorization is only advisable when you are called on to deliver a precise message, and you are already trained to memorize a great deal of text and deliver it flawlessly.

This delivery mode does offer some advantages over reading from a script. Specifically, there's no barrier between you and your audience, so you can maintain eye contact with listeners throughout your speech. This allows you to be more natural with gestures and in using visual aids. And like reading from a manuscript, you can control your word choice by precisely repeating what you've memorized; in

MEMORIZED DELIVERY CAN COME ACROSS AS SLICK... AND NOT IN A GOOD WAY

fact, memorization was a key feature of classical rhetorical training. In contemporary thought, however, it is no longer considered the best form of speech preparation and delivery in most situations.

Why? Because this mode of delivery also has distinct disadvantages. For one thing, memorized presentations often come across as slick and prepackaged—or "canned." Listeners may view the speech as a stale performance delivered the same way every time, regardless of the audience. As a result, they may take offense or lose interest.

Memorizing is also very challenging—especially with a long speech. In addition, people who speak from memory are typically wedded to their text; the presentation can grind to a halt if the speaker forgets so much as a single word or sentence.

Because this delivery mode's disadvantages outweigh its advantages, we recommend avoiding it unless you have a specific background in memorizing large bodies of text (as a trained actor, for example) *and* your speech situation requires it.

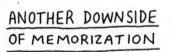

...but then, the most famous line, one of the most famous lines in all of Shakespeare's plays, comes when Brutus...er... I mean Mark Antony addresses the, er...
...citizens... in the, er...
Forum! He takes the pulpit and says: "Friends, Romans, countrymen, lend me your eyes..."
Aaagh! I mean <u>ears</u>! Sorry!

This leads me to my next point, which is... er.................
Um........Aaaagh! Well... er.....
....
.... Sorry!

ANOTHER DOWNSIDE OF MEMORIZATION

Speaking from an Outline

In this mode of delivery—the preferred mode in most speech situations—you deliver your speech by referring to a brief outline that you prepared in advance. Typically, you will initially want to prepare and practice with a full-sentence working outline. Next, like most speakers, you'll want to condense the working outline into a briefer speaking outline (complete with delivery cues) recorded on sheets of paper or note cards (for more information on outlines, see Chapter 11).

You should be able to glance at this brief outline and instantly remember what you want to say. And if you've made the note cards easy to read (for example, by using large print and spaces between lines), you can maintain eye contact with your audience.

Using this brief outline to deliver your speech will allow you to speak *extemporaneously*, meaning you will write the outline ahead of time, learn the material in the outline, and then speak spontaneously in the presentation with only the outline available for reference.

Speaking from an outline offers the best aspects of reading from a script and memorizing your speech while avoiding the disadvantages of those two other delivery modes. You can glance quickly at the outline just long enough to spur your memory, so there's no barrier between you and your audience, and your eye contact does not

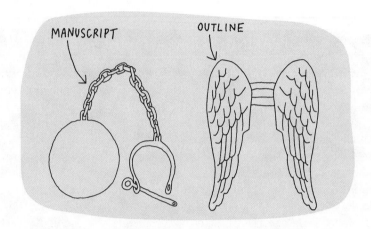

suffer. Also, you don't have to worry about forgetting your place, because the outline is at hand to remind you.

Equally important, when you speak from an outline, your delivery becomes more *conversational*. You sound as if you are talking with your listeners instead of reading a speech *at* them. Finally, with this delivery mode, you choose your words flexibly, as you do during a conversation. Thus, you can adapt your message as needed to the audience at hand. For instance, if you notice that a listener looks confused, you can provide further explanation for the point you're discussing.

Of course, speakers need to practice delivering from their outlines to give the best possible presentation. This practice is extremely beneficial in more than one way; research indicates that practice and preparation can lessen the anxiety that speakers feel when it is time to present.[1]

Impromptu Speaking

In different situations, you may be called to speak unexpectedly. **Impromptu delivery** means that you are generating your speech content in that moment, without time to prepare in advance. These kinds of speeches are both quite common and very challenging for inexperienced speakers. They occur with regularity in a variety of situations: you might be called on to speak at a meeting at the last minute, to comment in a class, or to offer a spur-of-the-moment toast at a wedding or party. You also use impromptu delivery while fielding unexpected questions after a presentation.

While such situations can seem terrifying for new speakers, it is possible to handle them effectively if you follow a few simple guidelines for impromptu delivery. The key is to remember that even in a spontaneous speaking situation, you can still speak from a mental outline that you draft quickly and keep in your mind, just as you would with a physical outline in an extemporaneous situation. (Or, if you have a few moments to collect yourself, you might try to jot down your main points.) You can pull together a mental outline by quickly asking yourself the following questions:

- *What is the question or topic?* Begin by thinking carefully about the precise nature of the question or topic you have been asked to address. In speech parlance, this is sometimes referred to as *thinking about the call of the question/topic.* Ask yourself, "What is the specific topic to speak about, or question to answer?" Be precise here.

- *What is my answer or view?* As you are developing a mental outline, consider what you think about the topic, or what you think the answer to the question is.

- *How do I support my position?* Consider what reasons support your view or your answer.

Your answers to these questions should quickly yield a precise thesis or topic statement, as well as a preview of the organization and body of the speech. This entire process can actually occur in just a matter of seconds.

Since this is an impromptu speech, people will not expect a carefully prepared introduction; thus, a direct one will suffice (for example, "I'm delighted to tell you what our division has been developing this year"). Your conclusion need only summarize your points and restate your position (for example, "So, that's what we've been working on this year; I hope you're all as excited about these new products as we are").

USING VOCAL DELIVERY SKILLS

To deliver a high-impact speech, you need to think about more than just your mode of delivery; you need to draw on a variety of speaking skills, both vocal and nonverbal. In this section, we examine the importance of **vocal delivery skills**—that is, the effective use of your voice when delivering a speech. Developing vocal delivery skills involves careful consideration of the use of volume, tone, rate of delivery, projection, articulation, pronunciation, and pausing.

VOCAL
DELIVERY
SKILLS

Volume

Volume refers to how loud or soft your voice is as you deliver a speech. Some speakers are not loud enough, while others are too loud. A guiding rule for volume: be loud enough so that everyone in your audience can hear you, but not so loud as to drive away the listeners positioned closest to you.

Most speakers' biggest challenge in terms of volume is speaking loudly enough. Since audience members don't have the option of "turning up the volume," you will need to provide that volume yourself when there is no microphone available. If you speak too softly and don't project enough, your listeners may have trouble hearing you, and they may even see you as timid or uncertain—which could damage your credibility.

Yet speaking too loudly presents a different set of problems. A student named Jason once gave an informative presentation in one of our classes. During his speech, many listeners in the front row began leaning back in their chairs. He was speaking so loudly that his listeners were trying to put some distance between themselves and him.

When you begin preparing your delivery, think about your volume level. How loud is your natural speaking voice? If you aren't certain, ask some friends or relatives to give you an assessment. Then consider your audience for the speech presentation—as well as your speaking forum. How will the size of the audience or the room affect you? Finally, focus on visual cues from your audience while you deliver your speech to help you determine whether your volume level is appropriate, and adjust your volume as needed.

Tone

The **tone** of your speaking voice derives from *pitch*—the highs and lows in your voice. If you can mix high and low tones and achieve some tonal variety, you'll add warmth and color to your vocal delivery. By contrast, if your tone never varies (called speaking in a *monotone*), listeners may perceive your presentation as bland, boring, or even annoying (in the case of a relentlessly high-pitched voice).

How much tonal variety should you aim for to make your voice interesting and enticing? Follow this guiding rule: use enough tonal variety to add warmth, intensity, and enthusiasm to your voice, but not so much variety that you sound like an adolescent whose voice is cracking. As you practice your speech, try dropping your pitch in some places and raising it in others. If you're not sure whether you're achieving enough tonal variety, practice in front of a trusted friend, family member, classmate, or colleague. Then solicit his or her feedback.

Additionally, consider using *inflection*—raising or lowering your pitch—to emphasize certain words or expressions. For instance, try a lower pitch to convey the seriousness of an idea or end on a higher pitch if you are posing a question. Like italics on a printed page, inflection draws attention to the words or expressions you want your audience to notice and remember.

Rate of Delivery

Your **rate of delivery** refers to how quickly or slowly you speak during a presentation. As with other vocal delivery skills, going to one extreme or another (in this case, speaking too quickly or too slowly) can hurt your delivery.

Consider the example of Lou, a student at Harvard University who had a very slow rate of delivery. While giving a talk during a seminar on music theory, he noticed that many of the students (as well as the teacher) seemed inattentive. He also became aware that those listeners who *were* paying attention began interrupting him—not with questions about the content of his speech but with queries about his next point. Clearly, they were trying to move him along, which probably meant they were irritated and distracted.

Do you fall into the "slow speaker" category? Do people tend to finish your sentences for you—during conversations or while you're delivering a public address? Although people who try to finish your statements may seem rude, their behavior sends an important signal that you need to step up your rate of delivery. Fail to catch that signal, and you risk losing your audience's interest and appreciation.

Of course, swinging to the other extreme—talking too fast—presents the opposite problem. Overly fast talkers tend to run their words together, particularly at the ends of sentences, preventing their audiences from keeping up with what they're saying. Listeners often have a difficult time following fast talkers not because they are disinterested or impatient but simply because they cannot comprehend what is being said. And in the worst-case scenario, potentially interested audience members can transform into defeated listeners in the face of a fast talker's verbal onslaught (see page 112).

The guiding rule for achieving an appropriate rate of delivery is this: speak fast enough to keep your presentation lively and interesting, but not so fast that you become inarticulate. You can also ask a friend or relative to listen to you and give you feedback about your rate of delivery. Finally, resist any temptation to speed up your delivery to fit an overly long speech into the allocated time. Instead, shorten the content of the presentation.

GOOD POSTURE AIDS PROPER PROJECTION

GOOD SPEAKING POSTURE   BAD SPEAKING POSTURE

Projection

Have you ever observed someone singing without a microphone and wondered how the person's voice managed to reach people near *and* far? What about actors on a stage who speak their lines quietly yet can still be heard by everyone in the theater? These individuals use **projection**—"booming" their voices across their speaking forums to reach all the members of their audiences.

To project, use the air you exhale from your lungs to carry the sound of your voice across the room or auditorium. Projection is all about the mechanics of breathing. To send your voice clearly across a large space, first maintain good posture: sit or stand up straight, with your shoulders back and your head at a neutral position (not too far forward or hanging back). Also, exhale from your diaphragm—that sheet of muscle just below your rib cage—to push your breath away from you.

Articulation

Articulation refers to the crispness or clarity of your spoken words. When you articulate, your vowels and consonants sound clear and distinct, and your listeners can distinguish your separate words as well as the syllables in your words. The result? Your audience can easily understand what you're saying.

Articulation problems are most common when nervousness increases a speaker's rate of delivery or when speakers are being inattentive. Whatever the cause of any articulation issues you may have, focus on this rule to get better results: when you deliver a speech, clearly and distinctly express all the parts of the words in your presentation. This advice applies to the vowels and consonants of your words as well as each syllable, and make sure not to round off the ends of words or lower your voice at the ends of sentences.

Pronunciation

Pronunciation refers to correctness in the way you say words. Are you saying them in a way that has been commonly agreed on? If you pronounce terms incorrectly, your listeners may have difficulty understanding you. Equally troublesome, they may question your credibility.

Elizabeth, a banking professional, related this story about the problems that can arise when a speaker mispronounces words:

> In my job I was required to work with lawyers, because they drew up the trust documents for their clients. I worked with

lawyers, but I was no lawyer myself. Sometimes they can be a little arrogant about their position, thinking that if you didn't go to law school, you shouldn't be working in a law-related field. I worked hard to earn their respect. But I noticed that when I used some legal terms or words with them, they occasionally would look at each other and smile. Like they were sharing a private joke. One such word was *testator*. That's the person who creates a testament like a trust or a will. Whenever I used that word, I always said "TES-tah-tore," so that it sounded like it would rhyme with "matador." And the lawyers would smirk—but nobody ever corrected me. Some time later I was embarrassed to learn that the word is pronounced "tes-TAY-ter."

It is especially important to take special care when pronouncing proper names. Taking the time to find out how to properly pronounce an unfamiliar name (be it that of a person or a place) will strengthen your credibility. On the other hand, mispronouncing such names can damage your credibility or even offend your audience. A student named Gabriel learned this lesson the hard way when he pronounced the last name of Supreme Court justice Sonia Sotomayor as "*SOTE-a-MAY-or*" (as in the mayor of a city) instead of "*So-to-my-ORE.*" Students in Gabriel's class concluded that Gabriel hadn't cared enough to pronounce Sotomayor's name correctly; several pointed out that he could have easily found out how to say it by watching news reports or asking one of his Spanish-speaking classmates.

How can you ensure that your pronunciation is accurate? The guideline here is simple: if you're not certain how to pronounce a word you want to use in your speech, find out how to say it *before* you deliver your presentation. For names of public figures (like Sotomayor), search for radio or television interviews with the subject to find out the preferred pronunciation. For other words, you can ask for guidance from your instructors, classmates, coworkers, or friends who might be familiar with the term. Better still, refer to a reputable dictionary, which will provide phonetic spellings for each word as well as a general guide to pronunciation. Many online dictionaries and other resources provide useful audio clips that demonstrate proper pronunciation.[2]

Pausing

Used skillfully, **pausing**—leaving gaps between words or sentences in a speech—affords you some significant advantages. Besides enabling you to collect your thoughts on a subject, it reinforces the seriousness of your subject because it shows that you're choosing your words carefully. Pausing can help you create a sense of importance as well. If you make a statement and then pause for the audience to weigh your words, your listeners may conclude that you've just said something especially important.

To get the most from pausing, use it judiciously—every so often rather than after every sentence. Otherwise, your listeners may wonder if you're having repeated difficulty collecting your thoughts, or they may think you're being melodramatic. In either case, your audience will begin to take you less seriously.

USING A SPACE TO MAKE A POINT

FILLING SPACE POINTLESSLY

When pausing during a speech, it's best to fill those pauses with silence rather than **verbal fillers** such as *you know* and *like* or **verbal tics** such as *um* and *ah*. Here's an example of what verbal fillers do to a speaker's delivery:

> *And so,* the library was closed . . . *you know.* But I had to study somewhere. *But . . .* I didn't get to study there, *and . . . but . . .* I had to go somewhere . . . *but . . . and . . .* I tried

the dorm reading room. *And, like* . . . it was so quiet there, *you know?*

And here's an example of what verbal tics sound like:

Um . . . the purpose of my speech is . . . *ah*, to . . . *um* make you see how . . . *um* . . . dangerous this action . . . *ah* . . . really is.

Everyone uses verbal fillers or tics at some point while giving speeches—it's hard *not* to. But using them too often can distract your listeners or make them wonder if you're tentative or ill-prepared. The best way to avoid overusing tics and fillers is by learning to be more aware of when you do use them. How? Try speaking in front of a friend who is holding a clicker or other low-level noisemaker; have your friend use the noisemaker every time you use a filler or tic. At first you may be surprised by how often you do so, but with some practice, you will develop better awareness and better habits.

USING NONVERBAL DELIVERY SKILLS

In addition to vocal delivery, you will need to consider your nonverbal behavior as part of the delivery of your speech. **Nonverbal delivery skills** involve the use of physical behaviors to deliver a speech. In this section, we discuss how specific elements of nonverbal delivery—eye contact, gestures, physical movement, proxemics, and personal appearance—can help you connect with your audience and leave a lasting impression.

NONVERBAL DELIVERY SKILLS

Eye Contact

To understand what **eye contact** is, you may find it helpful to think first about what it is not. Eye contact is not you looking at your audience members while they look at something else. Nor is it the

audience looking directly at you while you stare at your notes or nervously gaze at the ceiling for some divine guidance on what to say next. Rather, with true eye contact, you look directly into the eyes of your audience members, and they look directly into yours.

Eye contact enables you to gauge the audience's interest in your speech. By looking into your listeners' eyes, you can discern how they're feeling about the speech (fascinated? confused? upset?). Armed with these impressions, you can adapt your delivery if needed—for example, by providing a few more juicy details about a particular main point if you notice that your listeners look fascinated and hungry for more, or by reexplaining a key point if listeners look confused or overwhelmed.

Eye contact also helps you interact with your audience. For instance, by glancing at a particular listener, you may notice that he or she seems eager to ask a question, thus prompting you to stop and field queries from the audience.

Finally, eye contact helps you compel your audience's attention. Father Paul, a wise Episcopalian priest, once confided a secret of his effective sermonizing technique: "When I speak, I look right at my congregation. And when I do that, I make them look at me too. And it is harder not to listen to me when I do that . . . precisely because of that!"[3] When you and your audience establish eye contact, it becomes difficult for listeners to look away or mentally drift as you're talking.

From the audience's perspective, eye contact is critical for another reason entirely: in Western cultures, many people consider a willingness to make eye contact evidence of a speaker's credibility—especially truthfulness. An old saying holds that "the eyes are the windows of the soul," meaning that our eyes can betray who we really are or what we really think or believe. Of course, just because someone makes eye contact doesn't necessarily mean that he or she is telling the truth. Likewise, a speaker's failure to look directly at the audience may stem from causes other than dishonesty, such as nervousness or shyness. Still, as long as people *believe* that the eyes reveal the soul, they will associate a lack of eye contact with deception. To communicate honesty, expertise, and confidence, maintain frequent eye contact with your audience.

How you use eye contact depends on the size of your audience. With small audiences, try to establish and sustain direct eye contact with each listener at various points in your speech. With large audiences, this isn't practical. Therefore, you'll need to use a technique called **panning**. To pan your audience, think of your body as a tripod, and your head as a movie camera that sits atop the tripod. Imagine yourself "filming" everyone in the group by moving your "camera" slowly from one side of your audience to the other. With this technique, you gradually survey all audience members—pausing and establishing extended eye contact with an individual listener for a few moments before moving on to do the same with another listener.

Panning with extended eye contact gives your audience the sense that you're looking at each listener, even if you aren't. And it still enables you to gauge your audience members' interest, hold their attention, and interact with individual listeners if needed.

Gestures

Gestures—using hand movements to emphasize a point, pantomime, demonstrate, or call attention to something—can add flair to your speech delivery, especially when your gestures seem natural rather than overly practiced.[4] At the same time, be aware that gestures can also backfire. For one thing, not all your listeners will interpret the same gesture—a clenched fist, an open palm, a raised forefinger—in the same way.[5] For example, some people see a fist as a symbol for violence, while others consider it a show of forcefulness or determination. If an audience member interprets a particular gesture differently from what you intended, you may inadvertently send the wrong message to that person.

Another consideration is that gestures may communicate a message that is not consistent with your verbal speech message. Former President George H. W. Bush used the same gestures in nearly every presentation—often enough that creating a parody of his delivery style was easy work for comedians such as *Saturday Night Live*'s Dana Carvey. The gestures—alternating a jabbing fist with a thrusting open-palmed hand—may have proved effective during addresses calling for strength (for instance, a presentation urging Congress to "get tough" on crime). But when Bush wanted to communicate tenderness or sympathy—for instance, while expressing grief for the victims of a hurricane or when speaking lovingly of his family—the jabbing fist (which Bush perhaps used out of habit) sent the wrong message.

In addition to ensuring that your gestures reinforce your spoken message, avoid using distracting gestures born of nervousness—such as stuffing your hands in your pockets; jingling keys or change in your pockets; or fiddling with a watch, ring, or pen. These behaviors can distract audience members to the point that they'll start focusing more on your gestures than on your speech.

To get the most from gestures, follow these guidelines:

- Use gestures deliberately to emphasize or illustrate points in your speech.
- Remain aware that not all audience members may interpret your gestures in the same way.
- Make sure your gestures reinforce your spoken message.
- Avoid nervous, distracting gestures.

Physical Movement

Physical movement describes how much or how little you move around while delivering a speech. Not surprisingly, standing stock-still

MOVEMENT EMPHASIZES TRANSITIONS AND ENGAGES LISTENERS

X- - - - - - -
STAND
HERE
TO DELIVER
THE FIRST
POINT

X
STAND
HERE
TO GIVE
THE SECOND
POINT

X
MAKE
CONCLUSION
HERE

(sometimes referred to as the "tree trunk" approach) isn't very effective, nor is shifting or walking restlessly from side to side or back and forth ("pacing") in front of your audience. A motionless speaker comes across as boring or odd, while a restless one is distracting and annoying.

Instead of going to either of these extremes, strive to incorporate a reasonable amount and variety of physical movement as you give your presentation. Skillful use of physical movement injects energy into your delivery *and* signals transitions between parts of your speech. For example, when making an especially important point in your presentation, you can take a few steps to the left in front of your audience, then casually walk back to your original spot when you shift to the next major idea. One useful tip is to combine moderate movement with the panning approach to eye contact, discussed earlier in the chapter.

How much physical movement, if any, is right for you? Move as much as necessary to invigorate your speech (even if you must come out from behind a lectern or podium), but not so much that you confuse or distract your audience.

Finally, a brief note about speaking from a lectern or podium. Although the lectern might make you feel somewhat more comfortable, it usually acts as a barrier between you and your listeners. Thus, unless you must be at the lectern because of a microphone, we recommend that you come out from behind it at least part of the time, and thereby interact more fully with your audience. When you are at the lectern, be sure to avoid gripping the sides or top tightly with your hands; such a grip adds tension to your body and will be clearly visible to audience members.

AVOID STAYING ROOTED TO ONE SPOT

Proxemics

Proxemics—use of space and distance between yourself and your audience—is related to physical movement. Through proxemics, you control how closely you stand to your audience while delivering your speech.

The size and setup of the speech setting can help you determine how best to use proxemics. For example, in a large forum, you may want to come out from behind the podium and move closer to your audience, so that listeners can see and hear you more easily. Moving toward your audience can also help you communicate intimacy;[6] it suggests you're about to convey something personal, which many audience members will find compelling. Research has also shown that audiences perceive a strong association not only between closeness and intimacy but also between closeness and attraction,[7] and see closeness as an indication of the immediacy/nonimmediacy of the speech message.[8]

Of course, different people have different feelings about physical proximity. While some welcome a speaker's nearness, others consider

THE POETICS OF SPACE (A.K.A. PROXEMICS)

it a violation of their personal space or even a threat. Culture can also influence a person's response to a speaker's proximity. In some cultures, people consider physical closeness downright offensive or invasive.[9] In others, people consider it essential to positive relationships.

To determine how much space to put between you and your listeners, consider your audience's background, the size and setup of your forum, and your ability to move around the forum. When speaking, move close enough to your audience to interact with them and allow them to see and hear you, but not so close as to violate any listener's sense of private space.

Personal Appearance

By **personal appearance**, we refer to the impression you make on your audience through your clothing, jewelry, hairstyle, and grooming, and other elements influencing how you look.

Personal appearance in a public speech matters for two reasons. First, many people in your audience will form their initial impression of you *before* you even say anything—just by looking at you. Be sure that your appearance communicates the right message about you! Second, studies show that this initial impression based on appearance can be long lasting and very significant.[10] If you make a negative first impression because of a sloppy or an otherwise unappealing appearance, you'll need to expend a lot of time and effort to win back your audience's trust and rebuild your credibility.

The rule for personal appearance is to do what is appropriate for the audience you are addressing, given the occasion and the forum. If you're addressing a somber and formally dressed audience while eulogizing the life of a fallen friend, don't show up in brightly colored casual garb and loud jewelry. Likewise, if you're delivering a presentation to a potential client in an industry known for its relaxed and playful corporate culture, consider dressing down for the occasion rather than donning a blue pin-striped suit and power tie.

But in any speaking situation, you should always strive to look presentable through good grooming (tidy hair, nails, makeup, etc.) and an overall tidy appearance (avoiding holes in clothing, clothes that are inappropriately revealing, etc.). That way, you show respect for the audience, the situation, and yourself.

CHAPTER REVIEW

"How you say something is often as important as what you say."

As Hannah's story at the beginning of this chapter shows, how you deliver your speech and the verbal and nonverbal skills you use while making your presentation can spell the difference between success and failure. In this chapter, you learned the pros and cons of three modes of delivery—reading from a script, reciting from a memorized text, and speaking extemporaneously from an outline—and learned that extemporaneous delivery is preferred in most contemporary settings. You also discovered how to use many different elements of vocal delivery—voice volume, tone, rate of delivery, projection, articulation, pronunciation, and pausing—to create more impact in your speeches. And you learned how to use elements of nonverbal delivery—eye contact, gestures, physical movement, proxemics, and personal appearance—to further captivate and engage your audience. By using the right delivery mode as well as the right blend of verbal and nonverbal skills, you can get your message across to your listeners—and leave them wanting more.

Key Terms

delivery *387*
script *389*
impromptu delivery *394*
vocal delivery skills *396*
volume *397*
tone *398*
rate of delivery *399*
projection *401*
articulation *401*
pronunciation *402*

pausing *404*
verbal filler *405*
verbal tic *405*
nonverbal delivery skills *406*
eye contact *406*
panning *409*
gesture *410*
physical movement *412*
proxemics *414*
personal appearance *416*

Review Questions

1. Describe four different methods of speech delivery.
2. What are vocal delivery skills? Describe seven elements of vocal delivery discussed in the chapter.
3. Explain what is meant by nonverbal delivery. Describe five elements of nonverbal delivery discussed in the chapter.

Critical Thinking Questions

1. How can you make decisions about how to pronounce proper names that you've read but never heard? What about proper names that have more than one accepted pronunciation (Kirsten, Louis)?
2. What kinds of audience considerations should you take into account when making decisions about your nonverbal delivery? Can gender, culture, age, and other factors affect the way particular gestures are perceived?

3. Some actors are known for their unique vocal qualities (James Earl Jones, Kevin Spacey, Kathleen Turner, Holly Hunter, Christopher Walken, Scarlett Johansson). What makes these performers' voices so unique? What kinds of vocal delivery skills do they employ when they speak?

Activities

1. View a few political impersonations (Will Ferrell's George W. Bush, Fred Armisen's Barack Obama, Tina Fey's Sarah Palin, or Amy Poehler's Hillary Clinton) from *Saturday Night Live*. Does seeing particular delivery habits—Palin's winking, Obama's frequent use of the word *look*—exaggerated and lampooned change the way you perceive these politicians in real life?

2. Without practicing, make a brief recording of yourself explaining a simple and familiar task—for example, providing directions from your home to campus. Then make another recording of yourself describing a less concrete concept, such as the musical qualities of a favorite song. Take note of how often you use verbal fillers and verbal tics in each case. Do you think you would have used them as often if you had prepared an outline and rehearsed? Try it, and compare your results.

3. Check out a few stand-up comedy performances on YouTube or DVD. Take note of how the comics use nonverbal delivery skills—such as eye contact, panning techniques, and movement—to engage with their audiences. Which comics are most effective at using nonverbal delivery skills? Why?

Go to **bedfordstmartins.com/speakup**, where you'll find helpful study materials, videos, and speech-building tools.

USING PRESENTATION AIDS

14

Phil couldn't wait to deliver his speech about Harley-Davidson motorcycles to the rest of his public speaking class. The purpose of the speech was to inform his audience of the difference in quality between American-made motorcycles and machines made in Japan and Germany. A longtime Harley owner, Phil felt strongly that if his audience could actually *see* a Harley up close and *hear* the distinctive rumble of its engine, they would understand his point in a more visceral way. But how could he provide this experience without actually driving his Harley into the classroom?

Phil considered other possibilities, such as playing a recording of a Harley engine being revved up, showing enlarged photos of different Harley models, or playing some video footage he had taken from a recent motorcycle convention he had attended. He knew that any of these presentation aids would help him convey the unique character and quality of Harley-Davidson bikes. But to his mind, they still weren't as potent as showing his listeners an actual motorcycle. He decided to put some more thought into the situation and to talk with his wife, Claire, about it.

That evening, after listening to Phil's concerns, Claire had an idea about how she could help. She agreed to park the family Harley outside the classroom windows during Phil's talk. When the day of the speech arrived, Phil opened the window shades and invited his classmates to stand near him as he extolled the virtues of Harley motorcycles. Outside, Claire pointed to various parts of the bike as he mentioned them. Members of the audience had to shift their gaze from Phil in the classroom to Claire standing outside (looking a bit like Vanna White as she gestured and walked around the bike). But they saw enough to understand what he was saying, and they immediately grasped his passion for Harleys (not to mention his wife's love for him!). Through creative use of presentation aids—in this case, an actual bike and an assistant who focused his listeners' attention on various aspects of the machine—Phil was able to deliver an exceptionally engaging and interesting speech.

In this chapter, we take a close look at presentation aids, examining their advantages, the many different forms they can take, and strategies for using them effectively.

WHY USE PRESENTATION AIDS?

Speech communication experts have long believed that listeners are much more likely to grasp spoken facts and concepts if presenters also provide visual and other nonverbal cues.[1] Indeed, as early as the 1950s, studies showed that the use of audio and visual aids in a speech could increase learning by as much as 55 percent.[2] A **presentation aid** is anything beyond your spoken words that you employ to help the members of your audience understand and remember your presentation. Also known as *audiovisual aids*, presentation aids include all forms of presentational materials you might use to support and convey the points and subpoints in your speech.

Consider your own learning experiences over the years. For example, how did you come to understand difficult math concepts? Did your teacher expect you to know how to solve complex problems after merely lecturing you about algebra or geometry? Or did she *illustrate* the problems and concepts on the chalkboard—with plenty of examples? Most likely, you found the illustrations helpful—even essential—for grasping the concepts. Likewise, if you studied a language not native to you, did your teacher merely lecture you about the language in your native tongue? Or did he model the language for you, demonstrating correct pronunciation and accent and perhaps playing recordings of native speakers using the language? Again, you probably found the demonstrations and recordings crucial for mastering the basics of the new language.

Savvy use of presentation aids can gain you several important advantages as you deliver a speech.

Presentation Aids Can Make Your Speech More Interesting.

A colorful and attractive presentation aid can help you spice up any presentation, especially one on a slightly dry topic. For instance, a financial-services salesperson giving a talk on retirement savings

ADDING INTEREST WITH A VISUAL AID

displays a photo of an older couple looking relaxed, happy, and healthy. The salesperson could also provide graphs that show the makeup of sensible investments.

Presentation Aids Can Simplify a Complex Topic. If you are giving a speech on a technical or complicated topic, a presentation aid can help you simplify your message so that your listeners can better understand you. For example, a student giving a presentation on how to skydive shows a drawing of a simplified parachute, with labels highlighting each part of the equipment.

Presentation Aids Can Help Your Audience Remember Your Speech. Many individuals find visual information much easier to recall than spoken information. Thus, the right presentation aids can help you ensure that you leave a permanent impression on your listeners. For example, a speaker who had been sharing a lengthy list of reasons for changing the entrance requirements at a community college might hammer home his message by displaying a bulleted list of his main points at the end of his speech.

HELPING YOUR AUDIENCE REMEMBER YOUR SPEECH

TYPES OF PRESENTATION AIDS

A presentation aid can provide both audio and visual assistance simultaneously (as in a video recording of an exotic bird singing), audio assistance only (such as a recording of a Harley-Davidson motorcycle engine), or visual assistance only (for example, a photograph of a person on a surfboard). Traditional aids include the speaker him- or herself, assistants, objects, drawings, photographs, charts and graphs, and overhead transparencies. Computer and information technology have opened the door to even more sophisticated video, audio, and slideware. Below, we take a closer look at each type of presentation aid.

The Speaker

You yourself can be an effective visual aid, particularly if your topic calls for an explanation of an action. Consider Zoya, a student who loved

YOU CAN BE YOUR OWN PRESENTATION AID

rock climbing and gave a presentation on the sport's basics. During her speech, she covered some of the most common climbing moves and provided tips for taking lessons and finding the best climbing spots for beginners. To illustrate what she was talking about, Zoya wore the clothes, special shoes, and equipment (such as a harness, belay device, and carabiners) that she used while climbing. Through her attire, she served as a visual aid.

In addition to wearing clothing or other apparel or equipment related to your topic, you can also be a visual aid by demonstrating or acting out an aspect of your speech topic. Shenille, a college sophomore in a speech class, prepared an informative presentation about three styles of African dance. She described them and then demonstrated each one by dancing briefly before the audience.

Assistants

If serving as a presentation aid yourself would complicate things too much or prevent you from interacting with your audience, consider asking someone else to reinforce points from your speech or to help you demonstrate. For example, in speeches about life-saving techniques and the use of CPR, lifeguards teaching new recruits often ask an assistant to role-play the victim of a drowning accident, concussion, heart attack, or stroke. The lifeguard then demonstrates techniques and procedures on the assistant while the class watches. As we saw earlier in the chapter, using an assistant can also help you surmount unique challenges in using presentation aids—such as how to show a motorcycle to a classroom of students.

Objects

Any object can be a visual aid. For example, in a speech about James Bond movies, one student presented a collection of posters depicting all the actors who ever played 007, from Sean Connery to Daniel Craig. And in a January 2010 speech, Apple's CEO, Steve Jobs, used the iPad—a multipurpose tablet combining laptop, iPhone, and iPod functionality—to unveil a new generation of products from his company. To make sure his audience members could see the iPad from a distance, Jobs projected the tablet's display onto a giant screen behind him. These images, along with digital slides touting the tablet's many uses, helped Jobs convey how iPad users could connect to the Internet, communicate via e-mail and chat, download and play video files, and display or alter photographs.[3]

TURTLES

Of course, Jobs was speaking to an immense audience and needed projection technology to make the iPad accessible to all his listeners. If you want to use a small object as a presentation aid in a speech to your classmates, you won't likely need the same technology. Instead, consider walking closer to the audience and holding the object up for them to see.

But what if you have the opposite challenge: your object is too large or unwieldy to present in its entirety to your listeners? This situation calls for equally creative problem-solving. Consider Alan, a student who once gave a speech about the "physics of bowling." He explained everything about bowling—including the science behind the holes drilled into the balls, the effect of the rotation and angle of the bowler's arm on the ball's momentum, and the ball's impact on the pins. Naturally, Alan couldn't bring an entire bowling alley into the classroom. So, he came up with an ingenious alternative. He showed his audience three bowling balls—all with different kinds of holes. Then he rolled each of the balls down a slanted table and into the hands of an assistant. As he rolled the balls, he pointed out to his audience how each ball's speed and path differed based on its design and his technique.

ABSTRACT ART

Visual Images

As the old saying goes, a picture is sometimes worth a thousand words. When you are giving a speech, it can save time and improve clarity to present a simple visual representation rather than try to describe something. If you are trying to explain the layout of a room, for example, a scale drawing will provide your audience with a clearer image than would a recitation of the room's dimensions. There are several types of visual aids that can help audiences get a clearer image of what exactly you are talking about.

Maps. A map is a visual representation of geography and can contain as much or as little information as you wish. In addition to the map itself, you can add highlighting or labels to make the map more useful to your audience. For example, if you're giving a talk on the architecture of a particular city, you could show a map with the most important buildings labeled. In a presentation about competing in the Ironman triathlon in Hawaii, a speaker could use a map to show the route traveled for the race.

Photographs and Drawings. Photographs can help you provide an exact depiction. For example, if you're giving a speech about the *Mona Lisa*, you could provide a photograph of the painting and use it to point out certain aspects of Leonardo da Vinci's technique. Drawings enable you to emphasize and de-emphasize certain details about your topic. For instance, in a speech about how mosquitoes spread malaria, you could provide a drawing of the insect that details its proboscis as the tool for spreading disease. As with maps, you can add labels or other types of highlighting to a photograph or drawing to focus your audience's attention on specific details.

Diagrams. If you are trying to explain how something works or describe its parts, a diagram can be helpful. A **diagram** is a drawing that details an object or action, as well as arrangements and relations among its parts. Diagrams can be drawn by hand or rendered on computers, and typically include labels and important information in addition to visual images. Coaches routinely diagram plays to convey strategy to their players; you might also use an annotated diagram to

PHOTO OF COMPETITOR

DIAGRAM OF COMPETITOR

provide instructions or point out different elements of something, such as a cyclist's equipment.

Graphs

A **graph** is a visual representation of the relationship between different numbers, measurements, or quantities. Graphs are especially helpful when you are presenting a great deal of statistical evidence. Some common types of graphs are line graphs, bar graphs, and pie charts.

LINE GRAPH

BAR GRAPH

Line Graphs. A **line graph** uses lines plotted on a pair of axes to show relationships between two elements. For example, you could use a line graph to show the various elevations of the Ironman race or how much profit a company made over a ten-year period.

Bar Graphs. A **bar graph** consists of parallel bars of varying height or length that compare several pieces of information. For instance, you could use a bar graph to compare the weight loss of three different triathletes in a series of races.

Pie Charts. A **pie chart** (also known as a *circle graph*) is used to show how percentages and proportions relate to one another and add up to a whole. A pie chart resembles a pie that has been divided up into slices, with each slice representing a percentage of the total sum.

PIE CHART

VERBAL CHART

For instance, you could use a pie chart to show the percentages of different types of foods in a doctor-recommended diet for triathletes or how much your town spent in a given year on various services, such as education or road repair.

Lists, Tables, and Other Text-Based Visuals

In some cases, presenting text graphically can help your audience organize and understand information. For example, you could use a bulleted list to highlight the key ideas or most important "takeaways" from your speech, such as the steps in last-minute race preparation for the Ironman competition or a list of the parts that make up a motorcycle engine. You might use a simple **verbal chart** to list or compare the pros and cons of a particular issue or item.

Texts and graphics can be combined to convey both information and action. A **flowchart** is a text-based visual that demonstrates the direction of information, processes, and ideas. You might, for example, use a flowchart to show the steps in preparing for the Ironman competition or the process that a bank uses to decide whether to lend money to a mortgage applicant. It is important to use text-based visuals sparingly; you do not want to present your speech outline as a visual aid.

Audio and Video

In many speech situations, it can be particularly useful to demonstrate an action that cannot easily be described in words or presented in a still image. In such cases, you may wish to incorporate audio selections or video clips into your presentation to vividly explain, demonstrate, or illustrate a key point. We'll discuss several means of sharing audio and video, as well as practical considerations for doing so, in the section on technology. But first, let's consider the circumstances in which this type of content is most useful.

Audio. Presenting sound recordings or effects can greatly enhance a presentation if used well. In a speech about a particular musician or composer, for example, it would make sense to play a recording of his or her work for the audience. Audio can also make abstract concepts easier to understand. For example, Monica is preparing a speech about the effects of loud music on hearing. Because "loud" is a relative term, Monica decides to play audio recordings of different sounds at different volumes (the engine of a compact car, a radio turned up all the way, a jet engine during takeoff). Though Monica can't subject her audience to a roar as loud as a real jet engine, she arranges the *relative* loudness of the sounds to demonstrate noise levels by decibel and to help her audience understand the nature of sound and how it is measured.

Video. When is a video useful to your presentation? In any situation in which a demonstration of the speech subject in action or motion would enhance the audience's understanding more than a simple photographic

FLOWCHART

representation or a verbal description. For example, a photograph depicting Olympic ice skater Apolo Ohno (equally famous for both his soul patch and his prowess in short-course speed skating) might be useful for identifying him as a skater and a celebrity, but a video showing his surge during a race would be more useful if the speech was about explaining racing techniques in speed skating.

Equally so, video may be a better choice for your presentation aid if a moving image can better capture the scene or setting. For example, a photograph of a redwood tree on fire might be useful in a speech about forest fires, but a video would be a better choice if the camera moved with and followed burning embers floating in the wind to demonstrate how quickly a fire can spread.

Not all video clips are useful. Video works best when it is clear, compelling, and easy to see. For example, Meg is a bird-watcher, and she wants to give a speech about a particular type of seabird that nests near her home. Showing a grainy, hand-shot video clip of the fast-moving bird in flight would probably not add much to her presentation, since it would not provide a clear image of the bird or a real sense of how it moves. However, a color illustration or photo of the bird, along with an audio clip of its call, would greatly enhance her presentation.

USING TECHNOLOGY WISELY

You've got your speech prepared, and you've pulled together a collection of visual and audio aids that will support your points in an interesting way. Now you need to decide just how to present them. Should you download all of your audio and video onto a laptop and create a digital slide show, complete with video clips and audio? Or will a simple flip chart and tape player do the job more effectively? In this section, we'll take a look at various means of incorporating presentation aids—both low- and high-tech—and examine the pros and cons of each.

Using Presentation Software

Presentation software programs (sometimes referred to as *slideware*) are computer programs that enable users to create, edit, and present information, usually in a slide-show format. You can use presentation software to create tables, charts, graphs, and illustrations. Digital cameras, cell phones, and MP3 players have further transformed the world of presentation aids by enabling you to capture, download, and share photos, audio, and video cheaply and easily. If you have access to a computer as well as a digital projector and audio speakers, these programs make it relatively easy to incorporate all of your aids into a digital slide show and present it to your audience. Such digital presentations have become extremely widespread on college campuses, in communities across the world, and especially in business settings. Many students choose to use these programs to create digital presentations; indeed, some instructors may require a digital presentation for a public speaking course.

The most commonly used presentation software is Microsoft PowerPoint, but other programs, such as Adobe Flash, Impress, OpenOffice.org, and Apple Keynote, are also available. The instructions for using these programs vary, and change with each new version (refer to your program's user guide for technical guidance). Along with the general guidelines for any presentation aid, there are certain guidelines that you should keep in mind when developing a digital slide-show presentation.

Use It to Unify a Mixed-Media Presentation. If you have many different types of aids (pictures, data graphs, lists, video, and audio), presenting them in a unified way helps keep the audience focused on your message. Digital slide shows allow you to incorporate a variety of presentation aids and present them in one consistent frame. It also makes it easy to print out all or parts of your slide show for your audience members to take home. Such handouts are especially useful in informational presentations.

Remember, Content Is King. Don't let your speech be eclipsed by technological bells and whistles. As with any presentation aid, it's important to use presentation software to share material that supports your points. A slick digital presentation that lacks substance might look good, but it is unlikely to impress your audience (or your instructor). Your speech should be sound enough to deliver without any aids at all.

Don't Let the Software Steal the Show. Presentation software should be used to assist you in delivering your speech—it shouldn't deliver your speech for you. Remember that *you* need to be the center of attention, not your slides. Help your listeners focus on you and your message: avoid reading from your slides, move around as you speak, maintain eye contact with listeners, and limit the amount of text in your slides. Use your slides to show material; use your speech to talk about the material you show.

Using Other Technology

While presentation software may seem ubiquitous, it is far from the only option you have for sharing your aids. Not every forum is equipped for digital presentations, and your choice of technology—analog or digital—may be dictated by forum or budget as much as by content or personal choice. Furthermore, in many cases, traditional presentation aids are more appropriate and make for more dynamic presentations than their digital counterparts. Printed photographs, marker boards, and flip charts make it possible for a speaker to interact with visual aids, keeping the audience focused on the speaker rather than just on the aid. If you want to share a basic visual as part of your speech, these simple options are often the best choice.

You have similar options when it comes to audio and video. Although in recent years it has become possible to integrate audio and video into presentations using computer software and a digital projector, it may often be more convenient or downright necessary to present audio and video using more traditional means— a television set and a videocassette recorder (VCR) or digital video disc (DVD).

When it comes to incorporating audio and visual aids into a presentation, some speeches benefit from a mixed approach. A student named Justine knew this when she gave an informative speech to her classmates on the history of jazz. During her presentation, she showed actual instruments—a tenor saxophone and an electronic keyboard—and demonstrated a few riffs on each. She later played a vintage LP recording of a rare Charlie Parker selection using a record player. Finally, she played a digital recording of saxophonist Sadao Watanabe from an MP3 player with speakers attached.

GUIDELINES FOR DEVELOPING PRESENTATION AIDS

Effectively developing your presentation aids—that is, figuring out exactly what aids to use and the appearance and organization of the aids—is crucial to reaping their potential benefits, from making your speech more interesting to simplifying your topic and helping your audience remember your speech. Even if you already have a general idea of what you want your aids to do—for example, show the audience paintings from Pablo Picasso's Blue Period, or help them remember the most important aspects of the job-interview process— you still have many factors to consider when developing your aids for maximum impact. As you develop your presentation aids, we recommend that you pay special attention to the speech forum, the audience demographics and their prior exposure, being sure your presentation aids support your points, keeping your aids simple, and rehearsing with your aids. Let's address each of these important factors in turn.

Consider the Forum

Consider the **forum** as you're mulling over which presentation aids to use. Where will the audience listen to your speech? Is the forum equipped to handle presentation aids? For example, are there outlets available for a laptop computer and computer projector, a slide projector, a television monitor, or a video/DVD player? If you want to visit a Web site during your presentation and show it to your audience, is wireless access available? If you plan to use printed visual aids, do you have access to poster boards, flip charts, marker boards, or chalkboards?

Consider Your Audience

Because presentation aids become part of the message you are sharing with listeners during your speech, your analysis of your audience should drive your selection of those aids. This also means that analysis of audience demographics and listeners' prior exposure can help you select appropriate aids. Ask yourself, "Of all the possible aids for this speech, which one or combination of several would work best with this audience?"

Demographics. Think about the *demographics* of your audience. Demographics—such as listeners' age, gender, and place of birth—can easily predetermine audience members' response to a particular audio or visual aid.

For example, a student named Anna is giving a presentation on costume design in film. The main point of her speech is that on screen, clothing plays an important role in defining a character. As she speaks, she clicks through images from films in which costume designers' carefully chosen contemporary clothing offered the films' audiences insights into characters' personalities and experiences. In presenting this speech to a class of traditional-aged college students, Anna might include images of Ellen Page in the film *Juno* (2007) or of Zach Galifianakis in *The Hangover* (2009). But what if Anna were presenting her speech to an audience consisting mainly of people in their forties and fifties? She might make the same points and present all the same evidence, but instead choose images of characters from earlier films, such as *Annie Hall* (1977) or *Do the Right Thing* (1989).

Prior Exposure. As noted in Chapter 5, **prior exposure** to certain elements of your speech may positively or negatively influence your audience's response to those elements. This can be true of presentation aids as well. Consider Crystal, a student who gave a persuasive speech opposing abortion. She knew from interviews that many of her listeners identified themselves as pro-choice. Therefore, she avoided using graphic photos or images of abortion procedures, which these audience members had probably seen many times and would likely find offensive. Instead, Crystal chose other visual aids to make her argument that all life has value. For example, she showed pictures of healthy infants and the children and young adults they grew up to be. While she may not have persuaded all her listeners to change their viewpoints on abortion, her speech nevertheless proved thought-provoking and held her audience's attention.

How can you determine whether your audience has had prior exposure to the presentation aids you're considering—and what that exposure implies? Ask the same kinds of questions we introduced in Chapter 5:

1. *"Has my audience seen or heard this aid before?"* If so, proceed to the next question.

2. *"What was the result of this prior exposure?"* Were listeners persuaded to take the action the speaker advocated? If not, proceed to the next question.

3. *"Why was the prior exposure ineffective?"* Ask yourself how you can avoid repeating the mistakes made by the previous presenter, who failed to persuade his or her audience through those particular aids.

Make Sure Your Aids Support Your Points

Is your point something that can be enhanced by specific images or sounds? For example, if you're giving a speech on a particular city's architecture, a map would strongly support your message. A recording of a song about that same city would be less relevant to your speech.

Keep Your Aids Simple and Clear

Consider the following suggestions for making your presentation aids simple and clear:

- *Keep your aids simple.* A presentation aid works best when your listeners can simply glance at it or hear it once and quickly grasp what you're trying to communicate. If they have to stare at it, see it more than once, or listen to it several times, the aid is too complex and detailed.

- *Test the size of visual aids.* Make sure each visual aid is large enough to be seen by everyone in your audience. Remember: the bigger your audience, and the farther they are from you and your visual aid, the larger the aid should be.

- *Create contrast.* On visual aids, contrast increases readability. To create contrast, place dark colors against a light background or light colors against a dark background. For example, on a poster, place dark text against a lighter background.

TEST LEGIBILITY

- *Test the legibility of visual aids.* Be sure to check whether all the numbers, letters, words, sentences, and graphics in your visual aids are legible—that is, easily distinguished at a distance. For instance, ask a classmate, friend, or roommate to view a poster or projected slide from a distance and tell you whether he or she can see everything on it. If not, continue refining your visual aid—for example, by stepping up font size and adding white space between elements.

- *Test the volume and clarity of audio aids.* Be certain that your audio aids will be loud enough *and* clear enough (that is, free of static or other "noise") for all your listeners to hear.

Rehearsing with Your Presentation Aids

We strongly advocate that you create your aids while developing your speech—and then practice using them as you rehearse your presentation. Don't put yourself in the risky position of needing to create aids on the fly while delivering your speech. At the same time, we suggest that you prepare for surprises—including power failures and technology glitches (frozen programs, system crashes, or a failed Internet connection). As many hapless public speakers have discovered, technology can fail just when you need it most. Imagine how you'd feel if, during a key point in your speech, you turned on your computer to project an important photo and the device didn't work. To avoid this scenario, always prepare a hard copy of any presentation aids you plan to present through computers or other technology or equipment. To further cover yourself, make sure you practice giving your speech without using the aids.

When delivering PowerPoint or other sorts of digital presentations, make sure to practice a number of times with your slides, just as you would with speech outlines. To guard against any surprises, check that your media will work with the computers in the speech setting before it's time to speak, and bring hard copies of your aids with you on the day of the presentation. When incorporating a DVD player or VCR into a presentation, keep in mind basic principles of using aids: make sure to practice with the aids, ideally in the room where you will be presenting and on the same equipment; consider taping power cables to the floor to avoid tripping over them during your speech; and make sure you have the video cued to the right scene before beginning your speech.

USING PRESENTATION AIDS DURING YOUR SPEECH

Skillful development of your audiovisual aids isn't enough to ensure a successful speech. You also need to use the aids correctly during your presentation. Otherwise, you risk making all-too-common mistakes— such as distracting your audience by leaving aids for display after you're finished with them, or losing eye contact with your listeners while discussing an aid. The following strategies can help you exert maximum impact with your presentation aids.

Make Sure Everyone Can See and Hear Your Aids

Position stereo speakers so that all your listeners can hear the audio recordings you're playing. Position a computer screen so that everyone can see it. Place a printed graph, chart, or picture prominently on the wall or flip chart, so that your entire audience can view it.

Control Audience Interaction with Your Aids

To avoid distracting your audience unnecessarily, do not show or play an aid until you are ready for listeners to see or hear it. Then, when you're finished presenting the aid, put it away or shut it off. This strategy keeps your audience's attention focused on you instead of your aids—and helps ensure that listeners don't miss important parts of your speech.

You can control audience interaction with your aids in several ways. For example, if you are using an audio recording, cue up the desired track ahead of time so that you can play it promptly when you're ready. Avoid playing a tape or CD as background music to your speech. If you plan to tape or pin a chart to the wall, do so in advance, but fold half of the display over the other half and tape or pin it down. That way, you'll block the audience's view until you are ready to refer to the chart in your speech. At that point, undo the tape or pin, and reveal the entire aid.

Use the same technique when displaying a series of images on successive sheets of a flip chart. Insert blank sheets between each sheet containing an image. When you finish with one image, flip the page so that all your audience sees is a blank page.

This technique also works well with overhead transparencies, slide shows, and computer images in a PowerPoint presentation. Remove each image after you've discussed it, leaving a blank screen, or turn the equipment off and refocus the audience on you.

What about handouts? To ensure that they're informative rather than distracting for listeners, issue clear instructions about how to use them. For example, pass handouts out facedown and tell the audience not to look at them until you say so. Explain that you don't want listeners to get ahead of you. Of course, there will always be somebody in the audience who ignores this instruction and takes a peek. To keep these individuals focused on your speech, watch your audience during your presentation. Look for listeners who are paging through the handouts. Then adjust your delivery by increasing your volume or moving closer to those audience members to draw their attention back to you.

Maintain Eye Contact

Many inexperienced speakers look at their visual aids during their presentation instead of maintaining eye contact with their audience. Of course, you need to glance at visual aids as you present them—especially if you're referring to something specific on an aid. But this should be *only* a glance—not a gaze.

Remember the Purpose of Your Aids

Treat your presentation aids as tools that supplement your speech—not the main vehicle for delivering your speech. Your presentation contains your message, and you are the messenger. If you forget this, you risk seeing your audience focus on your aids instead of you. For instance, many inexperienced salespeople rely too heavily on brochures and handouts during a presentation. They assume—mistakenly—that good marketing materials are all they need to sell a product or a service. But a brochure can't answer listeners' questions or interact spontaneously with them. Only a human being can connect with audiences in these crucial ways. The best speakers understand that presentation aids support a speech—not the other way around.

CHAPTER REVIEW

"Listening can lead to understanding; seeing can lead to believing."

In this chapter, you saw how the right selection and strategic use of presentation aids enhances your audience's interest, comprehension, and retention of your speech. Aids can take many forms, including the speaker him- or herself; assistants; objects; visual images such as maps, photographs and drawings, and diagrams; graphs; and text-based visuals. Newer technologies offer speakers many compelling presentation tools, including audio and video recordings and slideware. You can display presentation aids in a variety of ways—such as in printed form or through presentation software and other technology. To get the most impact from your aids, you need to develop them with your audience's needs in mind. Then use them judiciously during your presentation to support your points—not to deliver your message for you. A key point to remember is that presentation aids supplement your message, but they can never replace you; *you* are the messenger!

Key Terms

presentation aid *422*
diagram *430*
graph *431*
line graph *432*
bar graph *432*
pie chart *432*

verbal chart *433*
flowchart *434*
presentation software *437*
forum *441*
prior exposure *443*

Review Questions

1. What are three key reasons for using presentation aids in a speech?
2. Describe at least seven types of presentation aids you might use in a speech.

3. According to the chapter, when is presentation software most useful?
4. What factors should you consider while developing your presentation aids?
5. What four things does a speaker need to keep in mind when delivering a speech with presentation aids?

Critical Thinking Questions

1. Are all presentation aids visual aids? What other senses might a good presentation aid engage?
2. What advantages does presentation software offer over more traditional presentation aids? Why do so many software-assisted presentations go wrong?
3. How might a speech's rhetorical purpose influence the types of presentation aids you use? Do some types of speeches work better with presentation aids, and if so, which types of aids?
4. Are good presentation aids a product of innovation, research, or both? How does selecting or creating presentation aids fit into the overall development of your speech?

Activities

1. Imagine that you have been tasked with preparing a presentation on your college for prospective students at a local high school. What kinds of presentation aids might you use? Would you use the same aids at a high school in another state? Would you use the same aids for a group of parents? Why or why not?
2. Television commercials are by nature persuasive appeals created from video and audio elements. With this in mind, consider a few television commercials that you have found especially memorable. How do they use presentation video and audio elements, such as music and images, to grab your

attention? How do these aids relate to the commercials' main points? How could you apply lessons from these effective commercials to your own presentations?

3. Think of ways that you, as the speaker, are a visual aid. How can you tailor your nonverbal delivery—things like your posture or your appearance—to reinforce your main point?

Go to **bedfordstmartins.com/speakup**, where you'll find helpful study materials, videos, and speech-building tools.

INFORMATIVE SPEAKING

15

"Effective informative speakers share information in an accessible, understandable, and compelling manner."

Suppose you have a work-study job at the campus health center. Your school has determined that it is in the best interest of campus health for all students to have access to influenza inoculations this year, and has arranged for free shots to be administered to students on campus in the coming weeks. The center director has asked you to deliver a brief presentation at the student union to inform students about the program.

An informative presentation teaches the audience something and increases listeners' understanding, awareness, or sensitivity to your topic. Your speech might include information about the way the flu spreads, its symptoms, and the dangers it poses, particularly in people under the age of twenty-four[1]. It would be helpful to talk about simple measures students can take to prevent the spread of the flu, especially among students who live in dense campus housing but also those who commute from homes shared with young children or pregnant women. You should also present information about the vaccine itself: whether it is a live virus or a "dead" one, how it is administered (an injection versus an inhaler), and any potential side effects. Finally, you'd need to go over the logistics of your school's program: where and when the shots will be given, what kind of information students will need to provide the professionals administering it, and how to go about getting an appointment.

Your goal should be to provide all the information students will need to decide whether or not they want to get the shot, as well as how to go about getting it if they decide to do so. Though the presentation is primarily informative, it may also contain a bit of persuasive power. You are, after all, pressing what you believe to be an important health concern, and hoping that students, armed with good information, will opt to take advantage of the program.

In this chapter, we take a close look at informative speaking. First, we examine specific techniques for informing. Next, we consider the common types of informative speaking. Finally, we address how to develop an informative speech, including strategies for analyzing your audience and simplifying complex information in your presentation.

TECHNIQUES FOR INFORMING

Most informative speeches rely on one of the following techniques for conveying information: definition, explanation, description, demonstration, or narrative. While some topics may lend themselves best to one of these techniques, in truth you will most often use a blend of techniques in your informative presentation.

Definition

Through **definition**, you break something down by its parts and explain how they add up to identify the topic. In short, you explain the essence, meaning, purpose, or identity of something. That "something" could be

- an object—for example, "What is a lever?"
- a person or group—for instance, "Who are the Hutus?"
- an event—such as "What was the Diet of Worms?"

- a process—for instance, "What is bookkeeping?"
- an idea or concept—for example, "What is obscenity?"

As we discussed in Chapter 8, there are four different types of definitions. An example of each is shown in the following table, which demonstrates how you might use each of the four types to define the word *obscenity*.

TYPES OF DEFINITIONS

Type	Explanation	Example
Dictionary	The meaning of a term as it appears in a dictionary	*Merriam-Webster's Collegiate Dictionary*, Eleventh Edition, defines *obscenity* as "something that is obscene"—that is, "disgusting to the senses."
Expert	Comes from a person or an organization that is a credible source of information on your speech's topic	According to Chief Justice Burger of the U.S. Supreme Court in the 1973 case *Miller v. California*, obscenity is expression that appeals to a "prurient" (sick or unhealthy) interest in sex or sexual matters, in a "patently offensive way," and which, when taken as a whole, "lacks serious literary, artistic, political, or scientific value."
Etymological	Understanding a word or concept by tracing its roots in the same or other languages	The word *obscenity* may derive from the Latin word *obscaenus*, combining the prefix *ob* (meaning "to") and the word *caenum* (meaning "dirt," "filth," "mire," and "excrement").
Functional	Defining a concept by examining how it is applied or how it functions	In practice, American law recognizes obscenity as hard-core pornography (and ironically, not as violence, disease, or other social ills).

*JUSTICE POTTER STEWART, CONCURRING
OPINION ON *JACOBELLIS V. OHIO* (1964).

Explanation

Through **explanation**, you provide an analysis of something for purposes of clarity and specificity by tracing a line of reasoning or a series of causal connections between events. In this process of interpretation, you may also offer examples to illustrate the information you're sharing. For instance, you might use explanation to help your audience understand

- the most common causes of running injuries
- how a bill becomes a law in the U.S. Congress
- what events and decisions led up to the outbreak of World War II
- how the engine in a hybrid car works
- what stages a couple experiences as they form and maintain an intimate relationship
- how photosynthesis works

Explanation works well when you're giving a speech about a process (such as how photosynthesis works), tracing the emergence of an important event (such as World War II), or explaining how an interesting object works (such as a hybrid engine).

Description

When you use **description**, you use words to paint a mental picture for your listeners, so that they can close their eyes and imagine what you are saying. If you provide sufficient information and detail, your audience may be able to experience vividly what you describe, and through multiple senses. For example, you might decide to use description to help your audience understand

- what the aurora borealis looks like
- what it's like to march on Washington, D.C., for a cause you believe in
- what the people you see (every day) on public transportation look like
- how you felt when you got your driver's license
- what the call of a blackbird sounds like
- how your city would look if people stopped littering
- what it's like to attend the Burning Man festival in Nevada
- what it looks like when humpback whales breach
- what a freshly applied tattoo feels like

You can exert maximum impact through description by using vivid language, presentation aids, and details that evoke the senses of sight, sound, smell, touch, and taste. This can be especially effective if you use it as a subpoint to engage listeners' imaginations and place them in the middle of what you're describing.

Demonstration

You might choose to provide a **demonstration** of a topic if your goal is to teach your audience how a process or a set of guidelines works. Demonstrations often call for both physical modeling and verbal elements, as you lead the audience through the parts or steps of whatever you are demonstrating. Your audience learns by watching your modeling and listening to your words. Because physical modeling often requires the use of props and visual aids, be sure to practice using these aids before you give your speech. And since you'll be teaching your audience, you need to be confident that you know your topic thoroughly.

Demonstrations could be helpful for a wide range of informative speeches. For example, you might use a demonstration to show your listeners how to

- take apart and rebuild a computer
- care for a bonsai tree
- create paper origami sculptures
- start an eBay store
- milk a goat
- breakdance
- practice self-defense
- properly display and store an American flag

For some of these demonstrations, you could bring the needed props to your speech forum. For instance, to demonstrate how to fold an American flag, you could easily bring in a large flag and—with an assistant—show the proper way to fold it for storage in accordance with military custom.[2] You could also improvise, asking members of your audience about the flags they've seen in advertising, used as decoration in their dorm rooms, or printed on T-shirts and other clothing, before noting that such seemingly patriotic displays are actually violations of the U.S. Flag Code.[3]

Demonstration coupled with repetition of the speech message has proven especially effective as a learning and memory-enhancement tool. For example, an organization called *Per Scholas* provides job training for low-income individuals. This program has been spectacularly effective with helping to train computer-repair technicians who have little or no previous formal education. The practice of demonstrating the repair process and repeating the message has been key to the success of this program.[4]

Narrative

A **narrative** is a story. When you use a narrative in an informative speech, the story enables you to both share information and capture the audience's attention. The story itself can take the form of a personal remembrance, a humorous anecdote, or perhaps a serious account of an event that happened in someone else's life—all told in a way that informs the audience about your topic. Used skillfully, narratives can help "humanize" a speaker for listeners and thus enhance the speaker's credibility, or ethos.

When might you decide to use narrative in an informative speech? Anytime you want to get your point across in an engaging, memorable way. For example, you could use narrative to:

- *Open a speech on the drama and dangers of the Daytona 500.* A poignant introductory story about Dale Earnhardt (known as the Intimidator) and his death in 2001 from a crash could help win your listeners' attention and stir up their emotions right from the start.

- *Emphasize the importance of communication in sustaining intimate relationships.* An entertaining narrative about a misunderstanding that you and your romantic partner ultimately cleared up through skillful communication could help you get the point across in a lighthearted but meaningful way.

- *Help your listeners appreciate the need for careful preparation before a job interview.* A story about how your friend failed to research the dress code of a company he was interviewing with and showed up in overly casual attire could leave a lasting impression on your listeners.

- *Reveal the difficulty of making an appeal from prison.* A story that follows and tracks the appeal process undertaken by someone who was convicted of a crime, incarcerated, and later found innocent could raise audience awareness.

Using narrative effectively takes careful thought and preparation. You need to choose a story that supports your message, rather than just throwing in a narrative simply to entertain or captivate your audience. Thus, select stories—and the details that go into them—based on audience analysis. To illustrate, if you were giving a speech about the Daytona 500 to an audience composed of people who had little knowledge of the race, you might need to explain who Dale Earnhardt was and why he remains such an important figure to NASCAR fans.

Even if you know the elements of the narrative well, you may also want to research background information and specific details of the story and weave the information you find into the speech.

Finally, remember that telling a compelling story in a way that also informs and educates your audience is a bit of an art. You want to come across as casual and natural (rather than over-rehearsed) but also authoritative, which requires extensive preparation and practice. It's almost as if you have to carefully practice acting unrehearsed. In fact, using narrative in a speech can be a risky call, but if you can pull it off well, it offers you and your audience real rewards.

TYPES OF INFORMATIVE SPEECHES

Informative speeches seek to share information, explanations, or even ideas with an audience. Unlike persuasive speeches, which seek to make an argument and therefore confirm or alter an audience's beliefs or actions, informative speeches are meant to give audience members knowledge they might not have possessed before the speech. Informative speeches can be about a wide range of topics: specific objects, individuals or groups, events, processes, and ideas. In this section, we take a closer look at each of these types of informative speeches.

Objects

If you're giving an informative speech about an object, you have a virtually unlimited range of possibilities to choose from. The one thing all objects do have in common, though, is that they're not human. The following table shows just a small sampling of the much larger universe of possible objects your speech could address.

TYPES OF OBJECTS SUITABLE FOR AN INFORMATIVE SPEECH

Type	Examples
Mechanical/Technological	motorcycle blender cell phone weapons system
Natural	flowering plant river elephant planet
Cultural	painting building book gourmet dish
Personal	jacket credit card ice skate necklace

In giving an informative speech about a particular object, you could use a number of different techniques. For example, suppose you're preparing a presentation about the benefits of chocolate—which is a food and therefore an object. In this case, you could easily use description to inform your audience about chocolate. You might, for instance, describe the smooth, creamy texture and sumptuous flavor of a high-quality chocolate truffle and the feeling of well-being that can come from eating it.

But depending on the purpose of your speech, you can use one or more of the other techniques as well. For example, you could use

- *definition* to clarify what chocolate is and how it differs from other consumable products derived from cacao beans
- *explanation* to trace the process by which chocolate bars are made
- *demonstration* to show how you might bake a chocolate cake
- *narrative* to convey chocolate's popularity as a romantic gift

Finally, note that an informative speech about an object may also have elements of process in it—especially if that object has moving parts. For instance, to deliver a presentation on how a motorcycle operates, you might explain how the bike's fuel and transmission systems work together to create the process of acceleration.

Individuals or Groups

Giving an informative speech about an individual or a group offers an equally wide range of possibilities. People are consistently fascinated by others, as we can clearly see from the popularity of celebrity-focused magazines, reality television, and the booming trend of personal memoirs. Human subjects, then, can make for fascinating informative topic material because of extraordinary physical or emotional characteristics or compelling life stories. Groups, likewise, are collections of people with whom your audience can identify; these can include famous politicians in the same party or musical performers who capture tremendous amounts of attention. To illustrate, you could focus your talk on

- *a famous politician, entertainer, sports star, explorer, or artist.* For example, you might give a speech about Shirley Chisholm, the first African American woman elected to the U.S. Congress (in 1968) and a candidate for president in the 1972 Democratic primary, nearly four decades before Barack Obama or Hillary Clinton.

A FAMOUS POLITICIAN

AN UNSUNG HERO

- *an unsung hero*—a person or group who did something great but never won recognition for the accomplishment. For instance, you could tell your audience about a member of a small tribe in the forests of Burma who survived persecution by the ruling junta.

- *a tragic figure whose life provides a cautionary tale.* For example, you might discuss Heath Ledger's untimely death from a prescription drug overdose, just as he was beginning to mature into a superb actor.

A TRAGIC FIGURE

- *an influential political party, artistic movement, sports team, or musical group.* For instance, you might discuss the adversities and triumphs of the 1999 U.S. Women's Soccer Team, which won that year's World Cup Championship.

AN INFLUENTIAL
SPORTS TEAM

As with objects, you could easily use description to deliver your informative speech about an individual or a group. For example, if your speech focused on Hollywood director Kathryn Bigelow, you could describe her personal qualities as well as her approach to directing. You might also use narrative to tell a story about a defining experience in her life that led to her decision to become a filmmaker. Or you could use explanation to trace the events that led her to *The Hurt Locker*, the film for which she became the first woman to win an Academy Award for directing.

BIGELOW, Kathryn

BORN IN SAN CARLOS, CALIFORNIA (1951)

SHE IS A SAGITTARIUS

FILM DIRECTOR (HER FILM, *THE HURT LOCKER*, WON THE ACADEMY AWARD FOR BEST PICTURE)

THE FIRST WOMAN TO WIN THE ACADEMY AWARD FOR BEST DIRECTOR

SHE STUDIED PAINTING AT THE SAN FRANCISCO ART INSTITUTE AND FILM AT COLUMBIA UNIVERSITY, NEW YORK

SHE ONCE MODELED FOR A GAP AD

SHE WAS MARRIED TO FELLOW FILM DIRECTOR JAMES CAMERON FROM 1989 TO 1991

Remember that while you will never be able to describe all of a person's life experience in a single speech, you can use life events to make a larger point about a person's character—what kind of person he or she is. You could even support such claims by using narratives supplied by the person's family, friends, associates, and even critics or enemies.

A presentation on a person or group might effectively incorporate information about an object or a process as well. Consider a talk on renowned inventor Thomas Edison. To convey Edison's innovative spirit, you could discuss not only the life experiences that led to his great achievements but also several of his most famous inventions— objects such as the lightbulb and the phonograph. Or you could lay out the process by which he developed one of his best-known inventions, including how he resolved problems that surfaced while designing a particular invention.

Events

An event is a notable or exceptional occurrence, either from the present time or from some point in the past. Here are just a few examples of events on which you could focus an informative speech:

- the signing into law of the Twenty-sixth Amendment, which lowered the voting age to eighteen years
- the discovery of a new planet or species
- the outcome of a high-profile murder trial
- the publication of an important new book
- an underdog's surprising victory over the front-runner in a sporting event
- the emergence in the business world of a new and different kind of company
- the unearthing of new evidence suggesting the origins of humankind
- a wedding, funeral, or religious ritual in your family
- the Republican or Democratic National Convention
- the Banzai Pipeline Masters Surf Invitational

- a commemoration of a tomb of the unknown soldier
- your town's extraordinary Fourth of July celebration
- Fashion Week in New York City

How do you decide what event would make a good topic for an informative speech? Look for events that your audience will consider exciting, newsworthy, historically important, or interesting because they are unfamiliar or surprising.

In delivering an informative speech about an event, you could easily use narrative to tell the story of how the event unfolded. You could also use description to explain how the event affected a group of people. Or you could employ a blend of both narrative and description. For instance, suppose you were presenting a speech about the day you became an American citizen. You might begin with a narrative about your experience as an immigrant, including anecdotes about your travels from your home country and your family's struggle to establish

BLENDING NARRATIVE AND DESCRIPTION

itself in America. You might then detail the process of applying for citizenship. Finally, you might describe your naturalization ceremony and how it felt for you to take the citizenship pledge.

Processes

Imagine that you're filing a tax return, changing a tire, planting a vegetable garden, or giving a friend a haircut. Or maybe you're thinking about how two countries resolve a border dispute, how Major League Baseball owners and the players' union negotiate the baseball salary cap for each team, or how marriages are arranged in a particular culture.

Each of these is a process—a series of steps or stages that lead to a particular outcome. You can detect processes both at the level of something localized and simple, such as changing a tire, and at a much broader level, such as the ways in which changes in labor and immigration laws and trade policies affect the cost of automobiles (including those same tires!) in different countries and markets. Thus, we sometimes suggest that processes can be seen at both the micro level and the macro level (the view of a process from fifty feet or one from five thousand feet). Many of the informative presentations you may find in a speech class will lean toward the micro level, something easier to explain and grasp; but that shouldn't discourage you from trying a topic such as the ways in which global warming occurs. When presented as a process, even larger topics can still be digestible for most audiences.

Remember that some topics do not lend themselves well to a discussion of process, simply because of their sheer technical nature (for example, a speech about how changes in the tax code affect the concept of the alternative minimum tax). Does this mean you should avoid a technical topic? No; but it does mean that if you are selecting a topic because it *is* process oriented, focus on subject matter that is within your audience's level of understanding, and try to break down the topic into smaller parts before showing how those parts work together as part of a larger process.

When you deliver an informative speech about a process, you will probably want to walk your listeners through the steps that make up that process, explaining how those steps are carried out and in what order.

Depending on your goal, use a variety of techniques to inform your audience about a particular process. For example, if you want listeners to understand how a particular object is made or how it works, you might use explanation to clarify what each step is and how it leads to the creation of the object.

By contrast, if your goal is to teach audience members how to perform the process themselves, combine both explanation and demonstration—that is, verbally and physically model the steps of the process.

To illustrate, suppose you're giving a presentation on cake decorating. You'd probably want to explain what tools are needed, and what kinds of icings are appropriate for particular styles of decoration. You might also demonstrate by showing the actual techniques used to produce a certain decoration—for example, a basket-weave design—through enlarged photographs or a video. If you are in a relatively intimate environment, you might even ice a cake as part of your presentation.

In deciding which process to focus on in an informative speech, take care to avoid overused topics (such as how to make the perfect PB + J sandwich) and topics related to alcohol (such as how to make Jell-O shots or brew beer at home). Instead, think about processes that would be interesting and fresh for your listeners. Also, consider how you might discuss the impact of an important process. For instance, suppose you're informing your audience about how the baseball farm system works. In this case, you could add interest to the topic by using a narrative to convey how the process changes young players' lives by giving them a shot at the big leagues.

Ideas

An idea is a theory, a principle, a belief, or perhaps a value. Ideas are relatively abstract compared to other informative speech topics, such as an object, a person, or a process. For example, it's harder to describe the notion of "freedom of speech" than it is to explain what the aurora borealis looks like or how a motorcycle engine works. The idea of freedom of speech is more difficult to explain for two reasons: first, it's an idea and not a physical object or process; second, there are limits to freedom of speech—indeed, this concept has several subtleties that restrict its application in many situations (for example, it is illegal to incite certain kinds of violence or to threaten to kill another person).[5]

Some ideas are also loaded because people have difficulty agreeing on their meaning. Consider the notion of "terrorism." Its meaning seems obvious to many after the 9/11 attacks and their repercussions. But are all violent acts against civilians or noncombatants terrorism? Are nation-states guilty of terrorism when their troops accidentally kill civilians? Why do people say things like "One man's terrorism is another man's freedom fight?" Like freedom of expression, terrorism is a more complex and abstract notion than it may initially appear.

Here are some additional ideas that may constitute topics for an informative speech about an idea:

- family values
- fairness

IDEAS FOR SPEECHES ABOUT... IDEAS

- the economic impact of globalization
- Murphy's law ("if something can go wrong, it will")
- the disadvantages of technology
- "It's better to give than to receive."
- the separation of church and state
- free agency in professional sports

Because ideas are so abstract, it's important to select an idea carefully as you consider topics for an informative speech. Otherwise, you may fail to connect with your audience during your presentation. Be sure to consider your audience's interests and level of education while weighing potential ideas to discuss in your speech. For example, if you want to inform your listeners about the economic impact of globalization, think about how much your audience already knows about the topic. If their knowledge is scanty, you'll need to provide more background on globalization during your speech, or you may decide to select another topic with which your listeners are more familiar.

Also ask yourself whether your audience members have had prior exposure to the idea you want to discuss in your presentation. If they have—and did not find the idea compelling—you may want to consider selecting a different topic.

Finally, consider how you might make particularly abstract ideas more understandable to your listeners during your presentation. In a talk on the impact of globalization, for example, you could draw the following analogy: "Globalization is like agriculture. In agriculture, the more evenly you spread seeds across a large field, the more certain you can be that crops will grow in every corner of the field. Likewise, the more you allow commercial activity to flourish across many countries, the more you'll encourage economic well-being among the world's populations."

Most informative speeches about ideas require the use of definition or explanation, both of which enable you to clarify the meaning of the idea you're discussing and to examine its various ramifications. For instance, while the meaning of terrorism is hotly debated in academic and political circles, most people define it as some form of calculated violence (or the threat thereof) against civilians or noncombatants, all for the purpose of creating mass anxiety and panic while publicizing a political or social agenda.[6] An informative speech on terrorism might *begin* with that definition. But to further *clarify* the idea of terrorism for your audience, you could separate each part of the definition and explain it individually. For instance, to clarify what "publicizing a political or social agenda" means, you could offer several examples of groups who have committed violent acts and then used the resulting publicity to advance their causes.

DEVELOPING YOUR INFORMATIVE SPEECH

To develop an informative speech, you use the same strategies described in earlier chapters. Those strategies include analyzing your audience's background and needs, deciding which supporting materials to include, and determining how to organize the content of your talk. In this section, we focus on how to analyze your audience and how to select a technique that will help you organize your informative speech. Appropriate audience analysis and organization help ensure that you prepare a solid foundation and structure for your speech.

Analyzing Your Audience

As with any type of public presentation, audience analysis is essential for developing a successful informative speech. Yet analyzing your audience for an informative presentation raises unique challenges. Specifically, you'll want to focus on where and how your audience is situated for the informative presentation, your audience's specific demographics, and especially any common ground between you and your audience.

To analyze your audience, start by considering the characteristics of your speaking situation. If you are presenting an informative speech in class, note any requirements for the topic, format, and content of the presentation. If you're planning to deliver your speech outside of class, consider the occasion for your speech. Also note the forum (the setting where you will be speaking), the time of day intended for your presentation, the size of your audience, and the expected length of your speech.

Next, remember to examine audience **demographics**—particularly those most likely to influence your listeners' interest and disposition toward your topic. These may include political affiliation, group membership, occupation or academic major, race, ethnicity, gender, sexual orientation, socioeconomic status, age, religious affiliation, and family status—just to name a few.

Also look for common ground you might have with your audience—such as shared values, interests, and experiences. By noting common ground while developing an informative speech, you can incorporate strategies to strengthen your credibility, or ethos.

Selecting a Technique

Your audience analysis also informs your choice of technique—or organizational pattern—for delivering the informative speech. Which technique would *most* help you inform your audience about your topic: definition, explanation, description, demonstration, narrative, or a combination of these? Your choice of technique is crucial because it helps you decide how you'll develop and organize the main points and supporting materials in your presentation.

For example, suppose you were considering using demonstration to present your informative speech. In this case, you would want to ask yourself the following questions:

- *Forum*: "Where will the audience be situated—and will there be ample space for me to move around as I give my demonstration?"
- *Audience size*: "How many people will be in my audience—and will they all be able to see and hear my demonstration?"

You should also consider audience size and details of the speaking forum when planning presentation aids for your informative

SELECTING A TECHNIQUE TO INFORM

speech. If you anticipate a small audience and cramped space, a PowerPoint presentation may be unnecessary; showing objects or offering simple handouts might create a more intimate setting. In a bigger forum with a large audience, you may be best served by projecting PowerPoint slides onto a large screen—or even several large screens—combined with adequate amplification of your voice. When speaking in such situations, make sure you plan carefully where you will stand; you may want to stand in the center of the room, directly before the screen or screens, and control the audience's interaction with the presentation aids by making the screen go blank after each point is made.

Conversely, let's say you were considering using explanation or description to deliver your speech. In this case, you would focus more on demographics to analyze your audience. Look for anything in your listeners' backgrounds and characteristics that may make it difficult for them to understand the explanation or description you're planning to offer in your speech. For instance, if you're planning to describe a Hmong wedding ceremony and your listeners have no knowledge of Hmong culture, you'll need to provide more details in your description. Or if you're planning to explain the events leading up to the assassination of U.S. president John F. Kennedy and your listeners are too young to have lived through the event, you'll want to provide a fuller explanation than you would for an older audience. Of course, cultural background and age are not exhaustive examples of demographics. You'll need to consider other characteristics as well to develop an effective informative speech.

What if you're thinking about using narrative to present your speech? Common ground becomes particularly important in this case. To tell a story that will interest and move your listeners, it helps if you have had some of the same life experiences or share some of the same values. When you and your audience have common ground, listeners will find it easier to believe you and identify with the narrative you're presenting.

Focusing on Your Goal to Inform

When developing an informative speech, it's particularly important to remain focused on your rhetorical purpose—to inform—at every phase. If you know your subject well enough not to have to do research, be sure to establish your own credentials—noting, for example, "As someone who's played in poolrooms all over this state for more than two decades, I am fairly well schooled in the rules of the game." You should also bear in mind that it's your responsibility to remain objective; if you find yourself choosing evidence to support a particular point of view, you are going beyond informing. Remember that it's easier to remain objective on some subjects (such as knitting or explaining how an engine works), while others will invariably wander into more persuasive territory (defining terrorism or freedom of speech). We'll discuss persuasion further in Chapters 16 and 17.

ORGANIZING YOUR INFORMATIVE SPEECH

Organizational Pattern	Pattern Description	Example
Spatial	Describes or explains elements or events as they occur in space	A speech to explain the trajectory of a meteor that may come dangerously close to Earth
Temporal (Chronological)	Moves from the beginning to the end by referencing points in time	A speech that describes a negotiation process, breaking down each of the bargaining steps as they occur in time
Causal	Explains the roots of a phenomenon or process	A presentation that explains how plate tectonics causes earthquakes and tsunamis
Comparison	Presents major similarities and differences between two items	A speech that compares the global reach and power of the United States with that of ancient Rome
Criteria-Application	Presents the topic as a condition (or series of conditions) that must be met in order for a conclusion to follow	A speech to explain how U.S. troops might be withdrawn from Iraq if certain criteria or benchmarks are met
Narrative	The speech as story, with characters and plot	A speech to describe racism by relating a personal instance involving a hate crime directed at or witnessed by the speaker
Categorical (Topical)	Main points constitute separate topics, each of which supports the thesis	A presentation to explain running a marathon, breaking it down into separate categories for training, nutrition, technique and style, and mental preparation

CLARIFYING AND SIMPLIFYING YOUR MESSAGE

As you prepare your informative speech, focus on clarifying and simplifying your message as much as possible. You'll help your audience understand and thus retain your message.

Clarity is something you'll want to strive for in every informative speech, no matter what your topic is or who your listeners are. If you

UNCLEAR

CLEAR

present a message that's confusing or use words that have vague meanings, it will be hard to connect with your audience.

In addition to clarifying your message, your audience analysis will help you decide how much you should simplify your informative speech. For example, if listeners have little knowledge of your topic, and the topic is complex, simplicity will be vital. A student named Jean once gave an informative presentation on a complex, experimental genetic treatment doctors and research scientists could use to fight cancer. Her audience was made up of students in her speech class—few of whom had sufficient background to follow the technical details in her speech. Jean wisely simplified things by reducing "treatment" to "gene therapy." She then further simplified her topic by describing a simple three-step process for introducing genes into cells to prevent disease.

To clarify or simplify complex messages, consider the following techniques:

COMPLEX

SIMPLE

ANTS

BULLET ANT
(Paraponera clavata)

Move from General to Specific. Ask yourself, "At a minimum, what do I want my audience to take away from my speech? What basic message should the audience carry away?" Your answer can help you narrow down a general or broad topic to a specific, simpler one—as in Jean's speech on gene therapy.

Reduce the Quantity of Information You Present. An informative speech may contain a tremendous amount of information for the audience to hear, process, and remember. An old adage still rings true here: "Less is more." Look for ways to pare down the details you present. Obviously, a speech about gene therapy could contain huge volumes of information. Jean effectively reduced the quantity of information she presented by boiling the details down to a three-step process.

Make Complex Information Seem Familiar. You can further clarify a complex message by using definition to explain difficult-to-follow terms and ideas. You can also avoid **jargon**—technical or insider terminology not easily understood by people outside a certain group or field. In addition, you can draw analogies between complex ideas and things your listeners are already familiar with and understand.[7] For example, Jean could have made an analogy between gene therapy (a new concept for her audience) and a vaccine against polio (something probably familiar to her audience).

Use Presentation Aids. Presentation aids can also help you clarify and simplify your message. For instance, a diagram of the three-step gene-therapy process Jean was describing could enable her listeners to better envision the process and thus remember it. Likewise, if you were giving a speech on various bird calls, you could play a recording of a particular call instead of relying only on lengthy descriptions or demonstrations of what the call sounds like.

Reiterate Your Message. Through *reiteration*, you clarify a complex message by referring to it several times, but with different words each time. For example, in an informative presentation about training for a triathlon, a speaker referred three times to the importance of using a heart-rate monitor. But each time, he used different words. For example, the first time he made the point, he said, "It's vital to use a heart-rate monitor to track your progress while you're training." The second time, he said, "Using a heart-rate monitor can really help you track your progress." The third time, he said, "The more you use the monitor, the more information you'll have on how you're progressing." By reiterating key points, you help your audience remember your message.

Repeat Your Message. Conveying a key point several times using the same words can also help ensure that your audience understands your message. For example, while introducing the gene-therapy process, Jean could say something like, "This three-step process offers the best hope for treating cancer in the future." Then, in the conclusion of her speech, she could say, "Let me repeat: this three-step process offers the best hope for treating cancer in the future."

SAMPLE INFORMATIVE SPEECH

SPIDER SILK: A MIRACLE MATERIAL DERIVED FROM . . . GOATS?

Rachel Parish
Southeastern Illinois College

Student Rachel Parish gave this informative speech in the 2007 finals of an annual national tournament hosted by Phi Rho Pi, a group that fosters public speaking and debate for junior and community college students throughout the United States. In this speech about an object, Rachel explains the astonishing strength and versatility of a material that may surprise her listeners—spider silk. Rachel's speech is organized categorically, or by topic, with the main points describing spider silk's properties, the means of producing it, and a number of its applications.

In the classic book *Charlotte's Web*, we find the story of a loving spider saving pitiful Wilbur from becoming bacon through messages spun in her webs. However, this is not the first time that such power has come from such a seemingly delicate medium.

In ancient Greece, spiderwebs were used to stop bleeding in open wounds. Aborigines use spider silk in small fishing lines. And how could we not mention Peter Parker's amazing ability to swing from buildings and catch the bad guys, all through the power of the web?

Now that last example may be fictional, but Spider-Man's formidable weapon, the web, is no less amazing in real life. Spider silk is one of the strongest fibers known; it is incredibly fine and tough, and as the November 9, 2006, *London Daily Mail* tells us, "When woven into a fiber, it is weight-for-weight five times stronger than steel." •

So we know that the spiderweb, or spider silk, is tough, and over the past decade we found it to have both practical and medicinal benefits for us. However, to date we've never actually seen any of the benefits. Why? Well, gathering large quantities of spider silk has been relatively impossible until now. You see, while we may not have a real-life Spider-Man, we do have Spider*goat*. This is a transgenic goat that's producing spider silk on a much larger scale than Charlotte ever could. •

Today, we'll learn the value of spider silk and how these scientifically altered goats are allowing its once unavailable advantages to become a reality. First, we'll look at the background of spider silk; second, the goat's role in production; and finally, its current and future uses. •

Let's first learn the value of spider silk and how these goats are allowing its once unobtainable potential to be a reality. According to BBCNews.com, July 12, 2006, "Spider silk has been admired by scientists for decades due to its unique combination of strength, toughness, flexibility, and light weight; its thickness is less than one-tenth the size of a human hair, but it has 400,000 pounds per square inch of strength." To put this in perspective, if you built a massive spiderweb where each strand was the width of a pencil, you could catch a 747 jumbo jet in full flight.

So if spider silk is indeed the strongest fiber on earth, why haven't we taken advantage of this miracle material before? The June 16, 2006, *Science and Technology* tells us that "spiders are incredibly hard to farm so silk can be harvested, mainly due to a spider's nature." • Basically, if you put two

---

• Rachel's attention-getter includes stories and compelling facts.

• "What's in it for them": a startling fact about goats plus the benefits of spider silk.

• Rachel quickly gives her thesis and previews her three main points, organized topically.

• Rachel establishes her sources' credibility here and throughout by citing publication title and date. She could add even more credibility by consistently including the author's name and credentials.

spiders together in a confined space, due to their cannibalistic nature, you'll suddenly find yourself with only one spider.

In addition, even when they are contained properly, you can only milk so much silk from a spider. A study this past November by Randy Lewis of the University of Wyoming showed that even when dealing with large spiders, on a good day you can only gather 1.5 mg of silk. Thus, even if you could get the cannibals to get along, a spider farm capable of raising enough useful silk would simply be impossible. •

However, all that has now changed. Last year, Nexia Biotechnologies—a Canadian research firm—began looking at normal farm goats as the key to bringing spider silk to the masses. According to Christopher Helman, in Forbes.com, February 19, 2001, Jeffrey Turner, a geneticist at Nexia, discovered that the silk gland of spiders and the milk gland of goats were almost identical, but the goat's is obviously much bigger. At the turn of the millennium, Nexia began implanting spider genes into goats in order to breed "spider goats" capable of producing spider silk in large enough quantities for commercial use. The end result was Webster and Pete, the first two goats born with the spiderweb gene.

So now that we've looked past the roadblocks to cultivating spider silk by showing the creation of a feasible silk resource thanks to Webster and Pete here, let's examine the process by which the spider gene was passed on to the goats. • According to the January 15, 2006, issue of the journal *Nature*, "Spider silk starts out as a substance called scleroprotein, which shoots out from the spider's web spinnerets. . . . [I]t dries into a thread, and when this thread hardens we end up with something that looks a little more familiar to us."

When Nexia discovered that the silk glands of spiders were similar to goats' mammary glands, Nexia applied this discovery to dairy goats. Taking a goat embryo, Nexia injected the spider gene controlling the creation of silk into the goat's mammary cells. These cells then took effect and activated the female goats when they started lactating, or creating milk for their young. When the lactation

• Here and throughout, Rachel offers a variety of supporting materials—mainly examples, expert testimony, and statistics.

• An effective transition signals the end of a previous point and introduces the next one.

period in the goat is over, these cells stop functioning and stop producing silk until the goat starts lactating again. According to *Materials Today*, December 2002, Jeffrey Turner reports that each transgenic goat is "capable of making 'literally miles' of this spider silk–based material." Fifteen thousand goats could produce enough silk to meet projected medical and industrial demands. Plus, because they're not cannibalistic, we're able to farm goats on a large scale. •

However, the spiders do have one advantage: the goats can't spin the silk they produce, so then there's a weaving process. As explained in the October 10, 2006, airing of *Modern Marvels* on the History Channel, "The goats are milked as they normally would be, then the milk is put into a centrifuge that spins rapidly. This causes the silk fibers to separate from the milk so they can be extracted. Salts are then added to the silk fibers to help them harden. Once this step is completed, you have what researchers have dubbed 'bio-steel.'" According to the June 3, 2006, *Journal of Biological Chemistry*, this new silk made from spider-enhanced goats is the same strength and composition as normal spider silk. The method is environmentally safe and the goats are not harmed in any way during the milking process. •

So we've examined the background of spider silk, its genetic switch to goats, and how it has evolved into bio-steel. But what benefits can we anticipate from this evolution? Will the use of goat silk bring us from the research lab to the battlefield and the operating room? •

Biotech Week, December 13, 2006, reports that bio-steel is now being used to construct bulletproof clothing for soldiers and police. Dr. Randolph Lewis, a biologist at the University of Wyoming, stated in the same issue of *Biotech Week* that Kevlar, the most popular fiber used in bulletproof vests, is very difficult to make and requires a chemical processing that is highly damaging to the environment. Unlike Kevlar, spider silk bio-steel is made in water-based conditions, and it's completely biodegradable. • In addition, in

Sidenotes:
- Rachel offers this explanation of a process within her larger topical organization.
- Rachel shows solid audience analysis by anticipating listener concerns: the process is environmentally safe and doesn't harm the goats.
- Questions act as a transition and keep listeners involved.
- Rachel returns to the theme of environmental safety.

tests performed in early 2006 at the University of Wyoming, it was proven that when woven into a bulletproof vest, spider silk was stronger and more durable than the now-outdated Kevlar.

Yet bio-steel's most promising benefits are medicinal rather than military. According to the Royal College of Surgeons of England, in "Secrets of the Spider Web," March 9, 2007, "the demand for spider silk in the medical profession is high with a myriad of potential uses such as scaffolds, bone grafts, or ligament repair." The real strength of bio-steel as an internal support is its great wall strength and its ability to naturally dissolve over time without the need of additional surgeries. In addition, the spider silk bio-steel can be used as wonderful, durable, and biodegradable stitches that can be used in the most delicate of areas due to the material's thinness and strength. What's more, as *Science*, June 23, 2006, reports, spider silk bio-steel provokes a very low immune response when introduced into the body. What does that mean for us? Well, heavy immune responses cause rejection of artificial medical implants, thus making bio-steel a much more successful option than any previous materials. •

• By outlining bio-steel's medical uses, Rachel again shows what's in it for listeners.

The main challenge for researchers is breeding enough goats to meet the demand for bio-steel. However, according to the October 31, 2006, *CBC News*, "If breeding continues as is, then the University of Wyoming's herd of goats alone will be bountiful enough to meet commercial demands by the end of 2008." In 2006 they produced over 5,200 pounds of spider silk, and just this past August the UW researchers received a quarter-million-dollar grant from the Department of Defense to expand their output, so the future of goat bio-steel looks very promising.

Today we looked at the background of spider silk, the goat's role in production, and finally its current and future applications. We can see the value of goat bio-steel for both military and medicinal uses, and in time perhaps we could imagine America's favorite web slinger changing from Peter Parker to Pete and Webster. •

• The conclusion brings the speech full circle with a reference to Spider-Man.

SAMPLE INFORMATIVE SPEECH

PRECISION-GUIDED TUMOR KILLERS

Elvia Anguiano
Moraine Valley College

Elvia's informative speech focuses on an experimental cancer treatment that may improve on current chemotherapy techniques. She uses a categorical (topical) pattern to explore the current methods and to describe the benefits, pitfalls, and possibilities for this new treatment. By praising the possible benefits of the technique while also exploring some potential drawbacks, Elvia informs her audience ethically by showing different sides of the topic.

Have you ever heard one of those parodies of medicine ads before? You know, one that goes something like: "If you suffer from back pain, then *BelieveAll* is the right medication for you. Before taking *BelieveAll*, ask your doctor. Some side effects include insomnia, kidney infections, heart attacks, infertility for men and women under thirty-five, uncontrollable flatulence, and spontaneous self-combustion." •

Parodies like these can be very funny, but real side effects are not. As many cancer patients will probably tell you, one of the scariest things about having cancer is the treatments themselves—because of their horrible side effects.

But it may no longer have to be this way. Today I'm here to tell you about an experimental new method of chemotherapy—precision-guided tumor killers, or PGTKs •—and the possibility of its eradicating tumors more effectively than traditional chemotherapy, without all the horrible side effects. •

So that you may all get an idea of the importance of this new method, keep the following estimates in mind: the National Cancer Institute's Web site, accessed September 30, 2006, estimated that in 2006 there would be more than 1.3 million new cases of cancer and over 500,000 deaths in the U.S. alone. Furthermore, an article in the March 23, 2007, *Chicago Tribune* noted that, as of right now, one in

• Humorous attention-getter will connect with many audience members.

• By using the acronym "PGTK," Elvia creates a memorable label. Since the label itself is a kind of jargon, she makes sure to explain this acronym a second time, later in the speech.

• Elvia offers a precise statement of her topic.

twenty people worldwide has cancer. By 2020, that number will be one in nineteen. Think of the hundreds of people you have seen today, all the people here that could now have cancer or one day have cancer. •

So that you may all better understand PGTKs, you need to learn a little bit more about traditional chemotherapy, what PGTKs are, how they work, and finally their future potential and current limitations. •

Today, chemotherapy is one of the most commonly used methods to fight cancer. To understand why its use has become so widespread, we need to learn what it is, how it works, and why it has such horrible side effects. To begin with, chemotherapy was first developed in the 1950s— as reported by the Web site of the American Cancer Society, accessed November 27, 2006—when some people were accidentally exposed to mustard gas in a government weaponry experiment and the exposure resulted in a lowered white cell count. This intrigued the scientists, who then injected mustard gas into cancer patients and were shocked at the remarkable improvements. This discovery led to the development of many other drugs that now treat cancer. Today, chemotherapy is a mixture of many of those drugs.

Now that we know what chemotherapy is, we will move on to how it works. • According to the American Cancer Society Web site, accessed September 30, 2006, chemotherapy may be administered into the body through three different methods: a pill, a shot, and through an IV. The chemotherapy then courses through the body, seeking any cells in the process of reproduction. It then poisons those cells so that when they try to reproduce, or split, they are unable to and therefore die off.

Although chemotherapy has been very effectively attacking cancer for the past sixty years, there is one major drawback: chemotherapy cannot tell the difference between actively reproducing cells of cancer and those of normal tissue. This is why so many chemotherapy recipients suffer

• Elvia offers statistics about cancer rates to show relevance to listeners.

• Elvia offers a preview of main points.

• Elvia offers a quick internal preview.

• An effective explanation of the chemotherapy process and its drawbacks.

• Analogy helps clarify a potentially complex idea— aptamers are like a car's GPS.

• Explanation of the process of the PGTKs' function highlights advantages as compared to the earlier explanation of traditional chemotherapy.

such horrible side effects, including fatigue, nausea and vomiting, pain, hair loss, blood clotting problems, and effects on vital organs. •

Now that we know a little bit more about traditional chemotherapy, we may move on to the new method: precision-guided tumor killers, or what I referred to earlier as PGTKs. These are hollow spheres that are one thousand times smaller than the size of a pinpoint. PGTKs are filled with small doses of chemotherapy and are studded with aptamers on the outside. According to Dr. Omid Farokhzad, aptamer researcher and assistant professor at Harvard Medical School, quoted in the August 2006 issue of *Popular Science*, "aptamers are like the GPS in your car. They allow the direct delivery of the PGTKs to cancer cells, leaving all normal cells in the body alone." •

PGTKs are designed to work in a very similar way to chemotherapy. The PGTKs are injected into the body. They then course through the blood searching for any cancer cell, using their GPS system. Once they find a cancer cell, they latch onto that cancer cell in a similar way to standard chemotherapy. After a while, the cancer cells absorb the PGTKs. Inside, the PGTKs open up and release the chemotherapy. Once poisoned, the cancer cells burst and die off. •

Having learned what the PGTKs are and how they are designed to work, we may now focus on why they may prove more effective and better tolerated than traditional chemotherapy. According to an April 10, 2006, issue of the *Proceedings of the National Academy of Sciences*, researchers compared these chemo-loaded nanoparticles to regular chemotherapy in mice with prostate cancer. They found that after a single injection of the PGTKs, complete tumor reduction was observed in five of seven mice with a survivability of 100 percent. In contrast, two of seven mice in the chemotherapy group had complete tumor reduction with survivability of only 57 percent.

Thus far, Dr. Farokhzad's research has been most effective in targeting prostate cancer cells. As he noted in an interview published in the November 10, 2005, issue of *Nano World News*, "we wanted to focus on a cancer model where a localized tumor has a localized way of being treated in clinical practice." And Dr. Farokhzad's research has been well received in the medical and scientific communities; in the last several years he and his colleagues have published numerous articles in leading peer-reviewed medical journals, including the July 2006 issue of the *American Journal of Drug Delivery*, the February 2007 issue of *Biomaterials*, and the October 2007 issue of *Nanomedicine*. •

• Citing several peer-reviewed sources helps support Elvia's credibility.

Expressing his high hopes for the future of PGTK therapy, Dr. Farokhzad noted in *Science Central News* on May 11, 2006, that "our system is both significantly more effective than traditional chemotherapy and remarkably less toxic, allowing the long list of chemotherapy side effects to shorten significantly, and allowing cancer patients to continue with their current lifestyles." Venture capitalists seem to agree. The November 27, 2007, issue of *Red Herring*, a business and technology magazine, reported that a biotechnology company called Bind-Biosciences, cofounded by Dr. Farokhzad, had raised approximately 16 million dollars in a second round of venture capital funding—all for the purpose of developing these nanoparticles further. The same article added that demand in the United States for nanotechnology-based medicines could grow to 39 billion dollars by 2011 and up to 82 billion dollars by 2016.

Having learned about PGTKs, it is time to look into the future potential and current limitations of this new system. Although the future uses for the PGTKs are focused mainly on treating cancer, they are not limited to it. Since the PGTKs really are hollow spheres, the medicine inside can vary. Also, researchers are working toward a system whereby the aptamers' target can be changed—just like the target on your GPS—expanding the use of the PGTKs to other diseases and procedures. For example, if you fill the PGTKs with small doses of Carbatrol and target the aptamers to nerve cells in the brain, you could treat epilepsy. Or, as reported on the National Cancer Institute's Web site, accessed October 1, 2006, if you fill the PGTKs with mercury and target a specific organ in the body, you could make CT scans and other imaging procedures much more accurate and the diagnoses of doctors much more accurate.

• Elvia acts as an ethical informative speaker by noting drawbacks of PGTKs.

Although the promise of PGTKs is extraordinary, there are some drawbacks. • As Professor Miqin Zhang—a material scientist at the University of Washington in Seattle—stated, one drawback is that the PGTKs must remain separate to do their job. If they should join together, they become toxic to healthy tissue. Another drawback that Professor Zhang mentions is that at different stages of development, cancer cells have different molecular makeup. So, the PGTKs could easily detect an early stage of cancer using their GPS system, but they may not be so successful at a later stage of cancer. Keeping these drawbacks in mind, scientists continue to do their research and their testing to confirm their findings.

• "Looking back . . ." indicates the start of the conclusion, followed by a summary of main points.

Looking back, we've learned a little bit more about traditional chemotherapy. We've learned about a new system known as PGTKs, their future potential, and current limitations. • Cancer patients suffer enough with the pain and fear of having cancer. They should not have to increase their pain and suffering because of treatments that are supposed to save their lives. Perhaps one day you or someone you know may have cancer, and in fact, you probably will know someone who does. Just remember that neither you nor they may have to suffer or die; should this treatment be perfected and approved, patients will gladly take it. The ads for these new medicines would not need to be parodied as yet another treatment with horrible side effects. Instead, this could be a case where the medicine is actually better than the side effects. •

• Clincher is a compelling hypothetical story that reconnects with the introduction.

SAMPLE INFORMATIVE SPEECH

ON THE BANK CRISIS
Franklin Delano Roosevelt

In recent years, our nation has faced a new banking crisis reminiscent of one from an earlier era in our history. Immediately after his inauguration in 1933, President Franklin D. Roosevelt (FDR) had closed down the nation's banks in an effort to stem the panics that had overtaken them. A week later, Roosevelt addressed the American public directly via radio in the first of what would come to be known as his "Fireside Chats." In this first "Fireside Chat," Roosevelt endeavors to explain the causes of the banking crisis and to explain the steps being taken by the federal government to stabilize the banks. Though the speech's primary goal is to inform, informative techniques also help Roosevelt accomplish persuasive goals such as restoring public confidence and convincing listeners to fully embrace the strategies for recovery laid out in the speech.

March 12, 1933

Address of President Roosevelt by radio, delivered from the President's Study in the White House at 10 P.M. today.

I want to talk for a few minutes with the people of the United States about banking—with the comparatively few who understand the mechanics of banking but more particularly with the overwhelming majority who use banks for the making of deposits and the drawing of checks. • I want to tell you what has been done in the last few days, why it was done, and what the next steps are going to be. I recognize that the many proclamations from State Capitols and from Washington, the legislation, the Treasury regulations, etc., couched for the most part in banking and legal terms should be explained for the benefit of the average citizen. I owe this in particular because of the fortitude and good temper with which everybody has accepted the inconvenience and hardships of the banking holiday. I know that when you understand what we in Washington have been about, I shall continue to have your cooperation as fully as I have had your sympathy and help during the past week.

• In this opening paragraph, FDR identifies his audience and clearly previews his speech.

• Understanding that his audience may not be experts in the ways that banks operate, FDR begins his speech in a way that clearly explains the complex realities of the banking business without condescending to his listeners.

First of all, let me state the simple fact that when you deposit money in a bank the bank does not put the money into a safe deposit vault. • It invests your money in many different forms of credit-bonds, commercial paper, mortgages, and many other kinds of loans. In other words, the bank puts your money to work to keep the wheels of industry and of agriculture turning around. A comparatively small part of the money you put into the bank is kept in currency—an amount which in normal times is wholly sufficient to cover the cash needs of the average citizen. In other words, the total amount of all the currency in the country is only a small fraction of the total deposits in all of the banks.

What, then, happened during the last few days of February and the first few days of March? Because of undermined confidence on the part of the public, there was a general rush by a large portion of our population to turn bank deposits into currency or gold—a rush so great that the soundest banks could not get enough currency to meet the demand. • The reason for this was that on the spur of the moment it was, of course, impossible to sell perfectly sound assets of a bank and convert them into cash except at panic prices far below their real value.

• FDR's audience is unable to rewind his message if they become lost or confused, so he reduces the details of the banking crisis down to a clear, simplified message.

By the afternoon of March 3, scarcely a bank in the country was open to do business. Proclamations temporarily closing them in whole or in part had been issued by the governors in almost all the states.

It was then that I issued the proclamation providing for the nation-wide bank holiday, and this was the first step in the government's reconstruction of our financial and economic fabric. The second step was the legislation promptly and patriotically passed by the Congress confirming my proclamation and broadening my powers so that it became possible in view of the requirement of time to entend [sic] the holiday and lift the ban of that holiday gradually. • This law also gave authority to develop a program of rehabilitation of our banking facilities. I want to tell our citizens in every part of the nation that the national Congress—Republicans and Democrats alike—showed

• Here, FDR is using chronological organization to assist his explanation of his administration's response to the crisis.

by this action a devotion to public welfare and a realization of the emergency and the necessity for speed that it is difficult to match in our history.

The third stage has been the series of regulations permitting the banks to continue their functions to take care of the distribution of food and household necessities and the payment of payrolls.

This bank holiday, while resulting in many cases in great inconvenience, is affording us the opportunity to supply the currency necessary to meet the situation. • No sound bank is a dollar worse off than it was when it closed its doors last Monday. Neither is any bank which may turn out not to be in a position for immediate opening. The new law allows the twelve Federal Reserve banks to issue additional currency on good assets and thus the banks that reopen will be able to meet every legitimate call. The new currency is being sent out by the Bureau of Engraving and Printing in large volume to every part of the country. It is sound currency because it is backed by actual, good assets.

• FDR gives a clear explanation of the strategies used to deal with the crisis.

A question you will ask is this—why are all the banks not to be reopened at the same time? • The answer is simple. Your government does not intend that the history of the past few years shall be repeated. We do not want and will not have another epidemic of bank failures.

• By anticipating questions the radio audience cannot ask, FDR addresses their concerns.

As a result we start tomorrow, Monday, with the opening of banks in the twelve Federal Reserve Bank cities—those banks which on first examination by the Treasury have already been found to be all right. • This will be followed on Tuesday by the resumption of all their functions by banks already found to be sound in cities where there are recognized clearinghouses. That means about two hundred fifty cities of the United States.

• Addressing the public's fear, FDR first provides concrete examples of the steps being taken to avoid another crisis.

On Wednesday and succeeding days, banks in smaller places all through the country will resume business, subject, of course, to the government's physical ability to complete its survey. • It is necessary that the reopening of banks be extended over a period in order to permit the banks to

• After providing several examples of exactly what will happen, FDR fully answers the question he posed above.

make applications for necessary loans, to obtain currency needed to meet their requirements, and to enable the government to make common sense checkups.

Let me make it clear to you that if your bank does not open the first day, you are by no means justified in believing that it will not open. A bank that opens on one of the subsequent days is in exactly the same status as the bank that opens tomorrow.

. . .

• FDR repeats the phrase "Let me make it clear," reinforcing the impact of his words as he dispels widespread fears about the banking crisis.

It is possible that when the banks resume, a very few people who have not recovered from their fear may again begin withdrawals. Let me make it clear that the banks will take care of all needs •—and it is my belief that hoarding during the past week has become an exceedingly unfashionable pastime. It needs no prophet to tell you that when the people find that they can get their money—that they can get it when they want it for all legitimate purposes—the phantom of fear will soon be laid. • People will again be glad to have their money where it will be safely taken care of and where they can use it conveniently at any time. I can assure you that it is safer to keep your money in a reopened bank than under the mattress.

• The phantom metaphor emphasizes that the fears causing bank runs are insubstantial and will soon be dispelled.

The success of our whole great national program depends, of course, upon the cooperation of the public—on its intelligent support and use of a reliable system.

One more point before I close. • There will be, of course, some banks unable to reopen without being reorganized. The new law allows the government to assist in making these reorganizations quickly and effectively and even allows the government to subscribe to at least a part of new capital which may be required.

• This signpost lets listeners know exactly where they are in the address.

I hope you can see from this elemental recital of what your government is doing that there is nothing complex, or radical, in the process. •

We had a bad banking situation. Some of our bankers had shown themselves either incompetent or dishonest in their handling of the people's funds. They had used the money entrusted to them in speculations and unwise loans.

• Here, FDR reiterates that what seems like a complex topic is actually easily explained and understood.

This was of course not true in the vast majority of our banks, but it was true in enough of them to shock the people for a time into a sense of insecurity and to put them into a frame of mind where they did not differentiate, but seemed to assume that the acts of a comparative few had tainted them all. It was the government's job to straighten out this situation and do it as quickly as possible—and the job is being performed.

. . .

After all, there is an element in the readjustment of our financial system more important than currency, more important than gold, and that is the confidence of the people. Confidence and courage are the essentials of success in carrying out our plan. You people must have faith; you must not be stampeded by rumors or guesses. Let us unite in banishing fear. We have provided the machinery to restore our financial system; it is up to you to support and make it work.

It is your problem no less than it is mine. Together we cannot fail. •

• A powerful clincher closes the speech and leaves the audience with a memorable takeaway—that it is up to them to ensure the success of the banking system.

CHAPTER REVIEW

"Effective informative speakers share information in an accessible, understandable, and compelling manner."

As the opening example about the speech on influenza vaccines suggested, informative speaking is about teaching your listeners something and increasing their awareness of your topic. You probably use informative speaking many times during a typical day—whenever you're defining, explaining, describing, demonstrating, or telling a story about something. Whether you're speaking informatively in everyday situations or delivering a formal presentation to a class or other type of audience, you can greatly enhance your effectiveness by applying the key practices presented in this chapter.

First, know how and when to use the five techniques for informative speaking: definition, explanation, description, demonstration, and narrative. Second, decide on the type of informative speech you want to give—whether it will be about an object, an individual or a group, an event, a process, or an idea. Third, use audience analysis to decide which technique you should use to organize your speech and how much to simplify your message. And fourth, stay focused on informing and maintaining an objective viewpoint.

When you apply these practices, you improve the odds of achieving your purpose in giving an informative speech. You enable your audience members to learn something new and important, and you hone their understanding, awareness, or sensitivity to your topic.

Key Terms

definition *458*
explanation *461*
description *462*
demonstration *463*

narrative *464*
demographics *479*
jargon *485*

Review Questions

1. Name and explain five techniques for informing.
2. What five types of subjects for informative speeches are offered in the chapter?
3. What basic steps must be considered as you develop your informative speech?
4. Offer six basic techniques that you can use to clarify and simplify your informative message.

Critical Thinking Questions

1. Are there any subjects on which you could give an informative speech without doing any research at all? How would you establish your credibility without outside evidence?

2. Have you ever felt that someone who claimed to be informing you was in fact pushing a personal agenda? What about the speaker's presentation tipped you off to a potential personal agenda? Did this feeling make you more or less receptive to the information he or she was presenting?

3. Is it possible to define and describe a complex idea, such as terrorism or freedom of speech, without becoming emotionally involved? Can an informative speech be emotional without becoming persuasive?

4. If you had to give a speech informing your classmates about influenza vaccines, what presentation aids would you use? Would a slide show be more beneficial than a handout? Why or why not?

Activities

1. Take a look at any persuasive speech (you can find some at the end of the next chapter or search at the library or online for any political campaign speech). Edit it down so that the focus of the speech is only on informing. How much of the speech is left?

2. Consider a subject on which you believe you are well informed (a sport you play, a television show you follow, or a hobby or skill that you have). Do you think you could prepare a fifteen-minute informative presentation on the subject without any research? Create a quick outline showing how you would do it.

3. Look up a "how-to" topic at the library or online (how to make compost, play blackjack, file your taxes). What kinds of sources do you find? Which ones do you find most helpful—and credible—and why?

Go to **bedfordstmartins.com/speakup**, where you'll find helpful study materials, videos, and speech-building tools.

PERSUASIVE SPEAKING

16

"Good persuaders make strategic choices in an ethical manner."

Jorge was excited: he had recently joined a fraternity at the university he attended, and he had an idea that he couldn't wait to share with the leadership council. His thought? To have the fraternity conduct a large fund-raising drive for an international hunger-relief program. Jorge had read an article in the newspaper about the program and considered it a very worthy cause. Moreover, when he was a child, his family had always supported such programs, and he knew how important such aid was to people in need. He felt certain that the fraternity would be interested in the project.

During a council meeting, he presented his idea to the fraternity's leaders, complete with statistics showing how aid programs help mitigate hunger throughout the world. He even provided a detailed breakdown of the work needed to conduct the fund-raiser. But to his surprise, he got a lukewarm response. Though the council members seemed somewhat interested during his presentation, they were noncommittal about dedicating the required resources to the project. And in the weeks following his speech, he didn't hear back from them; they just didn't seem to share his enthusiasm for the project.

Jorge didn't realize it, but he had made an error that's all too common among people seeking to persuade others to adopt their ideas: he had neglected to explain how his proposal would benefit his listeners—a key element in any persuasive speech. For example, during his presentation to the leadership council, Jorge could have pointed out that by conducting the fund-raising drive, the fraternity not only would help ease hunger, it would also enhance its reputation on campus and in the wider community. As a result, the fraternity would probably attract more members, solving a problem of declining membership that it had been experiencing in recent years. Because Jorge hadn't answered his listeners' question, "What's in it for us?" he failed to deliver that crucial bit of motivating power that makes a speech truly persuasive.

As Jorge discovered firsthand, knowing how to speak persuasively is a vital skill for all areas in life. Consider your own situation: Do you want to get a new policy adopted on campus? Advance in your career? Influence members of your community to support an important cause? Get your roommate to listen to the music you want to hear? Win a major contract for your company from a new customer? Get an extension on the deadline for a late paper? In these and many other cases, you'll need to master the art of speaking persuasively if you hope to generate the outcomes you want.

In this chapter, we introduce the topic of persuasive speaking. We start by explaining the nature of a persuasive speech. Then we show you how to select an appropriate thesis, main points, and supporting materials based on your audience analysis. We also consider the ethical obligations of a persuasive speaker and present several strategies for organizing a persuasive speech. In Chapter 17, we'll go into more detail about specific methods of persuasion.

THE NATURE OF A PERSUASIVE SPEECH

In a **persuasive speech**, you attempt to influence your audience members' beliefs, attitudes, or actions. To do so, you should consider three distinguishing characteristics of persuasive speeches.

Persuasive Speeches Attempt to Influence Audience Members

When giving a persuasive speech, your goal is to have an effect on audience members' beliefs, attitudes, or actions. You may attempt to strengthen or weaken audience members' commitment to a particular perspective on your issue or try to motivate them to take an active role regarding your topic.

Strengthen Audience Commitment. If audience members already agree with your perspective, you may try to *strengthen their commitment.* For instance, your classmates may already concur that there are not enough healthy food and drink options in campus vending machines. You could seek to convince them to take immediate action to address the problem.

Weaken Audience Commitment. If many members of the audience disagree with your perspective on an issue, you may attempt to *weaken their commitment to their viewpoint.* For example, suppose you support the removal of all fast-food outlets on campus. However, your survey reveals that most of your classmates like to eat at those establishments. Your speech is unlikely to succeed if you advocate a ban on campus fast food. Instead, you could try to weaken your audience's commitment to fast food; for example, you might attempt to persuade them that eating fast food less frequently has many benefits.

Advocate Audience Action. You may also seek to persuade audience members to *take a specific action.* Asking students to drink less caffeine, serve on the college's library improvement committee, or vote for an activity-fee increase would be examples of this type of

THREE GOALS OF PERSUASION

STRENGTHEN COMMITMENT

WEAKEN COMMITMENT

PROMOTE ACTION

speech. You might also advocate action in the community, such as volunteering to help assemble food bags for a local food bank.

Persuasive Speeches Advocate Fact, Value, or Policy Claims

In any persuasive speech, you will make one of three types of claims: a fact claim, a value claim, or a policy claim.

Fact claims assert that something is true or false. Factual claims that are debatable can make especially strong persuasive speech topics. For example, is human activity indeed the primary cause of climate change and global warming? Have charter schools improved student achievement in your state? Do first-person-shooter video games cause players to commit violent crimes? Because each of these questions is debatable, you could come up with an argument supporting either a "yes" or a "no" answer.

Value claims attach a judgment (such as good, bad, moral, or immoral) to a subject. Examples of persuasive speeches making these claims include "Physician-assisted suicide is immoral," "Full-body scanners are a justified intrusion on airline-passenger privacy," "It is better to cut funding for prisons than for higher education," and "It is unfair to deny marriage to same-sex couples."

Whereas many people can reach agreement on factual claims when presented with enough evidence, value claims are more challenging for persuaders to make. Audience members' ideas of right and wrong may be deeply held and stem from fundamental religious or philosophical beliefs—and thus be difficult to change. If you decide to make a value claim in a persuasive speech, select one that your audience is at least open to considering. For example, with enough evidence, you could probably convince your classmates that more rigorous graduation requirements would be good for the university. By contrast, you'd probably stand little chance of significantly changing their views on abortion.

Policy claims advocate action by organizations, institutions, or members of your audience. Examples include advocating that the government should increase Pell Grants to students or increase regulation of prescription drug abuse, or that your listeners should invest in stocks, eat more vegetables, or volunteer to assist at a homeless shelter.

Persuasive Speeches Use Strategic Discourse

To give an effective persuasive speech, you use **strategic discourse**—the process of selecting the arguments to support your thesis that will best achieve your rhetorical purpose in an ethical manner. Aristotle wrote that rhetoric involves "observing in any given case the available means of persuasion."[1] What he meant was that with any persuasive speech topic, there are many ideas that you might use to support your thesis. Your job is to make strategic choices—that is, to select ethical arguments that are *most* likely to persuade your particular listeners.

To make such selections wisely, audience analysis is essential. As we discussed in Chapter 5, you need to consider factors such as demographics, common ground, prior exposure, and especially audience disposition toward your topic. As you will see in the section that follows, when you know your audience well, you can tailor your message effectively.

NONSTRATEGIC DISCOURSE

THINGS I LIKE TO TALK ABOUT (EVEN IF NO ONE IS LISTENING):

* How wonderful it is that I am able to recite the entire script of an episode of *Star Trek* ("THE TROUBLE WITH TRIBBLES") from memory.

* If only TELEPORTATION was real.

* An introduction to the importance of VULCAN ANATOMY.

STRATEGIC DISCOURSE

THINGS THAT PEOPLE MIGHT ACTUALLY LISTEN TO ME TALKING ABOUT (BASED ON MY AUDIENCE ANALYSIS):

* Showing parallels between *Star Trek* and *Lost*.

* Convincing listeners to attend a *Star Trek* convention.

* Comparing *Star Trek's* "Prime Directive" with current U.S. foreign policy.

FRAMING YOUR ARGUMENT BASED ON AUDIENCE DISPOSITION

Your listeners' disposition—their attitude toward your topic—should affect your approach to persuading them. As we discussed in Chapter 5, your audience may be hostile, sympathetic, or neutral toward the topic of your speech, and you should adjust your thesis depending on which audience type you are addressing.

The starting point is determining where your audience stands on your issue. For example, suppose your goal is the adoption of an open parking policy on your campus. Under this policy, the best parking lots would no longer be reserved for faculty, staff, and administrators. Students and employees could park in the more convenient lots on a first-come-first-served basis. You might have the chance to advocate for your idea before several different audiences:

- a committee of faculty and administrators
- a student senate meeting
- a group of students who live on campus, most of whom do not own cars

Although you want to advocate open parking with each of these audiences, you wouldn't present the same speech to all three. Faculty and administrators may have a hostile disposition toward your idea because the current arrangement provides them with designated staff parking in prime locations. They might even believe that the current policy is fair, since they had to park in remote locations back when they were students. On the other hand, student senate members are

AUDIENCE DISPOSITION

THE LAND OF AUDIENCE DISPOSITION

likely to have a sympathetic disposition because they would probably appreciate open parking themselves and also need to take pro-student positions to get reelected. Finally, students who don't have a car may have a neutral disposition, given that parking policies do not directly affect them. They may support student rights in general, but they may not be motivated to invest much time and energy promoting open parking.

Once you know where your audience stands, you can tailor your thesis appropriately. Audience members have a **latitude of acceptance**, which is the range of positions on a given issue that are acceptable to them. Likewise, they also have a set of positions that are unacceptable, constituting their **latitude of rejection**.[2] Moreover, if your listeners are very concerned about the issue you'll be discussing in your speech, their latitude of acceptance will be narrower. If the issue is not very important to them, they will be open to a broader range of positions.[3]

Therefore, you're most likely to persuade your listeners to change their minds if the position you take on your speech topic falls within their latitude of acceptance and if they do not feel strongly about the issue under discussion. Conversely, you won't likely persuade audience members if your position falls within their latitude of rejection and if they have very strong viewpoints on your topic that differ from yours. Under these conditions, your speech may even produce a **boomerang effect**—pushing your listeners to oppose your idea even more vigorously than they already do.[4]

How does all this work in practice? Let's return to the example of your effort to promote open parking on campus. If you are addressing the faculty and administration (a hostile audience), a speech advocating a change to open parking is likely to fall within these listeners' latitude of rejection. Thus, it would be counterproductive to take that position in your speech. However, your audience analysis might reveal that these listeners would be willing to try the policy for a week or convert a single faculty lot to open parking. If these options fall within their latitude of acceptance, consider framing your thesis around one of them.

Conversely, when you address the student senate (a sympathetic audience), you can ask for much more. Their latitude of acceptance may include not only a vote in support of your proposal but also a willingness to give their time to your campaign. Thus, for this audience, you could select an ambitious thesis—such as asking student representatives to pass a resolution declaring their support *and* to meet with college administrators to promote your idea.

Finally, you would take still another approach for the students who do not drive to campus (a neutral audience). If you asked them to sign a petition advocating open parking, that would probably fall within their latitude of acceptance because they likely support benefits for students and because signing such a document requires little effort on their part. However, if you asked them to pass out flyers, this greater demand on their time might fall within their latitude of rejection.

TAILORING YOUR PERSUASIVE MESSAGE TO YOUR AUDIENCE

Once you have used your audience analysis to select an appropriate thesis, it's time to choose main points and subpoints that will fit your audience. In this section, we'll discuss some strategies for approaching this task and thus making your persuasive message more likely to succeed.

Appealing to Your Audience's Needs

Audience members have **needs**—objects they desire and feelings that must be satisfied. Human needs powerfully affect how we behave and how we respond to one another's ideas. Your message is more likely to succeed when it is relevant to the audience—that is, when it answers their question, "What's in it for me?"[5] Experts from previous eras, such as psychologist Abraham Maslow[6] and social critic Vance Packard,[7] have identified specific sets of needs, and these needs continue to be emphasized in many persuasive appeals.

Maslow's **hierarchy of needs** explains how more basic needs must be met before people will focus on less essential ones. The most basic human needs are physiological: we require food, drink, health, and shelter to survive. Once we've had these needs met, we attend to safety needs, which include economic security and protection from danger. If our physiological and safety needs are fulfilled, we seek to satisfy social needs, including love and friendship. From there, we strive for self-esteem, the feeling that comes from being respected and valued as contributing members of society. Finally, to satisfy what Maslow called self-actualization needs, we seek opportunities for creativity, personal growth, and self-fulfillment.

It is important to consider this hierarchy when analyzing your audience. If most audience members are struggling to pay their rent, it will be difficult to persuade them to donate to a political campaign, eat organic food, or sign up for an elective class in pottery. These activities may be worthy, but they will not help students who are dealing with late fees or the threat of eviction. To the extent that they cost money, these ideas are likely to fall outside audience members' latitude of acceptance, potentially resulting in a boomerang effect.

By focusing on needs that are of concern to audience members, your speech will be more likely to persuade. For example, let's say you want to give a speech convincing your classmates to exercise more often. Exercise fulfills a number of different needs: it can improve people's health, help them perform better at work and in school, increase their self-esteem, mitigate the dangers that come with obesity, and (if done in a social setting) provide opportunities to forge friendships and meet romantic partners. You should determine which of these needs are most important to your audience and then emphasize them in your main points and subpoints.

Connecting to Your Listeners' Values

Values are "core conceptions" of what is desirable for our own life and for society.[8] They guide people's judgments and actions.[9] Each of us has values that guide how we live—for example, being helpful, honest, logical, imaginative, or responsible. We also have ideas about what kind of society we want to live in, such as one that offers equality, freedom, happiness, peace, or security.[10] All of these are values. Because values play a central role in guiding our lives, adapting an argument to audience values is one of the most important considerations if your argument is going to be persuasive.[11]

A speech about airline safety provides one example of how a message can be tailored to audience values. Suppose you support more extensive security screening at airports. If national security is an important value for your listeners, and you document how extended screening would reduce the risk of terrorist hijackings, you would have a persuasive argument.

VALUES GUIDE AUDIENCE JUDGMENTS —AND SOMETIMES VALUES ARE IN CONFLICT

On the other hand, suppose efficiency and liberty are fundamental values to your audience. To persuade these listeners, you will need to explain how the screening you're advocating would not slow down airport lines and could be done with minimal intrusion on travelers. If you could prove a high risk of terrorist hijacking, you could also argue that even though efficiency and liberty are generally important values, *in this case*, the value of national security is paramount.[12]

Demonstrating How Your Audience Benefits

Audience members weigh the costs and benefits whenever they are deciding whether to take action in response to a persuasive appeal.[13]

They are most likely to support your proposal when you show how they will benefit from doing so, and when they feel that the costs involved are minimal, or at the very least, worth the benefits.

To step up your persuasive power, help your listeners visualize themselves experiencing the benefit they'll gain if they take the action you're advocating. Here is how one speaker showed the audience how they could benefit by volunteering their time for young children:

> Imagine yourself volunteering to help young kids in our community. You do not need to drive downtown to help. Students can volunteer to read to children at the Day Care Center in our library at story hour each day. The next time you are using the library in the afternoon, walk past the center and see what a good time the kids and your classmates are having. Share a story from your culture or a book you loved as a child. If you enjoy volunteering, you can even sign up for a community service course and earn academic credit.

In addition to demonstrating how your listeners will benefit from taking the actions you're advising, you may also want to show them that the costs of these actions are low. Explaining that costs are low can be particularly important when your listeners are seriously considering taking action—if this is the case, they probably already recognize the benefits of doing so, and showing them that taking action has limited disadvantages could be the final step in gaining their support.[14]

Acknowledging Listeners' Reservations

In analyzing your audience, you may discover reasons that your listeners are opposed to your thesis or at least uncommitted or neutral toward it. To address their reservations, consider using a **two-sided argument**. In a two-sided argument, you acknowledge an argument

MAKING A TWO-SIDED ARGUMENT

against your thesis and then use evidence and reasoning to refute that argument. For example, suppose you want to see a ban on alcoholic beverages at all campus sporting events. In this case, you know that fans who drink responsibly will likely oppose your idea, as will athletic department administrators concerned about the revenues that would be lost if alcohol sales were banned. To address responsible drinkers' reservations, you could acknowledge that they themselves aren't causing a problem, but then argue that the harm caused by irresponsible drinkers is so great that a ban is needed. To deal with administrators' reservations, you could agree that it's important for sports programs to raise revenues but then suggest alternative ways of doing so that don't involve alcohol sales.

A well-presented two-sided argument can help you change your audience members' attitudes in favor of your thesis and can strengthen your credibility.[15] That's because people are more likely to support an idea if they know that its proponent cares about their concerns and understands their views.

Focusing on Peripheral Beliefs

You'll be more likely to persuade your audience members if you avoid threatening their core beliefs. **Core beliefs** are viewpoints that people have held closely, often for many years. Such beliefs are particularly immune to persuasion—especially through merely one speech.[16]

Beliefs that audience members have not held quite so closely or for quite so long are **peripheral beliefs**. People may form peripheral beliefs by hearing a news report, reading a book or magazine, or listening to a statement made by a political or religious leader. These beliefs are more open to change by a persuasive message. Thus, you can boost your chances of success if you focus your appeal on your listeners' peripheral beliefs.

For example, suppose you want to persuade various groups of people at your college to devote one Saturday morning to work on a campus beautification proj-ect. You first address the Campus Peace and Civil Liberties Coalition. Its mem-bers typically devote Saturday and Sun-day mornings to antiwar activities. If you argue that their antiwar position is less important than campus beautifica-tion, you won't likely gain volunteers, since you'd be attacking their core beliefs. On the other hand, the coalition members' belief that antiwar activities must take place *every* Saturday and Sun-day morning is more peripheral. You would have a better chance of winning

these listeners' support if you maintained that devoting just one Saturday morning to do something to benefit the campus commu-nity would be a worthy cause—and that the coalition members could quickly return to their regular schedule of antiwar demonstra-tions afterward.

You can further enhance your persuasiveness if you show audi-ence members how they can stay true to their core beliefs. For instance, let's say you want to persuade your listeners to invest in the stock market. Some audience members may oppose stock invest-ments because they strongly believe that large corporations harm the environment. For these listeners, you could suggest investing in com-panies that are developing alternative energy sources. This action would enable them to stay true to their core belief.

ETHICAL PERSUASION

As we noted in Chapter 3, a public speaker must be ethical as well as effective. You want your audience members to accept your thesis, but you should earn their support with honest—not deceptive—persuasion. In this section, we highlight important ethical considerations for per-suasive speakers.

Help Your Audience Make an Informed Decision

Ethical speakers help their listeners reach well-informed decisions rather than manipulating them into agreement. Unfortunately, some persuaders use unethical tactics. For example, one study found that a detailed description of a single individual who had been on welfare for sixteen years exerted a greater influence on an audience's perceptions of welfare recipients than statewide statistics showing that 90 percent of welfare recipients go off the rolls within four years.[17] Use of vivid evidence that depicts an atypical situation would constitute an unethical half-truth unless the speaker informed the audience that the situation described is not the norm.

To persuade ethically, present solid, truthful claims that support your thesis. Scrupulously avoid arguments based on faulty reasoning, and include

FIND THE DIFFERENCE

all key facts you know of that would help your audience carefully weigh what you're proposing. Remember, you can always address counter-arguments to your position by using a two-sided argument.

Research Your Facts

As a public speaker, you have an ethical duty to research your topic so that you can be sure the facts you present to your audience are accurate. If your research reveals that a fact is supported by a consensus of credible sources, you can confidently use that fact in your speech. Conversely, if you find that the "jury is still out" on a claim you wish to make, don't present that point as an established fact. Instead, acknowledge that the point is being debated. Then use a two-sided argument to show why you believe that the support for your side outweighs the support for the other side. If you find that few credible sources support your claim and most sources disagree, do not include that point in your speech. Research other arguments for your position instead.

Note Any Biases

Some communicators stand to benefit personally if they succeed in persuading their audience. For example, a former homeland security official who advocated full-body scanners at airports was a consultant for a company that made these devices, and a health economist who discussed government health-care policies had received a contract from the government.[18] Audience members will understandably feel cheated if such potential conflicts of interest are not disclosed, because such facts are relevant to their decision of whether or not to believe a speaker. Therefore, you should practice **full disclosure** to your audience. This means that you acknowledge any vested interest you may have in your topic. For example, if you would receive a commission if your listeners purchased a product you were promoting, or you'd receive extra credit if you recruited students to participate in a professor's study, your audience members deserve to know that information. They will also be more likely to respect you if you're honest enough to reveal such biases.

Attribute Your Research Properly

Include citations *every* time you present ideas that you found from other sources. Make sure that quotations and paraphrases are accurate and that they represent the original author's point of view.

ORGANIZING YOUR PERSUASIVE SPEECH

In Chapter 9, we presented several patterns for organizing the main points in the body of your speech. In a persuasive speech, you want to choose a pattern that will clearly convey your message *and* maximize your persuasive impact. To select the most effective pattern, consider whether you will be making a fact, value, or policy claim in your speech.

Organizing Fact Claims

If you're planning to make a fact claim, you will be seeking to prove that something is true or false. In this type of persuasive speech, consider using a causal, comparison, or categorical pattern, depending on the main points you'll be presenting.

Causal Pattern. Many fact claims argue that one thing causes another. If this describes your fact claim, a causal pattern is ideal.

To illustrate, here is how a presenter might organize a speech claiming that fast food causes health problems:

THESIS   Fast-food restaurants are a significant cause of health problems in the United States.

MAIN POINTS

I. Low prices encourage frequent fast-food consumption.
II. Fast-food meals are high in fats and calories.
III. High-fat, high-calorie foods cause obesity, diabetes, and heart disease.

Comparison Pattern. When you want to claim that two situations are similar or different, a comparison pattern can help you support that claim. Here is an example of how a student used this pattern to persuade his fellow classmates that they should vote in an upcoming election because the candidates had substantively different positions on issues that would affect the lives of many students:

THESIS   There are significant differences between the two candidates for the legislature in our district.

COMPARISON PATTERN

MAIN POINTS

   I. One candidate does not support the minimum wage; the other proposes an increase.

  II. One candidate believes taxpayers already spend too much on colleges; the other supports increased financial aid.

 III. One candidate opposes contraceptive distribution at campus health centers; the other proposes to make contraceptives readily available.

Categorical Pattern. Sometimes each main point in your speech will reflect a different reason that you believe your fact claim is true. In this case, you can use a categorical pattern to organize your presentation. Consider the following example from a speech intended to convince listeners that climate change is actually happening:

THESIS The earth is experiencing climate change.

MAIN POINTS

   I. The changes in ocean temperature are consistent with computer models of climate change.

  II. Extreme weather is on the rise.

 III. Glaciers on every continent are contracting.

 IV. Coral reefs are disintegrating.

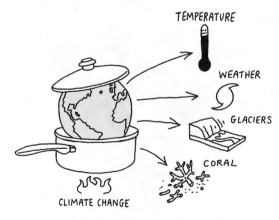

CATEGORICAL PATTERN

Organizing Value Claims

In making a value claim in a persuasive speech, you attach a judgment to your subject and then try to get the audience to agree with your evaluation. Two organizing patterns—criteria-application and categorical—can help you.

Criteria-Application Pattern. Recall that a criteria-application pattern has two main points. One establishes standards for the value judgment you are making; the other applies those standards to the subject of your thesis. Here is how you could use this pattern in a persuasive speech on the value of community service in college:

> **THESIS** Community service is a valuable part of the college experience.

> **MAIN POINTS**
>
> I. A college education should provide students with several benefits.
>   A. New knowledge and skills
>   B. Preparation for the workforce

CRITERIA-APPLICATION PATTERN

    C. Participation in new experiences

    D. Clarification of students' values and their place
       in the world

  II. Community service provides college students with
      the opportunity to gain all these benefits.

    A. It leads to higher grade-point averages and stronger
       communication skills.

    B. It provides valuable work experience and a chance to
       discover career interests.

    C. It offers an opportunity to experience new
       situations and work with people from diverse
       backgrounds.

    D. It encourages students to consider their values
       and see how they can help society.

Categorical Pattern. In some persuasive speeches, you may decide that it isn't necessary to explain how each main point supports the value judgment you are making because your audience already understands each point's relevance. In this case, you can use a categorical pattern.

To illustrate, suppose you want to convince your audience that advanced driver-training courses are beneficial. Your listeners probably know that they could judge the value of a driver-training course by considering factors such as reduced accident risk and lower insurance premiums. Therefore, you could organize your main points in a categorical pattern, such as the following:

THESIS   Advanced driver-training courses are beneficial.

MAIN POINTS

   I. They reduce the risk of accidents.

  II. They lower drivers' insurance premiums.

 III. They lower drivers' maintenance and gas costs.

 IV. The savings gained from the course exceed the cost of
     the course.

Organizing Policy Claims

When you advance a policy claim, you call for action. You might want audience members to do something in particular, or you might want to convince them that an organization or institution (such as state or local government) should take a particular action. For this type of persuasive speech, you can use any of these three organizational patterns: motivated sequence, problem-cause-solution, or comparative advantage.

Motivated Sequence. Developed by Alan Monroe over seventy years ago, this pattern remains popular.[19] It follows the stages of thinking that people often go through while solving a problem or considering new ideas.[20] A **motivated sequence** aims to establish five main points, as shown in the following example from a persuasive speech encouraging students to study abroad:

MAIN POINTS

I. *Attention* (creating a willingness to listen to your message). Few members of our class are looking forward to final exams next month. Do you think it would be more exciting if your finals were happening in Rome, Beijing, Sydney, or Buenos Aires?

II. *Need* (identifying a need relevant to your audience). Every member of this class plans to get a job after graduation. The job market is highly competitive.

III. *Satisfaction* (showing how your proposal will fulfill the need you identified). Participation in our college's Study Abroad Program will strengthen your credentials in the job market. Employers report that they are more likely to hire a candidate with international experience.

IV. *Visualization* (helping listeners form a mental picture of the benefits of your proposal). Imagine that you have returned to the United States after an amazing semester in Spain or Japan. At an interview for a job you really want, the interviewer asks if you have experience with other cultures. You answer yes, and you see the interviewer's interest perk up. The next day, the company makes you an offer.

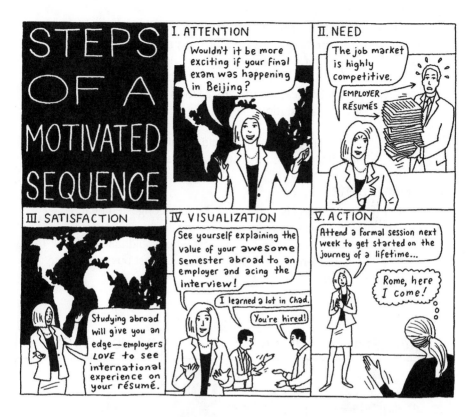

V. *Action* (clarifying what you want listeners to do). Attend an informational session on next year's Study Abroad Program in the Student Union next Wednesday. You can learn more about the exciting options open to you, hear from past participants, and ask questions. After that, I hope you will decide to make Montreal, Mumbai, or Madrid your home for next fall.

Problem-Cause-Solution Pattern. This pattern can be especially helpful if you are asking the audience to support a policy change by an organization or institution. Since your ultimate goal is new behavior on the part of the organization or institution, the problem-cause-solution pattern builds to the action you are advocating. Recall that with this pattern, the first main point demonstrates a problem that needs to be addressed. The second shows how current policies are not sufficient to eliminate the cause of the problem. And the third presents a solution that can minimize the problem.

Here is an example of how a speaker might use this pattern in a persuasive speech advocating the installation of public bike racks near bus stops and train stations.

THESIS   The local government should install secure bike racks near heavily used bus stops and train stations.

MAIN POINTS

I. *Problem*: Parking is scarce and traffic is congested near commuter bus stops and train stations in our county.

II. *Cause*: Many suburban commuters who would take mass transit live more than a mile from the closest bus stop or train station.

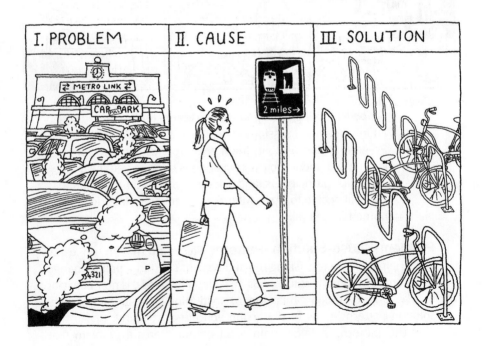

III. *Solution*: Providing secure bike racks will encourage alternative means of transportation to and from stops and stations, opening up parking spaces and alleviating traffic.

In the first main point, the speaker would establish that a *problem* exists—by showing that the roads near bus stops and around train stations are clogged with traffic, and that parking is scarce. In the second main point, he or she would explain that many commuters who rely on public transportation to get from the suburbs to the city still have to deal with local traffic congestion in order to catch their bus or train. In the final main point, the speaker would document how installing secure bike racks would allow some commuters to bike between their homes and their stop or station.

Comparative Advantage Format.
This format shows why the policy you are advocating would be more beneficial than existing policies. You would typically use it when there is no glaring problem or issue at stake but there *is* a reason that your proposal would be better than the status quo. Examples include arguing that the U.S. penny should be abolished or that college students should have a minor as well as a major.

With this format, the first main point in your speech outline explains your solution, and each subsequent main point identifies one advantage that your solution offers compared with the status quo. The subpoints for each advantage should include proof that your proposal would produce that benefit.

For instance, a speaker who wanted to persuade college students that they should have a minor could use the comparative advantage format as follows:

THESIS You should graduate with a minor.

MAIN POINTS

I. *Solution*: Research available minors on campus and select one that interests you.
II. *Advantage*: You can focus your studies on a subject you enjoy.

III. *Advantage*: You can strengthen your qualifications in your chosen career.

IV. *Advantage*: You can open the door to new career possibilities.

CHAPTER REVIEW

"Good persuaders make strategic choices in an ethical manner."

In this chapter, you learned how persuasive speakers strengthen or weaken their audience's commitment to a particular topic or motivate their listeners to take a particular action.

You also discovered strategies for developing a persuasive message for your audience, including choosing a thesis based on your listeners' disposition, relating your message to your audience's needs and values, demonstrating how the costs of your proposal are worth the benefits, and addressing audience reservations about your thesis.

Additionally, you found advice for developing your message in an ethical manner by helping your listeners make an informed decision, researching your facts thoroughly, disclosing any bias that you have, and properly attributing all your research sources.

Finally, you learned strategies for organizing your message, depending on whether you are making a fact, value, or policy claim.

Key Terms

persuasive speech *507*
fact claim *508*
value claim *508*
policy claim *510*
strategic discourse *510*
latitude of acceptance *513*
latitude of rejection *513*
boomerang effect *514*

needs *515*
hierarchy of needs *516*
values *517*
two-sided argument *520*
core belief *521*
peripheral belief *521*
full disclosure *525*
motivated sequence *530*

Review Questions

1. Describe three characteristics of persuasive speeches.
2. Describe five ways in which a speaker may adapt his or her message for an audience.

3. What four steps can you take to ensure that your persuasive speech is ethical?
4. Describe two ways to organize a persuasive speech for each of the following: a fact claim, a value claim, and a policy claim.

Critical Thinking Questions

1. How does using strategic discourse to craft a persuasive speech differ from preparing a speech in which you explain how you feel on a particular issue?
2. How would understanding Maslow's hierarchy of needs help you deliver more effective persuasive speeches? How could it hurt your effectiveness if you do not consider it?
3. Consider the way that talking heads and audiences for twenty-four-hour news channels tend to break along ideological and party lines. What does this tell you about latitudes of acceptance and rejection? How would you characterize the latitudes of acceptance and rejection for people who do not like to listen to commentators on either end of the political spectrum?
4. When organizing a persuasive speech, how can you decide which pattern works best?

Activities

1. Review the editorial page in several newspapers and consider their attempts to persuade you. How many make fact claims? Value claims? Policy claims? Can you tell what organizational pattern the writers are using?
2. Select any thesis for a persuasive speech that advocates action by the audience. How could you use each of the strategies for adapting your argument to the audience in a speech on the topic you have chosen?
3. Pay a visit to factcheck.org, a nonpartisan group that investigates claims made by politicians, news organizations, and interest groups to determine how truthful they are. Are you surprised by any of the

information presented there? What examples of unethical speech did you come across?
4. Consider any of the outlines presented in the examples in this chapter. Can you rework the main points (or add some new ones on that topic) to fit a different organizational pattern?

Go to **bedfordstmartins.com/speakup**, where you'll find helpful study materials, videos, and speech-building tools.

17

METHODS OF PERSUASION

"Persuasion happens when credible speakers provide good reasons and touch audience emotions."

Maya was both excited and nervous about delivering her upcoming persuasive speech. In her presentation, she planned to ask the audience to lobby for states to provide compensation for innocent prisoners who are exonerated by new DNA evidence. She felt passionate about the topic. Three years earlier, her uncle, David, had been released from a twenty-two-year imprisonment after DNA tests revealed that he hadn't committed the murder for which he was jailed.

But Maya knew she would face a challenge in persuading her listeners. After all, not many people are wrongly imprisoned, so why should her audience members take time out of their busy lives to lobby state governments for a new policy? In short, why should they care?

To build the most persuasive case possible, Maya decided to use three powerful tools: ethos (demonstrating her credibility), logos (presenting sound reasoning for her claims), and pathos (evoking intense emotion in her audience). She established her credibility by citing trusted researchers' findings on the accuracy of DNA testing and the inaccuracy of eyewitness accounts (which typically lead to wrongful convictions). She demonstrated solid reasoning for her proposal by presenting statistics about the difficulties exonerated prisoners face in finding paid work after their innocence is proven. And she evoked her listeners' compassion and empathy for exonerees by describing the harsh realities David had been enduring since his release from prison—including long stretches of unemployment.

Maya's presentation proved a resounding success. By skillfully blending ethos, logos, and pathos, she not only captured her listeners' attention but also convinced them that exonerees deserve to be compensated for the ordeal they suffered as a result of errors in the justice system. By the time Maya wrapped up her speech, some students were even jotting down the tips she was sharing for how to lobby state governments to introduce a new exoneree compensation law. Clearly, they had embraced her proposal and intended to take the action she recommended—solid evidence that she had given an effective persuasive speech.

You can use these strategies as successfully as Maya did. In this chapter, we discuss the use of ethos, logos, and pathos to create an effective speech.

ETHOS: YOUR CREDIBILITY AS A SPEAKER

Since ancient times, people have recognized that a speaker with **ethos (credibility)** has far more persuasive power than one without. A credible speaker is seen as knowledgeable, honest, and genuinely interested in doing the right thing for his or her audience. Ethos can help you win audience members' trust and persuade them to embrace your viewpoint. But what is credibility, exactly? By taking a closer look at what it consists of, we can get a deeper understanding of this crucial persuasive tool.

TRUSTING
TRUSTWORTHY

Understanding the Elements of Credibility

The ancient Greek philosopher Aristotle believed that practical wisdom and virtue are major components of ethos. Modern communication scholars use the term **competence** to refer to practical wisdom and the word **trustworthiness** instead of *virtue*. When audience members perceive a speaker as competent (knowledgeable and experienced) about his or her subject as well as trustworthy (honest and fair), they find it easier to believe the speaker's claims.[1]

Aristotle also urged public speakers to exhibit **goodwill** toward their audiences—by wanting what is best for their listeners rather than what would most benefit themselves.[2] According to contemporary researchers, speakers who demonstrate goodwill:

- understand their listeners' needs and feelings
- empathize with their audiences' views (even if they don't share them)
- respond quickly to others' communication[3]

THE SPEAKER HAS CREDIBILITY AND SHOWS EMPATHY

She really knows about the topic.

I can trust her.

She has my best interest at heart.

Any questions about volunteering at the food pantry?

I'm a single parent—what if I can't find the time?

That's a great point, and that's why there are opportunities for parents and kids to help out together...

Building Your Credibility

When you're just starting out as a public speaker, your audience members may not immediately recognize your credibility. You'll need to build your ethos through what you say during your speech—and how you say it. Here are some helpful strategies:

- *Share your qualifications to speak on the topic.* If you have some expertise in the subject, outline your credentials for your audience. In some cases, this might involve listing your educational qualifications and work experience ("I have a degree in finance and have worked in banking for six years"). In others, it might mean telling the audience about your personal stake in the subject, just as Maya did when she spoke about her uncle's having been exonerated of murder by DNA evidence in the story that opened this chapter.

- *Present strong evidence from reputable sources.* When you provide evidence for your claims, you indicate that you have carefully researched your topic, which communicates your competence. Citing a number of well-balanced and credible sources shows the audience the extent of your research and helps establish your credibility in the process.

- *Highlight common ground with the audience.* Reminding the audience of your shared experience can make your message—and you—more credible. A teacher speaking to parents of preschoolers, for example, might mention the anxiety he felt the first time he dropped his own young son off at day care before attempting to persuade them to ignore their child's crying during the first few mornings of school.

- *Choose your words carefully.* The words you select for your speech can also demonstrate your understanding of your listeners and thus your goodwill toward them. Be careful to use any technical terminology appropriately, to show you understand the subject matter, and make sure to avoid language that your audience might find insensitive or offensive.

- *Show respect for conflicting opinions.* Throughout your speech, use respectful language to refer to people who disagree with you. For example, "Some of you may not share my thinking on this, and that's okay. There are lots of ways to look at this issue."

- *Practice your speech until your delivery is fluent.* When you demonstrate effective delivery skills during your presentation—for example, by interacting comfortably with the audience—you are more likely to come across as trustworthy.

Avoiding Loss of Your Credibility

You have many strategies at hand for enhancing your credibility during a speech. But there are just as many ways to make a misstep and erode your ethos while you're giving a talk. Anytime you say something that shows a lack of competence, trustworthiness, or goodwill, you damage your credibility.

Such errors are common during political campaigns, especially during presidential elections. In 2004, for example, Senator John Kerry defended his vote on a large supplemental military appropriations bill by stating, "I actually did vote for the $87 billion before I voted against it."[4] His opponents used this comment to characterize him as a "flip-flopper" who lacked the decisiveness required to be president. In September 2008, Senator John McCain lost considerable ground in the presidential election after claiming that "the fundamentals of the economy are strong" when the United States was in the midst of a serious recession."[5]

In your speeches, careful preparation can help you avoid credibility-draining mistakes. Here are some common sources of this type of error:

- *Getting your facts wrong.* Your competence and preparation will be questioned if you present factual information that is just plain inaccurate. Mushers and dog-show enthusiasts would immediately recognize the error of calling the Alaskan husky a purebred dog, as these sled dogs are crossbred from diverse bloodlines. Likewise, a speaker who mixed up the Brontë sisters would alienate fans of Victorian literature, and social networkers would tune out a presenter who mixed up a tweet and a Facebook status update. One of the benefits of selecting a topic you know well is that you are less likely to present factual errors on a familiar subject.

- *Pronouncing words incorrectly.* Your experience in a topic area will be questioned if you mispronounce the names of key persons or concepts related to the topic. For example, a student who referred to hip-hop pioneer Afrika Bambaataa (*Bam-BAH-Tah*) as Afrika "*BOM-bait-a*" would not be credible to audience members who know that genre of music well,

KNOW YOUR FACTS OR RISK LOSING CREDIBILITY

and fans of renowned Italian tenor Andrea Bocelli
(*Ahn-DRAY-ah Bo-CHEL-ee*) would question the credibility of a
speaker who referred to him as *AN-dree-a Bo-SELL-ee*.

- *Failing to acknowledge potential conflicts of interest.* In
  Chapter 16, we noted the importance of disclosing your
  biases. If you fail to acknowledge a self-interest in your topic,
  it will hurt your credibility when it is revealed. For example,
  suppose a classmate advocated a thousand-dollar scholarship
  for all students who serve in student government and asked
  the class to sign a petition supporting this policy. After class,
  you read an article in the campus newspaper and discover
  that the speaker serves in the student senate—no wonder he
  wanted that scholarship policy! You would view that student
  more suspiciously the next time he presented a speech and
  might be less inclined to vote for him in the next election.

- *Stretching to find a connection with the audience.* Have you
  ever seen speakers attempt to speak a language they do
  not know well, try to adopt local or professional slang, or
  feign interest in the audience members' favorite sports team?
  They often end up mangling words or using terms incorrectly
  and get distracted from their message while worrying about
  possible mistakes. These errors only highlight how discon-
  nected a speaker is. You should always show respect to your
  audience, but the best choice is to be your authentic self.

Once a speaker's credibility has come into question, it's very difficult to repair the damage. Thus, before giving a speech, examine the
language you intend to use, and make sure that it communicates
competence, trustworthiness, and goodwill. However, even bulletproof ethos isn't enough to deliver an effective speech. You also need
to deliver a solid set of facts to prove the claims you're making.

LOGOS: THE EVIDENCE AND REASONING BEHIND YOUR MESSAGE

Reliable facts can further strengthen your credibility and help your
audience members make well-informed decisions—key effects of

A BUNCH OF LOGICAL PEOPLE

ethical public speaking. Sound reasoning that supports your claims is also essential if you hope to persuade audience members to change their beliefs or behaviors. When you present trustworthy facts to back your claims and clearly show how those facts have led you to those claims, you use **logos** effectively.

For example, suppose you want to deliver a persuasive speech arguing that diet soft drinks do not actually help people lose weight, a claim that might seem counterintuitive to many of your listeners. To convince them that you know what you're talking about, you'll need to supply proof, or **evidence**, of your claim. To further strengthen your logos, you'll have to show that the conclusions you've drawn from the evidence make sense. Is your train of thought logical? Or are you using **fallacious (faulty) reasoning** to twist or distort the facts in your favor?

In the following sections, we discuss how to use evidence and reasoning to build a persuasive message and how to avoid several common logical fallacies.

Using Evidence

When your audience analysis suggests that listeners may not accept a claim you want to make, you'll need to supply proof. One of the best ways to do that is to research evidence from credible sources (see Chapter 7) and then present that evidence in your speech. To use evidence effectively, apply the following principles:

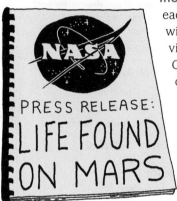

THIS JUST IN...

PRESS RELEASE:
LIFE FOUND
ON MARS

Identify Your Sources and Their Qualifications. Indicate who your source is for each piece of evidence you present, along with his or her qualifications, before providing the evidence during your speech. Concrete documentation strengthens your credibility.[6] To ensure your *sources'* credibility, use facts provided by unbiased experts.[7]

Give Listeners New Evidence. Use audience analysis to determine what evidence is likely to be new to your listeners. Facts that they're not yet familiar with are more likely to increase their perceptions of your credibility.[8]

Provide Precise Evidence. Precise evidence consists of specific dates, places, numbers, and other facts. Here's an example of this kind of precision:

> A study by Sharon Fowler and her colleagues at the University of Texas Health Science Center found that the risk of becoming obese or overweight for regular soft drink drinkers consuming 1–2 cans daily is 32.8 percent. For those who consume a comparable amount of diet soft drinks, the risk is 54.5 percent.[9]

This citation provides a specific percentage as well as the lead researcher's name and affiliation.

Look for Compelling Evidence. Audiences are more likely to be persuaded by compelling evidence that includes concrete or detailed examples. Such evidence engages listeners' senses, helps them visualize the point you're presenting, and increases the likelihood that they will remember the information.[10] For example, in your speech about diet sodas, you could include a compelling anecdote about a student who gained weight after switching from sugared to diet soft drinks.

<u>I AM PRECISE EVIDENCE</u>

Working smoke alarms cut your risk of dying in a house fire in half.*

<u>I AM COMPELLING EVIDENCE</u>

A fire started in the Jacksons' kitchen at 2 A.M. last night. Fortunately, a smoke detector woke the family and they escaped the blaze safely.

BEEP! BEEP!

*THE NATIONAL FIRE PROTECTION ASSOCIATION, "Smoke Alarms in U.S. Home Fires" (2009)

Characterize Your Evidence Accurately. Carefully word your claim so that it accurately reflects what your evidence proves. For example, if all the facts you've gathered strongly support the idea that diet drinks don't help people lose weight, then use those very words to state your claim about the drinks, rather than saying something like, "Diet soft drinks aren't as healthy as people think."

Using Reasoning

Reasoning is the line of thought that connects the facts you present and the conclusions that you draw from those facts. Persuasive speakers typically use **inductive reasoning**—generalizing from facts, instances, or examples, and then making a claim based on that generalization. The following table shows several examples of inductive reasoning from everyday life.

ARGUMENT GOING NOWHERE

ARGUMENT GOING SOMEWHERE

REASONING

EVIDENCE

INDUCTIVE REASONING

EXAMPLES OF INDUCTIVE REASONING

Fact	Claim
At three different locations at this university, food service was slow.	All food-service outlets at this school are slow.
Lonyae is good at football.	Lonyae would be good at soccer.
Two students in the back row just fell asleep.	This is a boring class.
Sarah waits until the last minute to study or write papers.	Sarah is likely to receive a low grade.

There are four types of inductive reasoning: example, comparison, sign, and causal. Let's explore each type in detail and consider how to use them effectively.

Example Reasoning. When you use **example reasoning**, you present specific instances to support a general claim. Your goal is to persuade the audience that your examples supply sufficient proof of your claim.

For instance, here's how you could use example reasoning to argue that endangered species are making a comeback:

> The Fortymile caribou herd, which ranges from central Alaska to the Yukon Territory, was down to 5,000 members in the 1970s. Now the number is up to 46,000.[11] In California, the number of peregrine falcons has increased from two known pairs to more than 150.[12] And there are now more than 6,000 breeding pairs of bald eagles in the lower 48 states, far more than the 400 pairs in the 1960s.[13]

To use example reasoning skillfully, be sure to provide enough instances to persuade your audience that your general claim is reasonable. The more examples you can find, the more confident you can be that your claim is correct.

Of course, in a short speech, you may have time to present only three or four examples to back up your argument. In this situation, you'll need to choose the most **representative examples**—that is, examples that are typical of the class they represent. To illustrate, if you wanted to present an even more compelling case that endangered species are making a comeback, you might want to cite several very different species that come from a variety of regions in North America.

If you're planning to use example reasoning in a speech you're researching, think about counterexamples your audience may consider. For instance, some listeners may argue that while certain species

REPRESENTATIVE EXAMPLES

We PEREGRINE FALCONS are enjoying life in California.

We BALD EAGLES are thriving in Maine and North Carolina and...

We CARIBOU are doing well in Alaska.

We PANTHERS are fine in Florida.

CLAIM: FORMERLY ENDANGERED SPECIES ARE THRIVING ACROSS THE U.S.A.

are recovering their populations, others are still endangered. Thus, they may view your claim that "endangered species are making a comeback" as inaccurate. If such counterexamples have merit, you may need to revise your claim to "*some* endangered species are making a comeback."

Comparison Reasoning. When you use **comparison reasoning**, you argue that two instances are similar, so that what you know is true for one instance is likely to be true for the other. For example, if you argue that long-term prohibition of marijuana can't succeed because prohibition of alcohol failed, you would be using this type of reasoning.

For comparison reasoning to work, your audience must agree (or be persuaded) that the two instances are in fact comparable. To illustrate, suppose you can show that marijuana use is similar to

NONREPRESENTATIVE EXAMPLES

CLAIM: FORMERLY ENDANGERED SPECIES ARE THRIVING ACROSS THE U.S.A.

alcohol use, and current marijuana law closely resembles earlier alcohol-prohibition law. By emphasizing these similarities, you can make a more convincing argument that marijuana prohibition will likely prove just as ineffective as alcohol prohibition did.

To further strengthen your comparison reasoning, make sure your audience accepts the "known facts" as true. For example, perhaps your listeners would argue that alcohol prohibition in the United States wasn't actually a failure if it reduced alcohol consumption significantly. In this case, you might have to note other ways in which such prohibition could be considered a failure. For example, it led to the rise of organized crime, as entities such as the Mafia took over bootlegging operations to counter government raids on speakeasies.

During the public debate on U.S. military policy in Afghanistan, advocates on both sides of the issue used comparison reasoning.

For example, pointing to the Soviet Union's unsuccessful conflict in Afghanistan from 1979 to 1988, Professor Gary Leupp of Tufts University used the "graveyard of empires" analogy—comparing this war to other failed wars in Afghanistan—to argue that the war could not be won:

> Soviet troops peaking at over 100,000 in 1987, with the advantage of supply lines from the neighboring USSR, and including numerous ethnic Uzbeks and Tajiks who could speak local languages and had some understanding of local culture, could not repress the rag-tag CIA-supplied [Afghan Mujahadeen] guerillas and secure control of the country. Nor . . . could an honor roll of would-be conquerors from Alexander the Great in the third century B.C.E. to the British in the nineteenth century defeat the hardy, fiercely independent Afghan tribesmen.[14]

Conversely, in testimony before Congress during his service as head of the U.S. Central Command, General David Petraeus compared the current war in Afghanistan not with earlier wars in that country but with the more recent conflict in Iraq:

> Nonetheless, while certainly different and, in *some* ways, tougher than Iraq, Afghanistan is no more hopeless than Iraq was when I took command there in February 2007. Indeed, the level of violence in Iraq and number of violent civilian deaths were vastly higher than we have seen in Afghanistan. But, achieving progress in Afghanistan *will* be hard and the progress there likely will be slower in developing than was the progress achieved in Iraq. Nonetheless, as in Iraq, in Afghanistan, hard is not hopeless."[15]

Which comparison is stronger? That would depend on how each speaker develops his main points. For Leupp to present a compelling case, he has to convince his listeners of the parallels between U.S. and Soviet involvements in Afghanistan and show that the Soviets even enjoyed advantages the United States does not. On the other

THE CURRENT CONFLICT IN AFGHANISTAN Vs. HISTORICAL CONFLICTS IN AFGHANISTAN

THE CURRENT CONFLICT IN AFGHANISTAN Vs. THE CURRENT CONFLICT IN IRAQ

hand, Petraeus could strengthen his comparison by further proving the relative success of U.S. troops in Iraq following the 2007 surge and emphasizing ways in which the levels of violence and dysfunction in Afghanistan are less than those the United States has successfully dealt with in Iraq.

Sign Reasoning. When you use **sign reasoning**, you claim that a fact is true because indirect indicators (signs) are consistent with that fact. For example, you might claim that college students are facing serious financial challenges, as evidenced by students working longer hours.

This type of reasoning is most effective if you can cite multiple consistent signs of the fact that you are claiming. For instance, you could strengthen your claim that students' financial challenges are rising by also noting an increase in student loans and a higher rate of students dropping out of school. But as you're researching your speech, look for signs *inconsistent* with your argument. To illustrate, if you discover that students are spending more money on entertainment and clothes, you may find it more difficult to convincingly claim that signs prove that financial struggles are on the rise.

Causal Reasoning. When you use **causal reasoning**, you argue that one event has caused another. For instance, you would be using causal reasoning if you claimed that playing violent video games leads children to get involved in violent and illegal activities.

You can strengthen your causal reasoning in several ways. One way is to explain the link between cause and effect. For example, you might contend that when children play violent games, they empathize with the violent character they control in the games. Thus, they are more likely to emulate that character in their everyday lives. Another way to use causal reasoning effectively is to support the cause-effect link with evidence from credible sources. For instance, you could use quotations from the American Academy of Pediatrics or a Senate Judiciary Committee Report to bolster your argument about violent video games' impact on children's behavior. Finally, you could show a correlation between the cause and effect—for example, by presenting statistics indicating that as the number of hours children spend playing violent video games increases, so does the number of violent incidents in which they get involved.

Causal reasoning can be tricky, as it is easy to misinterpret the evidence or come to the wrong conclusion. We'll take a look at errors in causal reasoning and other common reasoning errors in the following section.

SUPPORTING CAUSAL REASONING

1. EXPLAIN THE LINK BETWEEN CAUSE AND EFFECT

2. PROVIDE CREDIBLE EVIDENCE

3. DEMONSTRATE A CORRELATION

* U.S. SENATE JUDICIARY COMMITTEE REPORT, "CHILDREN, VIOLENCE, AND THE MEDIA" (1999)

557

Avoiding Logical Fallacies

Reasoning is fallacious (faulty) when the link between your claim and supporting material is weak. We have already discussed several fallacies in Chapter 3 in the context of unethical persuasion: hasty generalization, post hoc fallacies, personal attacks, and bandwagoning. In this section, we explain the logical error in some of these fallacies and highlight other oft-committed fallacies that you'll want to avoid in your speeches.

Hasty Generalization. When using example reasoning, be sure to avoid **hasty generalization**. This fallacy occurs when a speaker bases a conclusion on limited or unrepresentative examples. For example, it would be fallacious to reason that jobs can be created in any city whose leaders put their mind to it based on the example of Austin, Texas. Austin has a number of unique job-creation advantages that other cities may not be able to match—it is the home of a first-rate university, a highly educated population, the state capitol, and a "robust venture capital scene."[16]

Causal Reasoning Errors. One common error in causal reasoning is the **post hoc fallacy**. The fallacy lies in the assumption that just because one event followed another, the first event caused the second. But a correlation, in itself, does not prove causality. For example, suppose you're considering making an argument that parents should delay their children's entry into kindergarten a year because statistics show that children who start school at six perform better than those who begin at five. Through further research, however, you might find that although delayed entry is indeed *correlated* with better performance, there is no proof that one factor *causes* the other. In fact, further study reveals that these statistics *may* be misleading because students who begin school later are typically already more advantaged to begin with, with many being the children of affluent, college-educated parents. In short, it is unclear which factor causes certain students to perform better: the fact that they started school a year later or the fact of their parents' socioeconomic status. If you still wanted to advocate students starting a year early and avoid the post

POST HOC FALLACY

hoc fallacy, you would need additional conclusive evidence of a link between age and performance.[17]

It's also important to watch out for **reversed causality**, in which speakers miss the fact that the effect is actually the cause. In this example, high academic potential may cause parents to delay their child's entry into school by one year. Highly educated "helicopter" parents could be more likely to maneuver for every possible advantage for their children, and perceive that they will perform better relative to their classmates in school and sports if they are a year older than most of their peers.

Ad Populum **Fallacy.** You've committed the ***ad populum* (bandwagon) fallacy** if you assume that a statement (such as "The earth is ten thousand years old" or "Young people are less politically active today than they were fifty years ago" or "Homegrown terrorism is a major problem in the United States") is true or false simply because a large number of people say it is.

The problem with basing the truth of a statement on the number of people who believe it is that most people have neither the expertise nor the time to conduct the research needed to arrive at an informed

AD POPULUM FALLACY

opinion about the big questions of the day. For this reason, it's best to avoid using public-opinion polls to prove facts.

Straw Person Fallacy. You commit the **straw person fallacy** if you replace your opponent's real claim with a weaker claim you can more easily rebut. This weaker claim may sound relevant to the issue, but it really isn't. You're presenting it just because it's easy to knock down, like a person made of straw.

During the impeachment trial of former U.S. president Bill Clinton, some of his defenders committed this fallacy when they argued that an extramarital affair is part of private life and not a sufficient justification for impeaching a president. However, Clinton's political opponents maintained that whether the president had an affair was irrelevant: the important thing was that he had lied under oath, an action that *did* justify impeachment in their minds.

Slippery Slope Fallacy. You've fallen victim to the **slippery slope fallacy** if you argue against a policy because you assume (without proof) that it will lead to some second policy that is undesirable. Like the straw person fallacy, this type of argument distracts the audience from the real issue at hand. Here's one example of a slippery slope argument:

> We can't legalize same-sex marriage because the next thing you know, people will be marrying their pets.

In this example, the speaker can't support his or her claim: in states or nations that have extended marriage rights to gay men and lesbians, no one has in fact tied the knot with Fluffy or Fido.

SLIPPERY SLOPE FALLACY

False Dilemma Fallacy. You fall prey to the **false dilemma fallacy** if you claim that there are only two possible choices to address a problem, that one of those choices is wrong or infeasible, and that therefore your listeners must embrace the other choice. For example:

> Either we provide a public option for health insurance or the 46 million Americans who cannot get insurance will be one illness away from bankruptcy.

The weakness in a false dilemma argument is that most problems have more than just two possible solutions. To illustrate, in the health insurance example, there are numerous options for addressing the problem of uninsured Americans. For example, the Kaiser Family Foundation noted thirteen health-care reform options,[18] In addition, bankruptcy law could be revised to provide the seriously ill with other options for managing their economic hardship.

FALSE DILEMMA FALLACY

Appeal to Tradition Fallacy. You've committed the **appeal to tradition fallacy** if you argue that an idea or policy is good simply because people have accepted or followed it for a long time. For example:

> We must continue to require general education courses at this college. For the past fifty-three years, the students at State U have taken general education.

This argument is weak because it offers no explanation for why the tradition of general education courses is a good thing in the first

APPEAL TO TRADITION FALLACY

place. The fallacy lies not in advocating something that is historic or traditional, but in presenting history and tradition as proof. A speaker defending tradition must show why the tradition is worth preserving. A speaker might support the point in the example above by noting the benefits students gain from taking general education courses versus taking additional classes in their major (or taking more classes of their choice), or by showing how students with broad general education backgrounds have more career options after college.

PATHOS: EVOKING YOUR LISTENERS' EMOTIONS

When used with ethos and logos, emotional appeals—known as **pathos**—help you to put a human face on a problem you're addressing. When you stir your listeners' feelings, you enhance your persuasive power. Indeed, some experts have referred to human emotions as "the primary motivating system of all activity."[19] Thus, a heartwarming example of a person who benefited greatly from taking an action you're recommending in your speech can be a very compelling complement to statistical evidence indicating the total number of people who could benefit. An emotional appeal can be an effective, ethical component of a strong persuasive speech; however, these kinds of appeals can also be abused, so it is important to use them responsibly.

Using Emotional Appeals

Humans have the capacity to experience a wide range of emotions—including empathy, anger, shame, fear, and pity—and each of these feelings provides an opportunity to enhance your use of pathos in a persuasive speech. For example, in a presentation in which she advocated greater freedom in doctor selection for health maintenance organization (HMO) patients, a speaker used this emotional appeal:

> Trey McPherson was born with half of his heart shrunken and nearly useless, a condition that causes most children to die in infancy.
>
> Fortunately, Trey was not one of these victims because he was treated by a leading pediatric heart surgeon. After two surgeries, Trey's parents were able to experience the joy of seeing their ten-month-old son climb out of his crib at the hospital. Except for a bandage on his tiny chest, it was difficult to tell that Trey had recently experienced open-heart surgery. Unfortunately, many babies are not as fortunate as Trey. Although this skillful surgeon's patients have far-above-average survival rates, many pediatric cardiologists in the New York area find their "favorite surgeon is frequently off limits because of price if a child belongs to an HMO."[20]

This example evokes a variety of emotions. It stimulates listeners' *anger* and *pity* at the thought of small children denied the best available care. It prompts them to *empathize* by imagining how they would feel if a loved one with a serious disease were forced to accept low-quality medical care. And it brings *joy* at the thought of how Trey's parents must have felt when their child recovered from surgery.

But notice that this emotional appeal is accompanied by sound reasoning. The speaker provides evidence that Trey's access to excellent care is atypical, which justifies the anger she evokes.

A **fear appeal**—an argument that arouses fear in the minds of audience members—can be a particularly powerful form of pathos.[21] But to be effective, a fear appeal must demonstrate a serious threat to listeners' well-being.[22] And to be ethical, it must be based on accurate information and not exaggerated specifically to make your argument sound more persuasive.

A fear appeal is also more likely to succeed if your audience members believe they have the power to remedy the problem you're describing.[23] Consider messages by National Park Rangers advocating

HOW A FEAR APPEAL SUCCEEDS

safe storage of food in parks. The rangers provide statistics showing how often bears have broken into cars or tents when people have left food out. They augment these statistics with videos depicting bears smashing car windows and climbing inside the vehicles to get food. These images usually strike fear into viewers' hearts. But then the rangers show how easy it is to store food safely in lockers or bear-proof canisters. Because audience members realize they *can* readily adopt these practices, they *do* adopt them.

Effective *word choice* (see Chapter 12) can also strengthen the power of an emotional appeal. When a speaker's language connects with the values and passions of audience members, the persuasive impact of a message is enhanced. Political consultants on both the right and the left carefully consider the exact words that are used to express an idea to the voters. Emory University psychology and psychiatry professor Drew Westen notes that "every word we utter activates what neuroscientists call networks of association—interconnected sets of thoughts and emotions."[24] The selection of metaphors, for instance, has a significant influence in framing how audience members perceive an issue. For example, labeling participants in armed conflict as "freedom fighters" primes the listener to have a more favorable view of the cause for which they are fighting.[25] Westen's counterpart, Dr. Frank Luntz, has had a highly successful career assessing the instant response of focus-group members who are exposed to different words used to communicate the same basic message, and recommending optimal word choice for his clients.

During the public debate on health-care reform, Luntz concluded that opponents of the Democratic plan would have more success using the phrase "government takeover" of health care rather than referring to it as a "government controlled" or even a "government run" program.[26] On the other side of the issue, Westen advised Democratic supporters of health-care reform against using the phrase "universal health care," which created an image of bureaucracy and impersonal clinics in the minds of voters in the center of the political spectrum. Conversely, he found that the message "people who are retired, ill, or temporarily out of work shouldn't risk losing their life savings because of one illness" was very effective.[27]

While you are unlikely to be able to afford a high-priced consultant to help you choose the words that will be most compelling to your classmates, you can use your audience analysis to inform the language you select. If you express the key points of your message with words that relate to the values, needs, and aspirations of your audience members, your ideas are more likely to resonate. For example, in a classroom speech that took a stance on a campus issue, Taja advocated moving the campus's print newspaper to an online-only format. Her audience analysis revealed that many students already read plenty of news and blogs online; however, these same students were concerned that losing the printed newspaper would break a long tradition and result in less reliable reporting. Thus, Taja argued that "the online format we all rely on today could not be a better match for the campus newspaper's long tradition of excellent reporting," framing the change as a move from one medium to an ever better one rather than a complete overhaul of the paper's tradition of excellence. As was true for Taja, the words you choose to express your message can strengthen your persuasive appeal. However, they must also be used in an accurate and ethical manner.

Ensuring Ethical Use of Pathos

As we've discussed, emotional appeals, when combined with ethos and logos, can be very effective. But emotional appeals can have a dark side, too. If you fail to establish a sound connection between your point and the emotion you are invoking, you may succeed in persuading some of your audience members, but your appeal will not be logical and will certainly not be ethical. This is unacceptable. History is replete with persuaders (witness Adolf Hitler) who used pathos to achieve unethical and even horrific ends. Recall the old adage

UNETHICAL USE OF AN EMOTIONAL APPEAL

"With great power comes great responsibility," and don't use emotional appeal to manipulate your audience.

Let's take the HMO example previously discussed. The key to that appeal to pathos was that the speaker used sound reasoning to connect a relatively rare health emergency—a baby born with a damaged heart—with a broader challenge facing many potential patients: access to a wider selection of qualified physicians. If the speaker had failed to make the logical connection between the points, however, she would have been acting unethically. How might that happen? Suppose she could not provide evidence that access to a wide range of doctors would actually help families in Trey's situation and other health crises as well. In that case, her speech would merely be an emotional ploy to manipulate the audience into accepting her argument.

There are numerous examples of fear appeals that are premised on "facts" that are blatantly untrue. One instance involved an anti-vaccination advocate who contended that the H1N1 vaccine was part of an effort by the "global elite" to cut world population, asserting that the vaccine was "an extremely vicious cocktail of avian, swine, and human influenza viruses."[28] Climate scientists lost credibility after inaccurately stating that the Himalayan glaciers, which feed many rivers in Asia, could melt by 2035.[29] Fear appeals that exaggerate the health consequences of drug use (such as claims that marijuana use is similar to playing Russian roulette) have rarely succeeded;[30] indeed, poorly substantiated claims may even have a boomerang effect.[31] To present a convincing fear appeal and preserve your own ethos, you must substantiate with credible evidence the harmful consequence you predict.

Ethical speakers must also ensure that the language they select accurately describes the ideas they are discussing. Though compelling *word choice* can be used as an ethical persuasive tool, it can also cross the line into manipulation, exaggeration, or untruth. The **loaded language fallacy** is committed when emotionally charged words convey meaning that cannot be supported by facts presented by the speaker. For example, a speaker arguing against a proposal to tax sugar-sweetened beverages referred to the plan as a "healthy

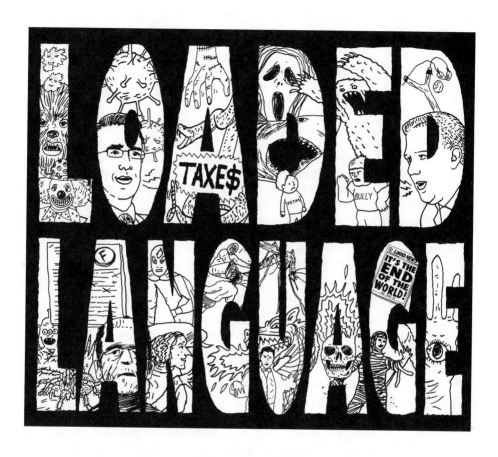

choice tax" and implied that consumers would pay sales tax on orange, apple, and grape juices, which are included in the U.S. Department of Agriculture's Food Pyramid for healthy eating.[32] The charge evoked anger in many audience members who agreed with the speaker that taxing such healthy choices would be absurd. The ethical problem was that the actual proposal only applied to sugar-sweetened fruit drinks, not to the 100 percent fruit juices included in the food pyramid.[33] Audience members were persuaded by the *loaded language* that described the proposal inaccurately, not by a credible argument against the true plan.

SAMPLE PERSUASIVE SPEECH

EXTRA CREDIT YOU CAN LIVE WITHOUT

Anna Martinez
California State University–Fresno

Anna Martinez selected student credit card debt as the topic of her persuasive speech. Based on her survey of the audience, she determined that it would not be feasible to argue that students should not use credit cards. She selected a different thesis that was within their latitude of acceptance: to encourage students to be more careful credit card consumers.

Anna's speech is targeted to an audience of college students, and she refers to information gleaned from her survey to support her points. Anna consistently uses evidence to support her claims. And she has a clearly organized speech in a problem-cause-solution format.

There is a dangerous product on our campus. It is marketed on tables outside the student union and advertised on the bulletin board in this classroom. Based on my audience survey, it is likely that most of you have this product in your possession right now. By the end of my speech, this product may be costing you more than it is right now. The dangerous product is credit cards. •

• Suspense-building attention-getter.

Today, I would like to discuss the problems created by college students' credit cards and hopefully persuade you to be a careful credit card consumer. If your credit card situation is anything like mine—and over two-thirds of this class indicated that they are currently carrying a balance on one or more cards—take note: you can save money.

My husband and I paid for our own wedding. More accurately, we used our credit cards to charge many of our wedding expenses. And thanks to Visa, we are still paying for our wedding every month! We have saved money with some of the suggestions I will present today, and you can do the same.

To that end, let's cover some of the problems created by students' credit card debt, then analyze causes of the problem, and finally consider steps you can take to be a careful credit card consumer. •

We'll start with a look at the problems created by these "hazardous products."

Credit card debt on campus is a significant and growing problem.

Many students have credit card debt. According to Matthew Scott, in *Black Collegian*, April 2007, "College financial aid provider Nellie Mae reported that 76 percent of undergraduate students had credit cards in 2005, with an average balance of $2,169. An alarming 25 percent of undergraduates had credit card balances totaling $3,000 or more." In *Business Week*, September 5, 2007, Jessica Silver-Greenberg noted that "the freshman 15, a fleshy souvenir of beer and late-night pizza, is now taking on a new meaning, with some freshmen racking up more than $15,000 in credit card debt before they can legally drink." If you are not sure how your own balances compare, you are not alone. The previously mentioned Nellie Mae study found that the average balance reported by students was 47 percent lower than the average balance computed from data provided by credit bureaus. •

High credit card use can change our lives for the worse. According to the April 2007 *Black Collegian* article, Rhonda Reynolds of Bernard Baruch College built up $8,000 worth of debt and was unable to make even the minimum payment. Her account went into collections. *Business Week*, March 15, 1999, provided another example. Jason Britton, a senior at Georgetown University, accumulated $21,000 in debt over four years on sixteen cards! Jason reports that "when I first started, my attitude was 'I'll get a job after college to pay off all my debt.'" Then he realized that he was in a hole because he could not meet minimum monthly payments. He had to obtain financial assistance from his parents and now works three part-time jobs. •

You probably do not owe $20,000 on your credit cards, but even smaller balances take their toll. Robert

Notes:
- Anna includes her thesis, connects with the audience, establishes credibility, and previews her main points.
- Anna consistently uses research sources to support her points.
- Supporting material: examples.

Frick, associate editor for *Kiplinger's Personal Finance* magazine, March 1997, states that if you make the minimum payments on a $500 balance at an 18% interest rate, it will take over seven years to pay off the loan and cost $365 in interest.

High credit card debt can also haunt your finances after you graduate. Matthew Scott, previously cited, notes that credit bureaus assign you a credit score, which is "your economic report card to the rest of the world." That score will "determine the interest rates you pay for many forms of credit and insurance." He also notes that prospective employers will check your credit score and use that number to decide whether or not you are responsible.

Many people in this class are carrying student loans, which will need to be paid back upon graduation. When you add credit card debt to student loan payments, rent, utilities, food, that payment on the new car you want to buy, family expenses, etc., the toll can be heavy. Alan Blair, director of credit management for the New England Educational Loan Marketing Corporation, in a 1998 report on the corporation's Web site, noted serious consequences for students who cannot balance monthly expenses and debts, including "poor credit ratings, inability to apply for car loans or a mortgage, collection activity, and at worst, a bankruptcy filing." •

• Relating the problem to a college audience.

Don't let this happen to you. After all that hard work earning a degree and finally landing a job where you don't have to wear a plastic name tag and induce people to get "fries with that order," the last thing any of us need is to be spending our hard-earned money paying off debt, being turned down for loans, or, worse yet, being harassed by collection agencies.

• Transition to main point II.

Credit card debt is hazardous to students' financial health, so why are these debts piling up? Let's move on to the causes of this problem. •

The reality is that credit card issuers want and aggressively seek the business of students like ourselves. As Jessica Silver-Greenberg writes in her previously cited September

2007 article, "over the next month, as 17 million college students flood the nation's campuses, they will be greeted by swarms of credit-card marketers. Frisbees, T-shirts, and even iPods will be used as enticements to sign up, and marketing on the Web will reinforce the message."

Card issuers actually troll for customers on campus because student business is profitable. Daniel Eisenberg, writer of the column "Your Money" for *Time* magazine, September 28, 1998, notes that "college students are suckers for free stuff, and many are collecting extra credit cards and heavier debts as a result." Eisenberg refers to a U.S. Public Interest Research Group survey, which found that students who sign up for cards at campus tables in return for "gifts" typically carry higher unpaid balances than do other students. Jessica Silver-Greenberg, in an October 15, 2007, *Business Week* article, writes that "college kids are a potential gold mine—one of the few growing customer segments in the saturated credit-card market. And they're loyal, eventually taking three additional loans, on average, with the bank that gives them their first card." •

Companies use "sucker rates" to induce students to apply for credit. *Business Week*, March 15, 1999, wrote "credit card marketers may advertise a low annual percentage rate, but it often jumps substantially after three to nine months. First USA's student Visa has a 9.9% introductory rate that soars to 17.99% after five months. Teaser rates aren't unique to student cards, but a 1998 study by the Washington-based U.S. Public Interest Research Group found that 26% of college students found them misleading."

So it appears that credit card companies will not stop demanding student business any time soon. What can we do about it?

My proposed solution is to be a careful credit card consumer.

Why not get rid of your credit cards before it's too late? All right, maybe you won't go for that solution. My survey indicated that most of you enjoy the flexibility in spending that credit cards provide. •

• Supporting material: explanation of why card issuers market to students.

• Anna notes that her listeners are likely to reject her strongest suggestion. Anna then advocates a solution within her audience's latitude of acceptance.

So here are some other ways you should be credit card smart. One practice is to shop carefully for the best credit card deals. The companies that are not spending their money giving away pizzas and iPods on campus may be able to offer you a better deal. In her September 7, 2007, *Business Week* article, Silver-Greenberg recommends that you beware of offers from South Dakota or Delaware corporations. Those states are "considered 'safe harbors' for credit card companies because they have no cap on interest rates or late payment [fees]."

A second solution is to read the fine print on credit card applications to learn what your actual interest rate will be. Alison Barros, a staff writer for the Lane Community College *Torch*, October 29, 1998, quoted Jonathan Woolworth, consumer protection director for the Oregon Public Interest Research Group, who wrote that "students need to read the fine print and find out how long those low interest rates last. Rates that are as low as 3% can jump to 18% within three months, and the credit card company doesn't want the student to know that."

Here is an example of the fine print on an ad that begins at 1.9% and soon rises. If you read the fine print, you note that the rate can rise to more than 20%. •

• Anna shows a visual aid here.

• *Second* and *third* are examples of signposts.

Third, even if you can only make the minimum payment on your cards, pay your bills on time. • Silver-Greenberg's September 5 article indicates that students' "credit scores can plunge particularly quickly, with one or two missed payments, because their track records are so short." She further cautions students to be aware of "universal default" provisions in their credit agreements—these provide that if you miss a payment on one card, other credit card companies can also raise your interest rate (even if you have paid those cards on time), perhaps to 30%. *Business Week*, March 15, 1999, cautions that "because students move often and may not get their mail forwarded quickly, bills can get lost. Then the students fall prey to late fees." •

• Adapting the solution to a college audience.

Finally, you can keep money in your pocket and out of the credit card company's by paying attention to your credit report. If any agencies are "talking trash" about you with inaccurate information, be sure to have it corrected.

To sum up these solutions, even if you do not want to stop using credit cards, there are many ways to be a careful credit card consumer. Shop for a good rate and be careful to read the fine print so you know what the rate really is. Know what you owe, and take the responsibility to make payments on time. •

• Internal summary of main point III.

This morning, we have learned about a hazardous product on campus—credit cards. We have noted the problem of high student credit card debt, analyzed some of the causes of this problem, and considered several methods for being a careful credit card consumer. •

• Summary of main points.

If your instructor offers you a chance for extra credit in his or her class, take advantage of the opportunity. But when a credit card issuer offers you a free T-shirt or phone card if you will sign up for their extra credit, just say no. When you pay off a credit card with a 19.9% interest rate, that "free" T-shirt could turn out to be the most expensive clothing you will ever buy. •

• Clincher sums up Anna's speech with irony.

SAMPLE PERSUASIVE SPEECH

WOMEN WITH DISABILITIES: HOW TO BECOME A BOAT ROCKER IN LIFE

Sue Suter

Sue Suter, the former U.S. Commissioner of Rehabilitation and president of the World Institute on Disabilities Services, delivered this speech to the New Zealand Rehabilitation Association Conference on Ethics in Rehabilitation in 1993.

Unlike classroom speakers, who should precisely follow the format presented by the instructor and textbook, professional speakers tend to develop their own unique style of crafting a speech. Nevertheless, Ms. Suter does an excellent job of modeling good public speaking practices. Her speech below—excerpted from the longer version that Suter delivered—is organized topically around main ideas. She uses diverse supporting materials (including examples, studies, poetry, humor, and anecdotes). And she relates her speech to the audience, indicating how each person can take an active role as a "boat rocker."

I'd like to begin with a favorite quote of mine that applies here. It's from a book called *What's Right with America*. And it says:

> Most of us Americans sail steadily through life on an even keel. But there are some, very few Americans who are boat rockers. They go through life making a fuss when things aren't right. And fighting the fights for us that we don't always fight for ourselves.

Ladies and gentlemen, this is not a "woe is me" speech. It is, however, about boat rocking. And it is about universal truths that women with disabilities have learned through a common experience. •

• Suter uses a quotation to gain audience attention and then reveals her topic.

A few days ago, while preparing for this speech, a friend and I talked about differences between the women's rights and the disability rights movements. At one point, my friend asked the question: which did I consider myself first—a woman, or a person with a disability? I said that I thought of myself as a woman first. That's an important distinction—one that's too often lost on those who are not members of the disability community. •

• Main idea: gender matters.

I contracted polio when I was two years old. I don't remember it. But I do remember my parents telling me about the advice that the doctor gave when it was time to take me home from the hospital. He told them, "just put her in bed. She's going to be staying there the rest of her life."

When I was in college, I decided to go after a master's degree in clinical psychology. But my career counselor advised against it. He warned that it was hard enough for a woman with a disability to get married. Having an advanced degree would only intimidate a man more.

When our son was born, the day before he and I were to leave the hospital, a social worker visited me to inquire how I was going to possibly care for a newborn infant. •

These were well-meaning professionals who believed that they knew what was best for me. But my life would be much different, and I probably wouldn't be with you today, if their advice had been followed.

Many articles about people with disabilities assume that gender has no influence. It does. As one interviewee put it, using a metaphor from baseball, "I'm a disabled woman now; two strikes. I'm almost out." Actually, there are three strikes against women with disabilities. The dual discrimination as women and as people with a disability. Plus, as William John Hamma and Betsy Rogovsky noted in their research, there's a special treatment meted out when the two intersect.

In a study of 130 undergraduate students in the United States, each was asked to describe what they saw in two photographs. One showed a forty-five-year-old man in a wheelchair. Most students imagined the cause of his disability as related to war, or job, or sports-related injuries—highly admirable. When they were shown a picture of a woman in a wheelchair, no one mentioned wars or jobs or sports. Instead, their answers centered on carelessness, like falling down stairs, or diseases—perhaps, by implication, diseases that were contagious. In other words, signs of weakness. •

Judy Heumann has often noted that "women with disabilities, in the richest and the poorest countries, are the poorest of the poor." That's a reality. Another reality is the impact of labels. Passive, child-like, lacking minimal skills.

Even the absence of labels takes its toll. The images of being independent, leader, married, child-bearer, sexual, or an employer. When a group of college students was asked in a survey to describe women with disabilities, none of those attributes were listed. Why?

Many of the women with disabilities in this room can claim those same titles as their own. I'd like to add my name to theirs. But why don't others see these qualities?

• Supporting material: examples of gender- and disability-based stereotypes.

• Supporting material: a study.

Women with disabilities are seen neither as mothers and nurturers, nor as professionals. Women who write about women with disabilities call this rolelessness!

The American comedian Lily Tomlin once played a character named Crystal. She was quadriplegic. And she asked her doctor, "What about sex?"

"I think you can have a baby."

"That's not what I asked." •

• Supporting material: a wry and humorous example.

Rolelessness. Women with disabilities are seen as asexual beings. Women with disabilities can have a baby. That's biology. The tough part is imagining that people with disabilities are capable of sexuality. There's a lot of truth to the old saying "Hormones know no handicap." •

• Main idea: disabled people are ordinary people.

Overcoming rolelessness means revealing that we are ordinary. I'll say it again. Overcoming rolelessness means revealing that we are ordinary. We must fight the Third Reich mentality that says the greatest goal is the perfection of the human race. •

• Style: use of repetition and also the phrase "Third Reich mentality."

• • •

More than anything else, the world needs to rediscover the normal. Disability is a normal part of being human. People with disabilities are ordinary people. This is not a form of denial. It is a fundamental recognition of our undeniable worth and our inseparable membership in the human race.

Yet women with disabilities are often devalued by the institutions they should be able to count on most—their families and the women's movement. One feminist activist said, "Why study women with disabilities? They reinforce traditional stereotypes of women being dependent, passive, and needy."

To that I ask, who is an accomplice to that image? Who is abandoning the universal ideals of freedom and dignity for all women in exchange for the easy path of appeasement? Appeasement has been defined as feeding your friends to the alligator in hopes that he'll eat you last. Everyone loses with that strategy.

• • •

Part of demonstrating our ordinariness means getting involved in situations that have nothing to do with disabilities. It's not enough to be invited to serve on a subcommittee for architectural accessibility. We need to aggressively seek positions on the finance committees and planning committees, as well. To get involved with parent-teacher groups. To volunteer at the local shelter for homeless people. To run for office. In essence, to claim a shared ownership in every issue that everyone holds in common.

Breaking into those roles takes an empowering action called cliff jumping. •

• Main idea: the importance of cliff jumping.

There's a poem by S. Wilde that reads:

"Come to the cliff," he said.
I said, "I am afraid."
"Come to the cliff," he said.
I went.
He pushed me.
And I flew. •

• Supporting material: a poem.

One of my first experiences with cliff jumping came when I attended my first day in junior high. My first day in a regular classroom after six years in a special ed school. There were a tense few moments of wondering how I'd be accepted. I was scared to death. Then my teacher took one look at me and said in front of the whole class, "What the hell happened to you?" Talk about an icebreaker. But later I figured it ended up being one of the best introductions I ever had. The disability issue was handled right up front. That freed up the rest of the time for me to get to know my classmates, and for us to find that we had many more similarities than differences . . .

Another kind of cliff jumping happened well into my professional career. I moved from running a relatively small state rehabilitation agency to head up the Rehabilitation Services Administration in Washington, D.C. And it was one of the best decisions I ever made. It overcame a kind of geographical isolation I hadn't recognized existed. •

• Supporting material: examples of cliff jumping.

I commuted to Washington because my husband and son were in Springfield. I cried for a week before I started the job. I hated leaving my family. But I learned that careers grow when people are willing to risk leaving their own backyard. And we made it an adventure for our family.

Finally, I returned to Illinois. I was recruited by the governor to run the state's Department of Public Aid. And then I became the first person with a disability to be nominated by a major party to run for a statewide office.

That was tough. Getting out to meet people. Wondering how they'd welcome me. Having to crawl into small commuter planes that are rightfully "puddle jumpers" so that I could make the next engagement. Riding in parades and waving because I couldn't walk; riding in a car while other candidates walked and shook hands along the parade route went against every instinct I felt, but it was an accommodation I had to accept. I was also hoisted onto haystacks to address crowds.

We lost a close election. Yet looking back on all of it, one impression especially touched me. Most people, I'm convinced, saw the real Sue Suter. A major party candidate fighting in a tough election. Not some cripple to be pitied. That revelation meant a lot.

Cliff jumping is a part of being normal. Every time is scary. But they are among the most empowering events in our lives because they free us from the emotional impoverishment of isolation. And because they give us the freedom to follow our conscience and our dreams. And perhaps most importantly, they free us from labels. •

● Main idea: the importance of role models.

● ● ●

There's [a] lesson we can learn from the deaf community. It's about the fact that history is a vast warning system. Most of the speeches you'll hear in this conference will center on the evolution of the disability movement. Progress, one step at a time. Yet history can also be cyclical.

Years ago, almost 50 percent of all teachers for the deaf in the United States were deaf themselves. More than teachers, they were imparters of a graceful language of signs that were rooted in the deaf community; they were role models for entire generations of young deaf students.

Then, in 1880, the renaissance came to an abrupt end. At an international conference of rehabilitation professionals—much like this one—the school of thought called oralism won the day. American Sign Language was discouraged. Speech acquisition was made paramount, so many schools no longer used deaf teachers; they were now considered bad role models of communication. And perhaps the most blatant wrong committed at the Milan Conference of 1880 was that not a single deaf teacher was allowed to vote on the changes.

It was not so long ago that stories filtered from our own Illinois School for the Deaf about a young deaf girl who asked a hearing dorm counselor if she was going to die soon. She was nearing graduation, and she had only seen a few deaf adults. What happened to the others? This is an extreme example. But it points out the vital importance of role models. •

• Supporting material: an anecdote.

I never had a role model when I was growing up. I remember what my father said to me when I was in the second grade. He loved me very much. He wanted me to be prepared for the future. So he warned me that I would probably never get married. He told me that I should become a clinical psychologist. I eventually did. Then he said that I should work to be the best so that I could be independent, because some day there might not be anybody around to take care of me.

Hard words for a seven-year-old girl to hear. But my father loved me. And he wanted me to be prepared. What a difference it would have made, for myself and my parents, if there was a family next door where the mother also wore braces. A role model. A person with a disability who was married, who raised children, who was nurturing and independent in her own right. Maybe even a corporate leader.

Middle-class college students aren't the only ones who need to know that those labels can also belong to a woman with a disability. People like you and me need that affirmation, as well. Would having a role model like that next door have changed my life? Maybe not. But it would have made me feel better. More normal. More ordinary.

• • •

We can dwell on the injustices of dual discrimination. We can churn until we turn a rut into a grave. Or we can empower ourselves: •

- by holding claim to our citizenship in the community of humanity . . .
- by reaching beyond parochial disability issues that others feel safe in allowing us to govern . . .
- by wrestling for control over the language that defines us . . .
- by treating the needs of women with disabilities as civil rights issues . . .
- by empowering ourselves as full-fledged citizens . . .
- and by simple acts of ordinary living that can mentor and nurture others looking for a role model. •

If there's one thought that I'd like to leave with you, it's that we can make a difference. I've seen it happen over and over.

For example, when women with disabilities in Chicago reached their limit putting up with poor health care, the Rehabilitation Institute of Chicago opened a new Women's Center. And with the help of their executive director, Judith Panko-Reis, the center has recently received a hundred-thousand-dollar grant to keep the operation alive.

A few years ago, there was a bill in our state legislature to increase wages for personal attendants, so that high turnover rates could be reduced. Many prominent rehabilitation organizations came to the legislative hearings in support of the bill. But it was one consumer, named Terry Gutterman, who made the issue understandable to legislators by simply asking them to "imagine

• Main idea: empowering actions audience members should take.

• Audience involved in solutions.

giving the keys to your house to fourteen different people in a single year." That message got through—I believe—in large part because of one small action by one person. The bill passed.

Groups and individuals make a difference. And I believe with all my heart that it can happen again. We women with disabilities have the same hopes and dreams and ambitions as our nondisabled sisters. We are neither weak nor heroic. We are normal. And we are boat rockers. •

• Clincher: relating back to boat-rocking theme from introduction.

SAMPLE PERSUASIVE SPEECH

REMARKS AT THE BRANDENBURG GATE

President Ronald Reagan

After World War II, the Soviet Union occupied much of Eastern Europe, and Winston Churchill lamented that "an iron curtain has descended across the continent." Nowhere was the divide between democratic Western Europe and occupied Eastern Europe more visibly apparent than Berlin, Germany. In 1961, West and East Berlin were separated by the Berlin Wall, a 103-mile concrete and barbed-wire barrier. The historic Brandenburg Gate, commissioned by Prussian king Friedrich Wilhelm in the late eighteenth century and located on the boundary, was closed to east-west traffic.

President Ronald Reagan had a good working relationship with Soviet leader Mikhail Gorbachev. They had met at four summits in the 1980s, and Gorbachev's policies of glasnost *(greater political openness) and* perestroika *(economic reform) created hopes of a thaw in the Cold War between West and East. Nevertheless, in 1987, the Soviet Union still dominated Eastern Europe, and the wall continued to divide Berlin.*

On June 12, 1987, President Reagan traveled to Berlin to deliver a speech on the 750th anniversary of the city. He spoke to West German leaders and twenty thousand citizens, with the Brandenburg Gate in the background.[34] Ronald Reagan was one of the most effective public speakers in the history of the presidency, and this speech was one of his most significant. As you read the text of his message, consider how he challenged Mr. Gorbachev to take the next step in the direction of reform.

Chancellor Kohl, Governing Mayor Diepgen, ladies and gentlemen: Twenty-four years ago, President John F. Kennedy visited Berlin, speaking to the people of this city and the world at the City Hall. Well, since then two other presidents have come, each in his turn, to Berlin. And today I, myself, make my second visit to your city.

We come to Berlin, we American presidents, because it's our duty to speak, in this place, of freedom. • But I must confess, we're drawn here by other things as well: by the feeling of history in this city, more than five hundred years older than our own nation; by the beauty of the Grunewald and the Tiergarten; most of all, by your courage and determination. Perhaps the composer Paul Lincke understood something about American presidents. You see, like so many presidents before me, I come here today because wherever I go, whatever I do: *Ich hab noch einen Koffer in Berlin.* [I still have a suitcase in Berlin.] •

Our gathering today is being broadcast throughout Western Europe and North America. I understand that it is being seen and heard as well in the East. To those listening throughout Eastern Europe, a special word: Although I cannot be with you, I address my remarks to you just as surely as to those standing here before me. For I join you, as I join your fellow countrymen in the West, in this firm, this unalterable belief: *Es gibt nur ein Berlin.* [There is only one Berlin.] •

Behind me stands a wall that encircles the free sectors of this city, part of a vast system of barriers that divides the entire continent of Europe. From the Baltic, south, those barriers cut across Germany in a gash of barbed wire, concrete, dog runs, and guard towers. Farther south, there may be no visible, no obvious wall. But there remain armed guards and checkpoints all the same—still a restriction on the right to travel, still an instrument to impose upon ordinary men and women the will of a totalitarian state. Yet it is here in Berlin where the wall emerges most clearly; here, cutting across your city, where the news

• Reagan uses vivid language, tradition, and common ground to connect with the audience.

• By including lines in German that incorporate the words *Berlin* and *Berliner*, Reagan evokes John F. Kennedy's famous speech from twenty-four years earlier (*"Ich bin ein Berliner"*).

• Reagan's target audience includes Eastern Europeans who are listening from behind the Iron Curtain.

photo and the television screen have imprinted this brutal division of a continent upon the mind of the world. Standing before the Brandenburg Gate, every man is a German, separated from his fellow men. Every man is a Berliner, forced to look upon a scar. •

President von Weizsacker has said, "The German question is open as long as the Brandenburg Gate is closed." Today I say: As long as the gate is closed, as long as this scar of a wall is permitted to stand, it is not the German question alone that remains open but the question of freedom for all mankind. Yet I do not come here to lament. For I find in Berlin a message of hope, even in the shadow of this wall, a message of triumph. •

In this season of spring in 1945, the people of Berlin emerged from their air-raid shelters to find devastation. Thousands of miles away, the people of the United States reached out to help. And in 1947, Secretary of State—as you've been told—George Marshall announced the creation of what would become known as the Marshall Plan. Speaking precisely forty years ago this month, he said: "Our policy is directed not against any country or doctrine but against hunger, poverty, desperation, and chaos."

In the Reichstag a few moments ago, I saw a display commemorating this fortieth anniversary of the Marshall Plan. I was struck by the sign on a burnt-out, gutted structure that was being rebuilt. I understand that Berliners of my own generation can remember seeing signs like it dotted throughout the western sectors of the city. The sign read simply: "The Marshall Plan is helping here to strengthen the free world." A strong, free world in the West, that dream became real. Japan rose from ruin to become an economic giant. Italy, France, Belgium— virtually every nation in Western Europe saw political and economic rebirth; the European Community was founded.

In West Germany and here in Berlin, there took place an economic miracle, the *Wirtschaftswunder*. Adenauer, Erhard, Reuter, and other leaders understood the practical importance of liberty—that just as truth can flourish only when the

- Effective style: a scar as a metaphor for the wall.

- Reagan makes an emotional appeal for hope.

journalist is given freedom of speech, so prosperity can come about only when the farmer and businessman enjoy economic freedom. The German leaders reduced tariffs, expanded free trade, lowered taxes. From 1950 to 1960 alone, the standard of living in West Germany and Berlin doubled. Where four decades ago there was rubble, today in West Berlin there is the greatest industrial output of any city in Germany—busy office blocks, fine homes and apartments, proud avenues, and the spreading lawns of parkland. •

• Example reasoning supports the claim that Berlin is thriving.

Where a city's culture seemed to have been destroyed, today there are two great universities, orchestras and an opera, countless theaters, and museums. Where there was want, today there's abundance—food, clothing, automobiles—the wonderful goods of the Ku'damm. From devastation, from utter ruin, you Berliners have, in freedom, rebuilt a city that once again ranks as one of the greatest on earth. The Soviets may have had other plans. But my friends, there were a few things the Soviets didn't count on—*Berliner Herz, Berliner Humor, ja, und Berliner Schnauze.* [Berliner heart, Berliner humor, yes, and Berliner dialect.]

In the 1950s, Khrushchev predicted: "We will bury you." But in the West today, we see a free world that has achieved a level of prosperity and well-being unprecedented in all human history. In the Communist world, we see failure, technological backwardness, declining standards of health, even want of the most basic kind—too little food. Even today, the Soviet Union still cannot feed itself. After these four decades, then, there stands before the entire world one great and inescapable conclusion: Freedom leads to prosperity. Freedom replaces the ancient hatreds among the nations with comity and peace. Freedom is the victor. •

• Reagan makes a comparison of totalitarian and free societies.

And now the Soviets themselves may, in a limited way, be coming to understand the importance of freedom. We hear much from Moscow about a new policy of reform and openness. Some political prisoners have been released. Certain foreign news broadcasts are no longer being jammed. Some economic enterprises have been permitted to operate with greater freedom from state control. •

• Sign reasoning: possible indicators of reform.

Are these the beginnings of profound changes in the Soviet state? Or are they token gestures, intended to raise false hopes in the West or to strengthen the Soviet system without changing it? We welcome change and openness, for we believe that freedom and security go together, that the advance of human liberty can only strengthen the cause of world peace. There is one sign the Soviets can make that would be unmistakable, that would advance dramatically the cause of freedom and peace. •

• A call for action: one more step that would prove Soviet desire for reform.

General Secretary Gorbachev, if you seek peace, if you seek prosperity for the Soviet Union and Eastern Europe, if you seek liberalization: Come here to this gate! Mr. Gorbachev, open this gate! Mr. Gorbachev, tear down this wall! •

• Dynamic style at the climax of the speech; President Reagan is still remembered for this line.

I understand the fear of war and the pain of division that afflict this continent—and I pledge to you my country's efforts to help overcome these burdens. To be sure, we in the West must resist Soviet expansion. So we must maintain defenses of unassailable strength. Yet we seek peace; so we must strive to reduce arms on both sides. •

• In this call for action, Reagan requests mutual arms reductions.

Beginning ten years ago, the Soviets challenged the Western alliance with a grave new threat, hundreds of new and more deadly SS-20 nuclear missiles, capable of striking every capital in Europe. The Western alliance responded by committing itself to a counterdeployment unless the Soviets agreed to negotiate a better solution—namely, the elimination of such weapons on both sides. For many months, the Soviets refused to bargain in earnestness. As the alliance, in turn, prepared to go forward with its counterdeployment, there were difficult days—days of protests like those during my 1982 visit to this city—and the Soviets later walked away from the table.

But through it all, the alliance held firm. And I invite those who protested then—I invite those who protest today—to mark this fact: Because we remained strong, the

Soviets came back to the table. And because we remained strong, today we have within reach the possibility, not merely of limiting the growth of arms but of eliminating, for the first time, an entire class of nuclear weapons from the face of the earth.

• • •

But we must remember a crucial fact: East and West do not mistrust each other because we are armed; we are armed because we mistrust each other. • And our differences are not about weapons but about liberty. When President Kennedy spoke at the City Hall those twenty-four years ago, freedom was encircled, Berlin was under siege. And today, despite all the pressures upon this city, Berlin stands secure in its liberty. And freedom itself is transforming the globe.

• Causal reasoning: mistrust is the cause of the arms race.

• • •

As I looked out a moment ago from the Reichstag, that embodiment of German unity, I noticed words crudely spray-painted upon the wall, perhaps by a young Berliner: "This wall will fall. Beliefs become reality." Yes, across Europe, this wall will fall. For it cannot withstand faith; it cannot withstand truth. The wall cannot withstand freedom. •

• Reagan exemplifies his optimistic outlook with a vivid anecdote that echoes a key message of his overall speech— that the Berlin Wall should be torn down.

And I would like, before I close, to say one word. I have read, and I have been questioned since I've been here, about certain demonstrations against my coming. And I would like to say just one thing . . . to those who demonstrate so. I wonder if they have ever asked themselves that if they should have the kind of government they apparently seek, no one would ever be able to do what they're doing again.

Thank you and God bless you all.

CHAPTER REVIEW

"Persuasion happens when credible speakers provide good reasons and touch audience emotions." Once you have selected a topic for your persuasive speech, analyzed your audience, and chosen an effective thesis, you need to develop a message that compels your listeners to accept your thesis—and your ultimate goal of changing or strengthening audience beliefs, attitudes, or actions. You can do this by combining ethos, logos, and pathos.

Through ethos, you establish your credibility as a speaker. The audience must perceive that you are competent and trustworthy, and that you have their best interests at heart. You can also avoid losing credibility by avoiding statements that raise doubts about your knowledge, honesty, or goodwill.

Through logos, you use credible evidence to support your claims. You also present sound reasoning to establish these claims through the use of examples, comparisons, signs, and cause-effect relationships. When reasoning, it is essential to avoid logical fallacies.

Through pathos, you further strengthen your persuasive power by evoking your audience members' emotions—not to manipulate your listeners but to move them in an ethical and responsible manner to take the action you're proposing or adopt the belief you're advocating.

Together, ethos, logos, and pathos can help you win your listeners' heads (their reason), hearts (their emotions), and hands (their commitment to action). Master these three tools, and you'll greatly enhance your prowess as a persuasive speaker.

Key Terms

ethos (credibility) *540*
competence *541*
trustworthiness *541*
goodwill *541*
logos *546*
evidence *546*

fallacious (faulty) reasoning *547*
inductive reasoning *549*
example reasoning *550*
representative example *551*
comparison reasoning *552*
sign reasoning *555*

Review Questions

1. Explain the three primary elements of credibility.
2. Indicate six steps you can take to enhance your own credibility.
3. What are four mistakes you can make that may harm your credibility?
4. What are three fundamental components of a logical message?
5. Identify and explain seven logical fallacies.
6. What factors come into play when making an emotional appeal?
7. What kinds of practices can harm an emotional appeal?

Critical Thinking Questions

1. What role does audience analysis play in establishing your credibility? Is the speaker's responsibility to back up claims with solid evidence the same for a sympathetic audience as it is for a hostile or neutral audience?
2. As an audience member, how can you identify logical fallacies during a speech? How can you identify weak or misleading evidence? How do you react when a speaker's claims are based on unsound evidence or reasoning?
3. How should a speaker who favors a particular tradition develop a logical argument for that tradition that avoids committing an appeal to tradition fallacy? For example, how might a speaker build a case for the general education requirement described in the text

on page 563? In a broader sense, how can you build a strong and ethical argument for maintaining a tradition that you support?

4. What types of presentation aids can you use to build your credibility?

5. Reflect on your position on a controversial issue in society. What evidence could persuade you to adopt a more neutral position or change your mind? Who would be a credible source that could induce you to rethink your position? How can the answers to these questions help you in your own efforts as a persuasive speaker?

Activities

1. FactCheck.org is a nonpartisan organization that reviews political speeches, advertising, and commentary, and verifies the validity of the claims made in them. Visit the Web site and look at recent postings. What logical fallacies do they identify? What other logical errors do they note? Were any of them surprising to you? Why or why not?

2. Choose one of the sample persuasive speeches from the end of this chapter, or one of the sample persuasive speeches in the appendix. Create a speaking outline that shows how you would revise this speech to suit a different rhetorical purpose, such as informing. Revise one of the informative speeches in Chapter 15 or the appendix to create a persuasive argument.

3. Create a credibility checklist based on the bulleted list on pages 542–43. Review a persuasive speech in this text or one that you find on the Internet and see how many of the criteria the speaker fulfills.

4. Watch a few episodes of *The Daily Show*. For one episode, assess each comedic "bit" or segment and identify those that focus on pundits' and politicians' use of loaded language and fear appeals. Characterize a few of the fallacies being exposed.

Go to **bedfordstmartins.com/speakup**, where you'll find helpful study materials, videos, and speech-building tools.

SPECIAL-OCCASION SPEAKING

18

“Whether to mark a celebration, a milestone, or a passing, we all participate in special-occasion speaking as speakers or listeners.”

Speeches that praise, celebrate, memorialize, or otherwise commemorate special occasions have a long history. A Sumerian tablet dating back to about 2000 B.C.E. records the funeral utterances of Ludingirra, a teacher and poet, as he laments the loss of his father and his wife by eulogizing (or memorializing) their achievements and personal qualities. Indeed, **epideictic** rhetoric—speaking that praises or blames—was one of the three genres of oratory identified by the fourth-century B.C.E. Greek philosopher Aristotle.[1] Speakers typically used this form of address to celebrate timeless virtues during occasions such as funerals or holidays.[2] And ever since Aristotle's lifetime, people around the world have continued to use public speaking to help themselves and others celebrate joyous occasions, mourn the passing of loved ones, honor friends' or colleagues' achievements, and observe other milestones in their communities.

Think about the times you've been moved by a speech marking a special occasion. Perhaps on the most recent Memorial Day, you heard a speaker praising soldiers who fought in World War II and remembered your grandfather's tour of duty in Europe during that conflict. Maybe you've attended a gathering to observe the passing of another September 11 on the calendar, and the speaker's words helped you reflect once again on the magnitude of the terrorist attacks. You might also have attended a wedding, clapping and cheering along with the other guests as friends and relatives of the bride and groom offered toasts to the new couple. And if you've excelled at your job, perhaps you've been presented with an award, along with words of praise from your boss, during a department meeting or party. If you've attended a formal dinner for your company or a community organization, you may have listened to an after-dinner speech—a traditional presentation designed to entertain an audience after a meal. Certainly, you'll have the opportunity to listen to many speeches of congratulation and advice if you take part in graduation ceremonies after completing your college degree.

Special-occasion speeches mark some of the most important events in our lives—events that bring us together with others in our community; events that unite us in our humanity. As you go through your own life, you'll not only hear many such speeches but probably be called on to give one or more yourself. Even if you never have to deliver a formal presentation in an official capacity

(such as at work or in a civic setting), you will almost certainly be invited to "say a few words" at various points in your life. For example, your grandmother might ask you to say good-bye to your deceased grandfather during an intimate graveside service. Or you might be hosting a large gathering of family at your home during Thanksgiving, and you know that your guests expect you to start things off by sharing some inspiring words about the meaning of the holiday. Or perhaps you've arranged for your friend's band to play for the first time at a local pub, and he's asked you to introduce the performers to the crowd.

Whatever your special speaking occasion, you'll have to face that ever-daunting question: "What am I going to say?" In this chapter, we help you answer that question. We start by introducing six types of special-occasion speeches and discussing the purposes each type serves. Next, we offer some general guidelines for speaking at a special occasion. After that, we go into detail about each of the six types of special-occasion speeches, providing tips tailored to each type. And finally, we revisit a few preparation and delivery strategies discussed earlier in this book.

TYPES OF SPECIAL-OCCASION SPEECHES

Although there are various types of special-occasion speeches, the six most common are:

- *Speech of introduction.* Sometimes referred to as "the speech before the speech," this is a brief presentation designed to prepare an audience for the "main event"—a speaker, a performance, or an activity that will follow. A speech of introduction provides context and gives credentials for the main speaker or performer.

- *Speech of presentation.* Awards, honors, and special designations often require speeches before they are conferred. A presentation speech explains the background and significance of the award and the reasons why the recipient is deserving of it.

- *Speech of acceptance.* Recipients of honors, awards, or designations are often expected to give a short presentation of their own—something beyond a simple thank you. Recipients typically express gratitude for the award, extol the award's significance to them and others, and acknowledge others' support and contributions.

SPEECH OF INTRODUCTION

Good evening, ladies and gentlemen. Welcome to the first ever CARTOON ACADEMY AWARDS CEREMONY—coming to you in glorious 3D!

SPEECH OF PRESENTATION

It gives me great pleasure to announce that this first award for HUMAN BEING DOING BEST JOB OF ACTING LIKE A CARTOON CHARACTER goes to... ...LADY GAGA!!

SPEECH OF ACCEPTANCE

Thank you, Robert, er, Iron Man. Thank you, Cartoon Academy. Thank you to my local garden supply store...

- *Speech to memorialize or eulogize.* A **eulogy** comments on the passing of an individual, celebrates his or her life, and often shares personal reflections and stories about the deceased. A speech to memorialize uses the same approach but is expanded to honor the sacrifice and heroism of a group of individuals—often on a significant anniversary, such as Veterans Day or September 11.

- *Speech to celebrate.* Events that represent rites of passage— such as christenings, graduations, weddings, reunions, and retirements—often demand celebration speeches. These may take the form of a toast or special observance that focuses the audience's attention on the milestone achieved, and recognizes the joy and pride the partici- pants feel.

- *After-dinner speech.* At times, a speaker needs to use humor and good storytelling to lighten the mood of an occasion or soften up an audience. Though these presentations are called "after-dinner speeches" (in the tradition of Mark Twain), they can follow or precede a meal. Light in tone, they can help a speaker entertain his or her listeners or set

SPEECH TO MEMORIALIZE

the stage for an event that follows the meal, such as a fund-raising effort for a charitable cause.

At some events, you'll hear more than one type of special-occasion speech being delivered. Consider the Academy Awards—what most of us call the Oscars. This star-studded annual event begins with a *speech of introduction*. A master of ceremonies—perhaps Ellen DeGeneres, Jon Stewart, or Steve Martin—prepares the audience for the main event, often acknowledging the honored tradition of the Oscars while also telling jokes to loosen up the crowd. At some point during the evening, a well-known actor gives a *presentation speech* before announcing a life-time achievement award for a long-famous director or producer. Recipients of Oscars and lifetime achievement awards deliver *acceptance speeches* thanking the academy, exclaiming how much the award means to them, and acknowledging (sometimes seemingly endlessly) the support they've received from their families and colleagues. And later in the evening, a presenter might *eulogize* a recently departed luminary from the motion-picture industry.

Each type of special-occasion speech serves a unique purpose and evokes a different mood. But the six types all have something in common as well: to deliver any of them effectively, you must apply certain common skills (such as evoking your listeners' emotions and being mindful of their expectations). The following guidelines can help you establish a basic foundation of knowledge before we explore strategies tailored to each of the six types of speeches.

GENERAL GUIDELINES FOR SPECIAL OCCASIONS

A handful of general guidelines can boost your chances of delivering an effective special-occasion speech, no matter what type you'll be giving. These guidelines include appealing to your audience's emotions, ensuring that your delivery suits the mood of the occasion, adapting your speech to your audience's expectations, evoking shared values, and respecting time constraints.

Appealing to Your Audience's Emotions

Successful special-occasion speeches often evoke emotional responses, such as laughter, tears, joy, and pride. Since many special occasions are intimately connected with important human events, your audience will likely be predisposed to experiencing a particular feeling during the occasion. Your job in giving the speech will be to signal when it's time for that emotion to come to the surface.

For example, suppose you're about to deliver a eulogy at a graveside service for your grandmother—a loving family woman, an accomplished artist, and a dedicated supporter of important causes.

THE ELEMENTS OF AN EFFECTIVE SPECIAL-OCCASION SPEECH

Family members and friends are gathered around the headstone under a canopy of maple and oak trees. Everyone present is reflecting on your grandmother's life, and the sorrow of saying good-bye begins to settle around their hearts. The moment arrives for you to walk to the headstone and deliver the eulogy. You begin speaking. As you recall your grandmother's special qualities and achievements and talk about how much she meant to you, your eyes fill and your voice breaks at times. The combination of your words and the expression of your grief gives the others gathered around the gravesite permission to let their own feelings well up. By enabling your family and friends to begin experiencing and expressing their grief, you help them embark on the mourning process—something we all must do when we have lost a loved one.

Matching Your Delivery to the Mood of the Occasion

Whether joyous or solemn, lighthearted or serious, your demeanor and words should match the overall mood of the special occasion for which you're giving a speech. As the saying goes, there's a time and a place for everything: a time to be serious, and a time to be joyful; a time to tell stories, a time to show respect, and a time to share your own sadness. By ensuring that what you say and how you say it are appropriate for the occasion, you will enhance your effectiveness and impact.

For example, a eulogy calls primarily for a somber, sad tone, though an occasional lovingly humorous recollection about the deceased may also be appropriate and appreciated. At the graveside service for your grandmother, for instance, family members and friends smile through their tears and nod their heads knowingly when you help them recall her famous midnight excursions into the kitchen for some chocolate ice cream.

If you're the best man at your older brother's wedding and you're giving a toast at the reception, you'll of course evoke a different overall mood. You'll want to express your happiness that your brother has found a loving spouse as well as give voice to everyone's wish that the new couple will share a long and joyous life together. And depending on the traditions of your culture, you might introduce a bit of humor by hinting at the wild escapades your brother had in his younger years and expressing your satisfaction that he's finally settling down with

a wonderful partner. You decidedly would not go on and on about any hard and painful times the couple experienced while dating. Nor would you be critical in any way of their relationship.

Adapting to Your Audience's Expectations

Listeners' cultural background, age, values, and other characteristics all affect how they perceive a special occasion and what they expect from a speech delivered during that occasion. For example, a community of Christian Arab immigrants living in Chicago would likely want to attend a church funeral service after one of their community members died. Moreover, they would probably expect a mostly religious service with brief discussion of the deceased, including comments focused particularly on how he or she cared about the community and shared its traditions. (Fuller discussion of the person might come at a community dinner in honor of the deceased, later in the day.)

On the other hand, an audience of amateur comedians might expect a fun and lighthearted presentation at a roast for a fellow entertainer, during which the audience would be treated to funny stories about the individual being roasted. At this kind of event, it would run against audience expectations to bring up painful events from the person's childhood and thus bring an overly serious turn to the proceedings.

The lesson? Before giving any special-occasion speech, be sure you're familiar with your audience's expectations regarding what should be said during the speech and how it should be said.

Evoking Shared Values

Many effective special-occasion speeches appeal to values shared by members of the audience and the speaker. For instance, suppose you're presenting a plaque to Olivia, a fellow member of PeopleAid, an organization that helps homeless members of your community. The award is for Olivia's steady dedication to PeopleAid's mission: she has recruited an unusual number of volunteers to serve boxed lunches to the homeless at shelters throughout the community and led other valuable projects for the organization. Before handing the plaque to Olivia, you deliver a speech extolling her ability to embody PeopleAid's values, which include compassion for those in need and a strong work ethic. Your speech about Olivia reaffirms your listeners' own dedication to these values and inspires them to strive for the same high standards she has set.

Other special-occasion speeches may touch on values such as patriotism, fairness, shared sacrifice, and religious belief. To illustrate, let's say you're giving a speech at a ceremony recognizing the first anniversary of the death of Frank, a close friend who lost his life while serving in the U.S. Army in Afghanistan. The ceremony is held at the town hall near where you and Frank grew up. Neighbors and family members have gathered to remember Frank and honor the one-year anniversary of his death. In your speech, you note that "Frank felt the same love for his country that everyone in this room feels. We have all made sacrifices for that love. Frank lost his life, and we lost him all too soon. We will never forget our lost friend, brother, son, and neighbor." Through these words, you tap into the patriotism in your listeners' hearts and their sense of shared sacrifice—reminding them that you are all connected in a close community.

Respecting Time Constraints

Most special occasions are carefully planned affairs. Recall a wedding, christening, or retirement dinner you've recently attended. The occasion likely had a program, featuring certain events occurring at specific times. The program for a retirement dinner, for example, might look something like: "Cocktails at 4:00. Award ceremony at 5:00. Dinner at 6:00." The occasion may also have featured several speeches. Whenever refreshments, meal service, and multiple speakers are involved, skillful management of the overall program schedule becomes that much more important. If a specific event listed in the program gets off to a late start, or if one of the speakers uses up more time than the program has allotted, then the entire event can quickly go off the rails. For this reason, if you're giving a speech at such an occasion, make sure you know beforehand when you're scheduled to speak and what your time allotment is. Then be certain to stick to these logistics while delivering your presentation.

STRATEGIES FOR EACH TYPE OF SPECIAL-OCCASION SPEECH

While the general guidelines described in the preceding section can help you deliver an effective special-occasion speech, you'll also want to master strategies tailored to each of the six types of speeches. Pair these specific practices with the general suggestions, and you'll increase the odds of delivering a top-notch speech—no matter what the occasion.

Strategies for Speeches of Introduction

When you're giving a speech to introduce another speaker, a performer, or an event, you have three goals:

- Shift your listeners' focus from interacting with one another to paying attention to the upcoming event.
- Build anticipation and excitement in the audience for the upcoming topic and speaker or presentation.
- Introduce the person, performance, or event that's coming next.

When making an introduction, remember that you are not the main entertainment. Your primary goal is to facilitate what's coming next, and there is nothing more disastrous than an introductory speaker who goes on too long or tries too hard. So, take care not to upstage the speaker or

THE ART OF INTRODUCTION

event you're introducing. In particular, resist any urge to talk at length about yourself. And be sure to express some of your own appreciation for and anticipation of the upcoming event. The following tips can further help you keep your audience focused on the main event and effectively achieve your three-part goal in giving a speech of introduction.

Be Patient. When the time comes for you to start your introduction, many listeners may still be settling into their seats, finishing a meal, or simply chatting with each other. To help them gradually shift their attention to you, stand up and begin talking above the background noise and voices in the room. But be patient: it takes time for people to transition away from what they're doing at the moment.

Use Attention-Getters. To further focus your listeners on the upcoming speaker or event, use attention-getters to cut through any noise or conversation in the room, while making sure that you remain appropriate for the setting. Consider one of the attention-getters mentioned in Chapter 10, and especially consider incorporating a striking statement or a little bit of humor, or taking the opportunity to let listeners know that you're one of them.

Modulate Your Volume. Even if you are working with a microphone, you may need to speak loudly at first to overcome the prevailing noise in the room and grab listeners' attention. But after your speech is under way, be sure to lower your voice as the room quiets down. If conversation stirs again later during your speech, you can always raise your voice once more to an appropriate level.

Be Focused and Brief. Remember that your job is to prepare the audience to pay attention to the speaker or performance that will follow you. To that end, keep your comments focused on that next event. And make sure your introduction is concise. Otherwise, audience members may start seeing you as the main entertainment, or they may lose interest in the next part of the program.

Strategies for Speeches of Presentation

Like a speech of introduction, the presentation of an award or commendation precedes and facilitates what comes next for the audience. But unlike a speech of introduction, a presentation speech usually *celebrates* the person, organization, or cause being honored—whether it's a service commendation for a teacher at a local PTA meeting, an award at a sports team banquet, or even an Oscar or Emmy.

Thus, in a presentation speech, your role will be more fundamental than in a speech of introduction; you must provide your listeners with background and context for the honor to follow. This might seem unnecessary, as listeners probably already know what the honor is and why they are there to observe it. Yet your job is to highlight the significance of the award and to build excitement and even reverence for it. You can do this by describing in detail the importance of the award itself and the background and contributions of the recipient.

Handled skillfully, a presentation speech can inspire intense emotion in listeners and even move them to dedicate themselves to the

THE ART OF PRESENTING

award recipient's work. Strong and enthusiastic applause after you've presented the award or commendation is another sure sign that you've nailed the speech. The tips below can help you achieve this kind of impact.

Adopt the Persona of a Presenter. In this type of speech, you're not just announcing the conferring of an award or honor; you're also presenting it. To demonstrate your authority as a presenter, be sure to speak respectfully and knowledgeably about your subject.

Explain the Significance and Background of the Award or Honor. Most people in your audience will understand that they are there for the presentation of an award. But they may not know why the honor or award really matters. What is its significance? Does it have an interesting history you could share? In a nutshell, a major goal of your presentation speech is to make clear why your listeners should care about the award about to be bestowed.

Connect the Recipient's Background to the Award's Criteria. Every award has qualifications or criteria that a potential recipient must meet and perhaps exceed. But these may not be obvious to the audience. In your speech, be sure to explain the criteria—and then point out how and why the recipient has met or surpassed them. Consider using stories and examples of the recipient's achievements to dramatically (and perhaps humorously) show why he or she deserves this honor.

Use Appropriate Presentation Aids. A video or a slide presentation, perhaps with a light music or audio accompaniment, can complement your speech. Consider using presentation aids to explain both the criteria for an

Your Majesty, Your Royal Highnesses, Ladies and Gentlemen. The work I have done has, already, been greatly rewarded and recognized. Imagination reaches out, repeatedly trying to achieve some higher level of understanding, until suddenly I find myself momentarily alone before one corner of nature's pattern of beauty and true majesty revealed. That was my reward.

RICHARD FEYNMAN
1965 NOBEL PRIZE IN PHYSICS

award and how the recipient fulfilled the criteria. For example, if you're presenting an award for a person who has helped teach literacy to children in need, you could provide a short slide show depicting the recipient performing this work, along with audio snippets of children who benefited from the person's efforts.

Strategies for Speeches of Acceptance

Now imagine that you're the beneficiary of an award and the presenter has just handed it to you. What do you say now?

A high-quality acceptance speech is less about what you're saying ("Thank you; I couldn't have done this without the rest of the team") and more about how you're behaving while accepting the honor. By being there, you transform the presentation into a kind of public spectacle. The audience will expect you to show both humility and responsibility. You can fulfill those expectations by giving a brief, gracious, and heartfelt speech that expresses your gratitude while also recognizing others' efforts that contributed to your achievement. The following tips can help you attain this blend of important qualities.

Use Appropriate Volume and Articulation. Accepting an award can stir intense emotions within you, causing your voice to drop or break—and if you are using a microphone, such lapses will only be amplified. To overcome this challenge, anticipate the impact of strong feelings, and feel free to gather yourself for a moment or two before you start talking. Strive to speak with sufficient volume and clarity throughout, especially when thanking others during your acceptance.

Show Genuine Humility. Listeners can easily spot the difference between someone who's genuinely modest and humbled by an honor and someone who's just acting

SPENCER LYNN WILKISON
2007 EL PASO COUNTY
FAIR QUEEN

humble. Think about it: on at least several occasions, you've proba- bly seen a person stand at a podium and gush about how this award has "caught me off guard" and "left me speechless"—but then he or she pulls out a sheet of paper and gives a canned speech. Irritat- ing, isn't it? To avoid making this mistake, don't act surprised if you knew you would be receiving the award. But definitely express your genuine gratitude for the honor and for the people who helped you achieve it.

Remember That Less Is More. Going on too long while accepting an award can give the impression that you always talk about yourself and rarely exhibit interest in others. To avoid con- veying this impression, aim for brevity in your acceptance speech. Say enough to demonstrate your humility (perhaps through a bit of self-deprecating humor) and to acknowledge your deep apprecia- tion for the award or honor. Briefly thank those to whom you are indebted. And then sit down. Otherwise, the music may start playing, and your presenter may take you by the elbow and start ushering you offstage.

Strategies for Speeches to Memorialize or Eulogize

Because death is a part of life, at some point you will inevitably lose a beloved family member or friend. You may be asked to deliver a eulogy about the person at a memorial service after his or her passing. Your purpose during this type of speech is to review and celebrate the life of your loved one and to console your listeners while simultane- ously helping them to grieve publicly. It may seem that the two goals (consoling and facilitating grief) are in conflict, but consolation actually supports grieving—primarily because you can express these strong emotions as you encourage your audience to feel the same. Witness- ing a eulogist publicly expressing grief gives the audience license to do so as well.

Delivering an effective eulogy is about helping the living by show- ing your own emotion as well as extolling the departed loved one's virtues and achievements. The following tips can help you provide this assistance while giving this kind of speech.

Focus on Celebrating the Person's Life. Each person's life has both high and low points, good experiences and bad. Instead of focusing on negative memories in your eulogy, highlight the departed loved one's accomplishments, important relationships, and unique qualities, citing examples and stories familiar to your listeners. You'll establish common ground with your audience members and help them collectively celebrate the best of the person they've lost.

Use Humor Judiciously. At most memorial services, several people will stand up and say something about the deceased. If each of a series of speakers focuses unrelentingly on the profound sorrow of the occasion, the collective heaviness may become too much for the audience to bear. For this reason, consider providing a humorous (but appropriate) anecdote about the deceased at some point during your remarks to relieve the tension. Listeners may feel profound relief when they can laugh through their tears.

Don't Be Afraid to Show Your Own Emotions. The best way to give the audience permission to grieve openly during a memorial service is to show your own emotions. A display of feeling can set loose a flood of feelings in your listeners, which can provide a release that is just as healthy and productive as laughter after your lovingly humorous story about the deceased.

Strategies for Speeches to Celebrate

Life is as much about joy and celebration as it is about tragedy and loss. The birth of a child, a couple's decision to spend their lives together, a graduation, a rite of passage from youth to adulthood—these and other major milestones in our lives are all cause for happiness. And they're all marked by special occasions at which people deliver speeches to help celebrate the joyous event.

If you're delivering a speech of celebration at such an occasion, your role is to explain the significance of the occasion, acknowledge the joy everyone is feeling, and inspire the audience to take part in the celebration. The following tips can help you achieve this goal.

Aim for Brevity. Take enough time to remind your audience why the gathering is so important and joyful—but not so much time as to tire, bore, or distract the audience from the subject of the celebration.

Use Humor Appropriately. Different cultures define "appropriate" humor in different ways. Use audience analysis to determine whether humor is OK for the particular celebration or whether listeners would find it distracting or offensive. Never use humor to hurt; instead, use it to highlight endearing qualities of the people being celebrated. Tell stories about the celebrant that he or she knows are funny, and avoid making jokes about matters the person is embarrassed about or considers sensitive. Consider using humor in a self-deprecating way, so that the story you're sharing becomes funny instead of hurtful.

Strategies for After-Dinner Speeches

After-dinner speeches have a long and storied tradition in the United States, emerging in an age before television and other mass media had developed and when speaking was therefore a major form of entertainment. This tradition produced such literary giants as Mark Twain, who gave several hundred of these kinds of addresses, always after a meal. Like others who delivered these types of presentations, Twain usually salted his after-dinner speeches with entertaining stories, personal references, and a great deal of wit.

While after-dinner speeches in the United States have developed a unique flavor, other cultures also have their own after-dinner speaking traditions. Some scholars argue that the North American style of toasting arose from a long-standing tradition from Great Britain, centered in formal affairs and especially in traditional British men's clubs. And Russia has a tradition of sharing many toasts—studded with anecdotes and stories for each drink—at formal occasions and especially at group meals.

MARK TWAIN (1835 TO 1910)

It usually takes me more than three weeks to prepare a good impromptu speech.

To cease smoking is the easiest thing I ever did. I ought to know, I've done it a thousand times.

Always acknowledge a fault. This will throw those in authority off their guard and give you an opportunity to commit more.

It is my custom to keep on talking until I get the audience cowed.

Effective after-dinner speakers assume the role of entertainers and have a talent for amusing and delighting their audiences while occasionally making a more serious point. Indeed, many after-dinner speeches are given at gatherings designed to raise funds for a particular cause, such as a charitable organization or a politician's election campaign. These speeches are longer and more involved than simple toasts, and they require the ability to thrill and captivate an audience, often after listeners have consumed a full meal and perhaps a few glasses of wine. To overcome these challenges, apply the following strategies for delivering an effective after-dinner talk.

Focus on Humorous Anecdotes and Narrative Delivery, Not Jokes. In after-dinner speeches, the tradition has always been to employ witty stories and anecdotes as opposed to a series of one-liners or jokes with punch lines. Remember that your after-dinner speech should be a combination of anecdotal references and storytelling wrapped around a larger theme, not a stand-up comedy routine.

Practice Your Storytelling and Narrative Delivery. The success of your after-dinner speech hinges just as much on how you tell a story as it does on what you say in the story itself. Sufficiently rehearse your narrative so that you can feel comfortable and relaxed sharing it during the actual speech. Think of your after-dinner speech as a kind of performance, and understand that—like all performances—this one will benefit from lots of practice and polish.

Link Your Speech to the Occasion's Theme. If the dinner gathering has a serious theme—for example, the importance of raising funds to support cancer research—consider linking a lighter narrative to that weightier theme. You'll help the audience adopt a relaxed and receptive frame of mind while still accepting the urgency of the topic.

Adapt Your Delivery to Your Audience and the Occasion. Be prepared to make spontaneous adjustments to your structure and content based on what's happening around you. Look for opportunities to focus your wit or good-natured satire on something that another speaker or a member of the audience has said. For example, by commenting on a point that a previous speaker made or a question that an audience member has asked, you show that you're delivering an original rather than a canned or prepackaged speech. You thus let your audience know that you consider them worthy of a fresh presentation tailored specifically to them.

SAMPLE SPECIAL-OCCASION SPEECH

2002 MT. HOLYOKE COLLEGE COMMENCEMENT ADDRESS

Her Majesty Queen Noor

Her Majesty Queen Noor of Jordan is an international humanitarian activist and an outspoken voice on issues of world peace and justice. She chairs the Noor Al Hussein Foundation (NHF), the King Hussein Foundation, and the King Hussein Foundation International (KHFI). In this commencement speech, excerpted from the original version presented on May 26, 2002, at the women's college Mt. Holyoke in South Hadley, Massachusetts, Queen Noor connects with her audience and uses a modified problem-solution pattern; she describes current challenges to peoples around the world, outlines reasons why women are uniquely poised to help address these challenges, and then encourages the graduates to take an active role in tackling them.

Honored Guests, Faculty, Ladies and Gentlemen, and of course, the Graduates of 2002:

Thank you very, very much. It's an enormous privilege to be here on this truly magnificent campus, in the company of such distinguished fellow honorary degree recipients, of course the faculty of such an exceptional institution, family and friends of the graduates of the Class of 2002. •

• • •

• Queen Noor offers an appropriate opening to a commencement speech by complimenting the campus and acknowledging various groups attending the occasion.

Mt. Holyoke is certainly rich in good things. You have courses here I wish fervently had been available to me when I began my rather unusual career: your Speaking, Arguing, and Writing program would undoubtedly have helped diminish some of my agony over my early speeches and interviews; and your Center for Environmental Literacy could have provided excellent preparation for my extensive international work in the field of conservation. •

• Queen Noor connects with her audience by showing knowledge of courses offered at Mt. Holyoke.

My own university education, Princeton, did however offer some uncommon experiences that helped prepare me surprisingly well. One was the pioneering challenge of membership in the first class of women to enter Princeton. Quite the opposite from the supportive environment you have enjoyed here. When I arrived, the male to female ratio was more than 22 to 1—a situation which, as you might imagine, required the quick development of diplomacy and survival skills, and as it turned out excellent preparation for my work in more traditional societies in the Middle East. •

. . .

Holyoke is also rich in a long history of women's leadership. It is a place where you all can draw on the past to support your efforts to change the future. From your experience, here, and that of the distinguished Holyoke women who have gone before you into the wider world, you know that women can be leaders in any areas they choose.

Mt. Holyoke's position as a college dedicated to women's advancement in a region rich with history resonates especially with me, for I am a woman dedicated to progress in a region where the past and present are alive, and interact daily. • If you think Mt. Holyoke is old at 165, imagine, in Jordan, with every step we take forward into the future, we are reminded that we are treading pathways marked out over millennia, from the founding of the first human cities ten thousand years ago, through the flowering of the three great Abrahamic faiths, through the crossroads of trade and tumult over centuries. •

We do not let that slow our steps towards progress, especially where women are concerned . . . but on such ancient paths we tread carefully.

True progress, while it solves problems, must grow out of history and tradition; it cannot be dictated by fiat. It must respect and work with the culture of those expected to embrace it; it cannot be externally imposed. •

This has been a primary focus of my work over the past twenty-five years, combined with my efforts to bridge our cultures by addressing widespread misconceptions concerning Arabs and Muslims—particularly women. Few westerners realize that in the seventh century, Islam liberated attitudes

• Queen Noor builds credibility by contrasting her own challenges as a member of the first class at Princeton that allowed women and shows how the experience helped her develop skills for her current work.

• Queen Noor continues with her theme of empowered women, a theme that will continue throughout the address.

• Transition between a focus on campus and a focus on Queen Noor's work in Jordan.

• Queen Noor's claim is based on her experience and may resonate with conservative listeners.

towards women and granted them specific social, political, and economic rights long before Western societies did, such as the equal right to education, to conduct business, to own and inherit property, and not to be coerced into a marriage, instead introducing a marriage contract, a kind of early prenuptial agreement, to assure the rights of the woman in particular.

According to the Quran, God or Allah said, "I waste not the labor of any that labors among you, be you male or female—the one of you is as the other." And, the Prophet Mohammed said, "All people are equal. They are as equal as the teeth on a comb." •

• The claim—perhaps surprising to some listeners—that Islam has held progressive views toward women since the seventh century is bolstered by a quote from the Quran.

Women the world over, including in the Muslim world, have had to struggle with the limitations placed upon them by less enlightened members of their societies. Islam fought against this from the beginning, and today, conservative, intolerant, and restrictive interpretations of tradition and scripture clearly do not reflect the beliefs of the majority of Muslims nor the intentions of the Prophet himself.

But rather than dwell on the aberrant and oppressive beliefs of those who would twist the teachings of Islam—important as it is to correct the dangerous and false perceptions they have engendered—I would like to focus on the inseparable issues of women, leadership, and peace in our time•—vitally linked themes which I believe more accurately reflect the true message of Islam and the teachings and life of the Prophet Mohammed—a man who surrounded himself with strong women such as his first wife, once his employer, who later supported his mission . . . and his last wife who led troops into battle to defend the faith after his death. Even beyond the religious consideration, I think these are subjects of interest and crucial import to us all.

• Thesis statement.

Unfortunately, since the first time I was invited here [in 1996], circumstances have changed—for all of us. . . . Today, uncertainty reigns. And after the tragedy of September 11, for many of you, it is an uncertainty darker and deeper than what seems like the simpler worries of only last year—worries about jobs, the economy, and what to do after graduation. •

This new dimension of anxiety and uncertainty for many Americans and others after September 11 is nothing new in many other parts of the world. Just as many friends and relatives of the World Trade Center victims remain in wretched suspense about the precise fate of their loved ones, the women of Srebrenica in Bosnia have been waiting for almost seven years for news of theirs, since eight thousand Muslim men and boys were marched away and never seen again.

Just as many Americans now face anxiety over terrorism, citizens in both Israel and the West Bank live in a constant state of alert for attacks, whether by belt bomb or tank, and women, children, and men cannot walk freely in Afghanistan and in many other places in the world without fearing the very ground under their feet may explode from those insidious, deadly leftovers from yesterday's wars— land mines.

While Americans may worry about anthrax and even smallpox attacks, mothers in Africa worry about protecting their children from a whole range of much more common diseases, ranging from dysentery to AIDS. •

Recent events have highlighted for some in the U.S., although perhaps not yet enough for others, that they share the problems of the rest of the world, whether they want to or not. The continuing terrorist threats have jolted many into the realization that there is no security in isolation. Now, rather than going on the offensive, it's time to assess the role of the U.S. in the community of nations and cultures, to look together for positive ways to solve these problems, and to pursue peace.

And here at Holyoke, you know that women can lead that process. •

In the long history of a world full of war, women have always at least been paid lip service as the guardians of peace. From Aristophanes' comedic heroine Lysistrata, . . . to Emily Greene Balch, who helped found the Women's

• Queen Noor begins outlining problems that face the world.

• Queen Noor expands on world challenges by paralleling the situation in the United States with issues in Bosnia, Israel, the West Bank, Afghanistan, and Africa.

• Queen Noor directly addresses the graduates as part of the solution.

International League for Peace and Freedom and shared the Nobel Peace Prize in 1946, to another Nobel Laureate, Aung San Suu Kyi, recently released once again from house arrest in Burma, women have acted as symbols in the intermittent human battle against military oppression.

However, far too often, women have been commended in public for their commitment to peace, just before the doors to the negotiating room slammed shut in their faces.

And when they did get a foot in the door, they needed exceptional courage and resolve to introduce reform. I recall a story of the first woman on the staff of a large institution, who inquired about a particularly unjust labor practice. "Madam," she was told, "we have done it that way for one hundred years." "Sir," she replied, "your hundred years are up!" •

• An inspiring quote is likely to connect with the graduates and their loved ones.

This kind of initiative can make vital and lasting contributions to the search for peace in our world. Tapping the unique talents of women peace builders can, I believe, ultimately end global conflict.

And we desperately need new perspectives, for women's sake and for humanity's. Women are vital to the peace-building process, and peace is vital to the advancement of women.

Women know better than anyone else that peace is not merely the absence of hostilities, but must grow from a positive human security founded in equity, tolerance, and understanding. . . .

Women bear the brunt of war, but they have almost never been included in the process that launches or resolves conflict. And this is not only unjust but also unwise.

• Queen Noor outlines why women are particularly well suited to address the current challenges.

On the most basic level, peace begins in the community, and women hold together the community. • To exclude them undermines the very foundation of peace. For quite some time now, the glittering prize of the global marketplace has been held out as the incentive for peace building. But women on the ground in war zones know only too well how much cleaning up needs to be done before a society recovering from conflict can even begin to contemplate international commerce.

The two edges of the sword that most seriously threatens the world's women are violence and poverty. Conflict destroys infrastructure and diverts funds from development in areas women desperately need, increasing the poverty from which they already suffer disproportionately. And poverty is most often the underlying cause of conflict.

When given training, resources, and opportunity, women will most often invest in their families. And as they become genuine economic players, they also become active decision makers in social and economic affairs, improving their own status and influence as well as the overall quality of life and stability of their communities.

· · ·

In this way, we are making progress at the community level. But it is time to incorporate women, their voices, opinions, and ideas at the highest political levels. This process has begun, both through the example of highly visible women and through an increasing feminization of politics, as women bring their issues to the forefront of national and global consciousness. Politicians the world over are beginning to realize that women vote. A record number of women are running for governor in U.S. states this year. Women's movements are gaining momentum and visibility. Never before have so many women held so much power. •

It is no accident that NGOs have emerged as a major force for world change as women's issues are coming to the center of the world stage. . . . New networks are linking grassroots women's organizations to the political process, to make women's voices heard in the corridors of power.

• Examples of women who have made recent strides on the national and world stages.

Those of you who attended the "Afghanistan and Beyond" forum in the Gamble Auditorium in March heard some of those voices, such as the Revolutionary Association of the Women of Afghanistan, and Women Waging Peace, groups that use networking, political influence, NGO and private sector partnerships, and especially new technology to bring about change.

Women, for the best and the worst reasons, have extensive experience with reconciliation. Opposed to violence, whether by tradition, temperament, or training, they have always relied on creative strategies and an intuitive pragmatism to stop war.

• • •

Women leaders from Israeli and Palestinian territories have formed such coalitions as the Jerusalem Link to forge a common language for peace in the Middle East. Similar examples abound from Azerbaijan to the Andes. True, alliances may be born out of necessity, but in the long run such joint ventures encourage the development of peace-oriented leadership.

After all, it is not only physical infrastructure that must be restored after decades of betrayal and violence. Trust must be carefully interwoven into the fabric of society, threading together the views and needs of the citizenry. Agreements among official leaders are not enough. Acceptance and reconciliation must begin in the streets of war-torn communities. Women working for peace often find the middle ground that eludes political leaders—that ground on which peace is built in the daily lives of the people.

Let me add this, even though I realize this is long, but for the grandfathers, fathers, brothers, and sons in this audience, of course, I would never want to imply that it is only • Queen Noor adds women who pursue peace. •

• Queen Noor adds an inclusive note by noting that men have also made vital contributions to peace building.

• • •

Now, especially now, when peace seems more elusive than ever, it's time for all of us, governments, businesses, and private individuals alike, to commit ourselves to the bold and often dangerous work of peace builders, especially women. Women have long enough been the symbols of peace—the Goddess Pax, perched on a pediment above the parliament buildings of the world, often the first to be knocked down when the rockets flare.

Now it is time they took their rightful place as the makers of peace, in the negotiating and legislative chambers, using their all too intimate experience with war and their expertise in coalition building to create a new world community. To the men—or anyone—who says we must continue as we always have, it is time to say, "Sir, your hundred—or thousand, or ten thousand—years are up!"

You can and must add your voice to the many other women's voices around the world calling for peace, justice, and tolerance. • Thanks to the power of technology in the service of democratic principles, never before in human history have ordinary people had so much opportunity to do good.

• A direct call to action directed toward the graduates.

Given the intense commercialism of Western culture and the current anxiety about job prospects, it is easy to assume that college graduates are dyed-in-the-wool materialists, interested solely in personal gain and career advancement. But there is heartening evidence to the contrary. According to a UCLA study last year, more students are speaking out and acting against injustice than [at] any time since 1966. Most important, the survey also marks a record number of students volunteering their time, talents, and effort to help others. •

• Data from a study supports the claim that young people do volunteer and can make a difference.

• • •

With your energy, your education, and your intelligence, you have so much more to offer not only to the world of work but to the world at large. Those qualities are needed now more desperately than ever before.

I was impressed and heartened when I read about the graduation pledge that many of you have signed since February. I won't ask for a show of hands, or even try to do a mental tally of green ribbons, because such a pledge is a thoughtful, internal commitment. But I do congratulate you—any of you—who are trying to work out how to make a living while making a difference in the world. •

• As she nears her conclusion, Queen Noor reminds students of a pledge they have already made to volunteer work.

In the face of uncertainty, the essence of humanity is hope. You, the new graduates of Mt. Holyoke College, the next generation of women leaders, can nurture that hope. And you can build a future for us all.

God bless you and many, many, many congratulations. •

• The speech concludes with a final call to action and a warm offer of congratulations.

SAMPLE SPECIAL-OCCASION SPEECH

REMARKS AT THE FUNERAL OF CIVIL RIGHTS LEADER ROSA PARKS

Governor Jennifer Granholm

Michigan governor Jennifer Granholm was one of the speakers who honored Rosa Parks's life at her memorial service on November 2, 2005, in Detroit.

Governor Granholm's message demonstrates the style that is a hallmark of special-occasion speeches. She uses metaphors that exemplify Rosa Parks's leadership and strength, along with repetition, to emphasize key themes. Granholm's speech appeals to the broader audience that is celebrating Rosa Parks's life, not just the dignitaries who are attending the service. She challenges the audience to honor Ms. Parks by carrying on her quest for civil rights.

To Judge Keith and all of the members of the clergy; to all of the members of Congress who are here and our state legislators; to our heads of corporations and honored guests— I'm so glad you're here. •

• Granholm begins in a way typical for formal occasions: she acknowledges dignitaries attending the funeral.

But today, I want to address my comments not to you, the "titled" people. Instead, I'd like to talk, for a moment, with everyone out there who doesn't have a title—those who aren't credentialed. I want to use my time to speak to everyone who's never been elected. I want to speak not to the CEOs but to the secretaries of the company; not to the senators but to the janitors; not to those who were lucky enough to be ushered into this beautiful space today but to those who stood in line for hours waiting to get in. And to those of you who are outside who did not get in—this is your day. •

• Granholm extends the range of her address beyond the dignitaries. She hopes to connect with everyone who is celebrating Rosa Parks's life.

Rosa Parks was lain in honor in our nation's capitol, in the great Rotunda that's reserved only for war heroes and for presidents. But she was not a president. She was, though, a war hero. She was a heroic warrior for equality, and that alone, my God, surely is enough for a nation to celebrate.

But Rosa Parks was also a warrior for the everyman and the everywoman. She was a warrior with the soft armor of a seamstress; a warrior with the powerful weapon of the Sunday school teacher; a warrior wearing a warrior's helmet made of a crown of perfectly coiled braids; a soldier whose tank in this battle was a city bus; an improbable warrior leading an unlikely army of waitresses, and street sweepers, and shopkeepers, and auto mechanics; a warrior protected in this army by the piercing weapons of love and nonviolence, more powerful than any weapons or any army before or since. •

And so, perhaps what we are celebrating today—in addition to the fight, the noble fight—is how it was fought. Rosa Parks stands for every one of us improbable warriors, in every seemingly small moment where truth and justice are at risk. She offered every one of us this example of a splendid paradox—the paradox of quiet strength. No more quiet than strong; certainly no more strong than quiet, each reinforcing the other. •

Rosa Parks was powerful because she was improbable. She was unexpected. She was untitled. And what was true of Gandhi was certainly true of Rosa Parks: that her greatness lay in what everybody could do, but doesn't. We will all say today that the greatest tribute we could pay to our improbable warrior is to continue battling and to do so in a way that honors her life. • I, like you, imagine the day when the war will be won. The day when a brilliant eight-year-old chess player has the same chances in life, whether she lives in Livonia or off Livernois. We know that this war will be won when the son of a barber on Grand River receives from each of us the same looks of hope and words of encouragement as the son of a doctor in Grand Rapids. We know that the war will be won when the city of Bloomfield Hills and the city of Detroit have the same college graduation rates—and the same low prison incarceration rates as well. •

We know that we will be winning Mrs. Parks's war—our war—when it's yesterday's news when a newly elected governor, senator, or president is a woman or person of color—yesterday's news. We know we will be winning the war when people in the state of Michigan do not have to vote on whether diversity in our university classrooms is a good thing. We know

- Style: warrior metaphors and effective use of repetition.

- Language amplifies Rosa Parks's quiet strength.

- Appeal to audience to carry on Rosa Parks's legacy.

- Effective use of examples and repetition.

we will see signs that we are winning this war when love overwhelms fear and acts of quiet strength become our daily bread.

So—good night, Mrs. Parks, from the state of Michigan, to our own gently powerful hero. Because by your actions, you have given us our final marching orders. We are enlisted in this war.

On behalf of the state of Michigan, ma'am, we are reporting for duty. •

• Granholm concludes her speech by celebrating Rosa Parks and pledging that the state of Michigan will continue Parks's war for equality.

SAMPLE SPECIAL-OCCASION SPEECH

SPEECH TO ACCEPT THE 1949 NOBEL PRIZE IN LITERATURE

William Faulkner

Speeches to accept awards often demand of their speakers a mix of gratitude and humility, rejoicing and respect. Award winners in our culture should also be modest, though not falsely apologetic, and they should show wit and good nature where possible. There are few prizes better globally recognized than the Nobel Prize, and in this speech accepting the Nobel Prize in Literature, delivered in Stockholm in 1950, the great author William Faulkner speaks from the heart in words that remind the audience why he was a good speaker—and a great wordsmith.

• Faulkner acknowledges the importance of the award, but notes that it is less for him and more for his literary output.

I feel that this award was not made to me as a man, but to my work—a life's work in the agony and sweat of the human spirit, not for glory and least of all for profit, but to create out of the materials of the human spirit something which did not exist before. So this award is only mine in trust. • It will not be difficult to find a dedication for the money part of it commensurate with the purpose and significance of its origin. But I would like to do the same with the acclaim too, by using this moment as a pinnacle from which I might be listened to by the young men and women already dedicated to the same anguish and travail, among whom is already that one who will some day stand here where I am standing. •

• Although Faulkner addresses a crowd of dignitaries, he makes it clear that he speaks to a younger generation of artists. The words that follow will be for them.

Our tragedy today is a general and universal physical fear so long sustained by now that we can even bear it. There are no longer problems of the spirit. There is only the question: when will I be blown up? Because of this, the young man or woman writing today has forgotten the problems of the human heart in conflict with itself which alone can make good writing, because only that is worth writing about, worth the agony and the sweat. •

He must learn them again. He must teach himself that the basest of all things is to be afraid; and, teaching himself that, forget it forever, leaving no room in his workshop for anything but the old verities and truths of the heart, the old universal truths, lacking which any story is ephemeral and doomed—love and honor and pity and pride and compassion and sacrifice. • Until he does so, he labors under a curse. He writes not of love but of lust, of defeats in which nobody loses anything of value, of victories without hope and, worst of all, without pity or compassion. His griefs grieve on no universal bones, leaving no scars. He writes not of the heart but of the glands.

Until he relearns these things, he will write as though he stood among and watched the end of man. I decline to accept the end of man. • It is easy enough to say that man is immortal simply because he will endure: that when the last ding-dong of doom has clanged and faded from the last worthless rock hanging tideless in the last red and dying evening, that even then there will still be one more sound: that of his puny inexhaustible voice, still talking. I refuse to accept this. • I believe that man will not merely endure: he will prevail. He is immortal, not because he alone among creatures has an inexhaustible voice but because he has a soul, a spirit capable of compassion and sacrifice and endurance.

The poet's, the writer's, duty is to write about these things. It is his privilege to help man endure by lifting his heart, by reminding him of the courage and honor and hope and pride and compassion and pity and sacrifice which have been the glory of his past. The poet's voice need not merely be the record of man; it can be one of the props, the pillars to help him endure and prevail. •

• By asking "When will I be blown up?" Faulkner emphasizes that public fears of nuclear holocaust in the 1940s had replaced meditations on the essential internal conflicts we all feel as humans.

• Faulkner urges future writers and poets not to ignore the essential human conflicts.

• A bold, life-affirming statement made in the face of fears about nuclear Armageddon.

• Effective repetition: "I refuse to accept this."

• Careful word choice: Faulkner labels the necessity to write about the human condition a "duty" and a "privilege." These words elevate the calling of future artists to a responsibility and an obligation.

CHAPTER REVIEW

"Whether to mark a celebration, a milestone, or a passing, we all participate in special-occasion speaking as speakers or listeners." At some point in your life, you will almost certainly be asked to deliver a special-occasion speech, whether it's to mark a joyous or sorrowful event, present or accept an award, introduce another speaker or performer, or give a witty but evocative talk after a formal dinner. By applying the general guidelines described in this chapter as well as the strategies tailored specifically to each of the six types of special-occasion speeches, you can lay the groundwork for a successful presentation that will have your listeners remembering the event for many years to come. If you are asked to deliver a speech on such an occasion, be aware of the type of speech your audience will expect and follow specific strategies designed to tailor your special-occasion speech for both the occasion *and* the audience.

Key Terms

epideictic *595*   eulogy *598*

Review Questions

1. Name and describe six types of special-occasion speeches identified in the chapter.
2. What five guidelines should be adhered to when delivering a special-occasion speech?
3. What four strategies for speeches of introduction are offered in the chapter?
4. Describe four strategies for speeches of presentation.
5. What three strategies should you use when delivering a speech of acceptance?
6. What three strategies should you use when speaking to memorialize or eulogize?

7. Describe two strategies that can help you deliver a celebratory speech.
8. Offer four strategies for effective after-dinner speeches.

Critical Thinking Questions

1. What kinds of characteristics do hosts like Conan O'Brien and David Letterman share with famous speakers like Mark Twain? In what ways are after-dinner speeches and late-night monologues similar? Which one do you think would be more difficult to prepare and deliver, and why?
2. How does a eulogy differ from a celebratory speech? How are they the same?
3. Are there occasions when you might need to deliver a celebratory speech in front of a somewhat hostile audience? How might you change your speech in those circumstances?

Activities

1. Imagine that you have been tasked with delivering a speech of introduction for a controversial figure (such as Roman Polanski, Nadya Suleman, Mark McGwire, or Chris Brown). How would you handle introducing someone whom you dislike or do not respect, or whom the audience might view negatively? Craft an attention-getter for this type of speech.
2. Think back to the best toast you ever heard. Create a list of your favorite things about the toast and compare it to the strategies for celebratory speeches outlined in the chapter. How many of the chapter's strategies did the speaker employ?
3. Imagine that you have to give a special-occasion speech honoring someone important to you. Prepare three outlines: one for a speech of introduction for this person, one for a speech of presentation of an imaginary award, and one to toast the person on a life event (such as a wedding, graduation, or retirement). How do your three outlines differ?

Go to **bedfordstmartins.com/speakup**, where you'll find helpful study materials, videos, and speech-building tools.

GROUP COMMUNICATION

19

Jenny, Sam, Juan, Ashley, and Yolanda were all taking a course called Community Service 101, in which students receive credit for performing volunteer work. The instructor had organized the students into groups and charged each group with deciding on a volunteer project and contributing at least thirty hours of service per person. At the end of the term, each group would deliver a thirty-minute multimedia presentation informing the class about its project. Jenny, Sam, Juan, Ashley, and Yolanda were placed in a group, one of five in the class.

Throughout the term, Jenny, Sam, Juan, Ashley, and Yolanda experienced firsthand the challenges and benefits of working in a group. For example, they argued over what to call themselves, eventually settling on URP ("Unique, Realistic People")—though only after intense and uncomfortable debate. During their first few meetings, Sam and Yolanda kept interrupting each other, while Ashley tried to dominate the discussion. Eventually, Juan stepped in to bring things under control. He reminded the others that they needed to quickly select a volunteer project and work out a plan for implementing the project in order to fulfill the requirements of the course. Jenny, realizing that smoother cooperation would help them achieve this goal, also suggested that the group agree on rules for communicating and making decisions. They settled on several rules, including "No interrupting when someone is speaking, everyone gets a chance to contribute ideas, and all decisions must be unanimous."

As the project unfolded, URP's attention to effective leadership and productive participation enabled the group's members to select and carry out a worthy project—supporting an after-school program at a nearby elementary school. Through spirited but respectful discussions, each member was able to offer unique and valuable ideas for carrying out the project.

Despite the rocky start, the group's commitment to the mission and to one another paid big dividends. By the time URP was scheduled to deliver its presentation on the project to the rest of the class, Jenny, Sam, Juan, Ashley, and Yolanda had mastered the challenges of managing group dynamics. Their speech was a resounding success, as each member described a different aspect of how URP had carried out its project and what results the group had achieved.

Through their URP project, these students had discovered both the difficulties and the advantages of working in a **small group**—a limited number of people gathered for a specific purpose. This classroom experience showed them that **group dynamics**—the ways in which members relate to one another and view their functions—can determine whether a group achieves its mission.

Learning how to master group dynamics, work well with others in pursuit of a common goal, and communicate your group's achievement to others are valuable life skills. Although group interactions can sometimes be frustrating, you will inevitably be asked or decide to participate in a group at some point in your educational and professional lives—whether in the classroom, in your community, or at work.[1]

Why is working effectively in a group so important? Small groups offer important advantages over individual efforts. Often, people can achieve a better outcome by collaborating on a task rather than working alone. Each group member has unique experiences and perspectives to offer. By sharing their ideas, each member has the chance to spot poten-

tial problems or improvements in a plan that a lone individual might miss. And each person in a group has different strengths and interests. The group can divide up a project so that each member takes responsibility for the portions of the job he or she is best suited for.

But as we've seen with URP's story, to gain the benefits of collaboration, group members must interact productively. This chapter provides suggestions for managing key elements of group dynamics—including how to lead a group, how to participate in one, how to make decisions as a group, and how to present your findings or decisions to an audience.

EFFECTIVE GROUP LEADERSHIP

When the coach of a gold medal–winning Olympic team, the leader of a Nobel Prize–winning medical research team, or the director of a successful play is interviewed, that person is garnering recognition for being a successful leader; successful groups depend on capable participation by each group member, but the leader's actions are critical.

Why? Because it's difficult for any group to function without an effective leader. Somebody needs to organize group meetings, keep the group focused, encourage participation by all members, mediate conflict, and facilitate decision making. The leader need not have total control, but he or she must help the members reach a decision and achieve goals as a group. How do groups acquire leaders? Through several means, as we discover in this section.

Selecting a Leader

Groups gain leaders in various ways. Sometimes an external authority selects a **designated leader** to help the group quickly move forward

NO LEADER

WITH A LEADER

with its mission. For example, a mayor may appoint a blue-ribbon committee to investigate ways to improve mass transit and designate a leader to guide the inquiry, or an army lieutenant leading a mission who needs to send soldiers on reconnaissance may designate a leader from the group of troops selected.

In other situations, there may be an **implied leader**, someone with preexisting authority or skills particularly well suited to the task at hand. For instance, a marketing manager may decide to form a task force to evaluate her company's advertising strategies. At the task force's first meeting, she's the implied leader because she formed the group.

In still other situations, a group may have an **emergent leader**, one who comes to be recognized as a leader by the group's members over time. While not officially elected or even named as such, an

DESIGNATED LEADER

IMPLIED LEADER

Which one of these group members is the implied leader?

emergent leader usually comes to assume the role because he or she has the most time to commit to the group, demonstrates exceptional competence and goodwill, or simply takes the initiative and starts leading. Juan and Jenny did this for URP.

DESIGNATED LEADER   EMERGENT LEADER

Leading Meetings

Effective group leaders conduct meetings in ways that enable members to work together productively, contribute their ideas, and make well-informed decisions. If you're the leader of a group, consider these tips for facilitating group meetings.

Address Procedural Needs. Where and when will meetings take place? Who will start meetings and record notes? And how will notes be circulated to members who could not attend a particular meeting?

Model the Behavior You Expect. Avoid interrupting others or dismissing their questions or comments. Make group members feel they can interact comfortably with you. And resist any urge to dominate discussions or decisions.

Facilitate Discussion. Ensure that all members of your group have the opportunity to participate in each discussion. If some group members are not speaking during a meeting, strive to bring them into the discussion ("Anil, what do you think?" or "That's a good point, Sarah—you've clearly researched this carefully. But let's also give Tyler a chance to share his ideas.") While it's important to contribute when you have an idea that nobody else has raised, try to let other members speak first. If you make your position known early, members may hesitate to contradict you.

Keep Members on Task. If the discussion begins to stray from the item under consideration, keep members on task in a friendly manner. For example, "I agree with Harry that our department's holiday party is going to be a blast. But let's talk about how we're going to tackle reserving the space for the event."

Help Members Avoid Groupthink. Groupthink is members' tendency to accept ideas and information uncritically because of strong feelings of loyalty or single-mindedness within the group.[2] Groupthink erodes the lively and open exchange of ideas necessary for informed decisions. If one person advocates a course of action in your group and everybody else nods in agreement, try to broaden the discussion before moving the group toward making a final decision. For instance, ask a particularly insightful participant if he or she can think of any potential risks to the proposed course of action. If nobody is willing to offer any reservations, consider raising some concerns yourself: "I like Sangeeta's idea, but let me play devil's advocate for a minute. . . ." Be sure that the group has considered the pros *and* cons of the proposed options before selecting one.

Facilitate Decisions. When it seems that members of your group have thoroughly discussed the issue at hand, help them come to a decision. As leader, you will participate in the final decision, but your leadership role does not entitle you to make the decision for the group—never use your power to manipulate the group. Once the decision has been made, ensure that it is recorded and then move the group on to the next issue. Revisit decisions only when new circumstances make the original decision unfeasible.

Help Organize the Group's Presentation. Does your group need to present its conclusions? If so, who will serve as the speakers or speaker? How will the presentation be framed to best meet the audience's needs? As leader, you don't necessarily need to make all the decisions yourself, but you do need to coordinate the decisions on these topics.

Managing Conflict

No matter the situation or setting, disagreements inevitably crop up as a group works together on a project. Some conflict is helpful. For example, when members express honest disagreement about proposed plans of action, they can help minimize the risk of groupthink. But interpersonal conflicts that have nothing to do with the group's mission only create distraction. Whenever conflict arises in your group, strive to either minimize it or channel it in a productive direction. The following guidelines can help.

Refer to Ideas by Topic, Not by Person. Focus on the content of specific suggestions rather than attributing those suggestions to individual members. For example, suppose you're part of a group that's trying to get a candidate elected as head of the town council. Monique advocates a mass e-mail to build support for the candidate, but Tim thinks that leafleting would be better. Refer to these ideas as "the e-mail plan" and "the leafleting plan" rather than "Monique's idea" and "Tim's suggestion." When ideas get associated with an individual, that person may develop a feeling of personal investment in that option. He or she may thus become defensive if the proposal is criticized—even if it has real shortcomings.

Resolve Conflicts Quickly. If a conflict between group members becomes distracting, try to resolve it rather than allowing it to continue or repressing it. Give the members who disagree an equal opportunity to explain their perspective; let each person speak without interruption, and then ask other members for their views. If both people's ideas have merit, perhaps you can help the group find a solution that draws the best from each perspective. As leader, you may ultimately need to offer your opinion or vote in order to break a deadlock on an issue, but try to give the members an opportunity to speak before injecting your opinion.

Focus on Tasks, Not Disagreements. To help members concentrate on the task at hand and not interpersonal tensions that may be simmering, articulate desired changes in behavior rather than criticizing individuals: "Let's get back to discussing our project," not "Sally, your answers to Noah's questions are always so sarcastic."

A personality clash may better be solved by discussing the problem in private with the members who disagree rather than airing the conflict in front of the entire group. If there is a member who gets along well with the people experiencing conflict, he or she may be able to help them find a way to manage their disagreement.

Manage Disruptive Emotions.

Conflicts can spark intense and disruptive emotions within a group. Even after a conflict has been resolved, members may still feel angry, upset, or embarrassed and may withdraw from the discussion. If this happens, bring reluctant members back into the discussion by inviting their input on important issues.

EFFECTIVE GROUP MEMBERSHIP

While strong leadership is essential to effective group communication, productive participation by members is equally vital. To contribute your best to a group as a member, start by understanding the types of roles you can take on to support your group's success.

Three Types of Member Roles

We've identified three types of roles group members can fill.[3] Two of them—task-oriented and maintenance-oriented roles—are helpful. The third type—self-oriented—is not productive and should be avoided.

Task-Oriented Roles. These roles contribute to the group's ability to accomplish its goals through enhancing members' participation and the free flow of information within the group. In a group in which members are fulfilling these roles, you'll likely see people asking good questions and making constructive comments. There are eight task-oriented roles:

- *Initiators* suggest the group's goals and offer new ideas or propose new solutions.
- *Information providers* offer facts relevant to the issue under discussion. These facts might include researched evidence or examples based on personal experience.

I'm constructive!

- *Information gatherers* ask other members to share facts they know, or they seek out needed information from other sources.
- *Elaborators* add supporting facts, examples, or ideas to a point that someone else has made during the discussion.
- *Clarifiers* attempt to make the meaning of another member's statement more precise.
- *Evaluators* offer their own judgments about the ideas put forward during a discussion.

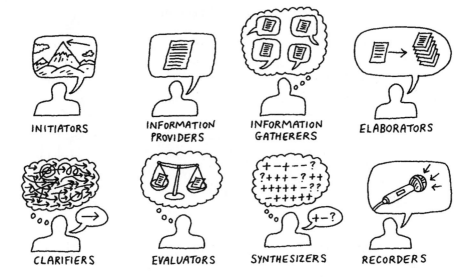

INITIATORS   INFORMATION PROVIDERS   INFORMATION GATHERERS   ELABORATORS

CLARIFIERS   EVALUATORS   SYNTHESIZERS   RECORDERS

- *Synthesizers* identify emerging agreements and disagreements among the group as a whole.
- *Recorders* take notes during the meeting, tracking major decisions and plans made by the group. They may send memos or e-mails to group members summarizing previous meetings, providing agendas for future meetings, or reminding people of tasks they agreed to work on between meetings.

Maintenance-Oriented Roles. These roles help sustain and strengthen efficient and effective interpersonal relations in a group. When members perform maintenance roles effectively, groups are more likely to work together comfortably as a team, support one another, and present findings or recommendations that reflect group consensus. There are five maintenance-oriented roles:

- *Harmonizers* decrease tension in the group, perhaps by infusing humor at just the right time or by making positive and optimistic comments.

I'm encouraging!

- *Compromisers* attempt to find common ground between adversaries within the group, and offer solutions that may be palatable to people on both sides of the conflict.
- *Encouragers* inspire other group members by complimenting their ideas and work.
- *Gatekeepers* facilitate the exchange of information among group members.
- *Norm facilitators* reinforce healthy group norms and discourage unproductive ones.

HARMONIZERS   COMPROMISERS   ENCOURAGERS   GATEKEEPERS   NORM FACILITATORS

Self-Oriented Roles. These roles accomplish little for a group and are motivated by the selfish ends of individual members. Groups with a heavy emphasis on these roles may experience incomplete findings, infighting, and dissension. There are four self-oriented roles:

- *Blockers* stop the group from moving toward its objective—by refusing to accept decisions the group has made or by arbitrarily rejecting other group members' ideas or opinions.
- *Withdrawers* refuse to make any contribution or to participate in the discussion. They may feel out of their element in the group or may be having difficulty following other members' comments and ideas.

- *Dominators* monopolize group interactions, interrupting others, arguing for the sake of arguing, and insisting on having the last word. This behavior may stem from feelings of insecurity, an aggressive personality, or some other factor.

- *Distracters*—the exact opposite of *harmonizers*— send the group in irrelevant directions with off-topic comments or extraneous conversation, perhaps because they have trouble concentrating on a topic or focusing on the completion of a process.

When you're participating in a group, focus on how you can fulfill task-oriented and maintenance-oriented roles (or encourage others to do so) and avoid playing self-oriented roles and discourage these roles in others.

BLOCKERS WITHDRAWERS DOMINATORS DISTRACTERS

Tips for Participating in a Small Group

In addition to fulfilling task- and maintenance-oriented roles, you can improve your effectiveness at group participation by applying the following practices.

Prepare for Group Meetings. If an agenda has been distributed for an upcoming meeting, think about the topics under consideration *before* you gather with other group members. Keep track of any necessary commitments you make for the meeting (such as researching the answer to a question or bringing your laptop), and be sure to fulfill them.

Treat Other Members Courteously. Courtesy begins with arriving at a group meeting on time (or at least informing the group if you will be late). Turn off your cell phone unless you are expecting a call that will help the group conduct its business. During the discussion, treat other members with respect, even when you disagree with their views. And if you do disagree with other members, be sure to focus on the issue at hand rather than on personalities. For example, if someone proposes an idea that you find questionable, don't say, "I'm not sure you have the patience to carry out this idea." Instead, try to learn more, perhaps by asking, "What's your experience in doing this sort of thing? Can you tell us more about the kinds of challenges we can expect?"

Listen Interactively. Inattention between members can cause tension in a group. Someone who doesn't feel heard may turn a deaf ear to another person's comments at later meetings. To avoid this problem, practice interactive listening (see Chapter 4). As other members of your group share their ideas and comments, try to understand their viewpoints and show that you're listening. Ask for clarification if you need it, and make sure you understand a point before you challenge it.

Participate, Don't Dominate. To gain the benefit of diverse perspectives, a group needs contributions from each member. When you have a relevant point to make, share your idea. Your participation is particularly important when you have experience with a topic or when you have a unique viewpoint that no one else has expressed.

At the same time, avoid monopolizing the discussion. If you find yourself speaking a disproportionate amount of the time, take a break and let other members contribute. You may even ask another member to chime in if it seems that he or she has an idea but is reluctant to speak.

Participate Authentically. A group functions at its best when members put diverse ideas and perspectives on the table. Therefore, be guided by honesty, not popularity, when considering problems and solutions. If you have an idea that you believe is important, don't be afraid to mention it, even if you're worried about how others might perceive it. And if you have concerns about another member's suggestion, explain your reservations to the group.

But balance candor with tact when questioning or challenging a colleague's idea. Critique the idea, not the person, in a manner that makes your concern clear. For example: "I'm not sure our group can afford to rent that facility for our project," not "Where in the world do you think we're going to get the money for that?"

And if others disagree with an idea you have presented, avoid overreacting. Instead, let others explain their position. If you disagree with what you're hearing, explain your position calmly and rationally. Conversely, if you think the other members' criticism is well taken, be honest and acknowledge that you agree.

Fulfill Your Commitments. For a group to achieve its goals, it's vital that members accept responsibility for performing certain tasks—both the ones assigned to them individually and the ones required of all participating group members. For example, you may promise to research the cost of an item that your group needs to purchase, or perhaps you've agreed to distribute notes from the last meeting to the group.

When you make commitments, the rest of your group will rely on you to fulfill them; if people drop the ball enough times, the group as a whole will find it more and more difficult to carry out its work. Moreover, in most situations, work assigned to another group member will hinge on work you've been assigned, so failing to follow up on your commitment will hurt not just you but also the other member.

GROUP DECISION MAKING AND THE REFLECTIVE-THINKING PROCESS

Although there is no single method that a group *must* use to make decisions, research has shown that the **reflective-thinking process** is a particularly effective approach.[4] The reflective-thinking process has five steps:

1. Define the problem.
2. Analyze the problem.
3. Establish criteria for solutions.
4. Generate possible solutions.
5. Select the best solution.

In this section, we take a closer look at each of these steps.

Define the Problem

Before your group can select a course of action, you must know exactly what problem (or objective) you will address. As a group, work to define the problem or goal as precisely as possible.

Analyze the Problem

Once your group has defined the problem, analyze its nature. What are the primary aspects of the problem? Which of these are most important for the group to focus on?

THE REFLECTIVE-THINKING PROCESS

Establish Criteria for Solutions

Decide which factors will be most important when weighing possible solutions to the problem your group will be addressing. Each proposed solution will have strengths and weaknesses, and establishing criteria will help you select the best overall solution.

Generate Possible Solutions

Create a list of potential solutions to the problem your group is addressing. Brainstorming (see Chapter 6) is an effective technique for building this list. Remember that during brainstorming, the goal is to generate as many ideas as possible without judging them. Research can also be a good way to find out how other individuals or groups may have handled similar problems.

Select the Best Solution

Once your group has developed a number of potential solutions, evaluate the advantages and disadvantages of each based on the criteria you've defined.

After a group has reached a consensus, it often needs to communicate its findings to others. In the following section, we explain how to plan and deliver effective group presentations.

DELIVERING GROUP PRESENTATIONS

To share its ideas with an audience, a group may select from several common approaches: a **symposium**, in which several or all group members speak to the audience in turn; a **panel discussion**, in which members engage in discourse with one another, observed by the audience; and a presentation by one member representing the group. In this section, we offer tips for using each of these three approaches.

Symposium

During a symposium, each group member takes responsibility for delivering a different part of the presentation, depending on his or her expertise or interest, or the needs of the group. For example, when a product team at a computer company proposes a design for a new handheld device to its research and development department, one member might describe the competing hand-held designs the team used as reference points for its own design. Then, another member could present the technical resources that will be required to manufacture the device. A third member might then present the group's thoughts about how to minimize the costs of producing the design.

If your group has decided to use this presentation format, plan your symposium carefully. Make sure everyone in the group agrees on the topic that each speaker will address and the time he or she will take. Be sure that all members know what will go into each presentation, so that no one unwittingly repeats points made by someone else (or forgets to mention important ideas).

When you participate in a symposium, avoid speaking longer than your allotted time. Otherwise, subsequent speakers may have insufficient time to deliver their parts of the presentation. Also, treat other speakers' ideas with respect. If you need to mention points on which group members disagree, present others' ideas in a professional manner, without judging the individuals advocating those ideas.

As you close your part of the presentation, make sure to briefly introduce the next speaker. Make use of any connection between topics in your transition, and as a courtesy to both the next speaker and the audience, introduce the speaker by name.

Like a speech by an individual, an effective symposium has an introduction, a body, and a conclusion. In addition to presenting his or her ideas, the first speaker should begin with an introduction that gains the audience's attention, reveals the topic of the presentation, establishes credibility, connects with the audience, and previews the main idea that each subsequent speaker will develop. The final speaker should conclude by summarizing each presenter's main idea and leaving the audience with a memorable clincher.

Panel Discussion

In a panel discussion, group members sit at a table and speak as if conversing among themselves, while the audience watches and listens. There may be time for audience questions after the discus-

sion, but the panel members' primary role is to speak, and the audience's primary role is to listen. For example, a professor might ask a team of students to come back the following semester and conduct a panel discussion for a new class about a research project they had conducted the previous year.

A panel discussion usually requires a **moderator**, who introduces the **panelists** (the other group members) and facilitates the discussion. The moderator's role is similar to that of a leader in a group discussion. He or she monitors the time, asks questions that keep the discussion moving, and ensures that each panel member has an opportunity to participate. A moderator may also participate in the discussion, though he or she should not dominate the presentation.

Panel members, too, should contribute to the discussion without monopolizing the presentation. It is particularly important to participate if you have special experience or expertise with the point being made. If you have less information on a given issue, or you have been speaking more than other members, give other panelists the opportunity to talk. And be tactful and professional when disagreeing with another member's point.

The atmosphere in a panel discussion is usually more casual than in a symposium, as panelists may interact with the speaker and make comments or ask questions. Talk about the panel discussion in advance with your group, so that you all know which questions or topics you want to bring up. That way, the group will be well prepared and can prioritize the most important issues to be covered.

Single Group Representative

Sometimes one person will be responsible for presenting on behalf of the entire group. If your group has selected this format, keep the following considerations in mind.

First, check that your group has discussed and decided on the best approach for the presentation. Which person is most qualified to present the group's opinions? Who would have the most effective delivery? Is this a topic that requires the ethos or authority of a group leader or a group member with particular expertise? Select the member who best meets these criteria.

PRESENTATION BY ONE MEMBER REPRESENTING THE GROUP

Second, if you're the person chosen to give the presentation, be sure that your group has carefully thought through all aspects of the speech. There's an important difference between a speech that you prepare, research, and deliver yourself and one that emerges from a group: in the latter instance, the group contributes substantially to the invention process. Get input from all group members before you start preparing the presentation, and solicit their feedback after you outline your speech.

Third, as you are delivering the talk, take care to distinguish whether you are representing your own views, the views of some members of the group, or a consensus of all group members. Be fair and accurate when summarizing other members' viewpoints. Acknowledge other members' good ideas rather than presenting them as your own.

CHAPTER REVIEW

"Several heads are better than one." The adage that opens this chapter and this section reflects the fact that people tend to make the best decisions when they share and discuss their ideas. In school, the workplace, and your community, you will inevitably find yourself participating in group discussions and presenting your group's conclusions.

An effective group discussion requires skillful leadership and constructive participation. The leader must manage key elements of group dynamics, including the flow of the discussion. He or she has to ensure that all perspectives receive consideration, encourage participation, keep the group on task, and minimize interpersonal conflict. Effective members focus on task- and maintenance-oriented roles and avoid self-oriented ones. They actively share their ideas, consider one another's viewpoints, constructively participate, and help the group reach a sound decision—perhaps through the five-step reflective-thinking process. These steps include defining and analyzing a problem, establishing criteria for solving the problem, generating multiple potential solutions, and choosing the best solution from the list.

Groups may present their findings in a symposium, during which each individual member presents part of the group's message. At other times, the group may use a panel discussion format, in which there is less formal structure and more give-and-take among members. In either case, thorough preparation will enable each member to know who will present which topics.

If you're called on to deliver a presentation for your entire group, preparation will again help you ensure that you're accurately reflecting the group's decisions, opinions, or findings.

Key Terms

small group *636*
group dynamics *636*
designated leader *638*
implied leader *640*
emergent leader *640*
groupthink *644*

reflective-thinking
   process *654*
symposium *656*
panel discussion *656*
moderator *658*
panelists *658*

Review Questions

1. Name and describe three types of leaders, and how they are selected.
2. What are the two main roles of the group leader?
3. What are the three main types of member roles in a small group?
4. What six strategies should group members employ to effectively participate in a small group?
5. Name and explain the five steps of the reflective-thinking process.
6. Name and describe the three common approaches to group presentations identified in the chapter.

Critical Thinking Questions

1. In what ways do the public speaking skills you have developed in this course increase your ability to participate effectively in groups? Offer specific examples.

2. Consider the group-member roles identified on pages 648–51 (task-oriented roles, maintenance-oriented roles, and self-oriented roles). Do you see yourself in any of the descriptions presented? Do your roles change depending on the nature and circumstances of the group you are in?

3. Does the reflective-thinking process described in this chapter apply only to group decision making? How might it help you make better decisions on an individual basis?

Activities

1. Watch a television reality competition that involves group projects (such as *Survivor* or *The Apprentice*). Write a brief report that provides five examples of how the individuals in these competitions conform to the group leader and member roles described in the chapter. Then, provide one example of how the group dynamic affects their outcomes on a specific task.

2. Make a list of individuals with whom you share a group identity (your coworkers, your family, your housemates). Is there a leader among them? How did this person come to be the leader? In different circumstances, do you think the leader and group roles would be the same?

3. Have you ever been part of a group that came to a bad decision? Having read the chapter, explain how you would modify your behavior to produce a better outcome if given the chance to do it over.

Go to **bedfordstmartins.com/speakup**, where you'll find helpful study materials, videos, and speech-building tools.

APPENDIX
Additional Sample Speeches

SAMPLE INFORMATIVE SPEECH

INVISIBILITY: SCIENCE FICTION NO MORE!

Josh Betancur
Santiago Canyon College

In this speech about the concept of invisibility and the processes by which objects might become invisible, student Josh Betancur demonstrates how ideas once in the realm of science fiction are now coming closer to reality. Josh uses evidence from a variety of scientific sources, supplemented by analogies and definitions, to support his clearly organized main points.

When the space shuttle *Copernicus* was exposed to tremendous amounts of radiation, scientists feared the crew would not survive. The battered craft made it back to earth. Astronaut Susan Storm was amazed she was alive but even more amazed with her newfound ability to become the invisible woman. By creating a force field, she was able to bend the light waves around her, so as not to be seen. Now this may sound like the fantastic stuff of comic books, which it is; however, this ability may someday become reality, for scientists at Duke and the University College London have just created an invisibility cloak. •

Heralded by the December 2006 *Science* magazine as the fifth most influential discovery of 2006, it will affect every aspect of our lives, from aesthetics, architecture, and entertainment, to [the] military, telecommunications, and transportation. •

To understand this exciting new use of technology, it is necessary first to consider the physical science of invisibility, second to review experiments attempting to render objects invisible, and finally to have a better look, so to speak, at the tremendous potential impacts of this technology on our lives in the future. •

Let's begin by considering what it takes to make an object invisible.

Prior to J. K. Rowling, H. G. Wells had everyone convinced that invisibility could be achieved by drinking a magic elixir. Unfortunately, scientists could never concoct a potion to make a person transparent to light.

Rather than focusing on science fiction, researchers have focused on scientific principles. In a personal interview on February 10, 2007, Professor Craig Rutan, the Physics Chair at Santiago Canyon College, explained that in order to make something invisible, two hurdles must be overcome. First, you must find a way to transport light around the object. For example, for this blackboard to be visible, light must travel toward it. If something blocks that light, the board will become invisible. So you must find a way to transport light around the object without interference. Second, you must never illuminate the object. •

Now that we know what is required for invisibility, we'll take a look at scientific efforts to make objects invisible. •

A demonstration of one technique was documented by Inami, Sekiguchi, and Tachi of the University of Tokyo in *Brochure of Demonstration at Laval (France) Virtual 2003*. These professors . . . created a technology known as optical camouflage. In order to overcome the first hurdle, this

---

Side annotations:

• Attention-getter presents a short fictional anecdote and a striking fact: invisibility may become scientifically possible.

• Josh connects with the audience by showing diverse benefits.

• Preview of three main points, organized topically.

• Evidence based on interview research.

• Transition between main points I and II.

technology manipulates light so that an object blends in with its surroundings. The team takes a picture of what lies behind the individual and projects it onto him, giving him the necessary camouflage.

In order to overcome the second hurdle, that the object cannot be illuminated, the team used a computer to enhance the image before projecting it onto a special material known as retroreflective material. Now, you've seen this used on bright road signs. According to Federal Highway Administration Publication 03-082, *Minimum Retroreflectivity Levels*, retroreflective materials use microsized glass beads, or prisms, to redirect the light from a car's headlights back to the driver. •

• Supporting material: analogy to road signs.

If light is neither absorbed nor refracted, then in theory, the object should disappear. However, work remains to be done before this can be feasible. As any highway traveler can attest, bright road signs can still be seen. This is because the surface projected upon is not perfectly flat. Folds in the material absorb and disperse the light, thus making the object visible. Other limitations include the fact that with current optical camouflage, onlookers must stand in one specific spot and look through a peephole in order for the invisibility effect to occur. Moreover, this technology is neither cheap nor easy to transport.

Optical camouflage is not the only process that scientists are analyzing. Another promising technology is an "invisibility cloak," created by scientists from Duke University and University College London. The January 2007 issue of *Discover* calls the cloak one of the top discoveries in physics for the year 2006.

Discover, November 2006, reports that Duke physicists David Smith and Dave Schurig used specially created "metamaterials" to cloak a small cylindrical object, shielding it from microwaves. Microwaves have a longer wavelength than visible light does, hence it is easier to shield an object from them. What are metamaterials? According to the Duke Web site of Professor Smith's research group, June 10, 2006,

• Supporting material: definition of *metamaterials*.

they are "artificial structures that display properties beyond those available in naturally occurring material." • On the Duke University Web site, May 25, 2006, Smith notes that the cloak acts "like a hole you've opened up in space." All electromagnetic waves are directed around the cloaked object, and they come out on the other side, much as water in a river "flows virtually undisturbed around a smooth rock."

In the November 2006 *Discover*, the Duke physicists compare this process to a mirage on a hot summer road. "When light rays from the sky hit the hot, thin air just above the surface of the asphalt, they bend. . . . Light travels faster in the hot, thin air close to the road than it does in the cold, dense air above, and that difference in speed is what causes it to shift direction as it crosses the boundary between the two." The rays that were moving from the sky to the road get redirected to your eye, the road "shimmers like water," and the mirage cloaks "the now invisible road behind an image of the blue sky." •

• Supporting material: analogies to a mirage and river water flowing around a rock.

The invisibility cloak is an exciting first step, but it will be a challenge to improve the technology to shield objects from visible light. As the Duke researchers explain in *Discover*, tiny metal shapes are stamped on the metamaterials. These shapes must be smaller than the wavelength that is directed at them. Microwaves are about three centimeters (or one inch) long—60,000 times the 500 nanometer wavelength of green light waves! The researchers state that it would be theoretically possible to make such tiny shapes for the metamaterials, but they would be difficult to mass-produce. Ulf Leonhardt, a theoretical physicist at the University of St. Andrews in Scotland, also notes that the current materials are rigid—more like a suit of armor than a cloak. •

• Supporting material: explanation of why the invisibility cloak faces challenges.

Although more work needs to be done, invisibility technology offers many potential benefits to society. •

• In the following paragraphs, Josh uses diverse sources to document benefits.

There are already some practical applications of optical camouflage. BBCnews.com explains on January 4, 2007, that the underside of a plane can be cloaked to allow pilots to see the ground as they land, that it could make windows where there are none, and that doctors could quite literally see through their hands. For these reasons, the August 2003 *Time* magazine deemed it to be the coolest invention of the year.

The invisibility cloak could impact our lives in ways that we can now only imagine. *News View Researcher* on November 14, 2006, asks us to imagine a forty-story building that would block a picturesque view of Central Park. Cover the building with the invisibility cloak and it only appears three stories tall. Could you imagine covering eyesores like air conditioners, power lines, or Dumpsters?

Ker Than, staff writer for LiveScience.com, writes on October 19, 2006, that "a cloak that deflects radio waves could render an object invisible to radar or improve cell phone reflections by rerouting signals around an obstruction."

These materials could also find their way into health-care. Costas Soukoulis, a senior physicist at Ames Laboratory, explains in the January 9, 2007, *Science Daily* that metamaterials may lead to the development of a superlens that can capture "details much smaller than one wavelength of light to vastly improve imaging for materials or biomedical applications, such as giving researchers the power to see inside a human cell or diagnose disease in a baby still in the womb." The previously cited LiveScience.com article notes that cloaking materials "might also be used to protect people from penetrating and harmful radiation. 'If you knew that you had radiation of a certain bandwidth frequency, you could have it skirt around some region that you wanted shielded,'" says Duke physicist David Smith.

And of course, the military is anxious to get their hands on this technology. MSNBC.com explains on December 5, 2006, that "a cloaked ship would be impervious to radar detection. A bunker could be rendered invisible, and soldiers could be turned into superspies." The obvious danger here is that hostile groups could acquire the technology. Moreover, how will people know where invisible things are so as not to run into them?

Today, we have ventured into the unseen world of invisibility by first examining the science of invisibility. Second, we looked at the process of optical camouflage and the physics behind the new invisibility cloak. Finally, we looked at the tremendous impacts that this new technology could have on all of our lives. Now, you may not be able to run out tomorrow and purchase a cloak, but in the not-too-distant future, our military will be stronger, cell phone reception clearer, and characters like Susan Storm and the invisible woman may no longer just be comic book characters. •

• Summary of main points and clincher tied to the introduction.

SAMPLE PERSUASIVE SPEECH

CHILD SLAVERY AND THE PRODUCTION OF CHOCOLATE

David Kruckenberg
Santiago Canyon College

Student David Kruckenberg presented this speech in the finals of the Phi Rho Pi national championship tournament in 2007.

David uses a problem-cause-solution format to address the compelling issue of child labor in the production of chocolate. He uses diverse reasoning strategies and consistently documents his claims with evidence. David's speech is well organized, with a clear preview and transitions between each main point. His audience-centered solution demonstrates how each of us can be personally involved in addressing the problem.

I was forced to stay in a large room with other children from a neighboring plantation. I tried to run

away, but I was caught. As punishment they cut my
feet; I had to work for weeks while my wounds
healed.

This moving testimony may sound like past history, when
slavery was prevalent. But these words are not a reminder
of the past; they're found in the April 24, 2006, *Forbes* magazine. These are the words of an enslaved boy working in
the cocoa fields of the country of Côte d'Ivoire, also known
as the Ivory Coast. And he is not alone. UNICEF reports in
February 2006 that child trafficking is on the rise in this
African region. •

• Attention-getter:
a shocking first-
person quotation
plus evidence the
problem is growing.

It may surprise you to learn that the last chocolate you
ate may well have been tainted with child slavery. Despite
the promises and agreements made in recent years by
chocolate companies, they continue to use child labor in the
production of their chocolate. We as consumers must communicate that this is unacceptable. •

• David connects
with the audience
and presents his
thesis.

To do so, we will first reveal the connection between
chocolate and child slavery, second examine why the problem continues, and finally discover just how much power we
have in bringing child slavery to an end.

How are chocolate and child slavery connected? •

• Preview statement
and transition to first
main point.

Cocoa bean production is limited to areas near the
equator, such as Central America, Indonesia, and the Ivory
Coast. The International Cocoa Initiative Web site, last updated February 8, 2007, explains that with almost a million
acres devoted to growing cocoa, the Ivory Coast accounts
for more than 40 percent of world cocoa production. Because growing cocoa is labor-intensive and labor is a significant part of the cost of production, the *Vancouver Sun* on
November 10, 2006, reports that many farmers in the Ivory
Coast have turned to using forced child labor to cut costs.

The conditions of these children are beyond comprehension. The International Cocoa Initiative details the hazards
they face each day: they must work long hours in the fields in
brutal conditions. They clear fields with machetes and apply
pesticides without protective gear. After harvesting the cocoa

pods, they must split them open with heavy knives. Once the beans are dried and bagged, they must carry these large loads long distances on their young backs.

Even more alarming is just how many children are forced to live this life. The *New York Times* of October 26, 2006, reports that more than 200,000 children in the Ivory Coast are forced to work in the cocoa fields. The *Chicago Tribune* of May 5, 2006, reports that in contrast to the rest of the world, this region of Africa has the highest rate of child laborers of all children five to fourteen years old; more than one in four are forced to work. Earth Save International, last updated February 14, 2007, says that these children are either enticed with promises of good wages and easy work or outright kidnapped. One example is a boy named Molique, who came to the Ivory Coast at the age of fourteen; despite the promises, he was never paid. When he asked to be paid, he was beaten. He had to scavenge for food and at night was locked up with the other kids. The *New York Times* of October 29, 2006, says that almost 12,000 children in the Ivory Coast have been trafficked far from their families' homes and into slavery. •

The growing use of child slavery is reprehensible, but why is it allowed to continue? The answer is our widespread and growing demand for chocolate. •

Unfortunately, child slavery continues because our demand for chocolate continues, enabling the Ivory Coast and the chocolate companies to ignore the problem. Farmers in the Ivory Coast invest in cocoa for its large profits. In order to maximize their gain, they cut costs by using the forced labor of children. These 600,000 farmers then turn to large export companies in the Ivory Coast to buy their cocoa. The *New York Times* of October 26, 2006, reports that these export companies are able to keep the price that they pay for cocoa low because they have so many farmers to choose from. The exporters then sell their cocoa to large chocolate companies such as Hershey's, Nestle, M&M/Mars, and Cadbury. •

The *Calgary Herald* of November 17, 2006, tells us that in 2001, almost all of the big chocolate companies signed

• Combination of examples to build pathos and statistics to document the extent of the problem.

• Transition to main point II.

• Causal reasoning.

the Harkin-Engel Protocol, agreeing that by 2005 they would certify that their chocolate was not tainted with child slavery; however, this deadline passed two years ago with the companies making excuses saying they need more time. But the September 20, 2006, *Seattle Post-Intelligencer* suggests that they're more concerned about the civil war in the Ivory Coast interfering with their supply of cocoa. Clearly the civil war is also the top priority with the Ivory Coast government. The Associated Press on June 15, 2006, explains that the government doesn't want to interfere with the supply of cocoa because export taxes are their primary source of revenue. The government uses this money to buy military arms and equipment. The Ivory Coast may not have blood diamonds, but [the nation] certainly possesses blood chocolate. •

• Blood chocolate— compelling analogy to blood diamonds.

Ultimately, the blame rests on us, because consumer demand for chocolate keeps the industry insulated from pressure. The World Cocoa Foundation, last updated February 14, 2007, tells us that North America and Europe consume nearly two-thirds of all cocoa products and that demand for confectionary products containing chocolate rises 4 to 5 percent each year. The sad truth is most consumers are not aware of chocolate's connection to child slavery. Because we continue to buy their chocolate, the industry feels no urgency to change. •

• Evidence shows that the speaker and audience members are part of the problem.

Now that we understand the problem and why it continues, we must ask what we can do, and the answer is simple. We must stop buying slave-produced chocolate.

But don't worry, I'm not suggesting that we stop buying chocolate altogether. There is an alternative, and it's called fair trade chocolate. TransFair USA, a nonprofit organization, is the only independent third-party certifier of fair trade products in the U.S. It allows companies to display the fair trade–certified label on products that meet strict standards. Some of these standards found on their Web site, last updated November 16, 2006, include a prohibition [on] forced child labor, safe working conditions, living wages, environmentally safe farming methods, a guaranteed minimum price,

• How the audience can be personally involved in the solution.

and direct trade between the farmers and chocolate companies, thus eliminating the manipulative exporters. •

If we as consumers change how we buy chocolate, the industry will have to respond. Currently, they're trying to distance themselves from the bad press associated with slave labor, and as a result the Ontario *Guelph Mercury*, February 3, 2007, reports that some have begun to buy into the fair trade market. For example, Business Wire, October 11, 2006, reports that Ben and Jerry's is expanding its fair trade–certified ice cream flavors. *Forbes* magazine, previously cited, says that fair trade has even made inroads into the Ivory Coast but still accounts for only about 1 percent of cocoa exports. •

• David explains how one solution can reduce the problem.

Economics teaches us that demand controls supply; they can only sell what we buy. A perfect example of this is the industry's response to the rise in demand for organic food products. The *Boston Herald* on October 16, 2006, reports that organic food sales have risen more than 15 percent in the last two years. With a multibillion-dollar market, the September 20, 2006, *Sacramento Bee* says that big companies like Wal-Mart and Frito-Lay have made organic food mainstream. If we demand more fair trade chocolate, the industry will have to supply it, and when the chocolate companies start buying more slave-free cocoa, farmers in the Ivory Coast will have to abandon slavery to keep their buyers. •

• Analogy to consumer-generated demand for organic products.

Today we have exposed the connection between chocolate and child slavery, examined why the problem continues, and finally discovered how we can bring it to an end. The next time you go to buy chocolate, remember the words of a child, quoted in the November 10, 2006, *Toronto Star*: "When the rest of the world eats chocolate, they're eating my flesh." The Ivory Coast may be seven thousand miles away, but we have a responsibility to protect all children. Fair trade chocolate may cost us a little more money, but that's a small price to pay to free thousands of children from slavery. •

• Clincher includes another compelling quotation that connects to the introduction.

SAMPLE PERSUASIVE SPEECH

BACK-TO-SCHOOL EVENT

President Barack Obama

On September 8, 2009, the first day of school for many students, President Barack Obama delivered an address at Wakefield High School in Virginia. The speech was broadcast to elementary and secondary students in classrooms across the country.

In this speech, President Obama encourages all students to take responsibility for their own education, explaining how education is essential for students to achieve their dreams and to contribute to society. Drawing on anecdotes from his own experiences as a student, along with fundamental American values, the president exhorts students to work hard, even when confronted by obstacles.

Although there was political controversy before President Obama delivered his speech, he received favorable reviews afterward. His message that students have a responsibility to work hard in school because education is central to our success as a nation addresses values that appeal to all Americans, regardless of political persuasion.

Hello everyone—how's everybody doing today? I'm here with students at Wakefield High School in Arlington, Virginia. And we've got students tuning in from all across America, kindergarten through twelfth grade. I'm glad you all could join us today. I know that for many of you, today is the first day of school. And for those of you in kindergarten, or starting middle or high school, it's your first day in a new school, so it's understandable if you're a little nervous. I imagine there are some seniors out there who are feeling pretty good right now, with just one more year to go. And no matter what grade you're in, some of you are probably wishing it were still summer and you could've stayed in bed just a little longer this morning. I know that feeling. • When I was young, my family lived in Indonesia for a few years, and my mother didn't have the money to send me where all the American kids went to school. So she decided to teach me extra lessons herself, Monday through Friday—at 4:30 in the morning.

• Obama uses personal anecdotes about his own school days to connect with his audience.

Now I wasn't too happy about getting up that early. A lot of times, I'd fall asleep right there at the kitchen table. But whenever I'd complain, my mother would just give me one of those looks and say, "This is no picnic for me either, buster."

So I know some of you are still adjusting to being back at school. But I'm here today because I have something important to discuss with you. I'm here because I want to talk with you about your education and what's expected of all of you in this new school year.

Now I've given a lot of speeches about education. And I've talked a lot about responsibility. •

• Note style here: the president uses a parallel format, repeating the phrase "I've talked about" to introduce a series of examples.

I've talked about your teachers' responsibility for inspiring you and pushing you to learn.

I've talked about your parents' responsibility for making sure you stay on track, and get your homework done, and don't spend every waking hour in front of the TV or with that Xbox.

I've talked a lot about your government's responsibility for setting high standards, supporting teachers and principals, and turning around schools that aren't working, where students aren't getting the opportunities they deserve.

But at the end of the day, we can have the most dedicated teachers, the most supportive parents, and the best schools in the world—and none of it will matter unless all of you fulfill your responsibilities. Unless you show up to those schools; pay attention to those teachers; listen to your parents, grandparents, and other adults; and put in the hard work it takes to succeed.

And that's what I want to focus on today: the responsibility each of you has for your education. • I want to start with the responsibility you have to yourself.

• Here, Obama clearly identifies and articulates his thesis.

Every single one of you has something you're good at. Every single one of you has something to offer. And you have a responsibility to yourself to discover what that is. That's the opportunity an education can provide.

Maybe you could be a good writer—maybe even good enough to write a book or articles in a newspaper—but you might not know it until you write a paper for your English class. Maybe you could be an innovator or an inventor—maybe even good enough to come up with the next iPhone or a new medicine or vaccine—but you might not know it until you do a project for your science class. • Maybe you could be a mayor or a senator or a Supreme Court justice, but you might not know that until you join student government or the debate team.

And no matter what you want to do with your life—I guarantee that you'll need an education to do it. You want to be a doctor, or a teacher, or a police officer? You want to be a nurse or an architect, a lawyer or a member of our military? You're going to need a good education for every single one of those careers. You can't drop out of school and just drop into a good job. You've got to work for it and train for it and learn for it.

And this isn't just important for your own life and your own future. What you make of your education will decide nothing less than the future of this country. What you're learning in school today will determine whether we as a nation can meet our greatest challenges in the future. •

You'll need the knowledge and problem-solving skills you learn in science and math to cure diseases like cancer and AIDS, and to develop new energy technologies and protect our environment. You'll need the insights and critical thinking skills you gain in history and social studies to fight poverty and homelessness, crime and discrimination, and make our nation more fair and more free. You'll need the creativity and ingenuity you develop in all your classes to build new companies that will create new jobs and boost our economy.

We need every single one of you to develop your talents, skills, and intellect so you can help solve our most difficult problems. If you don't do that—if you quit on school—you're not just quitting on yourself; you're quitting on your country.

• For supporting materials, Obama points to a series of examples and makes them personal for students.

• The president touches on personal goals as well as patriotic duty as he transitions to his next main point.

Now I know it's not always easy to do well in school. I know a lot of you have challenges in your lives right now that can make it hard to focus on your schoolwork. •

- Obama establishes common ground with the audience by acknowledging the challenges faced by many students and his own similar struggles.

I get it. I know what that's like. My father left my family when I was two years old, and I was raised by a single mother who struggled at times to pay the bills and wasn't always able to give us things the other kids had. There were times when I missed having a father in my life. There were times when I was lonely and felt like I didn't fit in.

So I wasn't always as focused as I should have been. I did some things I'm not proud of, and got in more trouble than I should have. And my life could have easily taken a turn for the worse.

But I was fortunate. I got a lot of second chances and had the opportunity to go to college, and law school, and follow my dreams. My wife, our first lady Michelle Obama, has a similar story. Neither of her parents had gone to college, and they didn't have much. But they worked hard, and she worked hard, so that she could go to the best schools in this country.

Some of you might not have those advantages. Maybe you don't have adults in your life who give you the support that you need. Maybe someone in your family has lost their job, and there's not enough money to go around. Maybe you live in a neighborhood where you don't feel safe, or have friends who are pressuring you to do things you know aren't right.

But at the end of the day, the circumstances of your life—what you look like, where you come from, how much money you have, what you've got going on at home—that's no excuse for neglecting your homework or having a bad attitude. That's no excuse for talking back to your teacher, or cutting class, or dropping out of school. That's no excuse for not trying. •

- While he sympathizes with students' struggles, Obama quickly follows up with a call for action.

Where you are right now doesn't have to determine where you'll end up. No one's written your destiny for you. Here in America, you write your own destiny. You make your own future.

• • •

But the truth is, being successful is hard. You won't love every subject you study. You won't click with every teacher. Not every homework assignment will seem completely relevant to your life right this minute. And you won't necessarily succeed at everything the first time you try. •

That's OK. Some of the most successful people in the world are the ones who've had the most failures. J. K. Rowling's first Harry Potter book was rejected twelve times before it was finally published. Michael Jordan was cut from his high school basketball team, and he lost hundreds of games and missed thousands of shots during his career. But he once said, "I have failed over and over and over again in my life. And that is why I succeed." •

These people succeeded because they understand that you can't let your failures define you—you have to let them teach you. You have to let them show you what to do differently next time. If you get in trouble, that doesn't mean you're a troublemaker; it means you need to try harder to behave. If you get a bad grade, that doesn't mean you're stupid; it just means you need to spend more time studying.

• • •

The story of America isn't about people who quit when things got tough. It's about people who kept going, who tried harder, who loved their country too much to do anything less than their best.

It's the story of students who sat where you sit 250 years ago, and went on to wage a revolution and found this nation. Students who sat where you sit seventy-five years ago who overcame a Depression and won a world war; who fought for civil rights and put a man on the moon. Students who sat where you sit twenty years ago who founded Google, Twitter, and Facebook and changed the way we communicate with each other. •

So today, I want to ask you, what's your contribution going to be? What problems are you going to solve? What discoveries will you make? What will a president who comes

• Obama offers a two-sided argument to make the point that success won't come easily.

• To reinforce his point, Obama cites examples that students can relate to.

• References to innovation, sacrifice, and rugged individualism are used to explain and illustrate fundamental American values.

• Obama uses rhetorical questions to prompt students to reflect on his remarks.

here in twenty or fifty or one hundred years say about what all of you did for this country? •

Your families, your teachers, and I are doing everything we can to make sure you have the education you need to answer these questions. I'm working hard to fix up your classrooms and get you the books, equipment, and computers you need to learn. But you've got to do your part too. So I expect you to get serious this year. I expect you to put your best effort into everything you do. I expect great things from each of you. So don't let us down—don't let your family or your country or yourself down. Make us all proud. I know you can do it.

Thank you, God bless you, and God bless America.

SAMPLE PERSUASIVE SPEECH

THE DEMOCRATIZATION OF EDUCATION
Shakira

The United Kingdom's Oxford University is one of the most prestigious colleges in the world. Its debating society, the Oxford Union, has hosted generations of scholars and leaders, including Winston Churchill, three U.S. presidents, Albert Einstein, and Mother Teresa. The society has also hosted its share of public figures, including Star Trek's Leonard Nimoy, talk-show host Jerry Springer, and Kermit the Frog.

Colombian pop star Shakira joined this roster of famous speakers on December 7, 2009. The artist is world famous for her Grammy Award–winning music and dance moves. But she displayed her serious side at this scholarly forum, delivering a compelling persuasive speech advocating universal education for all children.

As you read Shakira's speech, note how she relies on her own ethos (her experience establishing an education foundation in Colombia) and employs a wide variety of supporting materials and stylistic choices to make her case.

Thank you Oxford, and thank you Oxford Union.

It is truly an honor and a privilege to be here today, and that you have afforded me this opportunity to speak to you.

I must confess, I am somewhat mystified as to why you are here. I won't be singing . . . and there won't be any hip shaking.

So, how do I, a girl from Barranquilla, Colombia, come to occupy the same stage as Newton and Churchill? Lord knows I'm no Mother Teresa, but here I am, nonetheless.

I realize that the one point of view from which I can depart is that of an artist. After all, it is who I am. We artists depend on our imaginations.

When I first learned I was coming, I thought about the past and I imagined the future. From your minds, ideas will sprout that will give new shape to the world. I cannot help but fast-forward to what the world will be like in fifty years. What will be happening? Who will we be? How will we live? What challenges can we overcome?

I have a fantasy about this future that I want to share with you.

Let me put it this way, if civilization were a car, we would have been cruising at 20 miles per hour for millions of years only to hit light speed in the last hundred. ●

• Figurative analogy: Shakira weaves the image of driving a car throughout her speech.

What made us accelerate so quickly recently, and how can we continue this pace? There is only one explanation: the democratization of education. ●

• Thesis is presented clearly and early.

Think about it: just recently a fossil was discovered in Africa, the oldest human fossil at over four million years. Our ancestors may have been slightly smaller than they are now but not significantly so, particularly if you compare them to me since I am 5'3"—well, okay, 5'2".

From then to now, humans learned, slowly but surely, the tools and methods they needed to survive and thrive in what would become modern civilization.

. . .

We know that in the Middle Ages, education was reserved by, and for, a few, a handful of people with access to the precious resources of knowledge—writing, reading, libraries. The rest of the population, well, they weren't so lucky; they lived unexamined lives, carting stone and wood from one place to another, unable to participate in intellectual conversation.

• • •

There was no critical mass of thought that allowed humanity to truly advance, to rescue them from plague, to invent the vaccines that would extend their lives, to devise the sociological models that would allow society to flourish. •

• Shakira employs causal explanation as she describes the historically slow rate of intellectual growth.

These civilizations rose and fell and rose again; but in comparison to the present, the pace of development was incredibly slow—like a river one must stare at with unbroken concentration to detect the movement of the current.

But what they didn't anticipate was the Renaissance, the Enlightenment, and later the Industrial Revolution! Suddenly, a middle class emerged, and everywhere people began to engage with each other, sharing their knowledge—and instead of having a few thousand people thinking for everyone, there were millions of readers, writers, creators, artists, academics, teachers, and students, becoming a true collective of shared resources, an ongoing, endless exchange of our most vital resource: information.

But then, a hundred years or so ago, we really picked up the pace. Suddenly, we pushed down hard on the accelerator. Suddenly, we were aboard a space shuttle, speeding through the sky, piercing the boundaries of the earth's atmosphere, traveling thousands of miles to the moon, staking a flag on its surface, and sharing that breathtaking moment with the rest of the world through a device known as the television. Thank God for televisions.

• • •

We have achieved so much, and we owe it to one basic but transformational concept.

The democratization of education.

• Example reasoning: Shakira provides a list of modern realities brought about by education.

It is the airplane that brought me to England, the medicine that allows grandparents to meet their grandchildren, the philosophy that expands our individual liberties, and the technology that sent us to the moon. •

I do not subscribe to the idea that the older days were better days. I strongly believe that the best is yet to come, with universal access to education to feed our collective intelligence, with our commitment to meet and organize in places like this, among students like you—we could be so close to creating a network of intellects, an enormous think tank devoted to sharing the best ideas and inspiring each other to keep learning, keep informing, and keep advancing our world. And finding solutions to our common issues. Wouldn't that be great?

We have evolved so far in the course of human history, with so many technological advances in just the past century, how will we evolve in the next ten tears, or twenty years, or fifty years—now that we know that the world has shrunk and has become just one big neighborhood[?] •

• • •

• Shakira uses a rhetorical question to transition to her next main point.

Nine years ago, as part of the Millennium Development Goals, leaders from around the world made a pledge to transform the world so that every child would have access to a primary school by the year 2015. That is just over five years from now. Sadly, their actions have not met their promises. Sadly, at the current pace of change, we won't have universal access to education in a hundred years, let alone five. That is unacceptable.

Especially when the world has the resources to feed itself several times over, then, why are children starving? Latin America alone has three times the necessary abundance to feed its own population. •

• Here, she establishes the need for change by providing statistics and examples.

These children can't wait a hundred more years. They need us to cure a child with leukemia or AIDS with a simple pill or a breakthrough vaccine. We need to live in a world in which together, we can find a solution to global warming so we don't have to worry every single time a storm begins to form on the horizon. We need to find new ways to distribute food so no child goes to bed hungry.

And I know that education is our ticket.

How do I know? Because I've seen it.

I was born and raised in a country marked by civil conflict, social strife, and inequality. Growing up in the developing world, where education is perceived as a luxury and not as a right; where children beg for an education and parents are desperate to provide it; where if one is born poor, one is destined to die poor.

But the good news is that there is an exit strategy to break the cycle of poverty in which millions are trapped because of lack of access to education. •

• A bold statement offers a graceful transition from one main point (the bad news) to the next main point (the good news).

From the moment I turned eighteen, I decided to establish my own foundation in Colombia. And since then we have been working on providing high-quality education, nutrition for children, and occupational training for their parents; building schools that also work as community centers for families that have been displaced by violence, that have lost everything they had.

We found the way to keep kids in school and maintain parents' involvement in their children's education. Providing nutritious meals in schools, we have decreased the number of dropouts, and we have eradicated malnutrition among our students. •

• Here, Shakira establishes credibility through personal experience.

So we know that creating comprehensive models of education in areas where the population is vulnerable to extreme poverty and conflict transforms the minds and the lives of not only children but entire communities. And it works. Believe me, it works.

I'm still a student on all these issues, but I've come to learn that there are ways to change this. So no government can say that the challenge of bringing education to every child is an impossible task. Because we know how to enroll all those 75 million kids who don't have access to any kind of primary education, by:

Abolishing school fees

Hiring quality teachers

Providing uniforms and textbooks to children

And providing most importantly food, because no kid can learn on an empty stomach and because we've proven that it becomes the best incentive for parents to send their kids to school and reduce child labor.

Now I want to be clear about this, this isn't about charity. This is about investing in human potential. •

From an ethical point of view, from a moral point of view, it accomplishes a purpose. But also from an economic point of view, this could bring enormous benefits to all mankind. Universal education is the key to global security and economic growth.

• Shakira uses a two-sided argument to acknowledge, and then refute, the notion that investing in education is simply charity.

Security

We all want safer nations. And in a world where weak states are often a haven for violent extremists, getting more children into school can dramatically help reduce the risk of instability and lay the groundwork for more stable democratic political systems to emerge. •

A child who lives in extreme poverty away from school is ten times more likely to be recruited by a militant group than one who is receiving an education. For instance, in Colombia we have kids in our schools who were destined to be a part of the drug trafficking business or recruited by guerrillas; today, as we speak, they are going to college and, like you, are graduating soon. So yes, education promotes peace and stability worldwide. Isn't that what we all want?

• Shakira makes an appeal to audience values—in this case, security.

Economic Growth

On the other hand, education helps catalyze economic growth. One single year of primary education invested means a 10 to 20 percent increase in wages in their adult life. For every dollar invested in early childhood development programs, that same child will give back 17. So yeah, education also boosts economic growth. •

So I, for one, would definitely like to go faster. I want to go faster because, with so many challenges, faster is better. I want to go faster because faster is more just.

And they need us to do it all tomorrow. I say: let's do it today.

• Providing statistics shows the benefit of her proposal and bolsters her credibility.

• • •

Only by investing in our children, by tapping their potential that has remained untapped for too long, can they one day cure our diseases, or bring us to Mars, or secure us peace here on earth.

Because, it bears repeating, we are one world.

One civilization.

• Repetition of the word "one" makes her plea more memorable.

One conscience.

One engine.

One destiny. •

And so, if I have just one more thought to offer you and to add to our one collective conscience here today, it is this:

Education for all.

• Shakira connects with her audience by quoting the renowned philosopher and Oxford alumnus John Locke (class of 1656!).

John Locke, who I believe was one of yours, once said, "the only fence against the world is a thorough knowledge of it, and the earlier the better." • So yeah, the earlier the better. There is no time to waste. It is you who are in the driver's seat. It is your foot on the accelerator.

• Style: Shakira returns to her accelerator metaphor for clincher.

And please, step on it. •

Thank you very much. This has been a true honor.

SAMPLE SPECIAL-OCCASION SPEECH

1962 SYLVANUS THAYER AWARD ACCEPTANCE SPEECH

General Douglas MacArthur

General MacArthur delivered an acceptance speech when he was honored with the Thayer Award at the U.S. Military Academy in

1962. This award is given annually to a U.S. citizen whose service and accomplishments in the national interest exemplify personal devotion to the ideals expressed in the West Point motto: duty, honor, country. The version below excerpts the first two-thirds of the original speech text.

General MacArthur builds his speech around the motto of "Duty, Honor, Country." He explains what these ideas mean to him, and he uses repetition to emphasize the motto. The general uses stylistic devices such as description, metaphor, and simile to express his message. MacArthur presents an inspirational message to his West Point audience, encouraging them to live up to the USMA motto.

General MacArthur's speech refers to the military service and heroism of "men." In 1962, women were not allowed to serve in combat, nor were women accepted as cadets at West Point until 1976. Nevertheless, women also performed heroic service in wars; for example, many women worked as "Rosie the Riveters" in war production industries during World War II. Any contemporary speaker should not make gendered references to war heroes or to the accomplishments of cadets currently at West Point.

General Westmoreland, General Grove, distinguished guests, and gentlemen of the Corps!

As I was leaving the hotel this morning, a doorman asked me, "Where are you bound for, General?" And when I replied, "West Point," he remarked, "Beautiful place. Have you ever been there before?" •

No human being could fail to be deeply moved by such a tribute as this [Thayer Award]. Coming from a profession I have served so long, and a people I have loved so well, it fills me with an emotion I cannot express. But this award is not intended primarily to honor a personality but to symbolize a great moral code—the code of conduct and chivalry of those who guard this beloved land of culture and ancient descent. That is the animation of this medallion. For all eyes and for all time, it is an expression of the ethics of the American soldier. That I should be integrated in this way with so noble an ideal arouses a sense of pride and yet of humility, which will be with me always. •

Duty, Honor, Country: those three hallowed words reverently dictate what you ought to be, what you can be, what

• Attention-getter: an ironic anecdote—clearly, he's been to West Point before!

• MacArthur connects with his audience.

you will be. They are your rallying points: to build courage when courage seems to fail; to regain faith when there seems to be little cause for faith; to create hope when hope becomes forlorn. •

• The theme of MacArthur's speech is identical to the academy's motto: "Duty, Honor, Country."

Unhappily, I possess neither that eloquence of diction, that poetry of imagination, nor that brilliance of metaphor to tell you all that they mean.

The unbelievers will say they are but words, but a slogan, but a flamboyant phrase. Every pedant, every demagogue, every cynic, every hypocrite, every troublemaker, and I am sorry to say, some others of an entirely different character, will try to downgrade them even to the extent of mockery and ridicule.

• Functional definition of "Duty, Honor, Country" is made through a long series of examples.

But these are some of the things they do. • They build your basic character. They mold you for your future roles as the custodians of the nation's defense. They make you strong enough to know when you are weak, and brave enough to face yourself when you are afraid. They teach you to be proud and unbending in honest failure, but humble and gentle in success; not to substitute words for actions; not to seek the path of comfort, but to face the stress and spur of difficulty and challenge; to learn to stand up in the storm, but to have compassion on those who fall; to master yourself before you seek to master others; to have a heart that is clean, a goal that is high; to learn to laugh, yet never forget how to weep; to reach into the future, yet never neglect the past; to be serious, yet never to take yourself too seriously; to be modest so that you will remember the simplicity of true greatness, the open mind of true wisdom, the meekness of true strength. They give you a temper of the will, a quality of the imagination, a vigor of the emotions, a freshness of the deep springs of life, a temperamental predominance of courage over timidity, of an appetite for adventure over love of ease. They create in your heart the sense of wonder, the unfailing hope of what next, and the joy and inspiration of life. They teach you in this way to be an officer and a gentleman.

And what sort of soldiers are those you are to lead? Are they reliable? Are they brave? Are they capable of victory? Their story is known to all of you. It is the story of the American man-at-arms. • My estimate of him was formed on the battlefield many, many years ago and has never changed. I regarded him then as I regard him now—as one of the world's noblest figures, not only as one of the finest military characters but also as one of the most stainless. His name and fame are the birthright of every American citizen. In his youth and strength, his love and loyalty, he gave all that mortality can give.

He needs no eulogy from me or from any other man. He has written his own history and written it in red on his enemy's breast. But when I think of his patience under adversity, of his courage under fire, and of his modesty in victory, I am filled with an emotion of admiration I cannot put into words. He belongs to history as furnishing one of the greatest examples of successful patriotism. He belongs to posterity as the instructor of future generations in the principles of liberty and freedom. He belongs to the present, to us, by his virtues and by his achievements. In twenty campaigns, on a hundred battlefields, around a thousand campfires, I have witnessed that enduring fortitude, that patriotic self-abnegation, and that invincible determination which have carved his statue in the hearts of his people. From one end of the world to the other, he has drained deep the chalice of courage. •

As I listened to those songs [of the glee club], in memory's eye I could see those staggering columns of the First World War, bending under soggy packs, on many a weary march from dripping dusk to drizzling dawn, slogging ankle-deep through the mire of shell-pocked roads, to form grimly for the attack, blue-lipped, covered with sludge and mud, chilled by the wind and rain, driving home to their objective, and for many, to the judgment seat of God. •

I do not know the dignity of their birth, but I do know the glory of their death. They died unquestioning, uncomplaining,

• At the time of this speech, women were not allowed in combat. If the speech were given today, the men *and* women who serve would need to be recognized.

• MacArthur honors the Thayer Award and his audience by expressing his admiration for all U.S. soldiers.

• MacArthur employs strong style and reinforces his credibility: descriptive language and personal remembrance.

with faith in their hearts, and on their lips the hope that we would go on to victory. Always, for them: *Duty, Honor, Country*; • always their blood and sweat and tears, as we sought the way and the light and the truth.

• Repetition of theme throughout speech.

And twenty years after, on the other side of the globe, again the filth of murky foxholes, the stench of ghostly trenches, the slime of dripping dugouts; those boiling suns of relentless heat, those torrential rains of devastating storms; the loneliness and utter desolation of jungle trails; the bitterness of long separation from those they loved and cherished; the deadly pestilence of tropical disease; the horror of stricken areas of war; their resolute and determined defense, their swift and sure attack, their indomitable purpose, their complete and decisive victory—always victory. • Always through the bloody haze of their last reverberating shot, the vision of gaunt, ghastly men reverently following your password of *Duty, Honor, Country*.

• A long descriptive sentence filled with alliteration and vivid language evokes the harrowing conditions in Asia during World War II.

The code which those words perpetuate embraces the highest moral laws and will stand the test of any ethics or philosophies ever promulgated for the uplift of mankind. Its requirements are for the things that are right, and its restraints are from the things that are wrong.

• Allusions to religion can be effective, but should also be made with care and with audience analysis in mind. Otherwise, speakers might connect poorly with listeners who do not share their beliefs.

The soldier, above all other men, is required to practice the greatest act of religious training—sacrifice. •

In battle and in the face of danger and death, he discloses those divine attributes which his Maker gave when he created man in his own image. No physical courage and no brute instinct can take the place of the Divine help which alone can sustain him.

• MacArthur once again praises the commitment and devotion of soldiers.

However horrible the incidents of war may be, the soldier who is called upon to offer and to give his life for his country is the noblest development of mankind. •

• • •

NOTES

Chapter 1

1. NACE, "Employers Cite Communication Skills as Key, but Say Many Job Seekers Lack Them," *NACEWeb*, April 26, 2006, http://www.naceweb.org/press/display.Asp?year+&prid+235 (accessed June 20, 2006).

2. R. H. Whitworth and C. Cochran, "Evaluation of Integrated versus Unitary Treatments for Reducing Public Speaking Anxiety," *Communication Education* 45 (1996): 306.

3. D. J. DeNoon, "Help for Public-Speaking Anxiety," *CBS News Healthwatch*, April 20, 2006, http://www.cbsnews.com/stories/2006/04/20/health/webmd/main1523045.shtml.

4. J. Gatz, "What You Need to Succeed in the Workplace," *Job Web*, http://www.jobweb.com/resources/library/Workplace_Culture/What_you_need_to_18_01.htm (accessed June 15, 2006).

5. NACE, http://www.naceweb.org/Press/Frequently_Asked_Questions.aspx?referal=pressroom&menuID=276&nodetype=4 (accessed June 28, 2010).

6. Heldrich Center for Workforce Development, "Are America's Schools and Skills Making the Grade?" Press release, June 14, 2000, http://www.heldrich.rutgers.edu/publications/WTV/release614.000.doc (accessed November 11, 2001).

7. L. Feldmann, "Now Running for Office: An Army of Iraq Veterans," *Christian Science Monitor*, February 22, 2006, http://www.csmonitor.com/2006/0222/p01S03-uspo.htm.

8. M. I. Finley, *Politics in the Ancient World* (New York: Cambridge University Press, 1983), 59, 73.

9. D. Bodde, *China's First Unifier* (Hong Kong: Hong Kong University Press, 1967), 181.

10. A. A. Boahen, "Kingdoms of West Africa," in *From Freedom to Freedom*, ed. M. Bain and E. Lewis (New York: Random House, 1977), 69.

11. G. Welch, "The Authors Who Talked," in *From Freedom to Freedom*, ed. M. Bain and E. Lewis (New York: Random House, 1977), 39.

12. C. Brooks, R. W. B. Lewis, and R. P. Warren, *American Literature: The Makers and the Making*, vol. 1 (New York: St. Martin's Press, 1973), 1179.

13. A. Brinkley, *American History: A Survey*, 10th ed., vol. 1 (Burr Ridge, IL: McGraw-Hill, 1999), 103–4.

14. N. Gabler, "A Victim of the Third Great Awakening," *Los Angeles Times*, January 14, 2001, M1.

15. Brooks, Lewis, and Warren, *American Literature,* 84.

16. C. A. Brekus, *Strangers and Pilgrims: Female Preaching in America, 1740–1845* (Chapel Hill: University of North Carolina Press, 1998), 3.

17. Lincoln-Douglas Debates of 1858, *Illinois in the Civil War*, 2000, http://www.illinoiscivilwar.org/debates.html.

18. E. C. DuBois, *The Elizabeth Cady Stanton–Susan B. Anthony Reader* (Boston: Northeastern University Press, 1992), 8.

19. B. Harris, "Texans Take Bush Fight on the Road," *Los Angeles Times*, July 28, 2000, A16.

20. A. Ayres, ed., *The Wisdom of Martin Luther King, Jr.* (New York: Penguin Books, 1993).

21. M. Z. Muhammad, "Students Are the Vanguard of Million Woman March," *Black Collegian* 28 (February 1998): 10; "Million Man March Draws More Than 1 Million Black Men to Nation's Capital," *Jet*, October 30, 1995, 4.

22. R. M. Berko, A. D. Wolvin, and D. R. Wolvin, *Communicating: A Social and Career Focus*, 3rd ed. (Boston: Houghton Mifflin, 1985), 42.

23. J. Stewart, *Bridges, Not Walls*, 7th ed. (New York: McGraw-Hill, 1999), 16.

24. M. W. Lustig and J. Koester, *Intercultural Competence: Interpersonal Communication across Cultures* (New York: HarperCollins, 1993), 31.

25. J. H. Bodley, "An Anthropological Perspective," *What Is Culture?* 1994, http://www.wsu.edu/gened/learn-modules/top_culture/culture-definitions/bodley-text.html.

26. U.S. Senate, *Hearing to Receive Testimony on S. 1367, S. 1617, S. 1670, S. 2020, S. 2478, and S. 2485: Before the Subcommittee on National Parks, Historic Preservation, and Recreation of the Senate Energy Committee*, testimony of Arnoldo Ramos, 106th Cong., 2nd sess., May 11, 2000, http://energy.senate.gov/hearings/national_parks/5_11Cats&Dogs/Ramos.htm (accessed June 28, 2000).

27. N. P. Tetsinas, "The New Homeowners," *Boston Globe,* July 8, 2007, D9.

28. "The Myth of the Melting Pot," Washingtonpost.com, 1998, http://www.washingtonpost.com/wp-srv/national/longterm/meltingpot/maps.htm (accessed July 12, 2000).

29. H. El Nasser, "Analysis Finds Boom in Hispanics' Home Buying," *USA Today*, May 11, 2006, http://www.usatoday.com/news/nation/2006-05-10-hispanic-homeowners_x.htm?POE = NEWISVA.

30. Tetsinas, "The New Homeowners," D9.

31. Lustig and Koester, *Intercultural Competence*, 11.

32. "More Marches, a Growing Backlash," *Economist*, May 6, 2006, 30.

33. H. Maurer, "A Fracas over Immigration," *Business Week*, April 10, 2006, 28.

34. Letters to the Editor, "Immigration Divides the Nation," *Time*, May 1, 2006, 8.

35. Comtex News Network, "National Press Conference Held: No Human Being Is Illegal; AFSC Calls for Substantive Immigration Policy Solutions," *US Newswire*, May 24, 2006.

36. J. Bell, *Evaluating Psychological Information: Sharpening Your Critical Thinking Skills*, 2nd ed., 72, cited in *Critical Thinking as Described by Psychologists*, December 15, 1996, http://academic.pg.cc.md.us/~wpeirce/MCCCTR/bell1.html (accessed June 12, 2006).

37. C. Morris, *Psychology*, 1993, xv–xvi, cited in J. Bell, *Critical Thinking as Described by Psychologists*, December 15, 1996, http://academic.pg.cc.md.us/~ wpeirce/MCCCTR/bell1.html (accessed June 12, 2006).

38. NCA, "NCA Credo for Ethical Communications," 1999, http://www.natcom.org/index.asp?bid = 514.

39. P. Bizzell and B. Herzberg, *The Rhetorical Tradition* (Boston: Bedford/St. Martin's, 1990), 35.

40. *USA Today*/Gallup Poll, November 20–22, 2009, www.pollingreport.com/values.htm (accessed June 28, 2010).

Chapter 2

1. L. G. Davis, *I Have a Dream . . . The Life and Times of Martin Luther King, Jr.* (Westport, CT: Greenwood Press, 1973).

2. A. Ayres, ed., *The Wisdom of Martin Luther King, Jr.* (New York: Penguin Books, 1993).

3. Davis, *I Have a Dream*, 137.

4. K. D. Miller and E. M. Lewis, "Touchstones, Authorities, and Marian Anderson: The Making of 'I Have a Dream,'" in *The Making of Martin Luther King and the Civil Rights Movement*, ed. B. Ward and T. Badger (New York: New York University Press, 1996), 151.

5. Ayres, *The Wisdom of Martin Luther King, Jr.*, 62–63.

6. E. Rothstein, "A Resonance That Shaped a Vision of Freedom," *New York Times*, June 29, 2006, B7.

7. J. F. Wilson and C. C. Arnold, *Public Speaking as a Liberal Art*, 3rd ed. (Boston: Allyn and Bacon, 1974), 337.

8. P. Bizzell and B. Herzberg, *The Rhetorical Tradition* (Boston: Bedford/St. Martin's, 1990), 32, 310.

9. N. H. Rogers, "Good Public Speaking," June 13, 2006, http://eep.store .merchandizer.com/merchant/newsite/samples/pe/pe1201.htm.

10. J. Ayres, "Comparing Self-Constructed Visualization Scripts with Guided Visualization," *Communication Reports* 8 (1995): 193–99.

11. C. R. Sawyer and R. R. Behnke, "State Anxiety Patterns for Public Speaking and the Behavior Inhibition System," *Communication Reports* 12 (1999): 34.

Chapter 3

1. United States National Park Service, "History Continued," *Statue of Liberty National Monument*, August 14, 2006, http://www.nps.gov/stli/ historyculture/history-continued.htm (accessed March 14, 2007).

Chapter 4

1. J. Stewart, *Bridges, Not Walls*, 4th ed. (New York: Random House, 1986), 181.

2. Study by TCC Consulting (San Francisco), undertaken between 1987 and 1997.

Chapter 5

1. For research that supports Minh's claim, see "Women See Fuel Economy as Major Factor in Car Buying Decision," *United Business Media Newswire*, November 15, 2005, http://www.prnewswire.com/ news/index_mail.shtml?ACCT = 104&STORY = /www/story/11-15-2005/ 0004216674&EDATE (accessed March 15, 2007).

2. This statistic first emerged from two of Alfred Kinsey's studies: *Sexual Behavior in the Human Male* (1948) and *Sexual Behavior in the Human Female* (1953). Although there has been some controversy over Kinsey's methodology, subsequent studies have indicated that a significant proportion of the population self-identifies as GLBT or as having participated in homosexual activity. See, for example, Australian Research Centre in Sex, Health and Society, *Sex in Australia: The Australian Study of Health and Relationships*, published as the *Australian and New Zealand Journal of Public Health* 27.2 (April 2003); and C. F. Turner, L. Ku, S. M. Rogers, L. D. Lindberg, J. H. Pleck, and F. L. Sonenstein, "Adolescent Sexual Behavior, Drug Use, and Violence: Increased Reporting with Computer Survey Technology," *Science* 280 (1998): 867–73.

3. There is a wide range of literature on the complicated and controversial subject of the relationship between Pope Pius XII, the Catholic Church, and the Holocaust. For an overview of the subject, see Jose M. Sanchez, *Pius XII and the Holocaust: Understanding the Controversy* (Washington, DC: Catholic University Press, 2002).

4. For more on this speech, go to http://www.americanrhetoric.com/speeches/tedkennedytruth&tolerance.htm.

Chapter 6

1. For an example on the topic of evolution, see N. Wade, "The Evolution of the God Gene," *New York Times*, November 15, 2009, WK3.

2. P. Russell, "How to Mind Map," http://www.peterrussell.com/MindMaps/howto.php (accessed December 7, 2009).

3. B. Kirchner, "Mind-Map Your Way to an Idea: Here Is One Approach to Rooting Out Workable Topics That Move You," *Writer* 122.3 (2009): 28–29.

4. J. F. Wilson and C. C. Arnold, *Public Speaking as a Liberal Art*, 3rd ed. (Boston: Allyn and Bacon, 1974), 70–71.

Chapter 7

1. R. D. Rieke and M. O. Sillars, *Argumentation and Critical Decision Making*, 5th ed. (New York: Addison Wesley Longman, 2001), 136.

2. J. C. Reinard, *Foundations of Argument* (Dubuque, IA: Wm. C. Brown, 1991), 113.

3. Reinard, *Foundations of Argument*, 115.

4. N. Pastore and M. W. Horowitz, "The Influence of Attributed Motive on the Acceptance of a Statement," *Journal of Abnormal and Social Psychology* 51 (1955): 331–32.

5. Associated Press, "Dire Predictions for Swine Flu's Future," *CBS News*, July 24, 2009, http://www.cbsnews.com/stories/2009/07/24/world/main5185843.shtml.

6. R. Stein, "Flu Pandemic Could Be Mild," *Washington Post*, December 8, 2009, A01.

7. Pew Internet and American Life Project, *The Internet Goes to College: How Students Are Living in the Future with Today's Technology.* September 15, 2002, http://www.pewinternet.org/PPF/r/71/report_display.asp, 2–3.

8. Primary Research Group, *The Survey of American College Students: Who Goes to the College Library and Why?* April 2009, http://www. researchandmarkets.com/reportinfo.asp?report_id = 888965&t = d&cat_id =.

9. P. Lyman and H. Varian, "How Much Information?" 2003, http://www.sims.berkeley.edu:8000/research/projects/how-much-info-2003/.

10. G.-Q. Zhang and others, "Evolution of the Internet and Its Cores," *New Journal of Physics* 10 (December 2008).

11. M. J. Metzger, A. J. Flanagin, and L. Zwarun, "College Student Web Use, Perceptions of Information Credibility, and Verification Behavior," *Computers and Education* 41.3 (November 2003): 271–90.

12. W. L. Lym, "Tempting Students with Scholarly Research: Breaking the Fast-Food Research Diet," *College Teaching* 57 (Fall 2009): 237.

13. C. Chen et al., "An Assessment of the Completeness of Scholarly Information on the Internet," *College and Research Libraries* 70 (July 2009): 386.

14. ICANN, "Top Level Domains," December 16, 2003, http://www.icann.org/+lds.

15. R. Berkman, "Internet Searching Is Not Always What It Seems," *Chronicle of Higher Education* 46 (July 28, 2000): B9.

16. The Virtual Chase, "How to Evaluate Information—Checklist," March 6, 2006, http://www.virtualchase.com/quality/checklist.

17. D. Sullivan, "How Search Engines Work," *Search Engine Watch*, October 14, 2002, http://searchenginewatch.com/webmasters/article.php/2168031.

18. D. Sullivan, "How Search Engines Rank Web Pages," *Search Engine Watch*, July 31, 2003, http://searchenginewatch.com/webmasters/article.php/2167961.

19. University of California, Berkeley, Library, "Meta-Search Engines," *Finding Information on the Internet: A Tutorial*, August 23, 2005, http://www.lib.berkeley.edu/TeachingLib/Guides/Internet/MetaSearch.html.

20. J. Tanaka, "The Perfect Search: The Web Is Growing by Millions of Pages Every Year," *Newsweek*, September 27, 1999, 71.

21. University of California, Berkeley, "How Much Information?" 2000, http://www2.sims.berkeley.edu/research/projects/.

22. A. Clyde, "The Invisible Web," *Teacher Librarian* 29 (April 2002): 47.

23. R. Lackie, "The Evolving 'Invisible Web': Tried-and-True Methods and New Developments for Locating the Web's Hidden Content," *College and Undergraduate Libraries* 10.2 (2003): 65, 69.

Chapter 8

1. E. Moscoso and R. Carr, "Privacy Battle Is Being Waged on Many Fronts," *Austin American-Statesman*, March 22, 2004, A6.

2. D. Searcey, "Some Courts Raise Bar on Reading Employee Email," *Wall Street Journal*, November 19, 2009, A17.

3. J. Brown, "Pan, Tilt, Zoom: Regulating the Use of Video Surveillance of Public Places," *Berkeley Technological Law Journal* 23 (2008): 755.

4. D. G. Savage, "Employer Wins Text-Messaging Case; High Court: Public Workers' Privacy Rights Limited When Using Device Issued for Job," *Baltimore Sun*, June 18, 2010, 16A.

5. Cambridge University Press, *Cambridge Dictionaries Online*, 2006, http://dictionary.cambridge.org (accessed January 31, 2007).

6. M. Boyce, *Zoroastrians: Their Religious Beliefs and Practices* (London: Routledge, 1979), 2.

7. Boyce, *Zoroastrians*, 2.

8. Ontario Consultants on Religious Tolerance, *Zoroastrianism*, March 24, 2005, http://www.religioustolerance.org/zoroastr.htm.

9. College Board, "Breaking Down the Bill: What's It Going to Cost?" 2009, http://www.collegeboard.com/student/pay/.

10. J. Reinard, *Foundations of Argument* (Dubuque, IA: Brown, 1991), 111.

11. W. R. Fisher, *Human Communication as Narration: Toward a Philosophy of Reason, Value, and Action* (Columbia: University of South Carolina Press, 1987).

12. S. Hymon, "About Goldfishcam," March 15, 2006, http://www.latimes.com/news/local/la-031506fishcam_lat,0.1619074.

13. J. Barrett, "Campaigning for a Healthier America," May 10, 2005, http://www.msnbc.msn.comid/7752179/site/newsweek; M. Tanneeru, "Obesity: A Looming National Threat?" March 24, 2006, http://www.cnn.com/2006/HEALTH/DIET.FITNESS/03/24/hb.obesity.epidemic/index.html.

14. K. E. Rowan, "A New Pedagogy for Explanatory Public Speaking: Why Arrangement Should Not Substitute for Invention," *Communication Education* 44 (July 1995): 245.

15. M. Walton, "Jellyfish Lures Dinner with Flashing Red Light," *Science and Space*, CNN.com, July 7, 2005, http://www.cnn.com/2005/TECH/science/07/07/redlightlure/index.html.

16. Virginia Tech Transportation Institute, "New Data from VTTI Provides Insight into Cell Phone Use and Driving Distraction," July 27, 2009, http://www.vtti/vt.edu/PDF/2-22-09-VTTI-Press_Release_Cell_ phones_and_Driver_Distraction.pdf.

17. R. M. Felder and B. A. Soloman, "Learning Styles and Strategies," http://www.ncsu.edu/felder-public/ILSdir/styles.htm (accessed April 17, 2006).

18. Felder and Soloman, "Learning Styles and Strategies."

19. R. M. Felder and L. K. Silverman, "Learning and Teaching Styles in Engineering Education," *Engineering Education* 78.7 (1988): 677.

Chapter 9

1. J. C. McCroskey, *An Introduction to Rhetorical Communication*, 5th ed. (Englewood Cliffs, NJ: Prentice Hall, 1986), 185.
2. J. C. McCroskey, "The Effects of Disorganization and Nonfluency on Attitude Change and Source Credibility," *Speech Monographs* 36 (March 1969): 13–21; H. Sharp Jr. and T. McClung, "Effect of Organization on the Speaker's Ethos," *Speech Monographs* 33 (June 1966): 182–83.
3. L. M. Simons, "Inside Bollywood," *Smithsonian* 31 (January 2001): 50.
4. L. M. Simons, "Inside Bollywood," 55.
5. L. M. Simons, "Inside Bollywood," 49.
6. L. M. Simons, "Inside Bollywood," 52.

Chapter 10

1. P. Bizzell and B. Herzberg, *The Rhetorical Tradition* (New York: St. Martin's Press, 1990), 429.
2. K. Kohrs Campbell, *The Rhetorical Act*, 2nd ed. (Belmont, CA: Wadsworth, 1996), 264–65.
3. V. Havel, "Playwright-Dissident Vaclav Havel Assumes the Presidency of Czechoslovakia," in *Lend Me Your Ears: Great Speeches in History*, ed. W. Safire (New York: Norton, 1992), 629–34.
4. "Transcript: Rice's Speech on Transatlantic Ties," *Washington Post*, February 8, 2005, http://www.washingtonpost.com/wp-dyn/articles/A7965-2005Feb8.html.
5. A. Richards, "Keynote Address to the Democratic National Convention," in *Great Speeches for Criticism and Analysis*, ed. R. Cook and L. Rohler (Greenwood, IN: Educational Video Group, 2001), 79.
6. Bill & Melinda Gates Foundation, remarks by Bill Gates, Harvard Commencement, June 6, 2007, www.gatesfoundation.org/speeches commentary/Pages/bill-gates-2007-harvard-commencement.aspx.
7. Joke Central, Conan O'Brien on the Economy, www.mustsharejokes.com/page/Conan+O%27Brien+on+the+Economy (accessed February 15, 2010).
8. L. M. Forquer and others. "Sleep Patterns of College Students at a Public University," *Journal of Amerian College Health* 56 (March/April 2008): 563.

9. R. Clark, *Einstein: The Life and Times* (London: Hodder and Stoughton, 1973), 26.

Chapter 12

1. Testimony of Kevin M. Brown, Chief Operating Officer, American Red Cross, before the Committee on Ways and Means Subcommittee on Oversight, United States House of Representatives, September 25, 2007.
2. G. Lakoff and M. Johnson, *Metaphors We Live By* (Chicago: University of Chicago Press, 1980), 5.
3. C. R. Jorgensen-Earp and A. Q. Staton, "Student Metaphors for the College Freshman Experience," *Communication Education* 42 (1993): 125.
4. J. L. Stringer and R. Hopper, "Generic *He* in Conversation?" *Quarterly Journal of Speech* 84 (1998): 209–21.
5. D. Cameron, *Feminism and Linguistic Theory* (New York: St. Martin's Press, 1985), 68.

Chapter 13

1. K. Menzell and L. Carrell, "The Relationship between Preparation and Performance in Public Speaking," *Communication Education* 43 (1994): 19–26.
2. See, for example, http://www.merriam-webster.com/dictionary/nuclear.
3. J. S. Tuman and Reverend Paul Levine, personal communication, St. Francis Episcopalian Church, Turlock, California, in 1976.
4. V. Manusov, "Perceiving Nonverbal Messages: Effects of Immediacy and Encoded Intent on Receiver Judgments," *Western Journal of Speech Communication* 55 (1991): 236.
5. J. K. Burgoon and B. A. LePoire, "Nonverbal Cues and Interpersonal Judgments: Participant and Observer Perceptions of Intimacy, Dominance, Composure, and Formality," *Communication Monographs* 66 (1999): 107.
6. Much of the original research on proxemics was pioneered by anthropologist Edward T. Hall: E. T. Hall, *The Hidden Dimensions* (New York: Doubleday, 1966). See also M. L. Patterson, "Spatial Factors in Social Interactions," *Human Relations* 21 (1968): 351–61.
7. Patterson, "Spatial Factors in Social Interactions," 351–61.
8. J. K. Burgoon, D. Buller, and M. deTurck, "Relational Messages Associated with Nonverbal Behaviors," *Human Communication Research* 10.3 (1984): 351–78.

9. E. T. Hall, *Hidden Differences: Doing Business with the Japanese* (New York: Doubleday, 1987).
10. L. J. Smith and L. Malandro, "Personal Appearance Factors Which Influence Perceptions of Credibility and Approachability of Men and Women," in *The Nonverbal Communication Reader*, ed. J. A. Devito and M. L. Hecht (Prospect Heights, IL: Waveland Press, 1990), 163.

Chapter 14

1. E. Bohn and D. Jabusch, "The Effect of Four Methods of Instruction on the Use of Visual Aids in Speeches," *Western Journal of Communication* 42.3 (1982): 253–65.
2. H. E. Nelson and A. W. Vandermeer, "Varied Sound Tracks on Animated Film," *Speech Monographs* 20 (1953): 261–67.
3. Steve Jobs, Keynote Speech, January 27, 2010, http://www.apple.com/ipad/ (accessed March 15, 2010). Jobs spoke to a friendly audience of Apple enthusiasts and neutral but receptive industry analysts and media representatives at this conference.

Chapter 15

1. American College Health Association, College Health Resources, H1N1 Flu, http://www.acha.org/Topics/H1N1flu.cfm, link to YouTube video, http://www.youtube.com/watch?v=DzLPIc3yt2k, posted January 10, 2010.
2. Flag-folding etiquette is detailed by the American Legion, http://www.legion.org/flag/folding (accessed March 23, 2010).
3. U.S. Code, Title 4, Chapter 1, §3; §8(d), via Cornell University Law School, http://www.law.cornell.edu/uscode/html/uscode04/usc_sup_01_4_10_1.html (accessed March 23, 2010).
4. D. Russakoff, "Building a Career Path Where There Was Just a Dead End," *Washington Post*, February 26, 2007, A1.
5. D. M. Fraleigh and J. S. Tuman, *Freedom of Speech in the Marketplace of Ideas* (New York: St. Martin's Press, 1997).
6. J. S. Tuman, *Communicating Terror: The Rhetorical Dimensions of Terrorism* (Los Angeles: Sage Publishing, 2004).
7. K. E. Rowan, "A New Pedagogy for Explanatory Public Speaking: Why Arrangement Should Not Substitute for Invention," *Communication Education* 44 (July 1995): 236–50.

Chapter 16

1. Aristotle, *On Rhetoric*, trans. G. A. Kennedy (New York: Oxford University Press, 1991), 1355.

2. M. Sherif and C. I. Hovland, *Social Judgment, Assimilation, and Contrast Effects in Communication and Attitude Change* (New Haven: Yale University Press, 1961), 195–96.

3. Sherif and Hovland, *Social Judgment*, 195–96.

4. D. K. O'Keefe, *Persuasion: Theory and Research* (Newbury Park, CA: Sage, 1990), 36–37.

5. R. E. Petty and J. T. Cacioppo, *Communication and Persuasion: Central and Peripheral Routes to Attitude Change* (New York: Springer-Verlag, 1986).

6. A. H. Maslow, "A Theory of Human Motivation," *Psychological Review* 50 (1943): 370–96.

7. V. Packard, *The Hidden Persuaders* (New York: Pocket Books, 1964).

8. M. Rokeach, *Understanding Human Values* (New York: Free Press, 1979), 2.

9. J. S. Tuman, "Getting to First Base: Prima Facie Arguments for Propositions of Value," *Journal of the American Forensic Association* 24 (Fall 1987): 86.

10. M. Rokeach, *Beliefs, Attitudes, and Values: A Theory of Organization and Change* (San Francisco: Jossey-Bass, 1968).

11. J. Hornikx and D. J. O'Keefe, "Adapting Consumer Advertising Appeals to Cultural Values," *Communication Yearbook* 33 (2009): 38–71.

12. For an analysis of how this argument and other strategies may influence a change in audience values, see N. Rescher, "The Study of Value Change," *Journal of Value Inquiry* 1 (1967): 12–23.

13. M. Fishbein and I. Ajzen, *Belief, Attitude, Intention, and Behavior: An Introduction to Theory and Research* (Reading, MA: Addison-Wesley, 1975).

14. K. Horneffer-Ginter, "Stages of Change and Possible Selves: 2 Tools for Promoting College Health," *Journal of American College Health* 56.4 (2008): 351–58.

15. M. Allen, "Comparing the Persuasive Effectiveness: One- and Two-Sided Message," in *Persuasion: Advances through Meta-Analysis*, ed. M. Allen and R. W. Preiss (Cresskill, N.J.: Hampton Press, 1998), 96.

16. M. Rokeach, *Beliefs, Attitudes, and Values*, 3.

17. R. Hamill, T. Wilson, and R. Nesbit, "Insensitivity to Sample Bias: Generalizing from Atypical Cases," *Journal of Personality and Social Psychology* 39 (1980): 578–89.

18. C. Hoyt, "The Sources' Stake in the News," *New York Times*, January 17, 2010, WK8.
19. A. Monroe, *Principles and Types of Speech* (New York: Scott, Foresman, 1935).
20. R. E. McKerrow and others, *Principles and Types of Public Speaking*, 16th ed. (Boston: Pearson Education, Inc., 2007), 168.

Chapter 17

1. J. C. Reinard, *Foundations of Argument* (Dubuque, IA: William C. Brown, 1991), 353–54.
2. Aristotle, *On Rhetoric*, trans. G. A. Kennedy (New York: Oxford University Press, 1991), 1378a.
3. J. C. McCroskey and J. J. Teven, "Goodwill: A Reexamination of the Construct and Its Measurement," *Communication Monographs* 66.1 (1999): 92.
4. "Kerry Discusses $87 Billion Comment, September 30, 2004, http://www.cnn.com/2004/ALLPOLITICS/09/30/kerry.comment.
5. J. Bentley, "McCain Says Taxpayers Should Not Bail Out Wall Street, Criticizes Obama for 'Nasty' Campaign," September 15, 2008, www.cbsnews.com/8301-502443_162-4449233-502443.html; Chris Isidore, "It's Official: Recession Since Dec. '07," December 1, 2008, http://money.cnn.com/2008/12/01/news/economy/recession/index.htm.
6. H. Flesher, J. Ilardo, and J. Demoretcky, "The Influence of Field Dependence, Speaker Credibility Set, and Message Documentation on Evaluations of Speaker and Message Credibility," *Southern Communication Speech Journal* 34 (Summer 1974): 400.
7. J. C. McCroskey, "A Summary of Experimental Research on the Effects of Evidence in Persuasive Communication," *Quarterly Journal of Speech* 55 (April 1969): 172.
8. McCroskey, "A Summary of Experimental Research," 175.
9. D. J. DeNoon, "Drink More Diet Soda, Gain More Weight?" June 13, 2005, http://www.webmd.com/content/article/107/108476.htm#.
10. R. E. Nisbett and L. Ross, *Human Interference: Strategies and Shortcomings of Social Judgment* (Englewood Cliffs, NJ: Prentice Hall, 1980).
11. Canadian Broadcasting Corporation, "Caribou Comeback," November 30, 2002, http://archives.cbc.ca/IDC-1-75-1391-8983/science_technology/endangered_species/.

12. J. Doyle, "Extraordinary Comeback of the Peregrine Falcon: Predators to Come Off Endangered List," June 10, 1998, http://www.sfgate.com/cgi-bin/article.cgi?file = /chronicle/archive/1998/06/10/MN75129.DTL.

13. J. L. Eliot, "Our Majestic National Bird Is Flying High over Much of Its Former Range and May Soon Be off the Endangered List," *National Geographic*, June 2002, http://magma.nationalgeographic.com/ngm/0207/feature2/.

14. G. Leupp, "Obama and the Graveyard of Empires," December 26–28, 2008, http://www.counterpunch.org/leupp12262008.html.

15. *The New Afghanistan Strategy: The View from the Ground*, hearing before the Senate Committee on Foreign Relations, 111th Cong, December 9, 2009. Statement of General David H. Petraeus, emphasis in original.

16. B. Kiviat, "How to Create a Job," *Time*, March 29, 2010, 18.

17. P. Bronson and A. Merryman, "Should Children Redshirt Kindergarten?" *Newsweek* Nurture Shock Blog, September 3, 2009. http://blog.newsweek.com/blogs/nurtureshock/archive/2009/09/03/should-children-redshirt-kindergarten.aspx (accessed April 11, 2010).

18. Kaiser Family Foundation, "Side-by-Side Comparison of Major Health Reform Proposals," March 26, 2010, www.kff.org/healthreform/sidebyside.cfm.

19. S. Callahan, "The Role of Emotion in Ethical Decision Making," *Hastings Center Report* 18.3 (1988): 9.

20. G. Anders, *Health against Wealth: HMOs and the Breakdown of Medical Trust* (Boston: Houghton Mifflin, 1996), 108–9.

21. K. Witte and K. Morrison, "Examining the Influence of Trait Anxiety/Repression-Sensitization on Individuals' Reactions to Fear Appeals," *Western Journal of Communication* 64 (Winter 2000): 1.

22. P. A. Mongeau, "Another Look at Fear-Arousing Persuasive Appeals," in *Persuasion: Advances through Meta-Analysis*, ed. M. Allen and R. W. Preiss (Cresskill, NJ: Hampton Press, 1998), 66.

23. Mongeau, "Another Look at Fear-Arousing Persuasive Appeals," 66.

24. D. Westen, "Health Care Reform: It's How You Say It," July 1, 2009, Startribune.com, http://www.startribune.com/opinion/commentary/49631647.html.

25. D. Westen, *The Political Brain: The Role of Emotion in Deciding the Fate of the Nation* (New York: Public Affairs, 2007).

26. F. I. Luntz, "The Language of Healthcare 2009, http://www.politico.com/static/PPM116_luntz.html.

27. D. Westin, C. Lake, D. Mermin, K. Holland, and Z. Young, "How to Talk about Health Care Reform: Executive Summary of Research for Families USA, the Herndon Alliance, and the AARP" (June 10, 2008).

28. "H1N1 Flu Vaccine Is a 'Eugenics Weapon': Quebec ex-MD/Conspiracy Theorist," August 6, 2009, http://www.canadianmedicinenews.com/2009/08/h1n1-flu-vaccine-iseugenics-weapon.html.

29. "Off-Base Camp: A Mistaken Claim about Glaciers Raises Questions about the UN's Climate Panel," *Economist* 394 (January 23, 2010): 76–77.

30. W. DeJong and L. Wallack, "A Critical Perspective of the Drug Czar's Antidrug Media Campaign," *Journal of Health Communication* 4 (1999): 155–60; D. R. Buchanan and L. Wallack, "This Is the Partnership for a Drug-Free America: Any Questions?" *Journal of Drug Issues* 28.2 (1998): 329–56.

31. A. Lang and N. S. Yegiyan, "Understanding the Interactive Effects of Emotional Appeal and Claim Strength in Health Messages," *Journal of Broadcasting and Electronic Media* 52.3 (2008): 432–47.

32. U.S. Department of Agriculture, "What Foods Are in the Fruit Group?" http://www.mypyramid.gov/pyramid/fruits.html.

33. K. D. Brownell, T. Farley, W. C. Willett, B. M. Popkin, F. J. Chaloupka, J. W. Thompson, and D. S. Ludwig, "The Public Health and Economic Benefits of Taxing Sugar-Sweetened Beverages," *New England Journal of Medicine* 361 (October 15, 2009): 1599–605.

34. R. Ratnesar, "Twenty Years after 'Tear Down This Wall,'" June 11, 2007, http://www.time.com/time/world/article/9,8599,1631828,00.html.

Chapter 18

1. Aristotle, *On Rhetoric*, trans. G. A. Kennedy (New York: Oxford University Press, 1991), 1358a-b.

2. Aristotle, *On Rhetoric*, 7, 47.

Chapter 19

1. B. R. Patton and K. Giffen, *Decision-Making Group Interaction*, 2nd ed. (New York: Harper & Row, 1978), 2.

2. I. Janis, *Victims of Groupthink* (Boston: Houghton Mifflin, 1972).

3. K. D. Benne and P. Sheats, "Functional Roles of Group Members," *Journal of Social Issues* 1.4 (1948): 41, 49.

4. The reflective-thinking process was developed from the ideas of John Dewey, an American philosopher who was interested in problem solving.

GLOSSARY

abstract   A summary of an article's contents, often included in indexes.

abstract word   A generic term that can be ambiguous or confusing for an audience. To say "I have a pet" is less informative than saying "I have a gray tabby cat."

ad populum **fallacy (bandwagoning)**   A misuse of logic that deceives an audience by claiming that a fact is true because a majority of people believe that it is true. Another form of this fallacy (often used in advertising and marketing) is to imply that because a large number of people are engaging in an activity, everyone should engage in the activity. Bandwagoning is unethical if speakers fail to provide support for their claims.

advanced search   Provides commands for making Web searches more precise.

age   A demographic consideration that affects an audience's response to and understanding of a speaker's message. For example, avoiding popular culture references that are too old or too young for an audience is a good way to take age into consideration.

agenda-driven listening   The failure of a speaker to adequately entertain an audience's questions or comments for fear of straying too far from his or her speech points.

analogy   A comparison based on similarities between two phenomena—one that is familiar to an audience and one that is less familiar—that helps listeners use their existing knowledge to absorb new information.

appeal to tradition fallacy   Arguing that a practice or policy is good because people have followed it for a long time.

argumentative listening   The act of only listening to a message long enough to get material to feed one's own argument.

arrangement   One of the five classical canons of rhetoric, arrangement is the effective organization of ideas to present them to an audience. Arrangement is dictated by topic, purpose, and audience analysis.

articulation Speaking with crispness or clarity so that listeners can distinguish separate words as well as separate syllables and vowel or consonant sounds within words.

atlas A reference work that provides maps, charts, and tables relating to different geographic regions.

attention-getter Material intended to capture an audience's interest in the introduction of a speech. Techniques a speaker can use to get an audience's attention include telling a story or anecdote, offering a provocative statement, building suspense, letting listeners know the speaker is one of them, using humor, asking a rhetorical question, or providing a quotation.

audience analysis The process of learning about an audience's interests and background in order to create or adapt a speech to their wants and needs.

audience size The number of people who will be present for a speech.

audience surveillance Analyzing an audience's nonverbal and verbal responses while you give a speech.

bandwagon fallacy See *ad populum* fallacy (bandwagoning).

bar graph A type of graph consisting of parallel bars of varying height or length that compares several pieces of information.

biased language Words, phrases, and expressions that suggest prejudice or preconceptions about other people, usually referring to their race, ethnicity, gender, sexuality, religion, or mental or physical ability.

bibliographic information Details about a researched source, including the title, author, publication date, and page numbers or URL.

bibliography An alphabetized list of the sources a speaker cited in his or her speech; usually written in accordance with a particular style of documentation, such as American Psychological Association (APA) style or Modern Language Association (MLA) style.

body (of speech) The section of a speech that falls between the introduction and the conclusion and contains the main part of the speech. This includes all major and supporting points.

body clock (chronemics) The time of day or day of the week when an audience will be listening to a presentation. An audience is more prone to distraction at certain times of the day, such as lunchtime, and certain days of the week, such as Friday.

boomerang effect   The act of pushing an audience more firmly into their previously held beliefs as a result of the speaker choosing a position that falls on the extreme end of an audience's latitude of rejection. (See also **latitude of rejection**.)

brainstorming   A strategy for generating topic ideas in which a potential speaker lists every idea that comes to mind—without evaluating its merits—in order to develop a sizable list of ideas quickly.

brief example   A single sentence or an otherwise short point of an instance that supports or illustrates a more general claim.

categorical (topical) pattern   An all-purpose speech organization pattern in which each main point emphasizes one of the most important aspects of the speaker's topic; often used if a speaker's topic doesn't easily conform to a spatial, temporal, causal, comparison, problem-cause-solution, criteria-application, or narrative pattern.

causal pattern   A speech organization pattern that explains cause-and-effect relationships in which each main point is either an event that leads to a situation or a link in a chain of events between a catalyst and a final outcome.

causal reasoning   Arguing that one event has caused another.

channel   The medium through which a source delivers a message, such as projecting one's voice, using a microphone, broadcasting on the airwaves, or streaming on the Internet.

citation   A complete record of the source for a piece of evidence, including author, date, and where the evidence can be found.

classical canons of rhetoric   The five concepts that effective speakers must attend to while preparing a speech, according to Cicero. These concepts are invention, arrangement, style, memory, and delivery.

clincher   Something that leaves a lasting impression of a speech in the listeners' minds, usually used as the second element in a speech conclusion. To go out with a bang, a speaker can extend a story or an anecdote he or she used at the start of the speech, relay a new story or anecdote, end with a striking phrase or sentence, or conclude with an emotional message.

common ground   Beliefs, values, and experiences a speaker shares with an audience. A speaker seeks to establish common ground with an audience, whether verbally or nonverbally, so that listeners will be more receptive to his or her message.

common knowledge   Widely known information that can be found in many sources and that does not require citation.

comparison pattern   A speech organization pattern that discusses the similarities and differences between two events, objects, or situations; especially useful when comparing a new subject to one with which the audience is familiar.

comparison reasoning   Arguing that two instances are similar enough that what is true for one is likely to be true for the other. If a speaker argues that U.S. residents will eventually accept mandatory health insurance because they accepted mandatory car insurance, the speaker is using comparison reasoning.

competence   Knowledge and experience in a subject.

conclusion   The final part of a speech, in which the speaker summarizes the main points and leaves the audience with a clincher, such as a vivid quote, image, or call to action.

concrete word   A specific word or phrase that suggests exactly what a speaker means. For example, to say a man was wearing a "dark blue suit" is more concrete than saying he was wearing "clothes."

connotative meaning   An association that comes to mind when a person hears a word. For example, saying "he tackled the project" brings to mind competitive sports and is a more vivid way to convey competence and enthusiasm than saying "he was excited to start the project and knew he could do a good job."

constructive criticism   Thoughtful and tactful suggestions for improvement that take into account what a speaker is trying to accomplish. These kinds of suggestions allow speakers to build on their feedback and make improvements for future presentations.

context   The occasion, surrounding environment, and situation in which a speaker gives a presentation.

coordination   A feature of a well-organized speech in which certain points share the same level of significance. For example, each main point is coordinate with the other main points, each subpoint with the other subpoints, and each sub-subpoint with the other sub-subpoints.

core belief   A long- and closely held viewpoint that is particularly immune to persuasion.

credibility   An audience's perception that a speaker is well prepared and qualified to speak on his or her topic. Trustworthiness, dynamism, and goodwill are also elements of a speaker's credibility. (See also **ethos**.)

credible source A source that can be reasonably trusted to be accurate and objective.

criteria-application pattern A speech organization pattern that proposes standards for making a judgment about a topic, then applies those standards to a related topic. For example, if a speaker were arguing that a city should budget money to renovate a specific crumbling, historic neighborhood, the speaker would first define the criteria for a "historic neighborhood" and then discuss how his or her city's specific neighborhood is historic and, thus, worth renovating.

critical thinking The analysis and evaluation of others' ideas, as well as one's own assumptions, based on reliability, truth, and accuracy.

culturally relative The recognition that ideas about ethical behavior sometimes differ from society to society.

culture The values, traditions, and rules for living that are passed from generation to generation. Culture is learned, not innate, and pervades all aspects of a person's life.

decode To interpret a message by making sense of a source's verbal and nonverbal symbols. Decoding is performed by a receiver.

defeated listening Pretending to understand a message while actually being overwhelmed by or uninterested in the subject matter.

definition A technique used in informative speeches that explains the essence, meaning, purpose, or identity of something.

delivery The speaker's varied and appropriate use of vocal and nonverbal elements such as voice, eye contact, and gestures while presenting a speech.

delivery reminder A special instruction speakers include within a speaking outline to remind themselves about such things as body language, pauses, and stressing key points.

demographics Audience members' characteristics, including but not limited to age, gender, sexual orientation, race, ethnicity, religious orientation, socioeconomic background, and political affiliation.

demonstration A technique used in informative speeches involving both physical modeling and verbal elements, with the goal of teaching an audience how a process or set of guidelines works.

denotative meaning The exact, literal dictionary definition of a word.

description A technique of informative speeches that uses words to paint a mental picture for audience members so that they can close their eyes and imagine what the speaker is saying.

designated leader A person chosen by an authority figure to help a group quickly move forward with its mission.

diagram A drawing that details an object or action, as well as arrangements and relations among its parts.

diction See **word choice (diction)**.

dictionary A reference work that offers definitions, pronunciation guides, and sometimes etymologies for words.

dictionary definition A type of support that provides the meaning of a term as presented in a general or specialized dictionary.

disposition An audience's likely attitude toward a subject. In most cases, an audience can be divided into three groups: sympathetic, hostile, and neutral.

drawing A visual depiction that enables a speaker to emphasize or de-emphasize certain details about a topic through techniques such as labeling parts of the main picture.

emergent leader One who comes to be recognized as a leader by a group's members over time.

encode To choose verbal or nonverbal symbols to organize and deliver one's message.

encyclopedia A reference work that offers relatively brief entries providing background information on a wide range of alphabetized topics.

epideictic Speaking that praises or blames.

ethical absolutism The adoption of a code of behavior to which a person adheres in all circumstances.

ethical audience An audience that exhibits courtesy, open-mindedness, and a willingness to hold the speaker accountable for his or her statements.

ethical speech Speech that incorporates ethical decision making, follows guidelines to tell the truth, and avoids misleading the audience.

ethics A set of beliefs shared by a group about what behaviors are correct or incorrect.

ethnicity   Cultural background that is usually associated with shared religion, national origin, and language.

ethos (credibility)   Inspiring belief in an audience by conveying a sense of the speaker's knowledge, honesty, trustworthiness, experience, authority, or wisdom.

etymological definition   A type of support that explains the linguistic origin of a term or word—useful when the origin is interesting or will help the audience understand the word.

eulogy   A speech that comments on the passing of an individual, celebrates his or her life, and often shares personal stories about the deceased.

evidence   Information gathered from credible research sources that helps a speaker support his or her claims.

example   A sample or instance that supports or illustrates a general claim.

example reasoning   Presenting specific instances to support a general claim in the hope that the cited instances will be sufficient to convince listeners that the claim is reasonable or true.

expert definition   A type of support that provides the meaning of a term as presented by a person who is a credible source of information on a particular topic.

expertise   The possession of knowledge necessary to offer reliable facts or opinions about the topic in question.

expert testimony   A type of support consisting of statements made by credible sources who have professional or other in-depth knowledge of a topic.

explanation   A technique used in informative speeches that provides an analysis of something for the purposes of clarity and specificity by tracing a line of reasoning or a series of causal connections between events.

extemporaneous delivery   The ability, enabled by practice, to deliver a speech smoothly and confidently from a speaking outline without reading from it.

extended example   A detailed narrative that serves as a sample or instance that supports or illustrates a general claim.

eye contact   The act of a speaker and audience members looking directly into each other's eyes as they are speaking or listening.

fact claim A statement asserting that something is true or false, such as "Animal experimentation is necessary for human survival."

fallacious (faulty) reasoning A type of faulty, and thus unsound, reasoning in which the link between a claim and its supporting material is weak.

false dilemma fallacy A speaker incorrectly claiming that there are only two possible choices to solve a problem, that one of them is wrong, and that the audience should therefore support the speaker's solution. You can usually detect this fallacy if you know there are more than two choices.

false inference Deceiving an audience by presenting information that leads them to assume an incorrect conclusion.

fear appeal A form of pathos in which an argument arouses fear in the minds of audience members.

feedback An audience's verbal and nonverbal responses to a source's message.

figurative analogy An analogy in which the two entities being compared are not in the same category.

fixed-response question A survey question that gives a respondent a set of specific answers to choose from. Examples include true/false, multiple choice, or select-all-that-apply questions.

flowchart A type of chart that demonstrates the direction of information or ideas, or illustrates the steps in a process.

forum (location) The setting where a speaker delivers, and an audience listens to, a speech.

freedom of expression The right to share one's ideas and opinions free from censorship.

full disclosure The practice of formally acknowledging one's own vested interest in a topic before presenting one's arguments, to reveal and acknowledge any potential conflicts of interest.

full-text source The complete text of an article linked within an online periodical index.

functional definition A type of support that explains how something is used or what it does.

gender composition A demographic characteristic that considers how many men versus how many women will be in an audience.

gender-neutral term   A word that does not suggest a particular gender.

gender stereotype   An oversimplified, often distorted view of what it means to be male or female.

gesture   A hand movement used as a part of delivery that points, pantomimes, demonstrates, or calls attention to something.

goodwill   Speakers wanting what is best for their audience rather than what would most benefit themselves.

graph   A visual representation of the relationship between different numbers, measurements, or quantities. Common types of graphs include line graphs, bar graphs, and pie charts.

group dynamics   The ways in which members relate to one another and view their functions.

groupthink   The tendency of the members of a group to accept ideas and information uncritically because of strong feelings of loyalty or single-mindedness within the group.

half-truth   A statement that deceives an audience by revealing part of the truth, but mixing the truth with a lie.

hasty generalization   Misusing logic and deceiving an audience by asserting that a piece of evidence—one that applies to a limited number of cases—applies to all cases.

hearing   Passively receiving messages without trying to interpret or understand them.

hierarchy of needs   A theory that divides human needs into five levels and emphasizes that the most basic needs must be met before people will focus on less essential ones. Psychologist Abraham Maslow's hierarchy of needs begins with physiological needs, followed by safety, social, self-esteem, and self-actualization needs.

hostile audience   A type of audience that opposes a speaker's message, or the speaker personally, and so will probably be reluctant to accept the message.

hybrid search engine   A specialized online program combining a search engine and Web directory. (See also **search engine** and **Web directory**.)

hypothetical example   An imagined example or scenario that a speaker invites his or her audience to consider in order to help them follow a complicated point presented immediately afterward.

imagery   Mental pictures or impressions painted with vivid language.

implied leader   A person with preexisting authority or skills that make him or her likely to be recognized as a leader by a group, even if leadership has not been formally assigned.

impromptu delivery   A speech in which content is generated in the moment, without advanced preparation.

inductive reasoning   Generalizing from facts, instances, or examples, and then making a claim based on that generalization. If a couple has two bad experiences in a row at the same restaurant, they might conclude that they will always have bad experiences at that restaurant.

informative purpose   The rhetorical purpose that aims to educate and increase an audience's understanding and awareness of a topic.

interactive listening   The process of a receiver filtering out distractions, focusing on what others have said, and communicating that he or she has paid attention.

internal noise (internal distractions)   Thoughts that distract a sender or receiver from processing and retaining a message.

internal preview   A short list of ideas before a main point or subpoint that quickly summarizes points that will follow. Using an internal preview is akin to giving the audience an advance warning of what is to come.

internal summary   A quick review of what a speaker has just said in a main point or subpoint, used to help an audience remember a particularly detailed point.

Internet   A popular research tool connecting computers around the world and containing millions of Web sites and other resources of varying quality maintained by individuals, businesses, and organizations.

interruptive listening   The act of interjecting questions or comments before a sender is finished speaking. Both audience members and speakers can be guilty of interruptive listening.

interview   A means of gathering information—used for research or audience analysis—in which a speaker has a conversation with experts or select members of a future audience and records their responses. The interview can be conducted in many ways—for example, in person, by e-mail, or by instant messaging.

introduction   Occurs at the beginning of a speech and serves several purposes, including gaining the audience's attention, establishing speaker credibility, building common ground with the audience, presenting the thesis statement, and previewing the speech's main points.

invention One of the five classical canons of rhetoric, this refers to using a variety of techniques and sources to gather and choose ideas for a speech.

invisible Web Online information, sometimes password-protected, that cannot be easily accessed using typical search engines. Search tools that specialize in finding information on the invisible Web include Complete Planet (www.aip.completeplanet.com), GoshMe (www.goshme.com), Library Spot (www.libraryspot.com), and OAIster (www.oaister.org).

jargon Specialized or technical words or phrases familiar only to people in a specific field or group.

keyword A word or term related to a topic, including synonyms of the word. Keywords are often used in online or database searches.

latitude of acceptance The range of positions on a given issue that are acceptable to an audience.

latitude of rejection The range of positions on a given issue that are unacceptable to an audience.

lay testimony A type of support consisting of statements made by persons with no special expertise in the subject they are discussing.

legally protected speech Telling the truth or withholding information based on whether the law allows unethical speech. If you (unethically) use legal protection as your guiding principle for speaking, you can technically stay within the bounds of what is lawful but still speak unethically.

line graph A type of graph that plots lines on a pair of axes to show relationships between two elements.

listening Actively receiving and processing messages to understand their meaning and remember their content.

literal analogy An analogy in which two entities in the same category are being compared.

loaded language Using emotionally charged words to convey meaning that cannot be supported by facts.

loaded language fallacy The unethical use of emotionally charged words to convey meaning that is not supported by evidence.

location See **forum (location)**.

logos The sound reasoning that supports a speaker's claims and makes the argument more persuasive to an audience.

main point A key idea that supports a thesis and helps an audience understand and remember what is most important about a speaker's topic; main points are supported by subpoints. (See also **subpoints**.)

map A visual representation of geography.

marking a special occasion A rhetorical purpose that seeks to honor a person or event by entertaining, inspiring, or emotionally moving an audience.

memory (preparation) One of the five classical canons of rhetoric, memory is the process of preparing and practicing a speech to ensure confident and effective delivery. Originally, the canon memory referred to learning a speech by heart; however, in the twenty-first century, using notes and other memory aids is usually preferred.

message Verbal or nonverbal ideas that a source conveys through the communication process.

metaphor An implicit comparison of unlike objects by identifying one object with another. For example: "Her advisor was *a fount of knowledge*."

metasearch engine A type of search engine that searches with several different search engines at once. (See also **search engine**.)

mind mapping A strategy for generating topic ideas in which a person writes down an initial word or phrase and then surrounds it with additional words, pictures, and symbols to create an interconnected map of ideas.

mobile audience An audience that is not bound to sit or stand for the duration of a speech. Mobile audiences might be found at an exhibitor's booth or on a city sidewalk.

moderator In a panel discussion, the person who introduces the panelists and leads the discussion.

motivated sequence A persuasive organizational pattern that is structured around five main points: attention, need, satisfaction, visualization, and action.

narrative   A story a speaker tells to share information and capture an audience's attention. As used in informative speeches, the story can be a personal remembrance, a humorous anecdote, or a serious account of an event that happened in someone else's life.

narrative pattern   A speech organization pattern that uses a story, including characters and a plot, to support the speaker's thesis.

needs   The objects an audience desires and the feelings that must be satisfied.

nervous listening   Talking through silences during lapses in conversation.

neutral audience   A type of audience that has neither negative nor positive opinions about a speaker or message.

noise (interference)   External or internal phenomena that disrupt communication between a sender and a receiver. External sources include nearby loud noises, while internal sources might include wandering thoughts of the sender or receiver.

nonlistening   Failing to pay attention to what one is hearing, and thus failing to process, understand, and retain the message.

nonverbal delivery skills   Use of eye contact, gestures, and other techniques—such as physical movement, proxemics, and personal appearance—to deliver a speech.

nonverbal symbol   A means of communication without using words. Examples include gestures, facial expressions, eye contact, and images.

objectivity   A quality of credible sources by which they avoid bias—that is, prejudice or partisanship.

observational capacity   A source's ability to witness a situation for himself or herself, thus increasing the source's reliability.

omission   A form of false inference that deceives an audience by withholding important information.

open-ended question   A survey question that invites respondents to give answers of their own choosing, rather than offering them a limited set of responses.

outline   A written means of organizing a speech using sentences, phrases, or keywords. An outline includes the main ideas of a speech's introduction, body, and conclusion.

outlining Organizing the points of a speech into a structured form that lays out the sequence and hierarchy of a speaker's ideas.

panel discussion A form of group presentation in which group members engage in discourse with one another, observed by the audience.

panelist A participant in a panel discussion.

panning A form of nonverbal delivery in which a speaker looks out and surveys all audience members. As the speaker looks back and forth across the audience, he or she pauses and makes extended eye contact with an individual listener for a few moments before moving on to do the same with another listener.

paraphrasing Putting someone else's ideas into one's own words and giving appropriate credit to the original source.

pathos Appealing to an audience's emotions.

pausing Leaving strategic gaps of silence between the words and sentences of one's speech.

peer review The act of subjecting articles submitted to a scholarly journal to critical readings by other experts in a particular field.

periodical A weekly, monthly, quarterly, or annual publication, including newspapers, magazines, and scholarly journals.

peripheral belief A viewpoint that people do not hold closely as a core belief and that they may not have had for a long time; thus, they may be open to persuasion. (For contrast, see also **core belief**.)

personal appearance The impression a speaker makes on an audience through his or her clothing, jewelry, hairstyle, grooming, and other elements influencing how the speaker looks.

personal attack (*ad hominem* attack) Persuading an audience to dislike someone by targeting his or her character rather than the relevant issues.

persuasive purpose A rhetorical purpose that seeks to strengthen listeners' commitment, weaken listeners' commitment, or promote a particular action.

persuasive speech A speech that aims to influence audience members' beliefs, attitudes, or actions; to which end it employs strategic discourse and calls for the audience to accept fact, value, and policy claims.

photograph A visual representation that is an exact depiction of a person, place, object, or event.

physical movement How much or how little a speaker moves around while giving a presentation.

pie chart (circle graph)   Information arranged to resemble a sliced pie that helps a speaker clarify how proportions and percentages relate to one another and add up to a whole.

plagiarism   Presenting another person's words or ideas as one's own.

policy claim   A statement that advocates action by organizations, institutions, or members of the audience. For example: "Anyone opposed to animal experimentation should join an activist organization, such as the Humane Society, to help put a stop to this cruel and unnecessary practice."

political affiliation   A person's political beliefs and positions.

post hoc fallacy   Incorrectly naming the cause of one event as the event that immediately preceded it.

power wording   The unethical practice of paraphrasing evidence in a way that better supports one's own claim but misrepresents a source's point of view.

precise evidence   Supporting materials consisting of specific dates, places, numbers, and other facts.

presentation aid   Anything beyond spoken words that a speaker uses to help the audience understand and remember his or her message; includes presentational materials that can be seen, heard, or touched.

presentation software   A computer program that enables users to create, edit, and present information, usually in a slide-show format.

presentation time   The length of time a speaker has to deliver his or her speech.

preview   A brief statement of the main points a speaker will be presenting in his or her speech; tells an audience what to expect and helps them visualize the structure of a speech. Sometimes also referred to as a "road map" for the speech.

prior exposure   The extent to which an audience has already heard a speaker's message, which will affect an audience's interest or belief in what the speaker is saying.

problem-cause-solution pattern   A speech organizational pattern that identifies a problem, explains the problem's causes, and proposes one or more solutions, which often includes asking an audience to support a policy or to take specific action.

processing   Actively thinking about the meaning of the verbal and nonverbal components of a message. Processing is the first step in effective listening.

projection The act of "booming" one's voice across a speaking forum in order to reach all audience members.

pronunciation Correctness in the way one says words.

proxemics The use of space and distance between a speaker and an audience.

quotation book A reference work offering famous or notable quotations on a variety of subjects.

race Common heritage based on genetically shared physical characteristics of people in a group.

rate of delivery How quickly or slowly a person speaks while giving a presentation.

reasoning The line of thought that connects the facts a speaker presents and the conclusions he or she draws from the facts.

receiver One who processes a message to perceive its meaning.

recency A quality of credible sources that holds that because of our rapidly changing world, newer evidence is generally more reliable than older evidence.

reference work A compilation of background information on major topic areas useful for doing introductory research or discovering a specific fact.

reflective-thinking process A five-step strategy for group decision making: (1) define the problem; (2) analyze the problem; (3) establish criteria for solutions; (4) generate possible solutions; (5) select the best solution.

relaxation strategies Techniques to be performed before giving a speech to help relieve muscle tension and banish negative thoughts. These strategies include deep breathing, tensing and releasing one's shoulder muscles, or engaging in an enjoyable, unrelated activity, such as watching a movie or listening to music.

religious orientation A person's set of religious beliefs, which can shape his or her response to a speech.

representative example An instance that is typical of the class it represents. For example, if a speaker is arguing that Americans are getting tired of corrupt politicians, providing representative examples would mean citing instances from across the country rather than just examples from one or two states or regions.

research The process of gathering and recording information from libraries, the Internet, and interviews to increase a speaker's credibility and understanding of a topic.

research librarian A career professional hired to assist students and faculty with their research.

research objective The goal one needs to accomplish with research.

research plan A strategy for finding and keeping track of information in books, periodicals, Web sites, and other sources a speaker might use to prepare a presentation.

retention The ability to remember what one has heard. The second step in effective listening, retention is directly related to how much attention one pays during an event; the more attentive one is, the more one will remember.

reversed causality Missing the fact that the effect is actually the cause.

rhetorical purpose One of three goals of a presentation: to inform, to persuade, or to mark a special occasion. The rhetorical purpose is the reason why a speaker is giving a particular speech.

rhetorical question A question that a speaker expects listeners to answer in their heads; used to capture an audience's attention and get them thinking about a speaker's topic.

scaled question A survey question that measures a respondent's feelings on an issue by offering a range of fixed responses, such as numbers one (lowest) to ten (highest) or a list of options ("strongly agree," "agree," "neutral," "disagree," or "strongly disagree").

script A typed or handwritten document containing the entire text of your speech.

search engine A specialized online program that allows users to conduct keyword searches and then provides links to relevant Web pages. Examples include Google (www.google.com), Yahoo! (www.yahoo.com), Bing (www.bing.com), and Ask (www.ask.com). Also referred to as a "spider" or "crawler."

sexist language Language with a bias for or against a given gender.

sexual orientation A demographic characteristic that considers whether audience members may be straight, gay, lesbian, bisexual, or transgendered.

shared meaning A common understanding with little confusion and few misinterpretations. Achieving shared meaning is a priority of the transactional model of communication.

signpost A word or phrase within a sentence that identifies the section of the speech or indicates organizational features of the speech.

sign reasoning Arguing that a fact is true because indirect indicators are consistent with that fact. For example, a speaker might argue that the United States is in a recession, supporting that claim with evidence that people are making greater use of payday loan businesses.

simile An explicit comparison of objects using the words *like* or *as*. For example: "My grandmother's lap was *as soft as a pillow*."

situational audience analysis Quick audience analysis just before or during a speech, to be conducted if the makeup or responses of an audience were unknown before the speech or are different from what the speaker expected.

situational characteristic A factor in a specific speech setting that a speaker can observe or discover before giving the speech. Examples include audience size, time, location, forum, and audience mobility.

situational ethics The belief that proper ethical behavior can be informed by a person's circumstances, especially if those circumstances are extreme or unusual.

slippery slope fallacy Arguing against a policy because one assumes (without proof) that the policy will inevitably lead to another outcome that is undesirable. For example: "If we legalize marijuana, that will be the first step toward legalization of all drugs, which would create a public health catastrophe."

small group A limited number of people (three or more) gathered for a specific purpose.

socioeconomic status A measure of where individuals stand in terms of financial resources, education, and occupation in relation to other individuals.

source In models of communication, a person who creates and sends a message to receivers.

spatial pattern A speech organization pattern in which each main point discusses a topic's different aspects of location or geography. If a speaker were explaining how the three largest cities within a state contribute to that state's economy, the speaker might use a spatial pattern of organization.

speaking outline A type of outline containing words or short phrases representing the speaker's key ideas and giving reminders of delivery guidelines. Also referred to as an "extemporaneous outline" or a "delivery outline."

specific purpose A concise phrase consisting of the rhetorical purpose followed by the objective of a speech. For example, the specific purpose of a speech on traveling in the Yucatan Peninsula might be "to inform my audience of the educational and recreational opportunities in addition to the health and safety hazards of traveling in the Yucatan Peninsula."

speech anxiety (stage fright) Nervousness before a speech that results in a variety of symptoms, such as sweaty palms, dry mouth, or even nausea or hyperventilation. A speaker can manage anxiety by being prepared, practicing, being well-rested, and performing visualization and relaxation exercises.

speech critique Written or oral feedback for a presentation that identifies the presentation's main points and objectives, thoughtfully discusses strengths and weaknesses, and offers suggestions for improvement.

stationary audience An audience that will be relatively motionless while listening to a speech. Classrooms, lecture halls, and conference rooms often contain stationary audiences.

statistics Numerical data that help a speaker quantify points and help an audience understand how often a given situation occurs.

stereotype A critical generalization based on the false assumption that characteristics displayed by some members of a group are shared by all members of that group.

strategic discourse The process of selecting arguments that will best achieve a speaker's rhetorical purpose in an ethical manner.

straw person fallacy Substituting a real claim with a weaker claim that a speaker can more easily refute. If a mayor proposes that bike lanes be added to a city's main thoroughfares, but the city council argues that it would be prohibitively expensive to add bike lanes to every street in the city, the city council is committing this fallacy.

style A speaker's word choice, sentence structure, and clarity.

subordination A principle of speech outlining that dictates the hierarchy in the relationship of main points and supporting materials. Each subpoint must support its corresponding main point, and each sub-subpoint must support its corresponding subpoint. On an outline, supporting points are written below and to the right of the point they support. (See also **subpoints** and **sub-subpoints**.)

subpoint An idea gathered from brainstorming and research that explains, proves, and expands on a speech's main points.

sub-subpoint An idea gathered from brainstorming or research that explains, proves, and expands on a speech's subpoints.

summary A brief review of the speech's main points; used in the conclusion of a speech to help an audience remember what they've heard.

superficial listening Pretending to pay attention while actually succumbing to internal or external distractions, such as wandering thoughts or conversation.

supporting materials (supporting points) Examples, definitions, testimony, and statistics that support or illustrate a speaker's main points.

survey A series of written questions a speaker asks others to answer in advance of the speaker's presentation.

sympathetic audience A type of audience that is already inclined to believe a speaker's message or holds the speaker in high esteem, and so will probably respond favorably to the speech.

symposium A method of group presentation in which group members take turns speaking.

taking evidence out of context A form of false inference that deceives an audience by selectively choosing from a source's data or statements and presenting them in a manner that is inconsistent with that source's beliefs or conclusions.

temporal (chronological) pattern A speech organization pattern in which the speaker presents information in chronological order, from beginning to end, with each main point addressing a particular time within the chronology.

testimony A type of support consisting of statements provided by other people, the source of these statements often being researched in a library, found online, or recorded in an interview.

thesis statement A single sentence that conveys the topic and purpose of the speech. All the different parts of a speech, such as the main points and subpoints, should tie into the thesis statement. Sometimes also referred to as a "topic statement" for informative and special-occasion speeches.

tone The high and low qualities of a person's speaking voice. Moderate tonal variety is preferable to using a single tone—known as *monotone*—which is usually either low and mumbling or high-pitched and annoying.

topic The subject of a speech. Speakers should choose a topic based on their own and their audience's interests and knowledge level, as well as their ability to cover the topic during the allotted time frame.

top-level domain The designation at the end of a Web address that indicates the site sponsor's affiliation: commercial (.com), nonprofit (.org), educational (.edu), government (.gov, .uk), or other organization (.net). Based on the top-level domain alone, it cannot be determined whether an online source is credible. The credibility of the person or organization that created the site must be assessed.

transaction A communicative exchange in which all participants continuously send and receive messages.

transition A word or phrase that smoothly connects one idea or part of a speech to another.

trustworthiness The characteristic of exhibiting honesty and fairness. Oftentimes seen as one component of a speaker's ethos.

two-sided argument An argument in which the speaker acknowledges an argument against his or her thesis, then uses evidence and reasoning to refute that argument.

unprocessed note taking Writing down a speech word for word without thinking about what is being said. Unprocessed note taking hampers retention.

value claim A statement that attaches a judgment—such as deeming something good, bad, moral, or immoral—to a subject. For example: "Animal experimentation is inhumane."

values People's "core conceptions" about what is desirable for their own lives and for society. Values guide people's judgments and actions.

verbal chart Words arranged in a certain format, such as bullet points, to explain ideas, concepts, or general information.

verbal clutter Extraneous words that make a presentation hard to follow. To say "*In spite of the fact that* you disagree with me" is more verbally cluttered than "*Although* you disagree with me."

verbal filler A word or phrase such as *you know* or *like* that a speaker uses to fill uncomfortable silences.

verbal symbol A spoken, written, or recorded word that a source uses to convey a message.

verbal tic A sound such as *um* or *ah* that speakers use when searching for a correct word or when they have lost their train of thought.

vetting   Having content of books reviewed and edited by other experts in the field to ensure credibility.

visualization   A method of easing speech anxiety in which the speaker imagines himself or herself giving a relaxed, well-received speech from start to finish.

vivid language   Attention-grabbing and descriptive words and phrases that appeal to the senses.

vocal delivery skills   The use of one's voice to effectively deliver a speech. A speaker should consider volume, tone, rate of delivery, projection, articulation, pronunciation, and pausing.

volume   How loud or soft a speaker's voice is when delivering a speech.

Web directory   A searchable index of reviewed Web sites compiled by human editors and organized into categories and subcategories. Popular Web directories include the Librarians' Internet Index (www.lii.org), Academic Info (www.academicinfo.net/table.html), and Infomine (www.infomine.ucr.edu).

Web site   A group of one or more "pages" of personal, commercial, nonprofit, or other information organized within the World Wide Web and hosted on the Internet.

word association   A strategy for generating topic ideas in which one idea leads to another, then another, and so on, until the speaker happens upon an appropriate topic.

word choice (diction)   Taking into consideration the audience, occasion, and nature of one's message when choosing the language for a speech.

working outline   A type of outline containing full sentences or detailed phrases of all the main points, subpoints, and sub-subpoints in a speech. Also referred to as a "detailed outline" or "preparation outline."

worldview   The "lens" through which a person sees and interprets reality. Listeners' worldviews will affect how they respond to a source's message.

World Wide Web   An electronic, easily navigable global collection of text, graphics, audio, and video accessed through the Internet. A substantially more extensive source of information than any library print collection, but the credibility of the sources you find must be carefully assessed.

yearbook   A reference work that is updated annually and contains statistics and other facts about social, political, and economic topics.

Credits

INDEX